Chinese Companies and the Hong Kong Stock Market

Listing by companies from one country on the stock market of another country is a device often used both to raise capital in, and to increase bonding with, the target country. This book examines the listing by Chinese companies on the Hong Kong stock market. It discusses the extent of the phenomenon, compares the two different regulatory regimes, and explores the motivations for the cross-listing. It argues that a key factor, in addition to raising capital and bonding with the Hong Kong market, is Chinese companies' desire to encourage legal and regulatory reforms along Hong Kong lines in mainland China, in order to develop and open up China's domestic capital markets.

Flora Xiao Huang is a Lecturer in Commercial Law at the University of Leicester, UK.

Horace Yeung is a Lecturer in Commercial Law at the University of Leicester, UK.

Routledge economic growth and development series

Series Editor: Linda Yueh

Fellow by Special Election in Economics at St Edmund Hall and Director of the China Growth Centre, University of Oxford, UK

The aim of the series is to publish a series of books that applies rigorous economic analysis to the field of economic growth and development. The scope includes regional and country-specific studies, as well as cross-country comparisons, to examine the evidence surrounding the pressing and interesting questions on the growth prospects of developed and developing countries.

1 **Chinese Companies and the Hong Kong Stock Market**
Flora Xiao Huang and Horace Yeung

Chinese Companies and the Hong Kong Stock Market

Flora Xiao Huang and Horace Yeung

Routledge
Taylor & Francis Group
LONDON AND NEW YORK

First published 2014
by Routledge
2 Park Square, Milton Park, Abingdon, Oxon OX14 4RN

and by Routledge
711 Third Avenue, New York, NY 10017

Routledge is an imprint of the Taylor & Francis Group, an informa business

British Library Cataloguing in Publication Data
A catalogue record for this book is available from the British Library

Library of Congress Cataloging in Publication Data
Huang, Flora Xiao.
Chinese companies and the Hong Kong stock market/Flora Xiao Huang and Horace Yeung.
pages cm. – (Routledge economic growth and development series)
Includes bibliographical references and index.
1. Stock exchanges–China–Hong Kong. 2. Hong Kong Stock Exchange. 3. Business enterprises–China. I. Yeung, Wai Ho, 1982– II. Title.
HG5790.15.H65H83 2013
332.64'25125–dc23

2013015927

ISBN: 978-0-415-64277-4 (hbk)
ISBN: 978-1-315-88369-4 (ebk)

Typeset in Times New Roman
by Wearset Ltd, Boldon, Tyne and Wear

MIX
Paper from responsible sources
FSC www.fsc.org FSC® C013056

Printed and bound in Great Britain by
TJ International Ltd, Padstow, Cornwall

Contents

3 Stock market development in China and Hong Kong

As already discussed, cross-listing could spark regulatory competition among different markets, which may result in convergence between developed markets, or between undeveloped and developed markets. Bonding serves as a mechanism to encourage such convergence because an issuer can potentially benefit from a regulatory gap between weak/strong markets and then may bring back their foreign experience to the home country.[1]

When Chinese companies bond themselves to a strong market, an issue may arise: are there genuinely any differences in regulatory standards between the home market and the host market? Hence, there is a need to investigate whether there is indeed a "regulatory gap" between China and Hong Kong. Chapters 3 and 4 compare the Chinese stock markets with the Hong Kong Stock Market in order to consider whether the Hong Kong market is superior to that of China, and whether this is the reason which drives Chinese companies to list in Hong Kong. This chapter focuses on market development and the next chapter concentrates on securities regulation and enforcement.

A stock market cannot be created in the absence of certain path dependencies such as its historical background and political economy. In the view of Cassis, the rise or decline of a financial center cannot be understood independently from the economic and social environment of the country where it operates; from the weight carried by the financial sector in the economy; from political influence; and from the preference given to it compared with other activities, like industry.[2] All these elements, both institutional and anthropological, create an atmosphere which is unique to each center, and vital to its success.

Therefore, when comparing the market development between China and Hong Kong, a contextual approach is necessary. An assessment of the two markets in a broader context such as those of history, economics, and politics, could produce a more rounded picture and offer a supplementary explanation of the different paths of their market development.

This chapter starts by introducing the Chinese socialist market economy, which nurtures its stock markets, lays out three phases of their development, and analyzes the fundamental problems arising from the transition stage. The chapter then moves on to the Hong Kong market. Its economic and historical conditions

91 Jackson, Howell, and Roe, Mark (2009), "Public and Private Enforcement of Securities Laws: Resource-based Evidence" in *Journal of Financial Economics*, 93.
92 Armour *et al.*, op. cit.
93 Ribstein, Larry (2005), "Cross-listing and Regulatory Competition" in *Review of Law and Economics*, 1, p. 102.
94 The three are the premier international listing destinations for companies from all over the world. See Cookson, Robert (2011), "Hopes High that Prada's IPO will Set the Style for Hong Kong" in *Financial Times*, 2 February 2011.
95 Coffee (2002), op. cit., p. 1827.
96 Ramos, Sofia (2003), "Competition between Stock Exchanges: A Survey." FAME Research Paper No. 77. Online. Available at: http://ssrn.com/abstract=410727.
97 Coffee (2002), op. cit., p. 1760.
98 Ribstein, op. cit., p. 117.

Illustrations

Figures

Tables

Preface and acknowledgments

This book is essentially based on research carried out by Flora Huang during her days at SOAS, University of London, with additional contributions from Horace Yeung. China is an important case in the landscape of cross-listing, not only because of a number of overseas flotations, mainly in Hong Kong, but because of the relationship between the two jurisdictions under the "One Country Two Systems" ideology and a high degree of socio-political proximity. This study is capable of covering the perspectives of both jurisdictions by combining the expertise of Flora, who has spent most of her life thus far in China, and Horace, who was born and educated in Hong Kong.

Flora is indebted to Sanzhu Zhu, Nick Foster, and Peter Muchlinski, whose encouragement, guidance, and support throughout her years at SOAS enabled her to develop a conceptual plan into a real project. Without their tremendous help this project would have never been completed. She would also like to give her special thanks to Mathias Siems, Linda Yueh, Michael Palmer, and Lynn Welchman, who gave their valuable advice on the research direction. Furthermore, she is thankful to Chao Xi at the Chinese University of Hong Kong and Judge Baojian Geng at the Supreme People's Court of China for their inspirations during her fieldwork in Hong Kong and China. Lastly, she wishes to express her gratitude to Paul Jones, Gil Lan, Timur Gok, Beverley Yeung, Peer Zumbansen, Yue Xu, and Shujie Yao for their constructive comments on certain parts of the book.

Horace is indebted to Jennifer Payne for her guidance and patience throughout his years at Oxford. Special thanks are due to Dan Prentice, John Armour, and Philip Lawton for their detailed and helpful comments on certain parts of the book.

Flora's research was funded by the Central Research Fund of the University of London, Scholarship of Universities' China Committee in London, SOAS Postgraduate Additional Fieldwork Award, SOAS Conference Grant, and AHRC Skills Fund. Horace's research visits to Hong Kong were funded by Mansfield College and the Faculty of Law of the University of Oxford and the University of Exeter. The authors are grateful for the generous support of these bodies, which has made this project possible. We are also grateful for the excellent research facilities provided by SOAS, the Chinese University of Hong Kong,

Hong Kong Monetary Authority, as well as the Universities of Hull, Exeter, Oxford, and Leicester.

Last, but not least, the authors are thankful for the help of the editors of the Routledge series on Economic Growth and Development.

This book is dedicated to our families and friends for their love, support, and encouragement.

FH and HY
August 2013

Abbreviations

ABC	Agricultural Bank of China
ADR	American Depositary Receipt
AIM	Alternative Investment Market
APEC	Asia-Pacific Economic Cooperation
BOC	Bank of China
BRIC	Brazil, Russia, India, and China
BSAM	Bureau of State Asset Management
CCL	Chinese Company Law
CEO	Chief Executive Officer
CEPA	Closer Economic Partnership Arrangement
CIRC	China Insurance Regulatory Commission
CNOOC	China National Offshore Oil Corporation
CO	Companies Ordinance
CPPCC	Chinese People's Political Consultative Conference
CSL	Chinese Securities Law
CSRC	China Securities Regulatory Commission
EPS	Earnings per Share
EU	European Union
FDI	Foreign Direct Investment
FSA	Financial Services Authority
FSB	Financial Services Branch
FSMA	Financial Services and Markets Act
GAAP	Generally Accepted Accounting Principles
GBP	British Pound Sterling
GDP	Gross Domestic Product
GEB	Growth Enterprise Board
GEM	Growth Enterprise Market
GFCI	Global Financial Centre Index
HKCC	HKFE Clearing Corporation Limited
HK$	Hong Kong Dollar
HKEx	Hong Kong Exchanges and Clearing Limited
HKFE	Hong Kong Futures Exchange Limited
HKFRS	Hong Kong Financial Reporting Standards

HKMA	Hong Kong Monetary Authority
HKSAR	Hong Kong Special Administrative Region
HKSCC	Hong Kong Securities Clearing Company Limited
HKSE	Hong Kong Stock Exchange
IAS	International Accounting Standards
IASB	International Accounting Standards Board
ICBC	Industrial and Commercial Bank of China
ICC	International Chamber of Commerce
IFRS	International Financial Reporting Standards
IOSCO	International Organization of Securities Commissions
IPO	Initial Public Offering
LP	Legal Person
LR	Listing Rules
LSE	London Stock Exchange
M&A	Merger and Acquisition
MMT	Market Misconduct Tribunal
MoC	Ministry of Commerce
MoU	Memorandum of Understanding
NCSSF	National Council for the Social Security Fund
NDRC	National Development and Reform Commission
NPC	National People's Congress
NYSE	New York Stock Exchange
OECD	Organization for Economic Cooperation and Development
PBOC	People's Bank of China
PRC	People's Republic of China
PRP	Process Review Panel
QDII	Qualified Domestic Institutional Investors
QFII	Qualified Foreign Institutional Investors
RMB	Renminbi (Chinese currency)
SAR	Special Administrative Region
SASAC	State-owned Assets Supervision and Administration Commission
SCCLR	Standing Committee on Company Law Reform
SCRES	State Commission on the Reform of the Economic System
SCSC	State Council Securities Committee
SEC	Securities and Exchange Commission
SEHK	Stock Exchange of Hong Kong Limited
SEOCH	SEHK Options Clearing House Limited
SFC	Securities and Futures Commission
SFCO	Securities and Futures Commission Ordinance
SFO	Securities and Futures Ordinance
SHSE	Shanghai Stock Exchange
SMLR	Stock Market Listing Rules
SOE	State-owned Enterprise
SOX	Sarbanes–Oxley Act (Public Company Accounting Reform and Investor Protection Act of 2002)

SPC	Supreme People's Court
SPV	Special Purpose Vehicle
SZSE	Shenzhen Stock Exchange
TAC	Takeover Appeal Committee
TSE	Tokyo Stock Exchange
TVE	Township and Village Enterprise
UK	United Kingdom
UNCTAD	United Nations Conference on Trade and Development
US	United States of America
US$	United States Dollar
WTO	World Trade Organization
XFN	Xinhua Finance

Legislation and regulatory instruments

China

Hong Kong

UK

EU

US

Bilateral

Multilateral

1 Introduction

Cross-listing (or overseas listing) refers to the action of companies listing their shares in a country other than the one in which they are incorporated. It is not a new phenomenon. Companies currently listed on the London Stock Exchange (LSE) or the New York Stock Exchange (NYSE) are not necessarily incorporated locally. Some are incorporated in tax haven jurisdictions like Bermuda and the Cayman Islands. However, in recent years, the phenomenon of cross-listing has acquired a new importance. In a globalized world, barriers to cross-border capital flows have diminished and the circulation of information worldwide has been facilitated. These factors provide an opportunity to companies, especially in emerging economies, to be listed on leading stock exchanges, affording them the possibility to tap extra capital and enjoy other benefits. Cross-listing also gives investors the chance to put their money in overseas companies with substantial growth prospects. This is therefore a mutually beneficial scenario, as long as investors are adequately protected.

The People's Republic of China (China or PRC),[1] a rapidly growing market, is a place investors should consider carefully. Its growth and trade offer opportunities to gain economically. In recent years China has experienced the listing of a large number of its companies on the Hong Kong Stock Exchange (HKSE). It is often assumed that in most cases such cross-listing leads to significant positive returns on firm performance. Yet few studies have focused on the effects of cross-listing on markets other than those located in the US.

This chapter first provides the objectives of the book, the reasons why cross-listings need to be explored, and why the case of Chinese companies listing on the HKSE is studied. An outline of chapters is given in the second part.

1.1 Aim of the book and its justifications

The reasons for studying cross-listings in general and the China-Hong Kong case in particular are set out below.

First, the importance of cross-listing has greatly increased in recent years. A prominent example is the launch of the Agricultural Bank of China (ABC) in 2010 on both the Hong Kong and Shanghai exchanges, one of the world's largest IPOs ever. Thanks to the influx of Chinese companies, the HKSE has for three years topped the global rankings for IPOs.[2] Chinese companies now have an overwhelmingly important presence on the stock exchange. For example, in 2008, 465 Chinese companies (in a very broad sense) were listed in Hong Kong and their capitalization accounted for 60 percent of the HKSE's total market capitalization.[3] Equity funds raised by these Chinese companies in the same year amounted to HK$287 billion, which was 71 percent of the total equity funds raised through the exchange during the year.[4] As one of the world's fastest growing economies, China deserves attention. Cross-listings can be beneficial to parties such as investors, companies, and markets. As developed economies become saturated and growth slows, investors begin to look to economies which are growing more rapidly. At the same time, such economies and their companies need adequate capital for development. Cross-listing gives investors access to these companies and the opportunity for greater profit while giving them the safeguards of a well-established market. Meanwhile, the less developed home market can learn valuable lessons and receive beneficial influence from the experience.

Second, an abundant literature has examined the cross-listing phenomenon from different perspectives: such as motivation, firm performance, and corporate governance. But most of this literature is restricted to firm-level improvement, and ignores influences of the host country on the home country in a cross-border environment. The book tries to fill this gap by looking at harmonization in financial markets and rules by means of cross-listing. It proposes a market and legal developing explanation for Chinese cross-listing.

Third, the Chinese case is complicated by the fact that the Hong Kong market and the Chinese markets are linked under the "One Country Two Systems" ideology and a high degree of socio-political proximity, a relationship which must be understood in its political context. China uses the socialist system while Hong Kong, under China's sovereignty, has kept its own capitalist economic and political system. But the influx of Chinese companies into Hong Kong may result in greater harmonization between the two systems.

Based on the reasons mentioned above, the book provides a critical and comparative analysis of the cross-listing of Chinese companies in Hong Kong. Two main research questions arise: why do Chinese companies cross-list on the HKSE? What effects does this phenomenon bring about?

Specifically, these questions can be divided into several sub-questions, separated under the headings "Reasons" and "Effects."

Reasons

- Why do Chinese companies go public and why are many listed in Hong Kong? Do they choose the Hong Kong market either because Hong Kong is superior to China in terms of market development and regulatory framework, or because of political considerations?

Effects

- How do Chinese companies opt into the Hong Kong market? Does Hong Kong treat Chinese issuers differently? What are the influences of Chinese cross-listing on Hong Kong?
- What effects does cross-listing bring about on Chinese companies?
- What are the reciprocal influences of Hong Kong on China's market and legal system via cross-listing?
- What is the future of the Chinese and Hong Kong markets?

In line with these questions, the book sets out three hypotheses. First, overseas listing decisions of Chinese companies, in particular SOEs, are primarily motivated by political demands, rather than by a firm's desire to fund growth and expand business. Cross-listing may be used as part of national political objectives, such as copying and learning from Hong Kong with a view to establishing its own market and implementing legal reform. To achieve this goal, the government is expected to select certain SOEs in key industry sectors with stronger political connections for ease of control. In addition, the pace and the number of listings would be controlled by the state and be adjusted to satisfy political needs. Given that Chinese SOEs list overseas mainly to fulfill political objectives, the research also investigates whether Chinese overseas listings are associated with substantial bonding effects in financial performance and corporate governance.

Second, it hypothesizes that China is catching up with the Hong Kong capital market in terms of its legal and regulatory system. It predicts that a regulatory gap exists between the two jurisdictions, in particular in shareholder law and its effectiveness. But this gap has gradually reduced.

Third, it hypothesizes that cross-listing would lead to convergence between the Chinese and Hong Kong markets. The two systems are foreseen to continue to harmonize but a single model is unlikely to happen as long as their preconditions differ.

1.2 An outline of chapters

To tackle the above issues, the rest of the book consists of seven substantive chapters and a conclusion.

Chapter 2 sets out the theoretical foundations of this book. Concerning the differing depth and liquidity among markets, existing empirical evidence has shown a positive correlation between investor protection and the development of capital markets. Other factors, such as politics and culture, are also considered. These factors will be put in the context of China, in the sense that if a country does not have conditions favorable to the growth of the market, domestic companies' access to finance may be seriously prejudiced. This is the push factor. As regards the pull factor, past explanations for cross-listing tend to be confined to company-level benefits (liquidity and bonding). In fact, because a significant number of cross-listed Chinese companies are essentially state-owned, there is a need to look beyond these company-level benefits. This chapter aims to contribute to existing scholarship by laying down a new market and legal system level explanation for the Chinese case.

Chapters 3 and 4 compare the Chinese stock markets with the Hong Kong Stock Market in terms of market development, securities regulation, and securities enforcement. The purpose of this comparison is to consider whether China's markets are inferior to their counterpart, with the consequence that many Chinese companies list in Hong Kong.

Chapter 3 contextualizes Chinese and Hong Kong market developments in the broader settings of their political economy and historical background. It shows that the Chinese and Hong Kong stock markets possess distinct features which are very different from each other. China practices a socialist economy whereas Hong Kong mainly implements a laissez-faire economic policy. The main function of China's markets is to accommodate state-owned enterprise (SOE) reform, while the aim of the Hong Kong market is corporate financing and privatization (a more diversified ownership structure featuring foreign investors). It further argues that Hong Kong has had an established market for a long time with strengths in the legal and regulatory environments, while China's stock markets are much younger, and have experienced major problems such as the ownership problem, weak corporate governance, and weak shareholder protection.

Chapter 4 compares the securities regulatory frameworks of the Chinese and Hong Kong markets in the light of law that is either on the books or in action. It firstly evaluates securities regulation in China and Hong Kong with respect to investor protection. Then it moves on to consider regulatory authorities such as the China Securities Regulatory Commission (CSRC) and the Securities and Futures Commission (SFC) of Hong Kong, and evaluates the effectiveness of their actions.

Chapter 5 looks at the process and procedures which must be followed when Chinese companies cross-list in Hong Kong, with particular reference to the strategies deployed to protect investors. Such companies are subject to the law of the two jurisdictions, China and Hong Kong. Under Chinese law, companies which wish to go public must obtain CSRC approval. Under Hong Kong law, Chapter 19 of the Hong Kong Listing Rules requires overseas issuers to be incorporated in a jurisdiction where shareholder protection standards are at least equivalent to those provided in Hong Kong. Since Chinese companies fail to satisfy Chapter 19, Chapter 19A has been enacted exclusively for them. It includes certain additional requirements and some modifications and exceptions to Chapter 19. A critical analysis of Chapters 19 and 19A is given to argue that the HKSE may have compromised its standards in order to attract more Chinese business. In addition to initial compliance with the Hong Kong Listing Rules, in the post-listing period the SFC and the HKSE continue to play a crucial role in monitoring public companies. Furthermore, reflections are provided on the domestic public offering and listing of shares in order to consider whether

Chinese cross-listings intend to bond themselves to a stringent regime or avoid certain domestic listing requirements.

Chapter 6 discusses the benefits companies receive, and the problems they encounter, following a Hong Kong listing, by means of general empirical evidence and case studies. The first part of Chapter 6 deals with general empirical evidence. The second part contains case studies. Five representative samples of Chinese companies are taken: Tsingtao Brewery (Tsingtao), Kelon Electrical (Kelon), China Petroleum & Chemical Corporation (Sinopec), the Industrial and Commercial Bank of China (ICBC), and BYD.

Chapters 7 and 8 consider possibilities for the future of the Chinese and Hong Kong markets. A degree of convergence of the two markets can be achieved in three ways: Chinese legal and regulatory reform, dual-listing and regulatory cooperation/competition. Chinese legal and regulatory reform is the focus of Chapter 7, while the latter two are discussed in Chapter 8.

In Chapter 7 it is argued that cross-listing affects the Chinese legal system. Various factors oblige Chinese legislators to compete with international exchanges by enacting legislation in three forms. Regulatory competition and experimentation has resulted in certain amendments to the Company Law and the Securities Law. Board structure (independent directors and fiduciary duties) and mechanisms of shareholder protection (voting rights, derivative actions, and other shareholder rights) have been borrowed in an attempt to improve corporate governance and restrain opportunistic controllers. The second form is issuance reform, intended to promote market discipline and transparency. The third form is non-tradable share reform, which illustrates that China is moving towards Anglo-American dispersed ownership.

Chapter 8 discusses the potential role of dual-listing and regulatory cooperation in the integration of the two markets. Dual-listings of Chinese companies on both the HKSE and the SHSE constitute the driving force reducing the gap between China and Hong Kong's stock markets, both in terms of the size of markets and their regulatory quality. With respect to regulatory cooperation, several agreements at the national and regional levels are addressed. They cover cross-border enforcement, mutual assistance in information exchange, and mutual recognition of qualification of financial intermediaries. With respect to regulatory competition, when China approaches closer to its counterpart, a question arises: will Shanghai replace Hong Kong as the predominant international financial center in Asia? This question will also be considered.

Chapter 9 concludes this book. It locates cross-listings in Hong Kong from China in the broader discourses of liquidity, bonding, and market and legal development. The chapter offers conclusions based on the empirical and theoretical findings of this research.

Notes

1 In this book, China refers to the mainland, as opposed to Hong Kong and Macau.
2 Noble, Josh (2012), "Hong Kong Loses IPO Crown" in *Financial Times* (December 17, 2012).
3 Hong Kong Government (2009), *Yearbook 2008*, Hong Kong: Information Services Department, p. 67. Here, Chinese companies refer to those incorporated in China under the Chinese Company Law, as well as those incorporated outside China but with actual business based in China and controlled by Chinese shareholders.
4 Ibid.

2 Theoretical foundations

This book examines the phenomenon of Chinese companies cross-listing in Hong Kong and asks what the impact of this phenomenon is on the companies themselves, as well as the impact on the Chinese home market. First, there is a need to consider why companies want to cross-list. There are both demand side and supply side factors that cause companies to seek a listing overseas. In essence, this entails the investigation of the weaknesses in the domestic ("home") market which motivates companies to consider cross-listings, and the strengths in overseas ("host") markets which encourage cross-listing. Subsequently, to apply the theoretical framework to the case of Hong Kong and China, the reasons why Chinese companies are "pushed" overseas, and why they are mainly "pulled" to Hong Kong, are discussed. Focus is placed particularly on ascertaining the motivations of Chinese cross-listings, and the impact of them at company and market levels, as well as the relevant legal development.

This chapter attempts to answer the question of why companies want to cross-list in general by looking at both the demand and supply side factors. A company in a weak market will want to cross-list if it cannot realize the benefits which are offered by a strong market. At company level, its motive may be an attempt to seek out greater liquidity, or a desire to raise capital at a lower cost. At market level, a country will want to develop its domestic market with a view to facilitating better resource allocation. A strong market may be defined as one which is large and liquid. However, there are other attributes which are also important: for example, the quality of rules and the efficiency of regulatory agency. This chapter seeks to find out why there is a divergence of weak and strong markets around the world, and assess the state of the Chinese market. There are some factors within a country which are influential to the development of the national capital market. Certainly the supply side factors are important, too, with regard to the decision to cross-list. They include the liquidity factor, the bonding hypothesis, and a new explanation: "spurring."

2.1 Law and finance in the context of China

The correlations between law and financial development are at the core of law and finance studies.[1] La Porta *et al.* have examined legal rules covering the protection of corporate shareholders and creditors, the origin of these rules, and the quality of their enforcement, in 49 countries.[2] They have alleged that the legal environment, including both legal rules and their enforcement, is important in determining the size and extent of a country's capital market. This is because a good legal environment protects potential financiers against expropriation by entrepreneurs. Investors are willing to surrender funds in exchange for securities, and therefore expand the scope of capital markets. Based on their findings, they have claimed that countries governed by French civil law have the weakest level of investor protection and have smaller and narrower capital markets.[3] Such classification, using legal families with little regard to each particular country's "demand for law" in the first place, later attracted criticism from other scholars.[4] For example, the historical record of the US does not support the La Porta thesis. Millions of Americans had owned shares as the Great Depression began, but the introduction of federal securities regulation actually occurred later, in the 1930s.[5] While the subsequent interpretation of statistical results is controversial, the strong correlation found in the study between investor protection and the development of securities markets is less disputed.

2.1.1 ***Investor protection and stock market development – a causal link?***

La Porta *et al.* demonstrate a positive correlation between levels of investor protection and the development of capital markets.[6] Two core ideas evolve from their law and finance theory. The first one is "legal family": shareholder laws in common law countries are superior than those in civil law countries. The second one is that "law matters": legal doctrine is crucial to financial market development (while enforcement has been overlooked). One may argue a third idea of "market and law"; that is, whether there is a causality or a reversed relationship between market development and legal rules. In contrast to the La Porta *et al.* approach, Coffee and Cheffins have shown that in the UK and the US the opposite sequence has occurred whereby financial markets have developed first, followed by creation of a political demand for investor protection.[7]

Before a detailed analysis is given in Chapter 4, this part will briefly assess whether China's legal system offers adequate protection for investors. The commencement of Company Law in China on 1 July 1994 was a milestone in developing a formal framework regulating corporate activities.[8] But prior to this many companies had already been established. This is a distinctive feature of Chinese law, in which the formal legal framework is usually put in place at a relatively late stage. Likewise, even though stock exchanges in Shanghai and Shenzhen were established in the early 1990s, the first set of securities laws did not come into effect until 1999.[9] This pattern of development can be associated with the Chinese tendency to subordinate law to government authority, and exercise detailed administrative control over economic activities rather than permitting activities within a range defined by law.[10] Positive changes in the regulatory framework have recently been made through revisions to the Company Law and

Securities Law, both effective on 1 January 2006. Shareholders' rights have been further strengthened.[11]

The goal of corporate and financial laws should start from the mitigation of the agency problem and attainment of efficient markets. For the former, the focus is placed on how shareholders can be protected from opportunistic managers or predatory controlling shareholders, whereas the success of the latter hinges on the disclosure duties of companies and their managers. On the face of it, today's general regulatory framework of markets and companies in China seems no different from that of other developed markets.

A feasible way to compare China with the rest of the world is to turn the law into numerical indices.[12] Using a panel data set covering a range of developed and developing countries, Armour *et al.* have discovered that significant upward movement in the level of shareholder protection was made by China between 1995 and 2005.[13] It experienced a jump in its shareholder protection score from 5 to 6.5. According to their shareholder protection index of 2005, although the UK and US were the top performers (scores of slightly more than 7), China was more protective of shareholder interests than some developed countries, including Germany and Switzerland.

Although China seems to have improved its legal system, it is worth noting that the legal ideology between East and West might not necessarily be the same. "Rule by law" refers to the instrumental use of law by the state to govern, whereas the "rule of law" refers to a normative and political theory of the relationship of legal institutions and the political state focusing on a theory of limited government through the separation of powers among executive, legislative and judicial organizations.[14] The current situation in China seems to be the former. Indeed, Tomasic has alleged that the privileges of incorporation and limited liability under the Company Law in China were "jealously guarded by the state" and the state would closely monitor the actions of incorporated companies.[15] Milhaupt and Pistor have further alleged that China's commitment to the rule of law has been weakened by other governance mechanisms.[16] For instance, while the Company Law 1993 stipulated the conditions under which a company could issue shares to the public, they were complemented shortly afterwards by a set of regulations promulgated by the State Council and the China Securities Regulatory Commission (CSRC). MacNeil has confirmed this by indicating that there has been an extensive state regulation of company formation in the sense that approval must be obtained from the relevant government departments in addition to satisfying the requirements of the Company Law.[17] By contrast, the laws in China are rapidly changing. For example, the Company Law, which came into effect in 1994, was revised in 1999, 2004, and 2005. Although undeniably the laws have been revised and improved, whether those enforcing the laws can keep up with the changes is questionable. To investigate the legal and institutional conditions in China, one must look into the laws in action as well as the laws on the books.[18]

According to Tomasic and Fu, both the early Company Law and Securities Law were in many aspects almost immediately out of date after their passage, and it was left to the Supreme People's Court to issue interpretations of these statutes, and to regulatory bodies such as the CSRC to promulgate regulations, guidelines and interpretation to fill in the holes and gaps.[19] The traditional emphasis of Chinese legal culture has been on administrative and criminal sanctions, but not on civil liability and procedural law.[20] In terms of public enforcement, it is possible for the CSRC to bring criminal or administrative actions against those companies and their officers that have been engaged in market misconduct.[21] In terms of private enforcement, investors have had much less success in seeking compensation through the courts by way of civil actions, despite the existence of legal provisions that seem to allow for such actions.[22] In practice, Pistor and Xu have stated that the private enforcement of investor rights has been virtually absent in China, not because of a lack of demand for them, but because courts have restricted investor lawsuits.[23] Chapter 4 will examine the issue of enforcement further.

Both the Company Law regime and the stock markets in China were established from scratch in the early 1990s. Apart from the fact that market operation had already begun, a formal set of securities laws only came into effect in 1999. Undoubtedly, the laws on the books have improved over the years. However, China's commitment to building a market economy that respects private economic interests has been unconvincing. A conflict of interests persists between the state ownership of many listed companies, and enforcement by the CSRC. This clearly illustrates that the market, and indeed various economic activities in China, are not solely governed by legal institutions. Political and other considerations must also be taken into account.

2.1.2 Political, cultural and economic considerations

The adverse effect of politics in China lies in the fact that the market has been dominated by state-owned listed companies. This has led to sub-optimal enforcement and greater majority-minority conflicts. The reason why state-owned companies have paramount importance in China is because the state has been reluctant to let go of its control in these companies, as well as control of the economy. The compatibility of private economic activities and socialism has always been an ideological dilemma for Chinese leaders.

There have been numerous concerns over reinterpreting Marxism and leaping into a "socialist market economy with Chinese characteristics." Would the introduction of a capital market be consistent with socialist economic division and production? For Chinese leaders, the use of non-socialist development and the taste of capitalism are only tools to get China into the "socialist utopia."[24] In this sense, capitalist means can be borrowed and utilized for the building of socialism. Would the state-owned nature of Chinese enterprises be changed? Would workers be exploited by profit-oriented companies? Responding to economic reforms, substantive changes were made to the structure of the legal system by learning from other developed countries. But socialism is still the basic system. Law has essentially been a tool for the maintenance of state domination.[25] Labor orientation in social democracies might not be compatible with shareholder wealth-maximization norms, which are important for the growth of a stock market.[26] Indeed, the new Company Law in China still has the feature of social democracies in that it requires the presence of the representatives of workers on both the board of directors and the supervisory board.[27] Zhu has noted that since 1987 two main themes have been running throughout the development of securities regulation in China: one to ensure the primacy of socialist ownership, the other to restrict foreign ownership in SOEs.[28]

Heavy governmental intervention might not be desirable for the development of a strong capital market.[29] The Chinese state has a high degree of control over market regulation. In addition, it can exert influence through its company ownership. A distinctive feature that separates China's stock market from those in other countries is the phenomenon that two-thirds of the outstanding shares in China are not tradable. Any SOE converting into a shareholding company has to divide up its share into three roughly equal parts.[30] About one-third of the shares can be publicly issued, owned by individuals and legal persons, and freely traded. The remaining two-thirds are allocated to state shares and legal person shares which cannot be traded on the stock market.[31] Such shares have been issued to the founders of a corporation, business partners or employees, and have served two main purposes: to keep the control of SOEs that were floated on the market, and to maximize IPO proceeds.[32] All these arrangements have flowed from the stubborn rejection of privatization by the Chinese state. Instead, corporatization was adopted in which SOEs were converted to joint stock companies, featuring both state and non-state ownership. The goal was to improve managerial incentives by installing shareholders with the incentive and the ability to monitor those managers.

As Clarke has rightly pointed out, these diagnoses and the implementation of corporatization as a solution are flawed.[33] The chief purpose of corporatization is to promote higher efficiency through better management. The goal of the state owner in the new system is assumed to be profit, according to the traditional shareholder's value-maximization norm. Indeed, the state owner is still the direct owner of companies in a number of sectors. It is simply too difficult for the state, as the majority shareholder, to exercise effectively its monitoring role.

The separation of ownership and management of control, as claimed by Berle and Means in 1932, has been viewed by Chinese commentators as "a positive good to be pursued for its own sake" because it seems to be the necessary feature of a modern enterprise, as well as a feature of the many Anglo-American corporations that now dominate the world.[34] This requires a widely dispersed shareholder base. Unfortunately, in China, the sophisticated institutional investor sector did not emerge until the end of the twentieth century.

Cross-listing might be a feasible remedy to curb these problems by featuring an even more diversified pattern of ownership. In April 2007 the Hong Kong-listed arm of China National Offshore Oil Corporation (CNOOC) voted 52 percent to 48 percent to stop the Chinese oil company from continuing to deposit funds with its state-controlled parent.[35] The practice is widespread among many

Hong Kong-listed subsidiaries of state-controlled Chinese companies, and has attracted growing criticism from investors who are concerned that the parent company could run off with the money. CNOOC lost the vote following a campaign led by Institutional Shareholder Services, the US-based advisory group. The growing physical presence of foreign investors in the region brings about a rise in shareholder activism in an attempt to safeguard their own interests. This incident shows that by introducing foreign institutional investors, the idea of improving the corporate governance of SOEs might work. This requires a market where there is a high concentration of well-established institutional investors, which is absent in China. These investors can invest in the market only if they are registered under the Qualified Foreign Institutional Investor (QFII) program. As of November 2012, there were 165 QFIIs.[36]

The politics of China might adversely inhibit the growth of the Chinese market in two major ways. First, the state retains the majority ownership in many large state-owned companies. This, on the one hand, reduces the circulation of shares on the market. On the other hand, there is a severe corporate governance implication. As the owner, the state has failed to exercise a meaningful monitoring role and has hindered enforcement by public authorities. Second, the domestic market is still heavily regulated in China, with foreign participation restricted.

Furthermore, culture is important in market development. For example, Black has suggested that a culture of honesty is one of the essential ingredients of a strong market.[37] Moreover, what China lacks is a well-developed investment culture. One of the major aims of company and securities law is to protect investors, but at the same time these investors are not completely innocent if they buy stock in organizations of doubtful validity and practices.[38] Although investors have no obligation to conduct any research or investigation, such as reading the financial statements of a company, before putting any money into a company, the press describes the behavior of Chinese investors as "betting" or putting stock in "Lady Luck."[39] Other than the obvious explanation that people have limited alternative investment channels, share trading offers ordinary Chinese the chance to gamble. In fact, the stock market in China is like a casino. It was revealed that the chance for ordinary investors to profit from the Chinese stock market has only been 40 percent, less than the odds of winning in a casino (48 percent).[40] "Seven lose, two even, one wins" has been a favorite saying among China's share investors.[41] Standard legal protections are essential in a scenario where investors are too naïve to protect themselves.[42] There can be both governance and regulatory strategies. However, both are problematic in the context of China, largely because of the dominance of state-owned companies. First, absolute control in these companies is still retained by the state. Second, enforcement, both public and private, against these companies, has not been common practice, as briefly discussed above.

In addition, the corporate culture of China is not compatible with the best corporate governance practices. Chinese companies retain characteristics of small family businesses such as paternalism, personalism, opportunism, and flexibility, even when conducting large operations. There is not a culture of honesty. Corruption is widespread in China with evidence of excessive entertainment, embezzlement, bribery, and moonlighting.[43] Personal connections or *guanxi* have remained a key element of Chinese organizations. China's traditional business culture is characterized by discretionary power, secrecy, a substantial government role in large-scale production, and personal connections. Conversely, it is commonly asserted that securities markets depend on the rule of law, transparency, and interactions between private parties who are often strangers to one another. Therefore, Hutchens has referred to the development of securities markets in China as a "cultural revolution" which has stimulated the growth of professions and institutions previously unknown in China, such as accounting, the legal professions, and investment banking.[44]

In a nutshell, China needs a culture of honesty and a more mature investment culture. With regard to the former, like many other developing countries, corruption is common. Solving this problem will involve a lot of effort. Concerning the latter, considering that China's financial markets have a short history, investors will hopefully gain experience day by day.

On the other hand, the emergence of private institutions such as accountancy firms, which often takes place in line with economic growth, is an essential part of financial market development. Ironically, China is actually one of the oldest countries using an accounting system. Well over 2,000 years ago China was already applying a highly developed accounting and auditing system for financial and economic activities.[45] Under the rule of the Communist Party, the accounting system was a modified Soviet system called "state accounting." This was used as a tool for the implementation of the state's production quota and government budgets. Managers personally selected an accounting approach and decided on the content of accounting statements and even on the level of profit. Considering the long absence of a sound accounting framework, an official with the Chinese Institute of Certified Public Accounting stated that Chinese accountancy firms were lagging behind international standards regarding employee qualifications, services offered, and management standards, even in this market economy era.[46]

Intermediaries in the Chinese financial markets have predominantly been state-owned. Securities and investment fund management firms were established by state-controlled companies or directly by government agencies in the 1980s. Most restructured in the 1990s into shareholding companies with a state organization as the majority shareholder. Since government agencies remain in control of these firms, they have been vulnerable to administrative interference. Dozens of underwriters have been implicated in disguising the accounts of restructured SOEs, with the assistance of local officials, to allow them to list.[47] Even though some of them are not state-owned entities, they are controlled by the CSRC in respect of licensing, capital adequacy, and the conduct of business. The presence of intermediaries, in theory, should facilitate the operation of the market. For instance, the certification services performed by accountants and lawyers can alleviate the information asymmetry by saving investors time and money by verifying information professionally. Furthermore, the financial press allows the dissemination of information from companies, both favorable and unfavorable, in a short period of time. For this to occur intermediaries must be independent of issuers and investors. In China this might not be possible because intermediaries are often owned or controlled by the state, which is the most regular issuer of securities and is also generally the controlling shareholder in companies.[48] Hence, the intermediaries are in an awkward position when performing their roles as "gatekeepers."

In summary, there is an immediate need in China to strengthen the system of reputational intermediaries, including professionals such as accountants and lawyers as well as other financial services firms such as investment banks and securities analysts. Before the existence of domestic financial markets there was little or no demand for them. However, considering the current market size, ensuring an adequate supply of high quality personnel is crucial to the future development of the Chinese market.

2.2 Existing theories for cross-listing

This section starts with the capital demand of companies. In the past, their fund-raising activities were restricted to their home countries. However, changes such as technological development and harmonization of regulations have allowed them to break down national boundaries and raise capital overseas. There are two predominant models which will be investigated in turn. The traditional model takes liquidity into account. The newer bonding hypothesis considers legal factors. Companies choose to opt into jurisdictions with additional, and usually higher, standards. They can benefit by an increase in their share price and the ability to raise capital at lower cost. Other than the laws on the books, a credible commitment to high standards requires a genuine threat of legal enforcement.

Subsequently, and importantly, in the next section the concept of "spurring" will be introduced. This describes how cross-listing is capable of deepening a country's market and legal development, a perspective that arises in the particular context of China and has rarely been examined before. There is a need to discuss why China is a different case, and how spurring can fill in the gaps in existing theories.

2.2.1 Liquidity

The primary and most obvious advantage of flotation is the opportunity to raise new capital. Apart from the problem of information asymmetry, which is that investors might know very little about a foreign company (especially in the past when telecommunications were less developed), investors may still be willing to include the shares of a foreign company in their portfolios as a way of diversifying risk. From an investor's perspective, cross-listing mitigates some of the uncertainties and costs involved in making direct purchases in foreign markets.[49]

These problems include higher transaction costs, potentially poor financial information, and a greater likelihood of failed trades. All these are likely to be alleviated when a foreign company is listed on a prominent and high quality exchange. As a result, the integration of world financial markets generally results in a sharp increase in capital inflows into many countries.[50]

The impact of cross-listing on a company's cost of capital can be demonstrated by comparing and contrasting the Capital Assets Pricing Model (CAPM) of a local investment portfolio and a global investment portfolio.[51] In the former case, the risk premium is determined purely by the local market, whereas in the latter case it is determined by global capital markets. In general, even though an investor will face some non-diversifiable risks in world markets, many other risks are diversifiable. Therefore, with the help of the CAPM, it can be demonstrated that the risk premium of a global investment portfolio is lower because of a lower risk measure, known as beta.[52] This fall in the global risk premium means an increase in the value of companies whose costs of capital are determined in global markets. This makes the pools of capital overseas more attractive than the local ones.

In the context of China, the absence of a stock exchange had been a problem before the Shanghai and Shenzhen Stock Exchanges were finally established in the early 1990s. Nonetheless, their growth was inhibited. Companies continued to rely on alternative sources of finance, such as bank loans. This placed a heavy burden on the state-owned banking system. The need to diversify and deepen China's fundraising channels became acute.

At the beginning of the 1990s the Chinese government emphasized that its approach to the growth of a capital market was "experimental" and on a small scale.[53] The banking sector dominated the resource flows to enterprises. The equity market helped enterprises raise finance to a limited extent. Budgetary financing of capital expenditure as a percentage of GDP fell dramatically, from 15 percent of GDP in 1978 to less than 5 percent in 1992.[54] The share of bank loans financing fixed assets and working capital increased from 39 percent in 1978 to 73 percent in 1991.[55] Bank loans were the main external source of corporate financing, and the government budgetary allocation was relatively small. In 1992, when the domestic stock exchanges were launched, the state budget contributed to only 6 percent of SOEs' finance, whereas 30 percent came from domestic loans, mostly from banks or provincial governments.[56] The contribution from debt instruments was 21 percent. By contrast, merely 2 percent of SOEs' finance came from the equity market.[57] Self-raised funds remained the most important source of finance. SOEs were allowed to retain 40 percent of their profits to compensate for this circulating capital shortage, with the remaining 60 percent returned to the state. This form of internal finance was only useful when SOEs were actually generating significant profits. Unfortunately, the economic performance of SOEs was far from satisfactory.[58]

The situation has not changed since 1992. By far the two most important sources of financing channels remain self-fundraising and bank loans.[59] Even listed companies have not relied on the equity market, but instead on debt, and in particular, bank debt.[60] This somehow contradicts what the state claimed at the Fourteenth Communist Party Congress in 1992, when it suggested that "the state will actively foster financial markets, including bond and equity markets."[61] Recognizing that a financial system is the core of modern economies, developing capital markets has been one of the strategic tasks in China for reaching its GDP targets. The goal of financial reform, therefore, has been to establish gradually a diversified financial sector that could help raise funds more effectively and use them more efficiently.

China's original goal in developing its equity markets was to raise funds for SOEs and take pressure off banks to extend loans further. In practice, however, because of their poor operating and financial performance, SOEs had to rely on non-arm's length bank loans for their survival. Their inability to repay their loans frequently rendered the loans non-performing. The total loans outstanding to all types of financial institutions had grown from RMB190 billion in 1978 to RMB7.4 trillion by the end of 1998.[62] Estimates suggested that the proportion of non-performing loans was about 24 percent before the Asian financial crisis and 29 percent afterwards.[63] State-owned banks have remained the key commercial players throughout the reform period until now. These banks operate nationally with extensive branch networks, and are owned centrally by government agencies such as the Ministry of Finance. This has led to severe interference by government both at central and local levels, especially with regard to non-performing loans.

One root of the problem is clearly that the stock exchanges were launched but not used. The domestic market in China was heavily regulated. The CSRC imposed a quota system from 1993 to 2000 on the maximum number of shares that could be issued each year, with the intention of curbing the potential excessive investment demand in a pre-mature market where market participants had not developed an understanding of the market rules and their rights and obligations. Provincial governments and industry-supervising bodies were assigned issue quotas and they would recommend enterprises for listing within the given quotas. The CSRC would then give final approval on public offerings. For example, the quotas were US$800 million, US$600 million, US$1.8 billion and US$3.6 billion in 1993, 1994, 1996 and 1997 respectively.[64]

The quota system clearly had its function. As mentioned, first it prevented the budding market from being swamped with shares. Second, it allowed funds to be channeled towards important sectors such as natural resources, utilities, heavy industry, real estate, and finance. However, the system was also notorious for its vulnerability to political lobbying and corruption. For example, it was reported that at least 12 companies from Jiangsu province had bribed regulators to gain market listings during the 1990s.[65] This limited the access to capital for less financially- and politically-able companies.

The malfunctioning banking system, and heavily regulated experimental market, means resource allocation in China has been far from optimal. This pushed the state to look for a way out through cross-listing.

2.2.2 Bonding

The bonding thesis asserts that international companies can improve their corporate governance standards by cross-listing in a stringent legal and regulatory regime to bond themselves to higher accounting, disclosure, and legal practices. Hence, valuable information is available to investors at a lower cost. Strong legal protection is achieved through the enforcement of corporate and securities laws that protect minority investors, and is backed by extensive property rights and contract law.[66] All these elements are likely to be correlated because countries with sound accounting and disclosure systems are likely to also have strong legal institutions in place to ensure compliance with these systems.[67] From an agency theory perspective, companies from countries with poor legal standards can reduce the agency costs of external finance by subjecting themselves to higher standards. According to the survey conducted by La Porta *et al.*, a typical company outside the UK or US has controlling shareholders who enjoy high benefits of control at the expense of minority shareholders.[68] Although the study excluded China, many large and important Chinese companies remain predominantly owned by the state. These controlling shareholders, generally families or, in the case of China, the state, might be willing to bear the cost of better governance because it enables them to raise capital on better terms to fund their company's growth opportunities, as opposed to enjoying the high private benefit of control.

Even in the globalization era, investors still exhibit a strong bias for stocks in their own country. That is why many companies still limit listing their securities to their domestic exchanges, and why most exchanges mainly list and trade domestic companies. Investors prefer familiar stocks and they demand a level of informational transparency that is comparable to, or even higher than, that of their home country. Investors also value an understandable and accessible legal system. With higher cross-border transaction costs and the considerations above, it seems that investors, at least less sophisticated individual investors, are highly unlikely to purchase shares directly from overseas markets. In an extreme case such as China, even sophisticated institutional investors cannot participate directly in local markets unless they obtain prior approval. Investors can easily purchase foreign shares now because of cross-listings and are willing to do so because of what the bonding hypothesis posits. Cross-listing on a well-developed exchange commits the cross-listing company to respect minority investor rights and provide full disclosure.[69] Also, the company becomes subject to the enforcement powers of the local authority. All these may not be desirable from a liquidity viewpoint as higher compliance costs will inevitably increase the cost of capital. However, the bonding hypothesis claims the opposite; that higher standards can actually lead to a lower cost of capital due to the governance effects and resulting mitigation of agency costs. On the other hand, investors acquire the ability to exercise effective and low cost legal remedies that might not be available in the company's home jurisdiction.

2.3 Major motivation for Chinese cross-listing: market and legal development

Although liquidity and bonding seem to be capable of explaining the phenomenon of cross-listing generally, there are other factors worth considering, especially in the context of this book. Both theoretical and empirical research on cross-listing concentrates on companies and stock exchanges as the actors in the global market for cross-listings. This is understandable, as in a general situation the decision to list is made at the company level and the effects of listing are largely restricted to this level. For example, a German company cross-listing on the London Stock Exchange will have limited impact on the German market and legal institutions. By contrast, many cross-listed Chinese companies are predominantly state-owned. The action of the state to list not just one company, but a number of them, in Hong Kong, can have a wider agenda. Therefore, this book provides a third explanation, spurring, which describes how market-led and government-led initiatives can sometimes deepen the financial and institutional development of a country through cross-listing. The former is passive because market exposure to better law is the result of cross-listing, whereas the latter is active because the political decision to develop a market is the motivation behind the cross-listing.

In relation to the companies-exchanges dimension, markets in countries whose laws provide better protection to minority shareholders should, in theory, attract companies with dispersed ownership, whereas markets in low corporate governance countries can trade shares of companies with concentrated ownership. This is because good shareholder protection laws will limit the amount of rents insiders can potentially extract. In this case, there is no extra benefit to holding a large block of shares, thereby facilitating a dispersed ownership model. By contrast, when there are high private benefits of control, shareholders will accumulate large blocks of stock. This equilibrium of the good/bad markets can be broken by cross-listing if the gain in the process outweighs what shareholders might lose.[70] At the company level, the bonding hypothesis argues that managers/controlling shareholders will wish to bond themselves not to take private benefits to ensure access to external capital markets. In particular, when a company has access to valuable investment opportunities that require external finance, the value of having access to external capital can be large.

The weakness of the above explanation, especially in the context of the Chinese case, is that it tends to restrict the effects of cross-listing within the boundaries of a corporation. An exception might be a state-owned company. There are other wider concerns for the state than simply the return on the stake it owns in the company. To address this shortfall, some scholars have started to explore the benefits of cross-listing from a macro-level perspective.[71] These efforts lie especially in examining how developing economies benefit from cross-listing. A revised framework that analyzes the direct and collateral benefits is necessary (see Figure 2.1). This revised framework acknowledges the relevance of the traditional benefits of cross-listing, but in the absence of conclusive

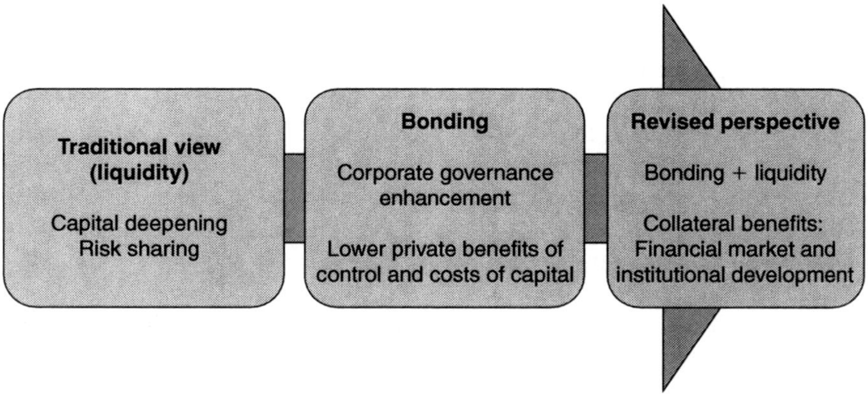

Figure 2.1 A summary of motivations for cross-listing.

empirical evidence of bonding also argues that the benefits can be catalytic and indirect. The potential indirect benefits are likely to be important in two key areas: financial sector development, and institutional quality. International financial flows serve as an important catalyst for financial market development, as reflected both in the straightforward measures of the size of the equity markets and in the broader concepts of financial market development, including supervision and regulation. The theoretical presumption is that foreign entry into the home market, China for example, increases efficiency, and that stock markets tend to become larger and more liquid after equity market liberalizations.[72] In this model, financial and institutional development can be market-induced, through the dissemination of best practices by superior markets to new players. By contrast, development can be facilitated by political decision.

2.3.1 Learning from, and cooperation with, Hong Kong

This section will seek to explain the necessity of a functional stock market in China. This need was driven by China's economic reform. Certain policy goals and features of the reform will be examined in light of the ideological dilemma between socialist state and market economy. The focus will be on how the Chinese state planned to overcome the hurdles of development.

Under Deng Xiaoping's direction of "crossing the river by feeling each stone," economic reform crept forward slowly and pragmatically. This pragmatic approach reflected the conventional Chinese wisdom of prudence. The speech made by Deng during his southern tour of China in early 1992 had the following remarks about the securities market:

> Securities, stock markets, are they good or evil? Are they dangerous or safe? Are they unique to capitalism or also applicable to socialism? Let's try and

> see. Let's try for one or two years; if it goes well, we can relax controls; if it goes badly, we can correct or close it. Even if we have to close it, we may do it quickly, or slowly, or partly. What are we afraid of? If we maintain this attitude, then we will not make big mistakes.[73]

In that same year, China defined its key economic reform objective as the construction of a "socialist market economy." The key strategy was to transform the SOEs into joint stock companies and allow them to raise funds through the stock market. The strategic role of the financial market in supporting sustainable economic growth was formally recognized in 2002, when the *Opinions of the State Council on Promoting the Reform, Opening and Steady Growth of Capital Markets* were issued. Promoting capital markets and increasing public awareness of their importance are regarded as national strategies. By contrast, the *Opinions* advocated the need to strengthen the legal and regulatory framework and step up enforcement efforts to maintain market order and protect investors' interests. From a macro view, the state emphasized that capital market reform should be conducted at a balanced pace, with global competitiveness as the key goal.

To put the vision into action, eight micro-development strategies were laid out.[74] Many of them require long-term commitments, a small part of which has been successfully implemented. For instance, in relation to a multi-layered stock market, a growth enterprise market was launched in October 2009 to cater for the financial needs of technological and small-to-medium sized companies. In March 2009 the State Council also made an official announcement on its goal of turning Shanghai into an international finance and shipping center by 2020. The twist in this announcement, according to commentators, was that the central government should know that Hong Kong is the main financial center.[75] In this sense it does not want Shanghai to compete with Hong Kong. It wants the cities to work together. As a matter of fact, it is not possible, at least for the moment, for Shanghai to truly evolve into an international finance center. In the absence of national reforms to make RMB fully convertible, the approach that Shanghai can take is to establish the city as a "RMB-based center." Furthermore, another big disadvantage of Shanghai when compared to Hong Kong, Tokyo, London, and New York, is that foreign companies are not free to list on the local stock exchange.

The Chinese government has put a lot of effort into liberalizing and internationalizing its market. The ultimate goal is to develop capital markets through market forces and proper regulation. Hong Kong is well positioned to speed up the reform process.[76] Increased participation in international markets will hasten the Chinese convergence with international standards. Hong Kong can serve as a platform for China to gain exposure and accumulate experience through interaction with international markets and players.

2.3.2 Legal transplants in Chinese legal reform

One point that may arise is, to what extent can China learn from Hong Kong? In the context of law, Comparativists are split between those who believe that a large portion of law in any society is a result of legal transplants,[77] and those who have serious doubts about their efficacy. For example, one scholar claims that "legal transplants are impossible."[78]

In the Chinese context, the emergence and development of the Chinese legal system is a prime example of the transplant phenomenon, in particular in securities regulation.[79] China is widely perceived as having an undeveloped legal system. Likewise, corporate governance standards within Chinese companies are often seen as either lacking or deficient in their operation. In contrast to this, Hong Kong is commonly seen as having a well-developed market economy with a set of regulatory legal safeguards in place, derived from Britain, and which meet Western standards. The important point is that Chinese companies listed in Hong Kong inevitably reflect the features of the two legal systems. In this sense, Chinese lawmakers should have had the luxury of selecting and adapting the most efficient elements of both models when developing Chinese securities law.

Subsequently, a question arises: in what sense are legal transplants successful? Kanda and Milhaupt define success as the situation which occurs when the imported legal rule is used in the same way that it is used in the home country, subject to adaptations to local conditions, while "failure occurs when the imported legal rule is ignored by relevant actors ... or the application and enforcement of the rule lead to unintended consequences."[80]

So, are Chinese legal transplants successful? Some scholars consider them to be a failure. For example, Professor Ruskola argues that Chinese legal reform has experienced many difficulties resulting from the politics of state policy determination and administration.[81] Xi claims that the absence of the requisite complementary institutions, both formal and informal, mitigates the transplant effects in China.[82] By contrast, others praise that Chinese legal reform is a triumph of legal transplants.[83] A typical representative is the amended Chinese Company Law which imports corporate governance mechanisms such as independent directors and derivative actions.[84] It is believed that the amendments improve the quality of listed companies and promote the stable and healthy development of Chinese capital markets.[85]

Which arguments are correct? Discussion of these matters are scattered throughout subsequent chapters. Chapter 4 compares securities regulation between China and Hong Kong in order to find out the degree to which China borrows the Western model with regard to shareholder rights law. It also explores the differences and similarities between the imported law and the original law. Chapter 7 discusses Chinese legal transplants in corporate and securities law, and the role of cross-listing in legal transfers.

2.3.3 Debates on regulatory competition/convergence

When companies have the discretion to choose where to list and are not limited to a single listing, competition between different countries and between different markets to attract listing may arise. There are at least two explanations for this competition. First, the number and size of listings is an important indicator for a capital market's depth and liquidity. Governments and policy-makers may seek to attract more listings, thereby gaining economic benefits from the expansion of financial services and professional services. Second, demutualized exchanges wish to maximize their revenues and share value.

Regulatory competition between countries and between markets may lead to two outcomes: a race to the top and a race to the bottom.[86] A race to the top may occur if there is a positive correlation between governance standards and market value, with issuers preferring high disclosure exchanges so as to improve their value. On the other hand, a race to the bottom may result from companies with controlling shareholders not wishing to improve their governance because they enjoy high benefits from private control. Such companies would choose not to list, or would prefer to list on an exchange with fewer listing requirements, and some stock exchanges may be willing to lower their standards in order to keep business.

Convergence may result from emulation generated by competition between regulatory systems. Many companies wish to grow in order to exploit global markets, and international shareholders require standard safeguards to protect their interests. From the view of countries and markets, they have an incentive to develop local securities laws in order to keep trading and their related revenues at home. They may therefore be forced to change their law so that they can foster a market/corporate-friendly regime, or a strong investor protection regime, or even a mixture of both.

Convergence can come from competition for securities market business between developed countries, but can also arise as a result of a country developing by learning from a more developed economy, adopting and adapting the latter's systems, which normally involves legal transplants mentioned above. The process of convergence can be reflected in two closely related areas: securities regulation and corporate governance. In securities regulation, especially disclosure requirements, the International Accounting Standards Board (IASB)[87] and the International Organization of Securities Commissions (IOSCO) have produced a body of international accounting standards to be adopted worldwide for cross-listings.[88]

In terms of corporate rules, the trend towards convergence has been documented by Hansmann and Kraakman.[89] They argue that the shareholder-oriented model of the company dominates because of the success of Anglo-American companies. This ideology is reflected in governance practice, e.g., the new principles of corporate governance of the Organization for Economic Cooperation and Development (OECD). However, the way in which rules can actually converge is complicated by the absence of a "role model." For example, while companies in the UK and the US share a similar dispersed ownership structure, market regulation and enforcement differ on either side of the Atlantic. The US is characterized by a powerful market regulator, while the UK model has emphasized self-regulation.[90] Public enforcement of securities law is strong in the US and relatively weak in the UK.[91] Private enforcement of corporate law in these two common law jurisdictions is also diverse. Numerous lawsuits are launched in the US, while private enforcement is rare in the UK.[92]

Indeed, convergence may encounter many impediments such as politics, culture, economics, and initial corporate structure.[93] The cost for listed companies complying with the internal governance law of the host country may exceed the benefits of cross-listing. From the standpoint of the host country, in order to avoid the decrease of foreign issuers, it has an incentive to exempt foreign companies from its internal governance law, or to avoid regulating internal governance.

2.4 Concluding remarks

Cross-listing can benefit various parties. Companies can obtain capital, enhance their values, and strengthen their public images. Exchanges profit from listing fees and trading volume. From recent statistics, the New York Stock Exchange, the London Stock Exchange, as well as the newcomer, the Hong Kong Stock Exchange, which have established themselves as brand names associated with high quality, are the clear winners.[94] The higher disclosure and governance standards adopted by these markets are the "product of a competitive desire to attract listings."[95] The economies of scale present in securities markets and financial services can lead to the emergence of regional or even global centers, with smaller centers in each country.[96] These global centers are capable of throwing abundant amounts of resources into technical infrastructure and the enforcement of rules to facilitate better bonding and thereby offer better value to both companies and investors. This competition can inherently result in a "winner takes all" contest that will leave only a few large pools of liquidity in major international financial centers.[97] Furthermore, on the home country side, cross-listing can affect the laws of the cross-listed companies' home jurisdiction.[98] First, companies that cross-list and become subject to the stronger shareholder protection rules of the cross-listing jurisdiction might demand changes in local laws that will make these rules convergent with those of the host jurisdiction. Second, in response to competition from overseas markets, local demands for legal changes will also arise to protect local trading. Therefore, cross-listing can serve as a means of spurring the development of the home market, although fundamental changes in some associated underlying factors such as law, politics, and culture, are necessary.

Concluding, this chapter has set out the motivations of a company to cross-list. These will be applied to the subsequent assessments of Chinese companies listing in Hong Kong in later chapters. To affirm bonding and spurring there will need to be a detailed discussion of specific listing rules applying to domestic companies in China and cross-listed companies in Hong Kong to investigate whether there is a regulatory gap. For the enforcement side there will also need to be a discussion as to whether the Hong Kong authority really does credibly commit to enforcing against mainland Chinese companies. For both Chinese companies, and the Chinese government, there will be an evaluation of whether the initial objectives of cross-listing have been achieved. For the companies, apart from the liquidity they have obtained, there are other objectives such as visibility and the introduction of foreign strategic investors to enhance management practices. For the government, Chinese leaders intend to use cross-listing as a catalyst to speed up the privatization process of large state-owned enterprises, as well as a spur to the development of domestic markets through regulatory competition. In the next chapter there will be an assessment of the market development in China and Hong Kong. Afterwards, in Chapter 4, a similar comparative assessment will be performed with respect to the regulatory quality of the two markets.

Notes

1 Siems, Mathias (2007), "Legal Origins: Reconciling Law & Finance and Comparative Law" in *McGill Law Review*, 52, p. 57.
2 La Porta, Rafael *et al.* (1997) in "Legal Determinants of External Finance" in *Journal of Finance*, 52; La Porta, Rafael *et al.* (1998), "Law and Finance," in *Journal of Political Economy*, 106; and La Porta, Rafael *et al.* (2000), "Investor Protection and Corporate Governance," in *Journal of Financial Economics*, 58.
3 Ibid.
4 See for example, Berkowitz, Daniel *et al.* (2003), "Economic Development, Legality and the Transplant Effect" in *European Economic Review*, 47; and Siems, op. cit. A mere categorization of a system as common law or civil law disregards deeper legal structures.
5 Cheffins, Brian (2003), "Law as Bedrock: The Foundations of an Economy Dominated by Widely Held Public Companies" in *Oxford Journal of Legal Studies*, 23, p. 18.
6 La Porta *et al.*, op. cit.
7 See Coffee, John (2001), "The Rise of Dispersed Ownership: The Role of Law and the State in the Separation of Ownership and Control" in *Yale Law Journal*, 111, pp. 65–6; Coffee, John (2007), "Law and Market: the Impact of Enforcement" in *University of Pennsylvania Law Review*, 156, p. 297; and Cheffins, Brian (2001), "Does Law Matter? The Separation of Ownership and Control in the United Kingdom" in *Journal of Legal Studies*, 30, pp. 483–4.
8 The Chinese Company Law ("the Company Law" hereafter) was adopted by the Standing Committee of the National People's Congress on 29 December 1993, effective as of 1 July 1994, revised on 25 December 1999 and 27 October 2005, effective as of 1 January 2006.
9 The Chinese Securities Law ("the Securities Law" hereafter) was adopted by the Standing Committee of the National People's Congress on 29 December 1998, effective as of 1 July 1999, revised on 28 August 2004 and 27 October 2005, and effective as of 1 January 2006.
10 MacNeil, Iain (2002), "Adaptation and Convergence in Corporate Governance: The Case of Chinese Listed Companies" in *Journal of Corporate Law Studies*, 2, pp. 297–301.
11 See Chapter 7 for more discussions.
12 One argument against the use of numerical comparative law is that "law is special, complex and cannot be reduced to numbers," despite its now-popular use across various areas of law. See Siems, Mathias (2005), "Numerical Comparative Law – Do We Need Statistical Evidence in Law in Order to Reduce Complexity?" in *Cardozo Journal of International & Comparative Law*, 13.
13 Armour, John *et al.* (2009), "Shareholder Protection and Stock Market Development: An Empirical Test of the Legal Origins Hypothesis" in *Journal of Empirical Legal Studies*, 6. But the indices constructed in the study refer only to the "law-on-the-

books." Separation investigations may be required to ascertain the quality of legal institutions.

14 Orts, Eric (2001), "The Rule of Law in China" in *Vanderbilt Journal of Transnational Law*, 34, p. 94.
15 Tomasic, Roman (1995), "Company Law and the Limits of the Rule of Law in China" in *Australian Journal of Corporate Law*, 4, p. 473. According to Art. 19 of the Company Law, a company must provide the necessary conditions for the establishment of the organization of the Communist Party of China and facilitate the carrying out of party activities.
16 Milhaupt, Curtis and Pistor, Katharina (2008), *Law and Capitalism*, London: The University of Chicago Press, p. 142.
17 MacNeil, op. cit., p. 302.
18 For the importance of legal enforcement, see Chapter 4. See also, for example, Coffee (2007), op. cit.
19 Fu, Jian and Tomasic, Roman (2006), "Legal Regulation and Corporate Governance in China's top 100 Listed Companies" in *Company Lawyer*, 27.
20 Chen, Zhiwu (2003), "Capital Markets and Legal Development: The China Case" in *China Economic Review*, 14, p. 454.
21 See Chapter XI of the Securities Law.
22 See for example, Art. 20 (for abuse of shareholder's rights) and Art. 152 (derivative suit) of the Company Law and Art. 69 of the Securities Law (for civil liability of false recording, misleading statements and material omissions made by issuers and securities companies).
23 Pistor, Katharina, and Xu, Chenggang (2005), "Governing Stock Markets in Transition Economies: Lessons from China" in *American Law and Economics Review*, 7, p. 191.
24 Based on this theory, the socialist system will evolve in four phases: from capitalism to the primary stage of socialism, then to the advanced stage of socialism and finally to communism. Hu, Yebi (1993), *China's Capital Market*, Hong Kong: The Chinese University Press, p. 67.
25 Liang, Bin (2008), *The Changing Chinese Legal System, 1978-Present*, London: Routledge, p. 19.
26 Roe, Mark (2003), *Political Determinant of Corporate Governance*, Oxford: Oxford University Press.
27 See Art. 45 and Art. 51 of China's Company Law 2005.
28 Zhu, Sanzhu (2000), *Securities Regulation in China*, New York: Transnational, p. 169.
29 The political story given by Roe, regarding the success of the US, is that low government involvement has always been a tradition, and that companies have experienced less interference as a result. See Roe, op. cit.
30 Green, Stephen (2003a), *China's Stockmarket: A Guide to its Progress, Players and Prospects*, London: The Economist, p. 15. About a third of equity will be transferred to state organs. These shares are either managed and represented by the Bureau of National Assets Management, or held by other state-owned companies. The ultimate owner of state shares is the State Council. Another third of every listed company's equity will be sold to domestic institutions (securities companies and SOEs with at least one non-state owner). These shares, which together amount to two-thirds of the total shares issued, are non-tradable. The remaining shares will be offered to the public.
31 Art. 36 of the Provisional Regulations on the Administration of Issuing and Trading of Stocks.
32 Beltratti, Andrea and Bortolotti, Bernardo (2006), "The Nontradable Share Reform in the Chinese Stock Market." FEEM Working Paper No. 131.06. Online. Available at: http://ssrn.com/abstract=944412 [accessed 20 December 2012].

33 Clarke, Donald (2003), "Corporate Governance in China: An Overview" in *China Economic Review*, 14, pp. 497–500.
34 Ibid., p. 498 and Berle, Adolf and Means, Gardiner (1991), *The Modern Corporation and Private Property*, London: Transaction Publishers.
35 See Tucker, Sunny (2007), "On Asia: Shareholder Activism Taking Root in Asia" in *Financial Times*, 13 April 2007.
36 For an updated list of these QFIIs and their investment statistics, visit the website of the State Administration of Foreign Exchange. Online. Available at: www.safe.gov.cn [accessed 20 December 2012].
37 Black, Bernard (2001), "The Legal and Institutional Preconditions for Strong Securities Markets" in *UCLA Law Review*, 48.
38 US Supreme Court Justice Louis Brandeis indicated that "there is no such thing as an innocent purchaser of stocks." Cited in Minow, Nell and Monks, Robert (2004), *Corporate Governance*, Oxford: Blackwell, p. 127.
39 See Lau, Justine and Mitchell, Tom (2006), "Investors are Betting on Chinese IPOs" in *Financial Times*, 31 May 2006; and McGregor, Richard (2007), "Chinese Put Stock in Lady Luck" in *Financial Times*, 12 May 2007. "With Chinese IPOs you have to ride the momentum, as long as you get out before it becomes too expensive, you will be fine," said Yang Liu, a China fund manager at Atlantis Investment Management.
40 Yeung, Horace (2010), "Just Another Casino? The Case of Launching the Growth Enterprise Board in China" in *International Company and Commercial Law Review*, 21, pp. 71–2.
41 Green, op. cit., p. 70.
42 Armour, John *et al.* (2009), "Transactions with Creditors" in Kraakman, Reinier *et al.* (eds.), *The Anatomy of Corporate Law: A Comparative and Functional Approach*, 2nd edn, Oxford: Oxford University Press.
43 According to the 2012 Corruption Index released by Transparency International, China was ranked 80 out of 176 countries (1 being least corrupt). The perceived level of corruption in China remained high. Online. Available at: www.transparency.org.
44 Hutchens, Walter (2003), "Private Securities Litigation in China: Material Disclosure about China's Legal System?" in *University of Pennsylvania Journal of International Economic Law*, 24, p. 622.
45 Hoepen, M. (1995), "Accounting in China: A Case of Vanishing Cultural Influence" in Blake, John and Gao, Simon (eds.), *Perspectives on Accounting and Finance in China*, London: Routledge, p. 354.
46 Lin, Thomas (2004), "Corporate Governance in China: Recent Developments, Key Problems, and Solutions" in *Journal of Accounting and Corporate Governance*, 1, p. 10.
47 Green, Stephen (2003b), "Better Than a Casino: Some Good News from the Frontline of China's Capital Market Reforms." China Project Working Paper No. 6. Online. Available at: http://ssrn.com/abstract=431200 [accessed 20 December 2012].
48 MacNeil, op. cit., p. 321.
49 Edison, Hali, and Warnock, Francis (2008), "Cross-Border Listings, Capital Controls, and Equity Flows to Emerging Markets" in *Journal of International Money and Finance*, 27, pp. 1019–20.
50 Ibid.
51 Stulz, Rene (1999), "Globalization of Equity Markets and the Cost of Capital" in *Journal of Applied Corporate Finance*, 12, pp. 10–12.
52 With the CAPM, the expected return required by the market on a risky security is equal to the risk-free rate plus a risk premium equal to the beta coefficient of the security times the market's risk premium. If a company has a low beta with respect to the world market portfolio, but a high beta with respect to its local market, the fall in the cost of capital will be substantial, as seen in the following equation: $ra = \beta a(rm - rf) + rf$, where ra is the expected return of the securities, rf is the risk free rate, and rm is the expected market return.

53 World Bank (1995), *China – The Emerging Capital Market: Volume II*, Washington DC: World Bank, p. 7.
54 Qian, Yingyi (1995), "Reforming Corporate Governance and Finance in China" in Aoki, Masahiko and Kim, Hyung-Ki (eds.), *Corporate Governance in Transitional Economies*, Washington DC: World Bank, pp. 232–3.
55 Ibid.
56 World Bank, op. cit.
57 Ibid.
58 In general, more than a third of the SOEs suffered continuous explicit losses. Another third registered implicit losses. Only a small proportion were profitable. See Cai, Fang *et al.* (2001), *State-owned Enterprise Reform in China*, Hong Kong: Chinese University Press, p. 2.
59 This is the conclusion from Allen *et al.*, according to their investigation of China's financing channels during the period 1994 to 2002. See Allen, Franklin *et al.* (2005), "Law, Finance, and Economic Growth in China" in *Journal of Financial Economics*, 77, p. 79.
60 It is worth comparing the situation of China with other bank-centered systems. See ibid., Table 8C.
61 See CSRC (2008), *China Capital Markets Development Report*, Beijing: China Financial Publishing, p. 284.
62 Lardy, Nicholas (1998), *China's Unfinished Economic Revolution*, Washington DC: Brookings Institution Press, p. 76.
63 Huang, Yiping (2001), *China's Last Steps across the River: Enterprise and Banking Reforms*, Canberra: Asia-Pacific Press, pp. 113–14. Chinese authorities did not release official data for reasons of confidentiality. Huang made the estimates based on a survey of various secondary literatures.
64 CSRC, op. cit., p. 166.
65 Green (2003a), op. cit., p. 161.
66 Coffee, John (1999), "The Future as History: The Prospects for Global Convergence in Corporate Governance and Its Implications" in *Northwestern University Law Review*, 93; Coffee, John (2002), "Racing towards the Top? The Impact of Cross-listings and Stock Market Competition on International Corporate Governance" in *Columbia Law Review*, 102; and Stulz, René, op. cit.
67 Ammer, John *et al.* (2005), "Look at Me Now: What Attracts U.S. Shareholders?" Board of Governors of the Federal Reserve System International Finance Discussion Paper No. 815. Online. Available at: http://ssrn.com/abstract=556208 (accessed 20 December 2012).
68 La Porta, Rafael *et al.* (1999), "Corporate Ownership around the World" in *Journal of Finance*, 64. It is especially true in China, where the large local companies are almost state-owned. In 2007 the combined profit of the 150 or so companies controlled by the central government was expected to have reached around US$142 billion. At the end of 2007 the list of the world's ten most valuable companies contained four groups controlled by the Chinese state. They are PetroChina, China Mobile, ICBC, and Sinopec. See Dyer, Geoff and McGregor, Richard, "China's Champions" in *Financial Times*, 17 March 2008.
69 Coffee (2002), op. cit., p. 1780. This may be controversial as foreign companies are often exempt from certain requirements, such as in Hong Kong, which operates dual standards. Also, the commitment of regulatory authorities to enforce rules against foreign companies is often in doubt. These will be discussed in later chapters.
70 For the association of private benefits of control and the decision to cross-list, see, for example, Benos, Evangelos and Weisbach, Michael (2004), "Private Benefits and Cross-listings in the United States" in *Emerging Markets Review*, 5; and Doidge, Craig *et al.* (2009), "Private Benefits of Control, Ownership, and the Cross-Listing Decision" in *Journal of Finance*, 64.

71 See for example, Kose, M. Ayhan *et al.* (2007), "Financial Globalization Beyond the Blame Game: A New Way of Looking at Financial Globalization Reexamines its Costs and Benefits" in *Finance and Development*, 44; and Kose, M. Ayhan *et al.* (2006), "Financial Globalization: A Reappraisal." IMF Working Paper (WP/06/189). Online. Available at: www.nber.org/papers/w12484 (accessed 20 December 2012).
72 Ibid.
73 CSRC, op. cit., p. 161.
74 They are: (1) maintain a fine balance between the government and the markets, strengthen legal and regulatory framework, and build fair, transparent and efficient markets; (2) create a fully multi-layered stock market to meet diverse needs; (3) improve the quality of listed companies; and so on. See CSRC, op. cit., p. 283.
75 Taylor, Phil (2009), "Anything but an Easy Ride for Shanghai" in *China Law and Practice* (June 2009).
76 SFC (2006), "Positioning of Hong Kong amid Reforms in the Mainland Financial Markets." Online. Available at: www.sfc.hk/sfc/html/EN/research/research/research.html.
77 For example, Watson, Alan (1993), *Legal Transplants an Approach to Comparative Law*, 2nd edn, Athens: University of Georgia Press, p. 6; and Watson, Alan (1996), "Aspects of Reception of Law" in *American Journal of Comparative Law*, 44.
78 Legrand, Pierre (1997), "The Impossibility of 'Legal transplants'" in *Maastricht Journal of European and Comparative Law*, 4. Also Legrand, Pierre (2001), "What Legal Transplant?" in Nelken, David and Feest, Johannes (eds.), *Adapting Legal Cultures*, Oregon: Hart Publishing, pp. 55–7. For Watson's response to Legrand's criticism, see Watson, Alan (2000), "Legal Transplants and European Private Law" in *Electronic Journal of Comparative Law*, 4.4. Online. Available at: www.ejcl.org/44/art44–2.html (accessed 20 December 2012).
79 The Chinese Company Law 1993 was modeled on American and other Western corporation codes. See Art, Robert and Gu, Minkang (1995), "China Incorporated: The First Corporation Law of the People's Republic of China" in *Yale Journal of International Law*, 20, p. 275.
80 Kanda, Hideki and Milhaupt, Curtis (2003), "Re-examining Legal Transplants: The Director's Fiduciary Duty in Japanese Corporate Law" in *American Journal of Comparative law*, 51, p. 890.
81 Ruskola, Teema (2000), "Corporations and Kinship" in *Stanford Law Review*, 52, p. 1693.
82 Xi, Chao (2009), *Corporate Governance and Legal Reform in China*, London: Wildy, Simmonds & Hill Publishing, p. 226.
83 For general discussions, see Tenev, Stoyan and Zhang, Chunlin (2002), *Corporate Governance and Enterprise Reform in China: Building the Institutions of Modern Markets*, Washington DC: World Bank.
84 For further discussion regarding Chinese legal transplants, see Chapter 7.
85 Wang, Jiangyu (2008), "An Overview of China's Corporate Law Regime." Online. Available at: http://ssrn.com/abstract=1222061.
86 Coffee (2002), op. cit., pp. 1811–16.
87 The IASB was founded on 1 April 2001 as the successor to the International Accounting Standards Committee. It is responsible for developing International Financial Reporting Standards (the new name for International Accounting Standards issued after 2001), and promoting the use and application of these standards.
88 Licht, Amir (1998), "International Diversity in Securities Regulation: Roadblocks on the Way to Convergence" in *Cardozo Law Review*, 20, pp. 231–2.
89 Hansmann, Henry and Kraakman, Reinier (2001), "The End of History for Corporate Law" in *Georgetown Law Journal*, 89.
90 Siems, Mathias (2008), *Convergence in Shareholder Law*, Cambridge: Cambridge University Press, pp. 38–40.

are discussed, as well as its successful growth into an Asian international financial center: China's Manhattan.

3.1 Development of China's stock markets

After the founding of the People's Republic of China in 1949, the main economic goal of the country was to establish a centrally planned economy. Securities activities were eliminated in the following 30 years.[3] Furthermore, the Cultural Revolution (1966–76) left China in chaos, isolated from the outside world. During this ten year period, China had all but dismantled the formal legal system which it had begun to create in the early twentieth century, and continued under Soviet influence in the 1950s. As a result, by the time China launched its economic reforms in the late 1970s, it had to rebuild its legal system virtually from scratch.[4] Since then, China has been reforming its highly centralized and unitary banking and financial structure. The legal system has also undergone substantial reforms to adapt itself to the changing environment. Along with the rapid growth of China's securities program, a regulatory regime has emerged. In a broad sense, Chinese financial law is a mix of the civil and the common law systems.[5]

3.1.1 The Chinese model: a socialist market economy

A "social market economy," a term which is frequently used interchangeably with the term "socialist economy with Chinese characteristics," is a concept first proposed by Deng Xiaoping in order to incorporate the market into the planned economy in China.[6] The ideology behind the Chinese economy has a profound effect on its legal development and the establishment of its stock markets. Hence, a brief review of the economic and political environment within which China's securities market has developed provides the background information essential to understanding this unique case.

A Economic reform and its impacts on the emergence of the securities markets

Since the country was established, the dominant feature of economic entities in China has been SOEs as the representatives of "the whole people." SOEs are the principal producers of energy, transportation, telecommunications, raw and semi-finished materials, and industrial and technical equipment. Despite their dominance in China's economy, SOEs suffered chronically from losses, inefficiency, and insufficient productivity. Chinese government statistics showed that in the 1990s approximately one third of SOEs were losing money, and even in debt.[7] Three problems underline the conditions of SOEs: lack of autonomy, lack of initiative, and lack of adequate incentives for efficiency and productivity.[8]

As a central element of its overall strategy to improve allocative efficiency, and promote the sustained growth of the economy, the government decided in

1979 to carry out unprecedented experiments with economic reform. The major goal of the reform was to eliminate the enormous waste and inefficiency in the Chinese economy at that time.[9] It was not carried out as a comprehensive program all at once. Rather, it was initiated and implemented as a series of experiments, touching almost all aspects of the economy including agriculture, industry, tax, price, economic structure, and opening to the outside world.[10]

A key component of the economic reform is SOE reform by corporatization through the establishment of shareholding companies.[11] This shareholding system was the prelude to the development of the securities markets. Corporatization (the conversion of SOEs into shareholding companies) and listing (the sale of shares of such companies in securities markets) were believed to be effective means to save the Chinese economy because they could serve four functions: (1) to relieve the state financial departments and banks from financing the enterprises which required investment funds; (2) to channel savings into social accumulation capital; (3) to provide the internal self-regulation for enterprises to assume its own profits and losses; and (4) to separate the government administration from enterprise management.[12]

However, considerable ideological obstacles existed. Some economists argued that the concept of establishing a shareholding system and issuing stocks was inconsistent with, even antagonistic to, the concept of socialist public ownership.[13] By contrast, others claimed that this corporate form could benefit the socialist economy even though it had been developed in capitalist economies.[14] This concept received endorsement from Deng Xiaoping, who was in favor of employing some capitalist methods to build socialism.[15] It was adopted by policy-makers, using the idea of "making foreign things serve China and achieve greater, faster, better and more economical results in building socialism."[16]

A far-reaching breakthrough came at the Communist Party Thirteenth National Congress in 1987. It was proclaimed that China, while a socialist country, was still in the first stage of socialism. It was thought at this stage that public ownership must continue to predominate, but at the same time a private sector might contribute production and employment that the state could not provide. This shift in policy reflected an intention to permit the coexistence of private ownership as a supplement to state ownership, which would continue to play the leading role in the Chinese economy. Released from the stringent ideological restraints imposed on it, a flourishing private sector soon emerged and provided the resources necessary to support the shareholding system.

B The stock markets in a socialist economy

> Are such things as securities and stock markets good or bad?....Can they only exist under capitalism? Cannot they also be adapted to socialism?
>
> (Deng Xiaoping[17])

In the view of Singh, stock markets in capitalist economies have a triple role.[18] First, it pools society's savings, previously dispersed among individual savers.

Second, these savings are then channeled selectively to companies with the best investment prospects. Third, the efficient use of assets embodying past savings are encouraged. The advantages are twofold. Companies can raise the capital they require from the public, and the public can obtain an investment opportunity other than merely placing their savings into a bank. But to Deng, the stock market was an experiment.[19] If it was a success, it could be popularized. If problems arose, it could be closed.

Chinese leaders have continuously expressed their concerns over the compatibility of the stock market and the socialist state of China. When ex-Premier Zhu Rongji made his first visit to the Shanghai Stock Exchange (SHSE), he delivered an extremely conservative speech emphasizing the importance of regulation.[20] As a radical economic reformer, he was suspicious of the stock market. Regarding the transition from the planned to the socialist market economy, Li Ruihuan, the former Chairman of the National Committee of the Chinese People's Political Consultative Conference (CPPCC), even called for more research on the complexities of the collision between "new, correct concepts and old improper concepts," as well as "the adjustment of interests between different sectors."[21] Apart from all these worries, the emergence of the securities market in China appears to be a "natural outcome" of conditions arising out of economic reform and the open-door policy."[22] Cao stresses that the restructuring of state enterprises and the establishment of a securities market have presented China with one of its most controversial ideological issues.[23]

3.1.2 Three phases of development

Phase I: Emergence (1978–91)

The birth and development of China's capital markets were closely linked to the reform of the SOEs. In SOE reform, the main focus was on granting greater autonomy to SOEs and implementing the responsibility system. But two problems in particular needed solutions.[24] First, economic growth required capital investment, and mechanisms had to be established to ensure that capital could be provided. Second, many of the companies operated by the state proved to be poorly managed and highly inefficient.

To cope with these problems, the securities market was established. It was meant to extricate the government from the funding problem arising from substantial budget deficits due in part to the heavy subsidies granted to loss-making SOEs. In addition, it was hoped that exposing companies to the rigors of the capital market would improve internal management and raise productivity. Stock markets could be a disciplinary tool providing a direct measure of management effectiveness. This permission was codified in the 1982 Constitution Law.[25]

At the same time, the development of capital markets impacted on SOE reform in a number of ways. Not only could it help to expand the financing channels available to enterprises, it could also change enterprises' ownership structure and internal governance structure.[26]

Stock markets in China did not appear overnight. Rather, there was a gradual process, which began with the issuance of share-like securities during the 1980s. The process was initiated in the township and village enterprises (TVEs), which sprang up in response to the economic reforms of Deng Xiaoping. In order to raise capital for the TVEs, a cooperative shareholder structure was introduced to augment whatever capital could be raised by the villages. The first such enterprise to issue share certificates was a Shenzhen TVE, named Bao'an County Joint Investment Company. A year later, Beijing Tianqiao Department Store became the first SOE to be restructured as a share-issuing company, in August 1984.[27] The same month also witnessed the incorporation of Shanghai Feilo Acoustics Co. Ltd., the first Chinese company to go public.[28]

China's GDP growth averaged 9 percent, and huge savings gave impetus to the emergence of a securities market.[29] To develop an alternative investment option for China's high level of savings, China launched the SHSE in December 1990 and the Shenzhen Stock Exchange (SZSE) in July 1991.

Phase II: Formation and initial development (1992–97)

In early 1992, Deng Xiaoping visited southern China to promote further economic reform and to advocate the establishment of a market economy in China. Following this, the State Economic Structure Reform Commission of the State Council (SESRC) took a major step by promulgating the *Standard Opinion on Limited Liability Companies* and the *Standard Opinion on Joint Stock Companies* (the *Standard Opinions*) on 15 May 1992.[30] The *Standard Opinions* provided for the establishment of limited liability companies and joint stock companies in China, and made it possible for Chinese companies to be listed on stock exchanges outside China. Local governments like Shenzhen had also adopted provisions in respect of business enterprises.

Though each of these laws and regulations had their own individual worth, the fact that they were enacted separately constituted a major problem. Each different law and set of regulations provided different standards for the organization and operation of different types of company. As an increasing number of companies became interested in being listed on stock exchanges within or outside China, the Chinese government felt compelled to adopt a company law that would provide standard requirements on a nationwide basis. Hence, the government worked towards a national company law, drafting seven versions over a ten-year period.[31] The government opened the path to reform by recasting Western corporate law, not as wedded to *laissez-faire* capitalism, but rather as a foreign construction readily adaptable to serving China in accordance with socialist principles.

On 1 July 1994, the Company Law[32] came into force, completing the initial stages of the establishment of the regulatory system and legal framework for China's stock markets. Following its adoption, a number of regulations and laws were enacted or amended in accordance with its general provisions. For example, there were amendments to the 1993 Accounting Law,[33] which set out the basic legal framework of accounting practice and standards, and the amended 1997 Criminal Law,[34] which contains newly created offences for crimes that violate financial and securities laws.[35]

During this period, the development of a securities regulatory framework in China had passed through two stages distinguished by creating the national securities commission. In the early stage, the People's Bank of China (PBOC) was designated as a watchdog to oversee the securities market in conjunction with various bodies of the central and local governments. Securities regulations enacted by certain local authorities were the main form of regulation. The second stage was the establishment of the Securities Committee of the State Council (SCSC) and the CSRC in October 1992.[36] This marked an important milestone, as China's capital markets started to align for the first time under a single centralized regulatory framework.

In the meantime, China opened up its capital market in two steps: first, creating the domestic B-share market; second, restructuring Chinese SOEs for overseas listing.

B-shares were created in 1991 for the sole purpose of enabling foreign investors to participate in the domestic markets. The aim was to have outlets available for the investment capital of non-mainland Chinese investors so that Chinese companies could have access to external sources of capital. The "foreign investors" in B-share regulation were initially defined to include institutional and individual investors from foreign countries, including Hong Kong, Macau, and Taiwan. The scope has now been extended to include Chinese citizens who reside permanently abroad. In the beginning, the experimental B-share scheme was limited to Shanghai and Shenzhen. It has now been extended to other parts of China.

Following the launch of the B-share scheme, a further step was taken to open up Chinese stock markets when nine Chinese companies were listed in Hong Kong in 1993. This was followed by the listing of several companies in the US and UK markets, and more companies on the Hong Kong Stock Exchange. Overseas listings provided more financing options for Chinese enterprises and led to the initial exposure of international investment banks to China. The listings also accelerated the restructuring of large SOEs and enhanced their reputation and competitiveness. China's experiment with listing has proved a definite learning curve for both company managers and the government. Failure of one model rapidly led to the development of new ideas and new models, as investment bankers, responding to investor demand, pushed the experiment forward. At the same time, major international companies were experiencing a trend toward the globalization of their operations.

Phase III: Further regulation and development (1998–present)

From 1998 onwards, with the promulgation of the Securities Law, the legal status of China's capital markets was formalized and strengthened. The Securities Law codified the regulatory practices that China had implemented in the past to regulate its emerging securities market. It also incorporated China's accumulated experience so far, and took on board lessons from the Asian financial crisis of 1997. However, there was no legal provision regarding the trading of state-owned shares, nor any provision regarding investment funds. This implied that Chinese legislators still struggled with certain fundamental socialist ideological issues and were cautious about new market practices.[37] Consequently, rules and regulations have been constantly amended, developed, and implemented, as exemplified by the amendments to the Company Law and Securities Law in 2005. These revisions resulted in profound changes in China's capital markets.

The role of the stock market in China is to enable the raising of huge amounts of capital for Chinese companies. By November 2012 there were a total of 2,494 listed companies in China's capital markets with a total capitalization of RMB19.93 trillion.[38] Wealth management is becoming increasingly popular among Chinese households, with the number of investor accounts increasing from 8.35 million in 1992 to nearly 138 million by the end of 2007.[39]

3.1.3 China at the transition stage

In the transition stage of an emerging economy, legal reform can take place by means of legal transplants from other developed economies. However, in the view of Black and Kraakman, and other scholars, emerging economies cannot simply copy the laws of other jurisdictions because these laws depend upon highly evolved market, legal, and governmental institutions and cultural norms that often do not exist in emerging economies.[40] To design and subsequently implement a suitable regulatory framework, the existing problems of the securities market must be diagnosed first.

According to its China Corporate Governance Report 2003, the SHSE has identified several shortfalls in its corporate governance practices; two are particularly important:

1 There is a conflict of interest when the government is both the referee and the player in regard to Chinese listed companies. On the one hand, the government enacts laws and regulations, sets up rules for the market, regulates the economic activities, and supervises the implementation of corporate governance institutions that it imposes on the companies. On the other hand, the government is a major shareholder of the company. Chinese listed companies have an improper shareholding structure with an overwhelmingly large percentage of non-tradable shares. In a majority of listed companies, non-tradable shares represent 60–80 percent of the total number. A few companies even have more than 90 percent shares that are not tradable.
2 China's legal and regulatory framework is far from mature. Apart from the fact that China's legal infrastructure is constantly improving, the Company Law and the Securities Law are especially inadequate in many aspects due to outdated concepts and limited practical experience at the time they were drafted. For example, there are a lack of measures to prevent controlling

shareholders from abusing the limited liability principle; there is inadequate protection for minority shareholders; there is excess reliance on administrative measures to directly limit the improper behavior of market participants.[41]

This report from the SHSE was released almost a decade ago. There have obviously been some developments since then in these two areas. For example, the government started a pilot program in 2005 in which 46 companies would convert their non-tradable shares into tradable ones.[42] Also, amendments to the Company Law and the Securities Law were adopted by the National People's Congress (NPC) on 27 October 2005. However, all these may only partially resolve the problems. According to a recent corporate governance report compiled by the Chinese Academy of Social Science, the ownership structure problem still exists.[43] Therefore, it is crucial to look at the root of these issues.

A The problem of ownership structure

Skepticism about China making a clean break with its socialist past and leaping into capitalism derives in large part from the Chinese leadership's stubborn rejection of privatization.[44] Zhu has noted that since 1987 two main themes have run throughout the development of securities regulation in China: one, to ensure the primacy of socialist ownership, the other, to restrict foreign ownership in SOEs.[45] To bring its state enterprises further within the market's orbit without privatizing their ownership structure, China created a comprehensive legal framework aimed at transforming state-run enterprises into merely state-owned ones, separating the government's ownership of an enterprise from its management and administration.[46]

With the establishment of the SHSE and the SZSE, large SOEs were increasingly transformed into joint stock companies. A distinctive feature that separates China's stock markets from those in other countries is the dichotomy of floatability of stocks, which refers to the phenomenon that two-thirds of the outstanding shares in China are not tradable. Any SOE converting into a shareholding company would have to divide up its shares into three parts, each roughly equal.[47] About a third can be publicly issued, owned by individuals and legal persons, and freely traded. The remainder would have to be allocated to state shares and legal person shares which could not be traded on the stock market. These two-thirds of shares would be issued to the founders of a corporation, business partners, or employees, and served two main purposes; to keep firmly in government hands the control of SOEs that were floated in the market, and to maximize IPO proceeds.[48] One of the major problems of Chinese stock markets has been caused by the large amount of shares in listed companies owned by the government and government entities.[49] The different categories of shares are shown in Table 3.1.

Originally, the objectives of the corporatization agenda were good, as outlined by Chen:

Table 3.1 China's share categories

Tradeable?	*Type of shares*	*Definition*
No (Private block transfer possible)	State Shares (G-shares after reform that are tradable)	About a third of equity is transferred to state organs. These shares are either managed and represented by the Bureau of National Assets Management, or held by other state-owned companies. The ultimate owner of state shares is the State Council. They are non-tradeable. But after reforms in 2005 the state shares became G-shares and are tradeable.
	Legal Person (LP) Shares	About a third of every listed firm's equity is sold to domestic institutions (securities companies and SOEs with at least one non-state owner) and become LP shares. These cannot be traded on the stock market.
	Employee Shares	Shares sold to firm's employees during the same process.
Yes	A-Shares	Renminbi (RMB)-dominated ordinary shares issued by Chinese incorporated shareholdings companies, and traded on the Shanghai and Shenzhen Stock Exchanges. Trading of A-shares has been restricted to investors from mainland China that are either institutions or individuals. (Note: An exception may be the foreign investors under the Qualified Foreign Institutional Investor Program.)
	B-Shares	RMB-dominated shares issued by Chinese incorporated shareholding companies and traded on the Shanghai and Shenzhen Stock Exchanges. B-shares are subscribed and traded in foreign currencies.
	H-Shares	Shares issued by Chinese incorporated shareholding companies and listed in the Hong Kong market. In a broad sense, this term also refers to shares listed overseas, e.g., in the US, the UK, and Singapore. However, in this book, H-shares are predominantly used to refer to those shares of Chinese companies listed in Hong Kong.

Sources: based on the CSRC Annual Report 2007, Green (2003) and Allen *et al.* (2007).

1. change the ownership structure of those SOEs that feature both state and non-state institutional shareholders in addition to small individual shareholders;
2. separate the state from business operation for enterprises so as to achieve full autonomy, not only in business structure but also in operational decisions; and for the state to limit its liabilities to those enterprises;
3. improve managerial incentives by installing shareholders with incentives and the ability to monitor managers.[50]

The most obvious impact of classification between tradable and non-tradable shares is the limited free float available, which made the domestic market extremely illiquid, volatile, and thus prone to market manipulation and insider trading.[51] The principal function of any market is to price goods or services. The specific market condition that regulators and exchanges attempt to create is called transparency. With a sufficient degree of transparency investors have a level playing field on which to make their investment decisions. Regrettably, according to Howie and Walter, the markets do not play this function for Chinese companies, for the simple reason that the different classes of stock trade in different and functionally independent markets.[52] In a comprehensive review of the empirical evidence as to whether state or private ownership more efficiently fosters economic progress, Djankov and Murrell find that investment funds, foreigners, and blockholders are the most effective in facilitating restructurings.[53] The least effective are found to be workers, diffuse individual investors, and the state.

Furthermore, as Clarke rightly points out, the diagnoses and the implementation of corporatization as a solution, are flawed.[54] The problem of the SOEs may have stemmed from the unity of ownership and control in the hands of the state. Theoretically, it is hard to determine which is superior between concentrated and dispersed ownership structures since each has its own agency problem. The conflicts of majority-minority shareholders are more imminent in the concentrated ownership system, while the conflicts between principal and agent are common in the latter system. Many developed Anglo-American countries like Canada and Australia also have concentrated ownership.[55] In China, however, the ownership problem is not arising from controlling shareholders, but from the state as a blockholder. In practice, a large number of corporatized SOEs remain dominated by a single state shareholder that exercises its control through formal channels, such as shareholder voting and appointment of key personnel.[56] Ironically, the state as the majority shareholder plays an ineffective role in monitoring the behavior of managers on a continual basis because the state is a collective body, so there is no body within it with sufficient and appropriate incentives to perform this role. There has not been any "real ownership." Meanwhile, the holders of tradable shares are typically minority shareholders with limited power to affect management decisions.

The problem is twofold. First, there is a majority-minority conflict. The interests of the state as the majority shareholder may not necessarily intersect with that of the minority shareholders, whose interest is purely profit-seeking. Second, there is a principal and agent conflict. With inadequate shareholder pressure, it is questionable whether trust can be put in managers. However, many Chinese firms are characterized by excessive Chief Executive Officer (CEO) power, insider control, and weak transparency.[57] Corruption remains widespread in China. An effective legal and regulatory regime is highly desirable.

B The problem of weak governance strategies

A standardized framework of investor protection is important when investors are too naïve to protect themselves. This appears to be a major concern for the present situation in China. It is claimed by many scholars that the interests of minority shareholders are not adequately protected in China because the state is the controlling shareholder in most listed companies.[58] The majority of Chinese listed companies are in fact former SOEs. Out of 1,160 listed companies at the end of 2001, approximately 1,103 were originally SOEs.[59] Similarly, statistics in Liu and Sun's study revealed that approximately 84 percent of public companies in the Chinese stock markets were ultimately controlled by the state in terms of equity ownership.[60] As observed by Xi, even to institutional investors, the concentrated ownership structure of Chinese listed companies is a barrier to exercise their voting power in a meaningful way under the basic "one share, one vote" system.[61]

When large shareholders effectively control a company, their policies may result in the expropriation of minority shareholders through: transferring resources from the company to controlling shareholders (i.e., "tunneling");[62] manipulating prices in transactions with other entities it controls such as related-party transactions;[63] controlling shareholders enriching themselves by not paying out dividends; or expropriation through the pursuit of non-profit-maximizing objectives by large investors.[64]

This is also the case in China. Various situations in which controlling shareholders may exploit minority shareholders in China are well documented. For example, a form of tunneling is that Chinese listed companies issue loan guarantees to their related parties (usually controlling blockholders), thereby expropriating wealth from minority shareholders.[65] Arguably, concentrated ownership, which is not rare among economies, does not necessarily result in tunneling. But the degree of controlling ownership accounts for a significant portion of it.[67] Another form of expropriation of minority shareholders could be achieved by related-party transactions, mentioned above. A corporate governance report by the SHSE revealed that approximately 40 percent of listed companies engaged in related-party transactions with their top ten shareholders, and that 78.94 percent of related-party transactions were related to SOEs in 2005.[68] A related-party transaction is not necessarily a transaction on unfair terms to the company, but given the lack of institutional safeguards that might ensure fair terms, there are legitimate grounds for concern.[69]

C The problem of weak regulatory strategies

In principle, disgruntled investors can enforce their rights through private civil actions. In practice, Pistor and Xu claim that private enforcement was rare in China before 2001, not because of a lack of demand for it, but because courts have restricted investor lawsuits.[70] Private litigation began to take off in 2001 in response to fraud uncovered at Yorkpoint Science & Technology and Yin Guangxia. Some 363 defiant investors commenced legal proceedings against Yorkpoint Science & Technology Co in the Intermediate People's Court of Beijing, Shanghai and Guangzhou in 2001.[71] Likewise, numerous investors prepared to file suits against Yin Guangxia.[72] This shocked key government officials as they always thought in terms of administrative measures instead of the judicial system. In September 2001 the Supreme People's Court promulgated a notice directing all lower courts not to accept private securities lawsuits.[73]

However, the Notice led to severe criticism from the public. Under pressure, the Supreme People's Court partially lifted the temporary ban in January 2002 by issuing a second Notice allowing lower courts to accept private securities litigation based upon false disclosure.[74] Later, Daqing Lianyi was involved in fraudulent disclosure scandals, which took the lead in the race triggered by the second Notice to sue listed companies.[75] In 2003, a third circular was promulgated setting out more detailed procedural rules for dealing with securities cases.[76] In the opinion of Zhu, these procedural rules, in conjunction with other relevant provisions of law, like the Company Law, the Securities Law and the Civil Procedure Rule, finally provided courts with the guidelines necessary to address claims from investors.[77] From this incident, Chen points out the inadequacy of the Chinese legal system, claiming that it is more like "crash-then-law" than "growth-then-law" in China.[78] China should have learned from the experience of other jurisdictions, given that it did not launch its capital markets until 1990s, a time when other developed markets had already accumulated considerable experience in relation to regulation.

While civil litigation can provide a remedy to disappointed investors, public enforcement, or even criminal liability, can serve as a strong deterrent to securities crime. Listed companies and securities firms are subject to a number of laws, with the CSRC as regulator. Additionally, the two stock exchanges can take enforcement action of their own in accordance with the listing rules. To illustrate the stages in a typical enforcement action by the CSRC, a time-line is used in Table 3.2 to highlight the major events.[79]

Table 3.2 Timeline of the CSRC's enforcement

Event 1:	A firm commits a fraud.
Event 2:	The CSRC learns of a possible fraud and makes an initial assessment of whether to proceed.
Event 3:	The CSRC begins an enforcement investigation.
Event 4:	The CSRC publishes an enforcement action.

Source: based on Chen *et al.* (2005).

A fraud is typically carried out over a 1–2 year period. The length of time between event 1 and event 4 is about 3–4 years.[80] Investors will not learn about an enforcement action until the final stage is reached.

A breakdown of enforcement actions in Chinese capital markets in the period from 1999 to 2003 is summarized in the work of Chen *et al.*, and consists of four panels of data including violation type, regulatory institution, report type, and the type of enforcement action.[81] From their statistics, more than half of the penalties were public condemnation. Fines, the most serious penalty, only accounted for about 11 percent of the sanctions.

The data coincides with Pistor and Xu's opinion that public law enforcement in the form of fines, or other more severe sanctions imposed by regulators, has been weak.[82] Public enforcement has been improved, but it is still not at a satisfactory level. According to more recent figures from 2007, the CSRC referred more than 60 people to the judicial system in relation to securities crime committed since 2003.[83] Only about ten of them have been prosecuted, and the average sentence was between six months and one year of imprisonment. Moreover, the fact that a typical investigation cycle can take three to four years underlines concerns about whether the authorities have the resources and political power to tackle violations within the stock market.[84] Legally, the difficulties in collecting evidence are strong barriers to successful criminal prosecutions against rule breakers, claim CSRC officials.[85] Even if a fines were imposed, the level of fines would not be sufficient to dissuade others from breaking the rules.[86]

Guo and Anderson have concluded that the CSRC and other regulators might be susceptible to political influence, local protectionism, and other forms of corruption.[87] Furthermore, what makes matters worse is that administrative and criminal penalties have not been severe enough to deter bad practices within Chinese companies and markets. The government is often reluctant to impose heavy administrative penalties for fear of negatively impacting on the company's performance; criminal prosecution is only invoked in particularly serious circumstances. As a result, potential violators may choose to flout the law because illicit gains are likely to be larger than any likely penalties. In light of the struggle between law and politics, Tomasic and Fu also add that it may be the case that a company chairman has a higher rank in the Communist Party than the investigating CSRC official, because senior managers of companies, and in particular SOEs, are usually appointed by the Party.[88] The CSRC is only a "quasi-government department," and not that powerful in the eyes of listed companies.

3.2 Development of Hong Kong's stock market

Hong Kong is frequently described as a place where East meets West, reflecting the territory's mix of its Chinese roots and a culture introduced to it during its time as a British colony. Geography and history have made Hong Kong a home to the largest concentration of Chinese outside China. This unique combination of East and West has built Hong Kong into a cosmopolitan metropolis with a remarkable level of prosperity and economic development, which, in turn, has generated important and perhaps unexpected secondary developments, including an important international securities market. It is one of the world's leading international financial centers, with a major capitalist service economy characterized by low taxation, free trade, and minimum government intervention under the ethos of positive non-interventionism.

3.2.1 The Hong Kong model: a laissez-faire economy[89]

It is argued that Hong Kong is one of the world's freest economies, although the Hong Kong government has always espoused policies of free trade and non-intervention. Scholars point to several economic factors that imply Hong Kong is far from being open and competitive.[90] For example, the transport and electricity sectors are highly regulated; housing, education and medical services, too, are dominated by the public sector.[91]

The policy of non-intervention does not mean that the government does not do anything. Instead, the role of government is limited to providing a business-friendly environment; the government leaves the economy to be led by market forces.[92] The rationale behind the policy of non-intervention is that "investors and entrepreneurs understand markets far better than officials and that private initiatives are a surer way to build Hong Kong's prosperity than any bureaucrat's blueprint."[93] Hong Kong has successfully transformed from an entrepôt, to a manufacturing center, to an international financial center. It owes its success to the market-led economy.[94]

The government's primary role is to provide the fundamental "software," such as personal liberty, the rule of law, a clean and efficient administration, and a level playing field for all business.[95] It must also provide the land and the infrastructural "hardware" like schools, roads, and airports that Hong Kong needs for its growth. The government also has a duty to protect and promote Hong Kong's commercial interests in national and international arenas through participation in, for example, the World Trade Organization (WTO) and the Asia-Pacific Economic Cooperation (APEC), and through negotiating and entering into bilateral arrangements with other countries.

It is in this spirit that the Hong Kong government has intervened sparingly in the market over the last 50 years, except for a few exceptions. Interventions have included the establishment of the linked exchange rate system, which stabilized Hong Kong currency against the US dollar,[96] and the development of the Mass Transit Railway System. One can argue that such initiatives have improved the business environment and that they are actually part of the policy of non-intervention rather than being exceptions to the rule.

However, since the 1998 Asian financial crisis, Hong Kong has been more interventionist in financial affairs than the purists would like. In particular, the financial turmoil started from a sub-prime crisis in the US in 2006 and has caused ruptures across many other countries in the form of financial failure and a global credit crunch. The Hong Kong government realizes that a free market without government intervention may lead to economic disaster.[97] The role of government is to create macroeconomic conditions to ensure a wise form of laissez faire, rather than free-for-all capitalism.

3.2.2 A brief history of its stock market

Before 1986

Hong Kong has experienced more than 100 years of stock market development. In 1891 the Association of Stockbrokers in Hong Kong was formed. It was later renamed "Hong Kong Stock Exchange" in 1914. A second stock exchange, the Hong Kong Stockbrokers' Association, was incorporated in 1921. The two exchanges then merged in 1947 under the name "Hong Kong Stock Exchange," which held a monopoly until 1969.

However, capital funding via the Stock Exchange was insignificant. In the period 1957–67, only 50–70 companies were listed, and less than 25 percent of them were actively traded.[98] In this period, the uncertainty over Hong Kong's political future affected investor confidence in Hong Kong. In 1969 reassurances from China in this regard increased confidence levels and the stock market boomed. In the same year, the Far East Exchange was opened. Another two exchanges, the Kan Ngan Stock Exchange and the Kowloon Stock Exchange, were established in 1971 and 1972 respectively. By 1972, the presence of the four exchanges hastened the development of Hong Kong's stock market and soon the community at large was investing in stocks.

The Stock Market Crash of 1973 and the oil crisis in 1974, led to the enactment of the Hong Kong government's first significant securities legislation: the Securities Ordinance[99] and the Protection of Investors Ordinance.[100] The Commissioner for Securities and the Securities Commission were also established to regulate and oversee the four exchanges. The need to strengthen market regulation and unify the four exchanges prompted the incorporation of the Stock Exchange of Hong Kong (SEHK) in 1986.

Since 1986

The closure of the Stock Exchange in the aftermath of Black Monday in October 1987 led to the Davison Report, which recommended a series of reforms for the securities and futures industry, including the establishment of the Securities and Futures Commission (SFC).[101] Since then a sophisticated regulatory framework has been established. A point to note is that the SFC does not impose too much regulation, since it was concerned that an over-regulated financial market would be unattractive to investors.

As part of the reforms stated in the Financial Budget of 1999, the SEHK and the Hong Kong Futures Exchange demutualized. Together with the Hong Kong Securities Clearing Company, they became wholly owned subsidiaries of Hong Kong Exchanges and Clearing Limited (HKEx). In March 2000 the merger was completed and HKEx went public on 27 June.

Since return of the sovereignty of Hong Kong from the UK to China, in 1997, as a Special Administrative Region (SAR), the "One Country Two Systems" concept has been working convincingly and Hong Kong remains an active international financial center.

3.2.3 Hong Kong as Asia's international financial center and "China's Manhattan"

A International financial center in Asia

Apart from its established stock market, Hong Kong has been an international banking center since 1900. Reed combines the number of banks in financial centers, affirming Hong Kong's leading role in finance (See Table 3.3).[102]

Cassis, in his comparative history of international financial centers, concludes that Hong Kong's success is attributable to the following elements.[103] First, Hong Kong was not starting from scratch. By the 1920s it had already emerged among the region's main financial centers and continued to play this role after 1945. Second, it had solid banking institutions dating from the nineteenth century and benefited from the presence of British overseas banks, especially the Hong Kong and Shanghai Banking Corporation. Third, it enjoys an advantageous geographical location, with lively ports, as well as being linked to the rest of the world by excellent transport, particularly air transport and telecommunications networks. Finally, its political regime has been stable, despite the troubles that plagued Hong Kong during the Chinese Cultural Revolution at the end of the 1960s and the uncertainty in relation to its handover to China in 1997.

Due to the positive determinants above, Hong Kong leads the way in Asian capital markets. Total market capitalization increased by 55 percent each year, until the credit crunch.[104] In recent years Hong Kong has been a high scorer in several international rankings, which serves as an indication of how well Hong Kong is recognized internationally.[105] From a path-dependent perspective, its success also perhaps reflects the fact that Hong Kong is not built upon one, or a few, but a spectrum of factors. For example, in terms of economic freedom Hong Kong is ranked first out of 179 countries;[106] in competitiveness Hong Kong ranks

Table 3.3 Ranking score of selected top international banking centers

	London	*New York*	*Hong Kong*	*Tokyo*	*Singapore*
1900	100	87	77	–	–
1915	99	100	84	–	–
1930	100	93	74	70	–
1947	100	92	78	–	76
1960	100	97	78	80	–
1970	100	99	76	86	–
1980	100	100	89	90	–

Source: Reed (1981).

first out of 59 economies.[107] Few would say that Hong Kong is not international. However, the international orientation of Hong Kong's financial services hinges on whether Hong Kong can continue to offer something unique to the global financial markets and how well Hong Kong links to the global financial markets.

B "China's Manhattan"

Hong Kong began as an entrepôt and a center of commercial activities, bridging China and the world economy in the mid-nineteenth century.[108] Since then it has taken a developmental route of its own, flourishing first as an entrepôt and a center of commerce and finance for Chinese business, then as an industrial city, and subsequently as a regional and international financial center. By the time Hong Kong was returned to China in 1997, this could be seen as part of a longer process of Hong Kong–China socio-economic integration that started in the 1970s so that, once again, Hong Kong holds a strategic position between China and the global economy. Today, Hong Kong plays a crucial intermediary role in the context of a rapidly growing and internationalizing Chinese economy, during a period in which China is also changing rapidly in terms of its geo-political reach. China has become "the factory of the world."

One eye-catching feature of the socio-economic changes in Hong Kong over the past two decades has been the significant influx of Chinese companies. It is a premier trading center for the shares of mainland enterprises. Hong Kong has some unique advantages such as its geographical proximity to, and cultural affinity with, the mainland. During the period 1997–2007, more than 70 percent of trading in the shares of mainland enterprises that were also listed in the US and UK, was conducted in the Hong Kong market.[109] The listing of mainland companies has widened the breadth of the Hong Kong Stock Market and provided more choice for investors.

In 1999 the SEHK revealed its intention to become the "Manhattan of China" by playing a bigger role in raising equity funds for China's economic development.[110] It envisioned China remaining the Exchange's main source of growth. This ambition was also reflected in the SFC blueprint that "Hong Kong will continue to play its unique role as a platform bridging the Mainland and the international marketplace."[111]

3.3 Concluding remarks

The development of a given market cannot be isolated from its historical background. Putting the Chinese and Hong Kong stock markets into the context of historic, economic, and political preconditions, the chapter shows that their patterns of market development are very different from each other.

China adopts a socialist market economy characterized by government planning. By contrast, Hong Kong largely evolves from a laissez-faire economy with minimum government intervention, despite ownership and control of several vital factors of production.[112] The emergence of the securities markets appears to be a natural outcome as a result of the political economy. The role of the Chinese stock markets is to raise funds for SOEs (corporatization without privatization)[113] while the main function of the Hong Kong market is to facilitate corporate financing and a more diversified ownership structure featuring foreign investors.

Compared to the 20-year history of China's capital markets, the Hong Kong market has undergone more than 100 years of development. It has long been positioned as an international financial center in Asia, and serves as a platform bridging the mainland and the international marketplace. Hong Kong takes advantage of the mix between East and West. It is rooted in China and enjoys investment and labor inflow from the mainland. But in the meantime, it benefits from a colonial legacy of common law institutions and a free market. In this respect, it is clearly ahead of its counterparts in China.

Unlike Hong Kong, China, as a late starter, where formal stock exchanges did not exist until the 1990s, has faced tremendous difficulties in developing its stock markets. Officials and scholars often claim that China needs a more developed legal system because "a market economy is an economy governed by law."[114] A constructive and practical approach to nurture the Chinese markets, which is still at the transition stage, would be to learn practices from a well-developed market. In this way, the fact that it is a late starter may not be a weakness, but an opportunity. Undoubtedly, there have been improvements in China's legal infrastructure and market institutions. However, despite a rapid growth in China's stock markets in recent years, there is still a long way to go before China will be able to develop mature securities markets.

Notes

1 See Coffee, John (1999), "The Future as History: The Prospects for Global Convergence in Corporate Governance and Its Implications" in *Northwestern University Law Review*, 93; Coffee, John (2002), "Racing towards the Top? The Impact of Cross-listings and Stock Market Competition on International Corporate Governance" in *Columbia Law Review*, 102; and Stulz, René (1999), "Globalization, Corporate Finance, and the Cost of Capital" in *Journal of Applied Corporate Finance*, 12.

2 Cassis, Youssef (2006), *Capitals of Capital*, Cambridge: Cambridge University Press, p. 5.

3 Wei, Yuwa (2005), "The Development of the Securities Market and Regulation in China" in *Loyola of Los Angeles International and Comparative Law Review*, 27, p. 488.

4 Chen, Albert (1992), *An Introduction to the Legal System of the People's Republic of China*, Singapore: Butterworths (Asia), pp. 29–33.

5 Wood, Philip (2005), *Maps of World Financial Law*, 5th edn, London: Allen & Overy, p. 45. He chooses five key indicators to help position worldwide legal systems. These are insolvency set-off, marketability of contracts, securities interests, commercial trust, and tracing.

6 Following Deng Xiaoping's triumphant tour of south China in late 1992, the Communist Party Committee's decision on the "socialist market economy" system of 1993 finally cast aside the concept of planned economy and marked the eventual adoption by the Chinese leadership of a more liberal and market-oriented reform strategy. See *Decisions of the Communist Party Central Committee on Some Issues*

concerning the Establishment of a Socialist Market Economy System, adopted by the Third Plenary Session of the CPC Fourteenth National Congress on 14 November 1993.

7 Wang, Wallace (1992), "Reforming State Enterprises in China: The Case for Redefining Enterprise Operating Rights" in *Journal of Chinese Law*, 6, p. 92. Money-losing enterprises typically resist declaring bankruptcy because the attitudes toward bankruptcy are so negative and because the workers would lose their jobs with little prospect of finding new ones in a competitive market.

8 Art, Robert and Gu, Minkang (1995), "China Incorporated: The First Corporation Law of the People's Republic of China" in *Yale Journal of International Law*, 20, p. 277.

9 More specifically, the reform was aimed at (1) moving the economy toward greater decentralization of decision-making; (2) increasing reliance on market forces and on material incentives for motivating desired economic behavior and resource allocation; and (3) opening the economy to external competition through foreign investment. See Xia, Mei *et al.* (1992), *The Re-Emerging Securities Market in China*, London: Quorum Books, p. 22.

10 Ibid, pp. 22–9.

11 Two steps were identified for SOE reform. The first was converting SOE's operational management mechanisms while leaving their fundamental ownership and organizational structure unaltered. The second step was corporatizing SOEs, in particular, large- and middle-sized SOEs, in a gradual and realistic manner. For more information about SOE reform, see Xi, Chao (2009), *Corporate Governance and Legal Reform in China*, London: Wildy, Simmonds & Hill Publishing, pp. 7–14.

12 Tan, Lay Hong (1998), "Legal Issues in China's Bifurcated Securities Markets" in *Company Lawyer*, 19.

13 Qian, Xuefeng (1993), "Riding Two Horses: Corporatizing Enterprises and the Emerging Securities Regulatory Regime in China" in *UCLA Pacific Basin Law Journal*, 12.

14 Wang, op. cit., pp. 119–21.

15 Deng, Xiaoping (1994), "Shehui Zhuyi he Shichang Jingji bu Cunzai Genben Maodun" [There is No Fundamental Contradiction between Socialism and a Market Economy] in *Selected Works of Deng Xiaoping (Volume III)*, Beijing: Foreign Language Press, pp. 151–3.

16 Meyer, Jennifer (1994), "Let the Buyer Beware: Economic Modernization, Insurance Reform, and Consumer Protection in China" in *Fordham Law Review*, 62, pp. 2131–2.

17 Speech made by Deng Xiaoping on his Southern Excursion in 1992.

18 Singh, Ajit (1990), "The Stock Market in a Socialist Economy" in Nolan, Peter and Fureng, Dong (eds.), *The Chinese Economy and its Future: Achievement and Problems of Post-Mao Reform*, Cambridge: Polity Press, p. 162.

19 See Green, Stephen (2003), *China's Stockmarket: A Guide to its Progress, Players and Prospects*, London: The Economist, p. 13.

20 Ibid., p. 21.

21 Keith, Ronald and Lin, Zhiqiu (2001), *Law and Justice in China's New Market Place*, Hampshire: Palgrave, p. 3.

22 Zhu, Sanzhu (2000), *Securities Regulation in China*, New York: Transnational, p. 4.

23 Cao, Lan (2000), "Chinese Privatization: Between Plan and Market" in *Law and Contemporary Problems*, 63. She claims that China has been ideologically circumscribed by "market socialism," market-based but only palatable to and compatible with socialism. Chinese officials view "corporatization," the conversion of a state-owned enterprise into a shareholder company, and "securitization," the subsequent sale of such shares on a securities market, as ideologically compatible with "socialism with Chinese characteristics."

24 Malkiel, Burton *et al.* (2008), *From Wall Street to the Great Wall: How Investors Can Profit from China's Booming Economy*, New York: W.W. Norton & Company, p. 103.
25 Preamble of the 1982 Constitution Law of the PRC.
26 As regards the effects of the stock market on SOEs, see Chen, Chien-Hsun and Shih, Hui-Tzu (2002), *The Evolution of the Stock Market in China's Transnational Economy*, Cheltenham: Edward Elgar, pp. 77–9.
27 CSRC (2008), *China Capital Markets Development Report*, Beijing: China Financial Publishing House, p. 3.
28 Ibid.
29 Zhang, Yichen and Yu, Da (1994), "China's Emerging Securities Market" in *Columbia Journal of World Business*, 29, p. 113.
30 Both *Standard Opinions* were promulgated by the State Commission for Restructuring the Economic Systems, and came into force on 15 May 1992.
31 *Asia Today*, 20 July 1994, "Zhongguo Gongsifa Jijiang Shishi" [The Chinese Corporate Law Will Come into Force].
32 The Company Law of the PRC was adopted at the Fifth Session of the Standing Committee of the Eighth National Peoples' Congress on 29 December 1993, and amended on 27 October 2005; the amendment came into force on 1 January 2006.
33 The Accounting Law of the PRC was adopted by the Ninth Session of the Standing Committee of the Sixth National People's Congress on 21 January 1985, and amended in 1993 and 1999; the amendment came into force on 1 July 2000.
34 The Criminal Law of the PRC was adopted by the Fifth National People's Congress on 1 July 1979, was amended on 14 March 1994, and came into force on 1 October 1997.
35 Arts. 170–191 Criminal Law 1997, dealt with crimes violating financial regulation.
36 In April 1998 the CSRC became the sole regulator of the national securities and futures markets by consolidating the supervisory functions of SCSC and PBC into the CSRC.
37 Zhu, op. cit., p. 221.
38 Data from CSRC. Online. Available at: www.csrc.gov.cn/pub/newsite/sjtj/ [accessed 20 December 2012].
39 CSRC, op. cit.
40 For example, Black, Bernard and Kraakman, Reinier (1996), "A Self-enforcing Model of Corporate Law" in *Harvard Law Review*, 109, p. 1913; Seidman, Ann and Seidman, Robert (1996), "Drafting Legislation for Development: Lessons from a Chinese Project" in *American Journal of Comparative Law*, 44, p. 34 ("The Law of non-transferability of Law holds that, save accidentally, no country can copy another country's law and achieve similar outcomes."); and Teubner, Gunther (1998), "Legal Irritants: Good Faith in British Law or How Unifying Law Ends Up in New Divergences" in *Modern Law Review*, 61, p. 14 ("Convergences are observable on the level of legal rules and institutions but the deep structures of law, legal culture, legal mentalities, legal epistemologies and the unconscious of law as expressed in legal mythologies, remain historically unique and cannot be bridged.")
41 For the detailed report, see SHSE (2003), *China Corporate Governance Report*, Shanghai: Fudan University Press. For more summarized key points, see Fu, Jian and Tomasic, Roman (2006), "Legal Regulation and Corporate Governance in China's top 100 Listed Companies" in *Company Lawyer*, 27, p. 281.
42 Yeung, Horace (2009), "Non-tradable Share Reform in China: A Review of Progress" in *Company Lawyer*, 30.
43 Lu, Tong *et al.* (2006), "Corporate Governance Assessment on the Top 100 Chinese Listed Companies" in *China Economist*, 3. Online. Available at: www.iwep.org.cn/cccg/en/publications.htm (accessed 22 June 2009).
44 Wedeman, Andrew (2003), "Corporate Capitalism in Socialist China" in Gomez,

Edmund and Hsiao, Hsin-Huang (eds.), *Chinese Enterprise, Transnationalism and Identity*, London: Routledge, p. 73.
45 Zhu, op. cit., p. 169.
46 Cao, op. cit., p. 34.
47 Green, op. cit. p. 15.
48 Bortolotti Bernardo and Beltratti, Andrea (2006), "The Nontradable Share Reform in the Chinese Stock Market." FEEM Working Paper No. 131.06. Online. Available at: http://ssrn.com/abstract=944412 (accessed 20 December 2012).
49 Allen, Franklin *et al.* (2007), "China's Financial System: Past, Present, and Future" in Rawski, Thomas and Brandt, Loren (eds.), *China's Great Economic Transformation*, Cambridge: Cambridge University Press.
50 Chen, Jinghan (2005), "Corporatization of China's State-owned Enterprises and Corporate Governance" in Brown, David and MacBean, Alasdair (eds.), *Challenges for China's Development – An Enterprise Perspective*, London: Routledge, p. 60.
51 For more criticisms, see Huang, Flora Xiao (2010), "Modernizing the Chinese Capital Market: Old Problems and New Legal Response" in *International Company and Commercial Law Review*, 21, p. 31.
52 Howie, Fraser and Walter, Carl (2003), *Privatizing China: The Stock Markets and Their Role in Corporate Reform*, Singapore: John Wiley & Sons, p. 177.
53 Djankov, Simeon and Murrell, Peter (2002), "Enterprise Restructuring in Transition: A Quantitative Survey" in *Journal of Economic Literature*, 40.
54 Clarke, Donald (2003), "Corporate Governance in China: An Overview", in *China Economic Review*, 14, pp. 497–500.
55 Morck, Randall (1996), "On the Economic of Concentrated Ownership" in *Canadian Business Law Journal*, 26, p. 69; Morck, Randall and Yeung, Bernard (2003), "Agency Problems in Large Family Business Groups" in *Entrepreneurship Theory and Practice*, 27, p. 369.
56 Clark, op. cit., p. 499.
57 Hua, Jinyang *et al.* (2006), "An Empirical Taxonomy of SOE Governance in Transitional China" in *Journal of Management and Governance*, 10, p. 413.
58 For example, Cheung *et al.* argue that minority shareholders in Chinese companies that conduct connected transactions with their controlling state-owned shareholders are subject to expropriation from such political connections. See Cheung, Yan-Leung *et al.* (2005), "Guanxi, Political Connections, and Expropriation: The Dark Side of State Ownership in Chinese Listed Companies." City University of Hong Kong Working Paper.
59 Green, Stephen (2003), "China's Stock Market: Eight Myths and Some Reasons to be Optimistic." The China Project Working Paper No. 6. Online. Available at: http://ssrn.com/abstract=431200.
60 Liu, Guy and Sun, Pei (2003), "Identifying Ultimate Controlling Shareholders in Chinese Public Corporations: An Empirical Survey." Royal Institute of International Affairs, Asia Program Working Paper No. 2. Online. Available at: www.chathamhouse.org/publications/papers/view/107671.
61 Xi, Chao (2006), "Institutional Shareholder Activism in China (Part I)" in *International Company and Commercial Law Review*, 17, p. 254.
62 Johnson, Simon *et al.* (2000), "Tunneling" in *American Economic Review*, 90, p. 22.
63 Clarke, Donald (2006), "The Independent Director in Chinese Corporate Governance" in *Delaware Journal of Corporate Law*, 31, p. 148.
64 Shleifer, Andrei and Vishny, Robert (1997), "A Survey of Corporate Governance" in *Journal of Finance*, 52. Also, La Porta, Rafael *et al.* (1998), "Law and Finance" in *Journal of Political Economy*, 106.
65 Berkman, Henk *et al.* (2009), "Expropriation through Loan Guarantees to Related Parties: Evidence from China" in *Journal of Banking and Finance*, 33, pp. 150–1.
66 Perera, Shalini (2010), *Corporate Ownership and Control: Corporate Governance*

and Economic Development in Sri Lanka, Series on Economic Development and Growth, Vol. 6, London: World Scientific Publishing, p. 180.

67 For general discussion, see Liu, Qiao and Lu, Zhou (2007), "Corporate Governance and Earnings Management in the Chinese Listed Companies: A Tunneling Perspective" in *Journal of Corporate Finance*, 13.

68 SHSE (2006), *Guoyou Konggu Shangshi Gongsi Zhili* [China Corporate Governance Report: the Corporate Governance of State Holding Listed Companies], Shanghai: Fudan University Press, pp. 50–3.

69 Clarke (2006), op. cit., p. 148.

70 Pistor, Katharina and Xu, Chenggang (2005), "Governing Stock Markets in Transition Economies: Lessons from China" in *American Law and Economics Review*, 7, p. 191.

71 Xi, Chao (2006), "Case Note: Private Enforcement of Securities law in China: Daqing Lianyi Co v Zhong Weida and Others (2004) Heilongjiang High Court" in *Journal of Comparative Law*, 1, p. 493.

72 Yin Guangxia announced false profits of US$89.6 million by fabricating purchase and sales contracts, export customs' declaration forms, tax-free documents, financial bills, and VAT invoices from 1999 to 2000. The audit report issued by the Shenzhen Zhongtianqin Accounting Firm and its signatory accountants was a gross misrepresentation. The news caused the company's stock to fall by the maximum permitted, 10 percent each day for ten days, and its market capitalization lost billions. The CSRC imposed administrative penalties on the company in April 2002. From then on, the Yinchuan Intermediate People's Court began to hear claims from 847 investors against Yin Guangxia. On 25 May 2005, the court ordered Yin Guangxia to compensate the minority shareholders to the total of 5.4 million shares from its surplus capital. The license of Zhongtianqin Accounting Firm was later revoked by the Ministry of Finance. See CSRC, op. cit., p. 176.

73 The Notice of the Supreme People's Court on Temporary Refusal of Filings of Securities Related Civil Compensation Cases (Fa Ming Chuan No. 406 [2001]), 21 September 2001.

74 The Notice of the Supreme People's Court on Relevant Issues of Filing of Civil Tort Dispute Cases Arising From False Statement in the Securities Market (Fa Ming Chuan No. 43 [2002]), 15 January 2002.

75 *Daqing Lianyi Co* v *Zhong Weida and Others* [2004], Heilongjiang High Court.

76 Several Provisions of the Supreme People's Court on Hearing Civil Compensation Cases Arising From False Statement in the Securities Market (Interpretation No. 2 [2003] of the Supreme People's Court), 9 January 2003.

77 Zhu, Sanzhu (2005), "Civil Litigation Arising from False Statements on China's Securities Market" in *North Carolina Journal of International Law and Commercial Regulation*, 31, pp. 381–2. Following the Circular in 2003, the "Orient Electron False Statement Case" has been finally resolved by the decision to grant civil remedies to 6,800 plaintiffs. This case gone on for four years and been labeled the Number One Case in China's securities market on account of: (1) it being the first case to follow the Circular; (2) the huge number of plaintiffs and compensation involved. See Liu, Ruidong (2007), "Quanguo Zhengquan Diyi An Chenai Luoding, 6800 Ren Jieshou Tiaojie" [The First National Securities Case Settled Down, 6800 Persons Accepted Mediation]. Online. Available at: www.chinacourt.org/html/article/200709/12/264338.shtml (accessed 20 December 2012).

78 Chen, Zhiwu (2003), "Capital Markets and Legal Development: The China Case" in *China Economic Review*, 14, p. 470.

79 This is a complete line of enforcement by the CSRC. However, there still exist some extreme situations such as cancellation of the case, and transferring the case to another court. According to two recent major circulars: the "Circular of the General Office of the State Council on Several Issues about Rigorously Cracking Down on

Illegal Issuance of Stocks and Illegal Operation of Securities Business (No. 99 [2006] of the General Office of the State Council)" and the "Circular of Relevant Issues concerning Suppression of Illegal Securities Activities (Zheng Jian Fa [2008] No. 1)" jointly issued by the Supreme People's Court, the Supreme People's Procuratorate, the Ministry of Public Security and the CSRC. The CSRC takes a leading role and invites other authorities to participate in establishing a coordinating group to crack down on illegal securities activities. The local government shall be responsible for the investigation, punishment, and the follow-up handling work of illegal securities activities.

80 Chen, Gongmeng *et al.* (2005), "Is China's Securities Regulatory Agency a Toothless Tiger? Evidence from Enforcement Actions" in *Journal of Accounting and Public Policy*, 24, p. 464.

81 Ibid.

82 Pistor and Xu, op. cit., p. 193.

83 Li, Qing *et al.* (2007), "Bamai Gaowen Gushi" [Diagnose the Market Fever], *Caijing Magazine*, 11 June 2007, issue 187. Online. Available at: www.caijing.com.cn/2007–06–11/100021866.html (accessed 20 July 2010).

84 It was announced on 23 May 2007 that a former deputy chief of a cement manufacturer had been fined for RMB200,000 for insider trading in the company's shares in June 2004. See Dyer, Geoff (2007), "Beijing Cracks Down on Insider Trading" in *Financial Times*, 24 May 2007.

85 Li (2007), op. cit.

86 In another case, Zhejiang Hangxiao Steel Structure was fined RMB400,000. A fine of RMB200,000 was imposed on the Chairman and President, as well as RMB100,000 on three other company executives. See Dyer, Geoff (2007), "Chinese Regulators Impose Fine" in *Financial Times*, 15 May 2007.

87 Anderson, Craig and Guo, Bingna (2006), "Corporate Governance under the New Company Law (Part 2): Shareholder Lawsuits and Enforcement" in *China Law & Practice*, May 2006.

88 Fu and Tomasic, op. cit., p. 283.

89 Laissez faire is characterized by free markets, little or no state intervention, and private ownership of property. This theory goes back to Adam Smith with his *Wealth of Nations* of 1776, a publication that expounds the belief that an economy can be corrected by an "invisible hand." It also applies to financial markets. It assumes that people will pay due diligence to whether what they are buying is worth what they are paying. See, generally, Chicago school of economics scholars such as Ronald Coase and Milton Friedman, who believed that laissez-faire government policy was more desirable than government intervention in the economy. Also see Alan Greenspan, the former US Federal Reserve Chairman, who was opposed to regulation during his 18-year reign. He did, however, concede there was a "flaw" in his market ideology after the credit crunch.

90 Williams, Mark (2005), *Competition Policy and Law in China, Hong Kong and Taiwan*, Cambridge: Cambridge University Press, p. 223.

91 Ibid.

92 Budget Speech by Donald Tsang, the former Financial Secretary of Hong Kong, 8 March 2000. Online. Available at: www.info.gov.hk/gia/general/200003/08/0308186.htm (accessed 20 December 2012).

93 Ibid., para. 17.

94 Ibid., para. 18.

95 Ibid., para. 20.

96 Ibid., para. 26.

97 Goodstadt, Leo (2010), "The Global Crisis: Why *Laisser-faire* Hong Kong Prefers Regulation." Hong Kong Institute for Monetary Research Paper No. 01/2010. Online. Available at: www.hkimr.org/cms/upload/publication_app (accessed 4 May 2010).

98 Uddin, Hamid and Wong, Ann (1998), "The Stock Market II: The Trading Market" in Ho, Simon *et al.* (eds.), *The Hong Kong Financial System: A New Age*, Oxford: Oxford University Press, p. 246.

99 This Ordinance was repealed by s. 406(1) of 5 of 2002 and combined in Cap 333 of Hong Kong Ordinances.

100 This Ordinance was repealed by s. 406(1) of 5 of 2002 and combined in Cap 335 of Hong Kong Ordinances.

101 SFC (2002), *Securities Regulation in Hong Kong*, Hong Kong: SFC, p. 5 ("Part II The Davison Report 1988").

102 Reed, Howard (1981), *The Pre-eminence of International Financial Centers*, New York: Praeger.

103 Cassis, op. cit., p. 275.

104 Ibid.

105 One example is the Global Financial Centers Index, compiled by the Z/Yen Group and the City of London (before March 2010) and the Qatar Financial Center Authority (since October 2010).

106 Heritage Foundation (2012), "2012 Index of Economic Freedom." Online. Available at: www.heritage.org/index/countries.cfm (accessed 20 December 2012).

107 IMD (2012), "World Competitiveness Yearbook 2012." Online. Available at: www.imd.org/research/publications/wcy/upload/scoreboard.pdf (accessed 20 December 2012).

108 For more discussion on the relationship between China and Hong Kong, see Chiu, Stephen and Lui, Tai-Lok (2009), *Hong Kong Becoming a Chinese Global City*, London: Routledge, p. 153.

109 Ibid., p. 6.

110 SEHK (1999), "The Way Forward." A Strategic Plan.

111 SFC (2007), "An Overview of the Major Events and Regulation of the Securities and Futures Markets between 1997 and 2007." Research Paper No. 36. Online. Available at: www.sfc.hk/web/EN/published-resources/research-papers/market-reviews (accessed 20 December 2012).

112 Williams, op. cit., p. 413.

113 The mere fact of share listing will inevitably facilitate a certain degree of privatization, but the focus is on corporatization (the conversion of SOEs into shareholding companies) and listing (the sale of shares of such companies in securities markets) as the Chinese government is still the majority shareholder of such companies. See Friedman, William (2002), "One Country, Two Systems: The Inherent Conflict between China's Communist Politics and Capitalist Securities Market" in *Brooklyn Journal of International Law*, 27; also Cao, op. cit., pp. 43–4.

114 Lubman, Stanley (2000), *Bird in a Cage: Legal Reform in China after Mao*, California: Stanford University Press, p. 174.

4 Weak and strong markets

A comparison of securities regulation and enforcement between China and Hong Kong

The previous chapter shows that the Chinese and Hong Kong stock markets evolved in different ways. This chapter turns to a comparison of their securities regulation and securities enforcement. It has several aims: to provide a comparative analysis of investor protection in both markets; to explore whether China's markets are weak compared to Hong Kong; and to test whether there is any "bonding."

It is structured as follows. The first part deals with the scope of comparison. Sections 4.2 and 4.3 apply comparative law methodology to the actual situation with a view to comparing the development of China and Hong Kong's stock markets in terms of securities regulation and enforcement. Finally, a conclusion will be drawn.

4.1 Scope of comparison

Comparative law is one method to compare and contrast norms, institutions, cultures, attitudes, methodologies, and even entire legal systems.[1] There are various methods in comparative legal studies, but the best approach serves the specific purposes of the research, taking into account the resources available.[2]

This chapter aims to investigate whether there is a regulatory gap between China and Hong Kong. The functional approach is better than other methods for this purpose because, for example, rule comparison seems impossible as capital market regulation is combined with numerous laws, rules, guidelines, and codes. It is over-complicated and time consuming to compare each Chinese rule to Hong Kong's. On the other hand, where rules or institutions are created for the purpose of solving human problems which are similar in two societies at the same stage of development, the functional approach is useful.[3] In relation to stock markets, corporate and financial regulations play similar roles in ensuring adequate information disclosure and strengthening shareholder rights in different jurisdictions, including China and Hong Kong. Meanwhile, regulatory authorities like the China Securities Regulatory Commission (CSRC) in China, and Hong Kong's Securities and Futures Commission (SFC), are responsible for regulating markets, and for facilitating and encouraging the development of markets. Thus, a comparison of legal rules and regulatory authorities whose functions are alike is feasible and may lead to a succinct description.

To study the relevant systems, the first step is to set up a structure. According to law and finance theory discussed in Chapter 2, it is often assumed that the quality of investor protection is correlated to the size and extent of capital markets.[4] Consequently, the difference in legal protection for investors might distinguish strong markets from weak ones. Effective investor protection should involve regulation of companies and markets. So the comparison will start from these two dimensions.

One shortcoming of a narrow functional comparison is that it only looks at law in the books and ignores law in action. It is important, therefore, to include a study of enforcement in a functional analysis. The value of enforcement is a key issue for understanding how financial markets deepen and broaden.[5] Enforcement could be run by regulatory agencies and can invoke strong criminal, financial, and reputational penalties which deter wrongdoing.

In this sense, regulatory authorities like the CSRC and the SFC are a determinant which influences the failure or success of capital markets. The key role of market regulators has been acknowledged by, for example, the Turner Review. The Review admits that the credit crunch revealed fault lines in regulation and supervision, and better prudential supervision of financial firms is essential to the health of financial services.[6] Black also suggests that institutions (market regulators and courts) are the preconditions for the establishment of a strong securities market. Therefore, the regulatory structures in China and Hong Kong, as well as their enforcement, will be examined in this chapter so as to explore how their laws function.

In summary, this chapter adopts mainly the functional method, but with an understanding of its weaknesses. It is structured according to two attributes: legal rules and regulatory authorities.

4.2 Comparison of securities regulation

The law governing capital markets involves regulations of companies and markets. In the company dimension, shareholders should have access to good information about the company and have confidence that the management of the company will not cheat them out of most or all of the value of their investment. In the market dimension, there must be mechanisms to ensure an orderly operation of the markets, fair dealing, and integrity. Thus, this section assesses securities regulation in China and Hong Kong's context through these two dimensions.

4.2.1 Regulation of corporate governance

Law can play an important role in reducing agency costs. Broadly speaking, it can be divided into two subsets: "governance strategies" and "regulatory strategies."[7] Governance strategies seek to facilitate the principal's control over their agent's behavior. By contrast, regulatory strategies subject managers to legal constraints on their ability to pursue self-interested behavior. Both strategies can be employed to control managerial performance.

In the following section, the legal regimes in China and Hong Kong's capital markets will be compared first; governance and regulatory strategies will then be compared.

A Overview of market regulation

1 CHINA

As addressed in Chapter 2, good law is correlated with capital market development, no matter what the causality is. In recent years China has attached great importance to the construction of market infrastructures. The current securities regulations fall into three inter-related categories constituting a comprehensive legal framework, with each subordinate regulation or rule serving as a necessary supplement to the laws and regulations of the higher level. They govern: securities offering, listing and disclosure; securities and futures trading; corporate governance, mergers, and acquisitions of listed companies; securities and futures intermediaries; supervision of securities investment funds; securities and futures markets supervision and legal liabilities.

i Level I: Laws Laws are developed by the National People's Congress (NPC) or its Standing Committee. By the end of 2005, such a legal framework had taken shape focusing on three pieces of legislation: the Company Law, the Securities Law, and the Securities Investment Fund Law.

- **The Company Law**
  The Company Law was promulgated by the Standing Committee of the NPC in 1993. It came into force in 1994 and was amended in 1999, 2004 and 2005.

  Since the late 1970s China has experienced economic reform and, in particular, SOE reform. The policies of practicing the shareholding system were outlined in a series of regulations jointly promulgated in 1992 by several central government-connected agencies. The aims of these regulations were the enhancement of the efficiency of state assets, the facilitation of efficient allocation of social resources, and the transformation of the enterprises into independent economic entities.[8] The promulgation of the 1993 Company Law was the culmination of all these regulations in China. It was designed to address problems within the state sector, especially the problem of the reform of SOEs.[9]

  However, the 1993 Company Law has been criticized by a number of scholars. Howson considers it a "disaster," a keen expression of conservative compromises or the wholesale avoidance of difficult issues implicit in China's transition from state ownership and the mandated allocation of capital to a "socialist market economy."[10] From a historical perspective, Xi argues that the old company law reflected the features of a planned economy such as regulations on the restructure of the SOEs, too much administrative intervention, and the rules of enterprise solely funded by the state.[11]

The amended Company Law in 2005 has significantly reduced the number of features of a planned economy and introduced some key elements of Western corporate law. For example, the amendment replaces the provision of "company operation under the state" with "business compliance with the laws and administrative regulations" in Article 5. Also, the amendment introduces the concept of fiduciary duties in Article 148 and the derivative action in Article 152.

- **The Securities Law**
  The Securities Law came into force on 1 July 1999 and was amended on 28 August 2004 and 27 October 2005. This is the first securities law in China. It is divided into 12 chapters and 240 articles regulating, among other things, the issue and trading of securities; takeovers by listed companies; securities exchange; securities companies; and the duties and responsibilities of the State Council's securities regulatory authorities.

  The 2005 Securities Law, which came into force on 1 January 2006, involves amendments to more than 100 articles of the old law. Significant amendments concern the expansion of the scope of the securities under regulation; separate regulation for different financial sectors among the banking, insurance, and securities industries; public offerings; forward trading; money and stock lending/financing; permitting SOEs and banking funds to enter the stock market; and a better protection of investors.[12]

- **The Securities Investment Fund Law**
  With the promulgation of the *Tentative Rules of Securities Investment Funds* in 1997, China's securities investment industry entered a rapid period of growth. In the same year the first three securities investment funds issued new shares, publicly, to raise funds from the market, marking a milestone development in the Chinese fund industry.[13] On 28 October 2003 China's Securities Investment Fund Law was promulgated, replacing the 1997 *Tentative Rules of Securities Investment Funds*.[14] This law lays down the regulatory principles and operational framework for securities investment funds, providing a legal environment for the future development of the Chinese fund industry. Most importantly, the Securities Investment Fund Law legally acknowledges the significance of the fund industry in the securities markets and encourages the existence of institutional investors, all of which has the advantage of enhancing the supervision and management of listed companies.[15]

ii Level II: The administrative ordinances Administrative ordinances are developed by the highest administrative authorities, such as the State Council, in accordance with the Constitution and other laws. By the end of 2007 there were 14 pieces of securities-related administrative ordinances in force, which included the *Ordinance on Administration of Futures Trading*, promulgated on 6 March 2007.[16] This ordinance is designed to regulate the trading activities of commodity futures and financial futures.

iii Level III: CSRC rules and regulations CSRC rules and regulations are developed by the CSRC in accordance with the laws and administrative ordinances of the State Council. These rules and regulations are subordinate to the laws and the administrative ordinances. They cover various documents relating to securities and futures issues. For example, the 2002 *Corporate Governance Code for Listed Companies* sets forth the basic principles for corporate governance of listed companies, the means for shareholder rights, as well as basic behavior rules and moral standards for management of listed companies.

2 HONG KONG

i Companies Ordinance (CO) The CO is the primary piece of legislation governing companies and their activities, from incorporation to winding up. "Company" means any company incorporated under the Companies Ordinance or one of its predecessors.[17] The CO also deals with non-Hong Kong companies; that is, companies incorporated outside Hong Kong but which have established a place of business in Hong Kong.[18]

The development of the CO has a close connection with Hong Kong's historical status as a colony of the UK. The first CO was enacted in 1865, and was derived from the UK Companies Act 1862. It was then combined in Chapter (Cap) 32 in 1933. In recent times the CO has been substantially amended. The amendments are often similar to those introduced in common law jurisdictions such as Australia, Singapore, and New Zealand, which have also adopted the UK corporate model. When interpreting its company law, the Hong Kong courts also refer to cases decided in these jurisdictions.[19]

The current statute, the 2004 CO, implements many of the recommendations in the 2000 Standing Committee on Company Law Reform (SCCLR) Report. The major change in the 2004 CO is the inclusion of the statutory derivative action.[20] Other changes are summarized by Tyler and Ho: the introduction of the one man/one director private company; a prohibition against incorporating a company limited by guarantee with a share capital; the removal of the right of dissenting shareholders of a public company to apply to the court to cancel certain alternations to the memorandum; simplification of the reduction of capital provisions and no longer any need for court approval where redesignation of the par value to a lower amount.[21] In fact, these changes largely reflect those made in the Companies Act (CA) 2006 in the UK.[22] This suggests that the Hong Kong legal framework is still significantly influenced by the UK model even after the handover of sovereignty.

In mid-2006, the Hong Kong government launched a major and comprehensive exercise to rewrite the CO. By updating and modernizing the law, the aim is to make it more user-friendly and facilitate the conduct of business to enhance Hong Kong's competitiveness and attractiveness as a major international business and financial center. On 12 July 2012, the Legislative Council in Hong Kong passed the new Companies Ordinance.[23] It will become effective on a day to be appointed and published in the *Government Gazette*, which is expected to be in 2014.

ii Securities and Futures Ordinance (SFO) Under Article 109 Basic Law, the government is to provide an appropriate economic and legal environment for the maintenance of the status of Hong Kong as an international financial center. Donald Tsang, then Financial Secretary (later appointed as Hong Kong's Chief Executive), announced in his Budget Speech in March 1999, a comprehensive market reform for the securities and futures market to enhance competitiveness in order to meet the challenge of an increasingly globalized marketplace driven by the advancement of technology and the emergence of a growing population of sophisticated investors. In that respect, the government has concluded that "the international character of Hong Kong necessitates a modern, flexible securities and futures regulatory framework that will enable Hong Kong to compete effectively."[24] The guiding principle of the new legislation is therefore "to provide optimal market regulation and afford sufficient protection for investors, while at the same time encourage, not stifle, healthy competition and market innovations."[25]

As a result of this process (initiated by the Davison Report), the primary legislation is now the Securities and Futures Ordinance (Cap 571). The SFO was enacted on 13 March 2002 and came into force on 1 April 2003. It serves as the legal framework for the regulation of the securities industry.[26] The SFO is the largest and most detailed ordinance in the history of Hong Kong. In total, it is composed of 409 sections and ten schedules.

iii Codes, guidelines, and circulars The SFC has now consolidated all SFC codes, guidelines, guidance, and related matters, into a "Regulatory Handbook," available in a continually updated form on its website. The Regulatory Handbook is divided into two volumes, the first of which addresses the SFC and its role in and approach to regulation. The second contains all the latest versions of the SFC's codes, guidelines, and guidance information. They are divided into seven parts: Part A Licensing of Intermediaries and Continuing Obligations of Licensed Persons; Part B Specific Requirements for Regulated Activities; Part C Regulated Investment Products; Part D Corporate Finance; Part E Enforcement Related; Part F SFO; Part G Miscellaneous.

In addition, the SFC has promulgated and continues to issue a wide range of circulars related to different aspects of the regulatory system such as the *Circular to Licensed Corporations and Associated Entities Anti-Money Laundering/Combating Terrorist Financing* in January 2007, and the *Circular to Intermediaries Licensed or Registered for Type 6 Regulated Activity* in December 2006.[27]

iv Rules governing the listing of securities on the stock exchange of Hong Kong Limited ("listing rules") Apart from the CO, which mandated information disclosure through the annual accounts, listed companies are also required to comply with a listing agreement. The Listing Rules reflect currently acceptable standards in the marketplace and are designed to ensure that investors have and can maintain confidence in the market.

The Listing Rules (Main Board) fall into four main parts: Chapters 1–6 set out matters of general application; Chapters 7–19A set out the requirements applicable to the issue of equity securities; Chapters 20 and 21 set out the requirements applicable to unit trusts, mutual funds, and other investment companies; and Chapters 22–37 set out the requirements applicable to the issue of debt securities. The listing agreement requires companies to fulfill a number of objective and subjective criteria. Further conditions which have to be met by infrastructure companies, mineral companies, overseas issuers, and Chinese issuers, are set out in rules 8.05B (2), 18.02, 18.03 and Chapters 19 and 19A.

v Corporate Governance Code[28] The Corporate Governance Code, included in an appendix to the Listing Rules, sets out the principles of good corporate governance and two levels of recommendations. The code establishes "aspirational" goals for directors, including attendance of non-executive directors at board meetings, and public disclosure of directors' fees and emoluments.

In 1998 the code was amended to include guidelines on the voluntary establishment of audit committees. Each committee requires a minimum of two members, who have to be non-executive directors. It is recommended that the majority of members be independent in nature. The primary function of these committees is to assist the board of directors to fulfill its oversight functions concerning financial reporting and internal control. The code has been constantly amended so as to maintain a high standard of corporate governance in the market. On 18 December 2010, the Hong Kong Stock Exchange published a "Consultation Paper on Review of the Code on Corporate Governance Practices and Associated Listing Rules" containing proposals to amend the Corporate Governance Code.[29] A new rule introduced in 2012 as a result of this consultation, was a requirement that the issuer must appoint independent non-executive directors representing at least one-third of the board.[30]

B Governance strategies

As discussed above, governance strategies exert control over managers through the terms of their relationship with the company and its shareholders.[31] They can be deployed to protect any vulnerable principal-agent relationship. Examples of these strategies include board structure, voting rights, pre-emption rights, takeover, and institutional investors. Hence, the following will summarize certain material differences between China and Hong Kong from a corporate governance perspective.

1 INDEPENDENT DIRECTORS

A key institution of corporate governance is an internal oversight body such as the board of directors. The function of the board of directors is to overcome the costliness of monitoring by individual shareholders.

In this regard, both China and Hong Kong adopt the independent director system, but the effectiveness of their implementation differs.

On 16 August 2001, the CSRC promulgated the *Guiding Opinions about Establishing Independent Director System in Listed Companies* ("the Independent Director Guidelines"). Pursuant to the Guiding Opinions, at least two members of the board of directors in Chinese listed companies had to be independent directors by 30 June 2002; and one year later, at least a third of any board had to be constituted of independent directors.[32] The fundamental impetus behind the introduction of independent directors in China is to protect small shareholders from exploitation by dominant shareholders.[33]

Despite the attention devoted to independent directors, it is unlikely that they can play their hoped-for role. In practice, according to a study by Liao *et al.*, Chinese listed companies implement the board independence requirements by adding extra members to the board rather than by replacing the original directors, even though the board size is already too large (more than 11).[34] As a result, the board structure remains unchanged to a large extent. In the view of Clarke, this system does not provide for mechanisms to ensure independence of directors.[35] One major problem exists in the nomination procedure.[36] Those who are entitled to nominate independent directors must individually or jointly hold more than 1 percent of the shares.[37] This implies that minority shareholders can hardly install their nominees without backing from the controlling shareholder.

Unlike Chinese law, in making their vote highly desirable as a way of insulating conflict-of-interest transactions from substantive scrutiny, Hong Kong's corporate law gives them a role that requires, in case of dispute, examination of the degree to which they actually were disinterested in the transaction in question. Chinese company law in this sense simply requires that directors meet some criterion of independence, but fails to provide a meaningful policing mechanism.

2 THE SUPERVISORY BOARD

The supervisory board is another crucial mechanism of corporate governance. Hong Kong has a single tier board system, while China adopts a two tier board structure. In the single tier system, such as that used in the US and the UK, there is only one organ, the board, that fulfills both the management and the monitoring functions. The separation of these functions is achieved by appointing independent directors who have specific competencies and tasks in situations of conflicts of interest.[38] In the two tier system, such as that operated in Germany, the shareholders delegate day-to-day management to a management board and entrust monitoring to a supervisory board.

The supervisory system in China was inspired by the German style of corporate governance.[39] But it is not the same as that used in Germany in terms of both legal powers and supervisory practice.[40] German supervisors have a much broader power base. In essence, the management board in a German company is largely responsible to a supervisory board, as directors are appointed and removed by the supervisory board and seek consent from the supervisory board regarding important business decisions. China's supervisory board does not have such powers. The powers granted by the law do not include any authority to control the appointment or business decision-making of the management board.

More importantly, unlike the German style, the Chinese supervisory board has an important worker participation function in addition to its monitoring role.[41] The political ideology of workers as a class, reflected in the principle of "democratic management" by the workers, has been embodied in the Chinese Constitution and other basic laws.[42] The two tier board structure may provide a mechanism through which the principle could be conveniently accommodated.

The amended Chinese Company Law 2005 requires listed companies to have a board of directors and a supervisory board. A supervisor may hold neither the position of director, nor that of senior officer.[43] The law defines the board of directors as a decision-making unit, and the supervisory board as a monitoring mechanism. Both are appointed by, and must report to, the shareholders of the company.

The Law also proscribes a list of responsibilities for the supervisory board, but fails to define the legal liabilities for it.[44] However, Ho criticizes the fact that the supervisory board in China has close relationships with the major shareholders, and so lacks independence and the necessary conditions for carrying out its monitoring duties.[45] They may even become part of the insider group. The supervisory board may therefore fail to perform its intended check-and-balance role.

3 VOTING RIGHTS

Voting rights empower shareholders, as a body, in corporate decision-making. But if there is a controlling shareholder, these rights may be less meaningful to minority shareholders. This is because the controlling shareholders can use their votes to appoint their own nominees to the board and thus shift decision-making from the large body of shareholders to the small board.[46]

The equal voting right system (one share, one vote) is adopted in China and Hong Kong. The amended Chinese Company Law requires the passing of any resolution by more than half of the votes held by the shareholders present in person, or by proxy at a shareholders' general meeting, except in cases of proposed amendments to the Articles of Association; merger; division; dissolution, alteration of form of the company; increase or reduction of registered capital. These situations require two-thirds of the votes held by shareholders present in person or by proxy at a shareholders' general meeting.[47]

Under Hong Kong law, an ordinary resolution is passed by a simple majority of votes cast by members present in person or by proxy at a general meeting, and a special resolution is passed by a majority of not less than three-quarters of votes cast by members present in person or by proxy at a general meeting.[48]

However, the one share one vote right is criticized by some scholars. The analysis of Chen *et al.* indicates that the largest shareholder is generally able to control a listed company as a result of the failure of small outside investors to attend the meeting and exercise their voting rights.[49] Their data shows that in China the largest shareholder, on average, constitutes 84 percent of the voting shares present at the general meeting, which means that the largest shareholder can essentially dictate everything in most scenarios and in most companies.

4 PRE-EMPTION RIGHTS

The fundamental objective of pre-emption rights is to protect shareholders against dilution of monetary value and against dilution of control.[50] In broad terms, pre-emption rights require a company which is proposing to allot equity securities to offer the opportunity to acquire those shares first to holders of the company's existing relevant shares in proportion to their existing holdings.[51] Franks and Mayer report a strong linkage between turnover of executive directors and the provision of new equity finance.[52] This illustrates that pre-emption rights can be a source of managerial discipline.

Article 35 of Chinese Company Law 2005 provides for pre-emption in respect of new capital raised by limited liability companies in China. The relevant provision provides for existing shareholders to have priority, unless all the shareholders decide not to do so. But the law does not specify in detail how this is to operate.

In contrast to China, company law in Hong Kong does not contain such rights. The Listing Rules do, however, require that all new issues of equity securities be first offered to the existing shareholders by way of rights unless they have agreed otherwise.[53] In this sense, if taking the law-in-action into account, China and Hong Kong positions are not materially different.

5 TAKEOVERS

It is thought that a company which is not being run in the interest of its shareholders will be vulnerable to a takeover bid.[54] The threat of the takeover will be a constant pressure on the boards of public companies to increase shareholder value. In line with this, the objectives of takeover regulation are: first, to facilitate takeover bids; second, to protect minority shareholders when control of their company changes so as to ensure that they have an opportunity of receiving sufficient information and a fair price for their holdings.

The legal framework for takeovers in China is contained in Chapter 4 of the 2005 Securities Law and the *Measures for the Administration of the Takeover of Listed Companies.*[55] And in Hong Kong, the *Code on Takeovers and Mergers and Shares Repurchase*[56] has been promulgated by the SFC regarding standards of commercial conduct and behavior considered acceptable for takeovers, mergers, and share repurchases.

Broadly speaking, both takeover regulations are modeled on the Takeover Code in the UK. For example, all of them impose a "no frustrating action" principle upon the managers of a target company, which prohibits them from taking, once a bid is launched or anticipated, any actions which might have the consequence of frustrating its success.[57] Similarly, both rules also require that any person who acquires more than 30 percent of the shares of a company is obliged to make a mandatory bid.[58] In addition, all shares of the same class are required to be treated equally.[59]

Unfortunately, the market for corporate control is not an effective mechanism for monitoring managerial behavior and corporate performance in China and Hong Kong. This is because controlling shareholders in most listed companies, in both places, are either the state or a family. In these situations the possibility of takeovers being a significant factor in corporate governance is essentially removed.[60]

6 INSTITUTIONAL INVESTORS

One of the most prominent trends in capital markets of recent years is the increasing importance of institutional investors. Given the weight of their shareholding, the way in which institutional shareholders use their power to influence the standards of corporate governance is of fundamental importance. They can threaten to sell their stocks if their longer term interests in the company are impaired, or they can directly influence the management by means of active corporate governance.[61] In the US, legal enforcement, both private and public, has been the major mechanism to protect investors, while in the UK the rise of institutional investors plays a crucial role in monitoring managers.[62]

In China, institutional investors remain relatively insignificant in the market and are yet to play an important role. On the one hand, retail investors dominate the tradable share market. By the end of 2007, investors in China's stock markets had opened a total of 139 million accounts. However, small investors, with less than RMB1 million in cash or share equivalent, accounted for about 99 percent of the total number of accounts.[63] Meanwhile, all investors tended to have relatively short investing periods with frequent trading patterns. The average turnover ratio in China's stock markets is nearly seven times higher than those in more mature markets.[64] Apart from that, overseas investors are still rare in China since their involvement is restricted by the Qualified Foreign Institutional Investor (QFII) program.[65] On the other hand, in the non-tradable share market, institutional investors are more like the confederation of the blockholders rather than the mouthpiece of minority shareholders. Taking the non-tradable share reform as an example, institutional shareholders were generally not a hurdle in the voting of compensation schemes, making the blockholders obtain liquidity rights with relatively low costs.[66]

Unlike China, the once-dominant position of retail investors in Hong Kong's capital market has been taken over by overseas institutional investors since 2000.[67] They have accounted for 40 percent of local market transactions in recent years.[68] They are from all over the world: Europe, the US, Japan, and Singapore. A high concentration of institutional investors from different countries can ensure that a comprehensive set of skills, experience, and knowledge, which is currently absent in China, is imported to the Hong Kong market.

C Regulatory strategies

Regulatory strategies constrain managers by forcing them not to make decisions, or undertake transactions, that would harm the interests of their principals.[69] Rules and standards constitute the most obvious use of law to address this agency problem. Indeed, law imposes substantial duties on directors. In addition, to function effectively, regulatory strategies will involve a third party agency, usually a court or regulator, to assess managerial conduct. From the company's viewpoint, third party enforcement consists of the derivative action and other mechanisms of minority shareholder protection.

1 FIDUCIARY DUTIES

Fiduciary duty is a concept developed from English equitable doctrines. Two core features are the duty of loyalty and the duty of care. The duty of loyalty usually includes the duties to act bona fide for the benefit of the company;[70] to exercise directors' powers for their proper purpose;[71] and not to allow any conflict between their duties as directors and personal interests.[72] The duty of care is basically a tort law concept. Company laws of most jurisdictions also impose this duty on directors; i.e., a director owes a duty to his or her company to exercise proper care in managing company affairs. Recently, there has been a trend toward a codification of such duties. For example, the UK Companies Act 2006 codified, in Sections 170–81, the equitable principles of fiduciary duty and the common law of negligence as they apply to directors.

China follows this trend of codification, while Hong Kong continues to use a common law approach.[73] Article 148 Chinese Company Law, as amended, clearly provides that directors have an obligation of loyalty and diligence towards the company. In Hong Kong, however, although directors' duties are stipulated in the Listing Rules,[74] they lack statutory force, which makes any breach of duty difficult to enforce under common law. In fact, many smaller company directors are ignorant of the concepts of corporate governance and duty. The role of a director is sometimes mixed up with that of a senior manager. This is a common problem with many directors in Hong Kong.[75]

As for China, the nature of legal demand affects whether the transplanted legal concept will function properly. The real question is how these requirements are to be given specific content and actually enforced in view of the weakness of the Chinese judiciary and the elusiveness of the legal concepts involved.[76] Lee believes that the introduction of the fiduciary concept without the concomitant incorporation of the English equity regimes is fatal.[77] It is likely that given the different market conditions and corporate culture in China, judges in China will respond differently. As Clarke has observed, the fiduciary concept comes from the law of trust, which in turn has no real counterpart in China.[78] In the Chinese context, the asset managers that the state was concerned with were essentially government officials at various levels, including SOE managers. The line between SOE and "superior administrative department" is difficult to draw. The duties of those managers were defined and enforced administratively.

2 DERIVATIVE ACTIONS

Minority shareholders face particular difficulties when they seek redress against director wrongdoings because the company may not be willing to pursue this in its own right. This is particularly true when a fraud is committed against the minority by those in control of the company. Under the *Foss v. Harbottle* rule in English law, the proper entity to bring an action is the company itself.[79] The derivative action is an exception to this rule. It can be brought by individual shareholders, acting on behalf of a company, against the company's director.

Derivative actions are related to the control of the corporate form. To put it simply, plaintiff shareholders theoretically act in the interests of all shareholders, thus employing a legal mechanism to address agency problems which exist between shareholders and management. This also has led many to argue whether it plays a crucial role in aligning the interests of managers and shareholders.[80] Indeed, according to empirical evidence, private shareholders' action has been a major part of the landscape in corporate governance in the US, but not in the UK.[81]

The statutory derivative action was introduced in Hong Kong in 2004.[82] A year later, China also codified such action in the amendments to the Company Law.[83] However, there is a lack of operational guidance and judicial explanation related to the derivative action in China. Some areas, such as litigation fee, recovery of expenses, security deposit, and liability of individuals, are still to be clarified.[84]

Broadly speaking, the system in China is stricter than that in Hong Kong. Two major differences exist.

The first regards the requirement for a plaintiff. Article 152 Chinese Company Law, as amended, grants minority shareholders the right to initiate derivative actions. It provides that, if any director, supervisor, or officer of a company violates any statutory provision that results in damage to that company, shareholders holding at least 1 percent of the company's shares for 180 consecutive days, either individually or in combination may require the supervisory committee or the board of directors to institute a lawsuit (in writing) at the People's Court. However, there is neither a minimum shareholding requirement nor a minimum holding period in Hong Kong. As long as a shareholder is a member of a company, he/she has rights to bring action.

The second difference is found in the time limit for the board to take action upon receipt of the request by shareholders. Under Chinese law, if the supervisory board or the board of directors refuses to take action or fails to institute such lawsuit within 30 days from such requirement, or where an urgent circumstance is involved and failure to institute such lawsuit will result in irremediable damages to the interest of the company, then such shareholders shall have the right to institute directly a lawsuit at the People's Court in their own names in the interest of the company.[85] Hong Kong law does not contain this time restriction for the board of directors.

In short, in terms of substantive law, Hong Kong can protect a broader range of minority shareholders. China is reluctant to copy this due to the presence of an abundant number of small retail shareholders.

3 PROTECTION OF MINORITIES

This may not be so relevant to a public company situation, where shareholders may be better off exercising their exit rights in a presumably well-functioning market.

Under Hong Kong law, a shareholder who complains that the affairs of a company incorporated in Hong Kong are conducted in a manner unfairly prejudicial to his interests, may petition the court either to wind up the company or make an appropriate order regulating the affairs of the company.[86] In addition, on the application of a specified number of members, the Financial Secretary may appoint inspectors who are given extensive statutory powers to investigate the affairs of a company incorporated in Hong Kong.[87]

In China, the law treats domestic companies and overseas listed companies differently. For domestic companies there is no specific provision in the amended Company Law to guard against the oppression of the minority by the majority. However, provisions of minority shareholder protection for overseas listed companies, especially Hong Kong-listed ones, are assumed to be similar to those in Hong Kong. The 1993 *Mandatory Provisions for the Articles of Association of Companies Listed in Hong Kong* (the "1993 Mandatory Provisions") provides that a company which wishes to list in Hong Kong must adopt in its articles of association minority protection provisions similar to (though not as comprehensive as) those available under Hong Kong law. These provisions state that a controlling shareholder may not exercise their voting rights in a manner prejudicial to the interests of the shareholders, may not relieve a director or supervisor of his duty to act honestly in the best interests of the company, and may not approve the expropriation by a director or supervisor of the assets or the individual rights of other shareholders.[88]

4.2.2 Regulation of market misconduct

A well-functioning market can ensure fairness and efficiency in order not to create prejudice to normal market activity and market integrity.[89] Market misconduct, also known as market abuse, generally consists of insider dealing, market manipulation, and disclosure of misleading or false information. It arises in circumstances where investors' interests have been unreasonably harmed by others. It prevents full and proper market transparency and undermines market integrity and investor confidence. Hence, market misconduct in different jurisdictions has long been subject to both regulatory and criminal penalties.

A General provisions

The term "prohibited trading activities" in the Chinese Securities Law, as amended, is similar to "market misconduct" in the SFO of Hong Kong.

In China, "prohibited trading activities" fall into these categories: insider trading, market manipulation, and false or misleading disclosure.[90] Prior to the Chinese Securities Law, as amended, a fundamental weakness in the legal system against market fraud, was that there were fewer provisions relating to civil liability and civil compensation than for administrative and criminal penalties.[91] One of the remarkable changes brought about by the amended Securities Law in 2005 is the strengthening of civil liability and civil compensation for market fraud. Securities companies and their staff, and securities investment consultancy organizations and their staff, are liable for compensation if they commit fraud and losses are caused by their actions.[92]

In Hong Kong, the SFO specifies six types of market misconduct, namely: insider dealing, false trading, price rigging, market manipulation, disclosure of information about prohibited transactions, and disclosure of false or misleading information.[93] The SFO sets up a dual system, civil and criminal, for regulating market misconduct under Parts XIII and XIV. Under the civil regime, market misconduct cases are referred to the Market Misconduct Tribunal (MMT), which can impose a range of sanctions such as ordering the disgorgement of profits, cease and desist orders, cold shoulder orders, and disqualification orders.[94] It can also impose civil fines of up to HK$10 million, or three times the profit gained or loss avoided as a result of the market misconduct, whichever is the higher. Under the criminal regime offences are punished with up to ten years' imprisonment and a fine of HK$10 million.[95] The SFO goes a step further by imposing a responsibility on directors, and responsible officers of participants in the market, to take reasonable measures to prevent their respective companies from acting in a way that constitutes market misconduct.[96] Failure to do so may attract civil and criminal liability.

B Insider dealing

Insider dealing is defined as the trading of securities by any person with potential access to confidential information about the company.[97] It upsets the fairness of information disclosure and consequently damages the integrity of the financial market. Major differences in insider dealing between China and Hong Kong are found in the definitions of an insider, what constitutes inside information, and exceptions.

In Hong Kong, an insider is defined as any person who is connected with a company in very broad terms, including any director, employee, substantial shareholder, or a company related to it.[98] Connected persons are potential insider dealers. It is not necessary that the connected person knows of the relevant connection for insider dealing to take place.

Unlike Hong Kong, the Chinese Securities Law adopts a closed-ended definition of insiders by specifically listing certain persons in Article 74. Apart from the possession of relevant insider information, China has set up an additional "personal connection" test to define insiders, requiring a causal link between an insider's position and the acquisition of the information. A "person with knowledge of insider information" would therefore be prohibited from trading only if that person has access to the information by virtue of their connection with the company whose securities are affected[99] by virtue of their office[100] or profession.[101] This approach brings numerous problems in practice. Huang criticizes two aspects in particular: first, the "person connection" test is uncertain of producing a conflict outcome; second, defining insiders by means of enumeration could cause potential crimes to be committed unintentionally.[102]

The definition of what constitutes inside information is also crucial to the prosecution of insider dealing. Pursuant to the SFO, the relevant information refers to specific information about the company, a shareholder or officers of the company, or the listed securities of the company or their derivatives.[103] This type of information is not the general information which insiders come across, but rather events which affect the company. There must be sufficient particulars in the information to comply with this requirement and it suffices if there is a probable consequence or reasonable belief that the event may happen.[104]

By contrast, Article 75 (1) of the Chinese Securities Law generally defines inside information as "information acquired in the course of securities trading, has not yet been disclosed, and concerns the company's business or financial affairs or may have a major effect on the market price of the company's securities." This definition is illustrated by eight types of information that are regarded as insider information. The "major events" listed in Article 67 also fall within the scope of inside information. However, some scholars cast doubt on the scope of this definition. For example, in the view of Huang, the listed types of information are relatively few because other kinds of information, such as front-running situations, may fall outside the definition of market information.[105]

To draw a better line between acceptable and unacceptable practices, the SFO provides a number of exceptions for activities which would otherwise be regarded as insider dealing.[106] For instance, the ordinance excludes acquiring qualification shares, performing an underwriting agreement, and where acting in the capacity of a liquidator, receiver, or trustee in bankruptcy provided the same is done in good faith.[107] The SFO also provides an exemption for a corporation from insider dealing activities where it has established effective information barriers (or Chinese walls).[108] However, Chinese Law does not contain such exceptions.

C Market manipulation

Market manipulation is another form of fraud. China and Hong Kong are broadly similar in this field.

Article 77 of the Chinese Securities Law 2005 prohibits four types of manipulation activities: carrying out combined or successive sales; collaborating with another person to mutually trade at a prearranged time, price, and method;

conducting securities transactions between accounts actually controlled by oneself; and manipulating the securities market by other methods.

Compared with the old Securities Law 1998, the amended law has made some important amendments on market manipulation.[109] First, it deleted provisions regarding the purpose of market manipulation activities, which had been restricted "obtain[ing] illegitimate benefits or ... shift[ing] risks to others." This purpose narrowed the scope of market manipulation and thus brought difficulties in enforcement because decisions had to be made to decide what kinds of activities were fit for this purpose. Second, it deleted the phrase "mutually buy or sell securities not held by them." The purpose of this amendment is to make the law concise and precise since this situation does not actually exist in reality. Third, it replaced the phrase "buying or selling securities from or to oneself without transfer of ownership of the securities by means of making oneself the other party to the transaction" by "conducting securities transactions between accounts actually controlled by oneself." This change came about as a result of the introduction in 2000 of the Real-Name Personal Saving Account System,[110] which stipulated that those opening an account at a financial institution would have to present their own identity cards and use real names.[111] Therefore, the old provision of trading securities with oneself without transfer of ownership is invalid in practice.

Under the SFO, market manipulation involves five specified types of market misconduct: false trading, price rigging, disclosing information about transactions prohibited by the ordinance, disclosing false or misleading information inducing transactions in securities and futures, and stock market manipulation.[112] The first four types of offence apply to both securities and futures, while the last type applies to securities transactions only. The provisions in the ordinance identify each type of specific market misconduct.

D Information disclosure

Mandatory disclosure and transparency of management are powerful tools of securities regulation for the reduction of information asymmetries in capital markets and the prevention of market abuses.[113] These issues are mainly dealt with in Hong Kong through comprehensive statutory and regulatory rules such as the CO, the Listing Rules, the Corporate Governance Code, and the Corporate Governance Report Rules. In China, the CSRC published the *Measures on Administration of the Information on Disclosure of Listed Companies* ("the Measures") on 30 January 2007, implementing the new Company Law and Securities Law's stricter new requirements on information disclosure. The *Measures* are regarded as a significant step forward in improving the quality of information disclosures by Chinese listed companies.[114]

1 WHO IS RESPONSIBLE FOR DISCLOSURE?

Part XV of the SFO requires mandatory disclosure of interests (including short positions) from individuals or companies who are interested in 5 percent or more of any class of voting shares in a listed company, including associated companies.[115] It also imposes mandatory disclosure requirements on directors and the chief executives of listed companies of their interests and short positions in any shares and their interests in any debentures of the listed company, including associated companies. This disclosure regime aims to provide investors with sufficient information to enable them to make informed investment decisions.[116]

In China, the *Measures* require disclosure of information by personnel at all levels of listed companies. First, listed companies, their issuers, directors, supervisors, and senior managers are responsible for ensuring the authenticity, accuracy, completeness, and timeliness of the information disclosed.[117] Shareholders, actual controllers, and purchasers of listed companies are responsible for giving companies timely and accurate notice regarding any changes in the information subject to disclosure, and they are also responsible for assisting companies with making appropriate disclosures.[118]

The *Measures* also define the information disclosure responsibilities of other market participants. For example, sponsors of security issues and securities service institutions are required to make special disclosure, including disclosure of their professional opinions.[119] Such individuals are further required to guarantee the authenticity, accuracy, and completeness of their disclosures, according to the market's operating rules and industry norms.[120] The *Measures* further prohibit illegal acquisition, provision, or transmission of listed companies' inside information by any institution or individual,[121] and set forth rules for media reporting of information on listed companies.[122]

2 WHAT INFORMATION MUST BE DISCLOSED?

In Hong Kong, accounting matters,[123] delegation of management,[124] service contracts,[125] and prospectuses[126] constitute the basic disclosure requirements for companies. Apart from this, there are continuing obligations and duties under both the general securities law and listing rules. The timely disclosure of financial information is a key requirement within them. The annual report and accounts must be sent to all registered shareholders within four months of the financial year end. The Listing Rule (Appendix 16) sets out specific content requirements for the report. The company must also publish and distribute half-yearly reports within three months of the closing of that period. Additionally, certain transactions shall be provided to shareholders or the prior approval of shareholders should be sought.[127] The *Rules on Corporate Governance Report* also sets out mandatory reporting[128] and recommended disclosures.[129]

In China, the *Measures* require listed companies to make timely disclosures of specified information such as their prospectus and periodic reports, both of which must contain all information that might materially affect investors' decisions, as well as listing announcements.[130] The *Measures* also set forth a timetable for these disclosures, based upon relevant laws and regulations.[131] In addition to the above disclosures, listed companies are also required to report any major events that may significantly impact upon the company's share price and which are not yet known to investors.[132] Companies must explain causes of such events, current status, and possible legal consequences. The *Measures* enumerate 20 types of event and the circumstances which would trigger such disclosure obligations.[133]

3 MANAGEMENT OF INFORMATION DISCLOSURE

The *Measures* also contain a new chapter on Management of Information Disclosure Affairs. This chapter requires listed companies to develop rules on managing information disclosure affairs, including rules defining in detail the information disclosure responsibilities of directors, supervisors, senior managers, and their various departments.[134] The *Measures* require each listed company's board of directors to adopt specific rules for managing information disclosures.[135] These rules will then be filed with the stock exchange and the local CSRC office at the company's place of registration. Hong Kong law also contains similar provisions. Rule 3 of the *Rules on Corporate Governance Report* encourages the company to include detailed additional details as to its internal control systems including how the system has been defined, and how to monitor and review it.

4.3 Comparison of securities enforcement

Apart from history and comprehensive substantive law, an established market also needs an efficient regulatory regime. The following part will discuss the regulatory structures of China and Hong Kong.

4.3.1 Overview of China and Hong Kong's regulatory regimes

A China

1 CSRC

Before 1992, all securities-related matters were supervised by the Financial Administration Department of the People's Bank of China (PBOC). The PBOC was also closely involved at the regional level through its branch offices. In October 1992, in order to strengthen guidance on the rapidly developing trade in securities, the State Council Securities Committee (SCSC) and its executive arm the CSRC were established to regulate China's securities and futures markets. In 1998 the SCSC terminated operations and its functions were transferred to the CSRC, which became the sole regulator supervising the nationwide securities and futures markets. Since its establishment, the CSRC has played an active role in regulating the issuance and trade of securities and the operation of stock exchanges.

Pursuant to Article 179 Securities Law 2005, the CSRC is mandated to perform the supervisory functions and duties. These include formulating rules and regulations of the securities markets; carrying out its supervision and administration of the issuance, listing, trading, registration, custody, and settlement of securities; carrying out supervision and administration of the securities activities of securities issuers, listed companies, stock exchanges, and securities companies; and so on.

2 SHANGHAI STOCK EXCHANGE (SHSE) AND SHENZHEN STOCK EXCHANGE (SZSE)

The Securities Law and the *Administrative Measures on Stock Exchange*[136] define a stock exchange as a self-regulatory legal person entity that provides the site and facilities for centralized securities trading and their supervision.[137] The two stock exchanges in China are located in Shanghai and Shenzhen. Both are under the supervision of the CSRC. The SHSE and SZSE were established in 1990 and 1991 respectively.

The major functions of these stock exchanges include: providing the site and facilities for securities trading; formulating business rules; accepting listing applications and arranging listing issues; organizing and supervising the activities of securities trading; supervising the conduct of the members and listed companies; managing and disclosing market information; and other functions permitted by the CSRC.

B Hong Kong

Hong Kong adopts a three tier regulatory framework. The first tier comprises the frontline operators of the market, i.e., two exchanges and their three associated clearing houses. Following their merger on 6 March 2000, all are grouped under the Hong Kong Exchanges and Clearing Limited (HKEx). The exchange bodies, the Stock Exchange of Hong Kong Limited (SEHK) and the Hong Kong Futures Exchange Limited (HKFE), bolster this role by embracing a self-regulatory approach to their own markets. This approach relates to the governance of members, issuers, and dealers (where appropriate). The SFC, being the statutory regulator overseeing the securities and futures market, is the second tier, and in fact the principal regulator. The bridge between the SFC and the two exchange bodies is the HKEx. The final tier is the government, which is not involved in day-to-day regulation of the securities and futures industry. The Financial Services Branch (FSB) of the Financial Services and the Treasury Bureau are responsible for this function.

1 FINANCIAL SERVICES AND THE TREASURY BUREAU

The FSB aims to maintain and enhance Hong Kong's status as a major international financial center by ensuring the provision of an appropriate economic and legal environment, and by ensuring that Hong Kong markets remain open, fair, and efficient. The FSB seeks to achieve the above objectives through the formulation of policy and the introduction of legislation, and assisting the Financial Secretary in overseeing the relevant regulatory authorities.[138]

2 THE SFC

The SFC is an independent statutory body established in 1989 by the Securities and Futures Commission Ordinance (SFCO). The SFCO and nine other securities- and futures-related ordinances were consolidated into the SFO, which came into force on 1 April 2003.

According to the SFC official website, the SFC, as the oversight regulator, is primarily responsible for detecting market malpractices with statutory implications, and, as set out in the SFO, its duties would include: maintaining and promoting the fairness, efficiency, competitiveness, transparency, and orderliness of the securities and futures industry; promoting understanding by the public of the operation and functioning of the securities and futures industry; and minimizing crime and misconduct in the securities and futures industry.[139]

3 HKEx

HKEx is the holding company for SEHK, HKFE, and their related clearing houses; namely Hong Kong Securities Clearing Company Limited (HKSCC), HKFE Clearing Corporation Limited (HKCC), and the SEHK Options Clearing House Limited (SEOCH).

In relation to market surveillance, HKEx focuses on trading operation and risk management, including; enforcement of trading and clearing rules; detection of trading malpractices by users (liaising with the SFC as necessary in relation to those which may involve statutory offences); maintenance of market transparency by monitoring price and turnover movements on a real-time basis, and requiring prompt disclosure of price-sensitive information; assisting in the risk management process by monitoring exceptional concentrations in positions and unusual price fluctuations; interaction with market participants, including the handling of disputes in relation to trading matters; and cross-market surveillance of HKEx's users.

4 SEHK

The Stock Exchange Unification Ordinance 1980 set the stage for the creation of the SEHK, which commenced trading in 1986. The SEHK, a wholly owned subsidiary of HKEx, is a recognized exchange company under the SFO. It operates and maintains the stock market in Hong Kong and is the primary and foremost regulator of Stock Exchange Participants with respect to trading matters and of companies listed on the Main Board and GEM of the Stock Exchange.

4.3.2 A comparison of supervisory structures

A Regulatory model

There are basically three models of securities regulatory practice: the US, the UK, and the hybrid models.[140] The US model is characterized by comprehensive securities law which provides regulatory rules for primary and secondary markets, issuers, underwriters, brokers, and investment advisers. By contrast, in the past, the UK model has emphasized listing requirements and the importance of self-regulation by securities participants rather than a substantial Securities Act. However, since the Financial Services and Markets Act 2000 (FSMA) in the UK authorized the Financial Services Authority (FSA) as the sole regulator for the financial markets, with strong enforcement powers, the role of self-regulation in the UK market has diminished.[141] The third model mixes the first two models, combining both the regulatory role of securities law and self-regulation. It is popular in emerging markets such as China.

In June 1993, before the Company Law was promulgated, the CSRC released preliminary rules on the content and form required for information disclosure by listed companies.[142] The rules cover share issues, prospectuses, annual reports, changes in shareholding, and the listing of shares. The Securities Law, as amended in 2005, reinforces the CSRC's position, requiring stock exchanges to report any abnormal trading in a timely fashion and to seek CSRC approval for the formulation of rules on listing, trading, and membership.[143]

This amendment is a double-edged sword. On the one hand, the reinforcement of the CSRC's role in securities markets is to ensure the functional operation of exchanges. On the other hand, the CSRC's tight control over the exchanges has limited their capacity for self-regulation and has thus constrained their independent operation.[144] Chinese stock exchanges function under the mandate of the CSRC. The formulation and amendment of the Constitution of a stock exchange is subject to the approval of the CSRC.[145] Also, the CSRC approves the appointment and removal of the general manager of the stock exchanges as well as the listing rules, trading rules, membership rules, and other relevant rules.[146] The exchanges can suspend, terminate, and resume bond and share trading, but only as allowed by CSRC-established procedures.[147] Furthermore, an application for listing shares on the stock exchange must first be submitted to the CSRC.[148]

By contrast, the securities market's regulatory body in Hong Kong intervenes less when regulating stock exchanges and listed companies based on a "positive non-interventionism" philosophy of economic policy during British rule. However, this policy has arguably been subject to a change in the post-handover era since 1997.[149] The SFO endows the SFC as the single financial regulator, hence reducing the role of self-regulation in Hong Kong markets.[150] The SFC retains a supervisory role over the Exchange, and in general leaves all frontline responsibilities in listing functions to the Exchange, with the exception of matters relating to takeovers and mergers, general listing policy matters, as well as many amendments to the Listing Rules.[151] The SFC also retains its power to suspend the trading of shares under the Statutory Rules. The enforcement of other securities-related regulations, such as the Securities Ordinance, the Protection of Investors Ordinance, and others, also rests with the SFC.[152]

B Legislative power

In China, the CSRC can formulate rules and regulations concerning regulation of the securities market according to law.[153] Such rules and regulations can be directly taken as references by the People's Courts in handling administrative cases.[154] In Hong Kong, the SFC only provides advice on legislation. The rules and guidelines made by the SFC would be submitted through the Hong Kong government to the Legislative Council. They must be approved by the Council before they come into force.

C Regulating the regulator

The Securities Law in China provides that the CSRC is supervised by the state's audit authority.[155] It also contains general provisions regulating the staff of the securities regulatory authority. For instance, Article 182 requires members of the securities regulatory authority to perform their duties faithfully, to "do their work according to law and be impartial and honest." They may not take advantage of their position to seek illegitimate gains or to divulge trade secrets. They may not serve in an organization that is under the regulation of the authority.[156] Abuse of duties, malpractice for personal gain, and the divulging of trade secrets, are punishable in accordance with the law.[157] However, the law lacks specific provisions on the method of bringing an accusation against the CSRC. Although a party concerned may apply for administrative review, or directly institute proceedings in a court,[158] it is doubtful whether administrative procedure can be applied in such disputes because the CSRC is not an administrative organ but rather an institution under the State Council.[159]

In Hong Kong, by contrast, there is a set of mechanisms which strictly regulate the SFC. The Securities and Futures Appeals Tribunal is a full-time review body which may review, on application, the merits of a range of regulatory decisions made under the SFO by the SFC, and may hear and determine any questions or issue arising out of, or in connection with, any review.[160] The Chairman of the Tribunal is appointed by the Chief Executive on the recommendation of the Chief Justice. In addition, the Chief Executive of Hong Kong appointed an independent Process Review Panel (PRP) to review and monitor the processes of the SFC in November 2000. The PRP determines if the SFC is fair and even-handed in handling investigation complaints as well as decision-making.[161] It comprises 12 members, including industry experts, academia, legal and accountancy professionals, representatives from the Department of Justice, the SFC's Chairman, and a non-executive director.

D Extra enforcement body

Other than the SFC, the Market Misconduct Tribunal (MMT), which was established in 2003 under Section 252 of the SFO, is an independent full-time body, the aim of which is to protect the interests of the investing public and reduce market malpractices. The MMT has jurisdiction to hear and determine any questions or issues arising out of or in connection with the proceedings instituted under the SFO. Its scope includes insider dealing, false trading, price rigging, disclosure of information about prohibited transactions, disclosure of false or misleading information inducing transactions, and stock market manipulation.[162] The MMT is chaired by a judge or former judge of the High Court who sits with two members appointed by the Chief Executive.[163] However, China does not have a specialized body to enhance the enforcement of market misconduct rules.

4.3.3 A comparison of enforcement capacities

To compare two legal regimes it is necessary to look at actual law enforcement, not just law in the books. The value of public enforcement is a key issue for understanding how financial markets deepen and broaden.[164] There is a positive link between the intensity of public enforcement and the size of a country's capital market.[165] Public enforcement assesses regulatory enforcement activities in the form of fines, or other sanctions imposed by the state regulator and stock exchanges.

The intensity of enforcement efforts by securities regulators differs widely among jurisdictions, but common law countries are assumed to be much more active enforcers than civil law countries. Scholars have attempted to test this assumption from different perspectives. La Porta *et al.* developed a public enforcement index, based on formal characteristics of the regulators such as their investigative powers and capacity to impose civil sanctions, to measure public enforcement strength.[166] Jackson and Roe adopted a resource-based approach that included looking at the regulators' staffing levels and budgets, and reached a similar conclusion.[167] Coffee has sought to explain the motivation of common law countries to invest more because their stock markets are larger, more valuable, national assets.[168] Another explanation is the social contract theory that social democracies in Continental Europe press managers to stabilize employment and to forego some profit-maximizing opportunities.[169]

Enforcement efforts can be sensibly measured in terms of inputs (i.e., budget and staff size) and/or outputs (i.e., enforcement actions brought or financial sanctions levied). Hence, this section will compare public enforcement in China and Hong Kong in accordance with these indicators.

A The baseline

As noted, the major regulatory agency of China's financial markets is the CSRC. The law vests the CSRC with the primary power to implement regulations and supervise markets. It uses three tools to punish listed companies. First, for lesser infractions, the CSRC may issue reprimands called "correction orders," in which a company or individual is told to correct certain behavior. However, correction orders are not formal administrative sanctions and thus do not make target companies eligible for civil lawsuits. Second, it issues more serious administrative sanctions which may take the form of formal warnings or fines.[170] Fines for companies range from RMB300,000–RMB600,000; individuals are subject to fines ranging from RMB30,000–RMB300,000.[171] Third, individuals who commit serious violations may also be barred from participation in the securities markets, and from serving as a senior manager or director of a listed company.[172]

Meanwhile, the two national stock exchanges play their self-regulatory role.[173] The law gives them the power temporarily to suspend trading in securities[174] and to de-list companies.[175] They have four regulatory tools at their disposal including: oral warnings (*koutou jinggao*), letters of oversight and supervision, notice of criticisms (*tongbao piping*), and public censure (*gongkai quanze*). Generally, public censure is made public, the less severe sanctions are considered to be non-public "internal oversight measures."

Under the Hong Kong regime, wrongdoers convicted of serious abuses can be subject to imprisonment. Licensees who are in breach of codes and guidelines face disciplinary actions such as reprimands, license suspension, a life ban from the industry, and fines. The SFC is empowered to impose civil fines of up to HK$1 million, or three times the profit gained or loss avoided.[176] The Stock Exchange works to both enforce the Listing Rules and promote compliance. Disciplinary action is a major regulatory response to rule breaches. Also, the MMT has jurisdiction to determine whether any market misconduct has taken place, the identity of any person who has engaged in the market misconduct, and the amount of any resulting profit gained or loss avoided.[177] Penalties are much more severe under the criminal route. Summary and indictable offences carry respective penalties of three and ten years' imprisonment, and fines of HK$1 million and HK$10 million.[178]

B Enforcement inputs

The value of the public enforcement of securities law can be assessed based on a regulator's budgetary resources and staffing levels. This methodological approach is used by some scholars such as Jackson and Roe, and Coffee.[179] Higher budgets and greater staffing levels allow the regulator to examine allegations of wrongdoing, to formulate its rule, to conduct market surveillance and review filings, and to act more often to remedy, prevent, and punish wrongdoing. Regulatory independence and high levels of agency authority are of little value to effective enforcement if the agency's budget is minuscule and its staffing levels thin.

Two measures of pubic enforcement inputs are feasible: the first is the size of regulatory staff scaled by stock market capitalization; the second is the securities regulatory budget scaled by stock market capitalization. Unfortunately, the budget of the CSRC in China is not available. All revenue and expenditures of the CSRC are included in the fiscal budget of the Central Government. The supervision fees levied by the CSRC on securities and futures market participants are paid directly into the National Treasury. Expenditures of the CSRC are covered by budgetary appropriation. But this data is not publicized. As a result of these data limitations this section only compares staffing levels in China and Hong Kong.

High staffing levels would make it easier for the public authorities to conduct market surveillance. In 2007–08, the average number of personnel in the CSRC was 2,379, while the SFC had 460 members of staff.[180] In the same period, the average market capitalization in China reached around US$3,128.5 billion, while Hong Kong had US$1,991.5 billion of capitalization.[181] The ratio of staff to market size was therefore 0.76 in China and 0.23 in Hong Kong. Therefore, in terms of the total number of staff, and staff/per US$ billion of market capitalization, China was superior to Hong Kong. So it seems that China is committed to enforcement and has devoted significant resources to this task.

C Enforcement outputs

Input data has its limitations simply because the fact that a securities regulator has ample resources does not guarantee that it utilizes them to bring enforcement actions, enact good rules, and hire competent people.[182] An alternative assessment criteria to determine enforcement capability could include an analysis of the number of actions brought, and the aggregate financial sanctions levied as a result. For the former, Table 4.1 shows securities enforcement actions brought by the CSRC and the SFC between 2001 and 2008. The total number of actions by the SFC was slightly higher, averaging 122 actions per year.[183] The CSRC was less active, with only 82.75 actions per year in the same period.[184] The contrast is more obvious when enforcement actions are scaled per US$ billion of stock market capitalization. This analysis reveals that enforcement in Hong Kong was more intense, nine times more than that in China. This is consistent with the perception that Hong Kong has a very tough public securities regulator.

Turning from the number of actions brought, to the aggregate monetary sanctions imposed, the data for 2008 for the SFC and the CSRC shows quite the opposite. In 2008 the number of actions brought by the SFC was 112, a similar

Table 4.1 China and Hong Kong securities enforcement (2001–08)

Year	*2001*	*2002*	*2003*	*2004*	*2005*	*2006*	*2007*	*2008*	*Total*
CSRC	29	17	35	49	43	57	405	107	742
SFC	92	90	69	99	198	156	161	112	977

Sources: various CSRC and SFC annual reports, and Liebman and Milhaupt (2008).

Note

The fiscal year end of the CSRC is the end of December, while that of the SFC is the end of March.

number to that brought by the CSRC, which took 107 actions in the same year. The SFC required the violators to disgorge illegal profits and to pay penalties totaling approximately US$19 million,[185] while US$47 million was confiscated by the CSRC;[186] in other words, monetary penalties in China exceeded those imposed in Hong Kong by a ratio of 2.5.

4.4 Concluding remarks

This chapter compares China and Hong Kong's stock markets from two approaches: securities regulation and regulatory authorities. From the above, three conclusions can be made.

1 Both jurisdictions have comprehensive shareholder protection legislation covering company and market regulation. Significant upward movement in the level of protection has been seen in China since the new Company Law and the new Securities Law were enacted in 2005. However, during the transplantation of Western law into China, scholars cast doubt on the effect of that law because state ownership of listed companies impairs the quality of governance and restrains the liquidity of the share market.[187]
2 China's CSRC is more powerful than Hong Kong's SFC. The CSRC can formulate rules and regulations which have a normative force similar to that of the law. Also, it can directly control stock exchanges and public companies. More importantly, unlike Hong Kong, there is no supervision of the CSRC. Inevitably, the significant power exercised by the CSRC restricts self-regulation of the stock exchange and limits the autonomy of listed companies.
3 Probably the most striking contrast is found in the differences between enforcement inputs and outputs. As regards inputs, China's staffing level is substantially higher than that of Hong Kong. This may indicate a commitment to enforcement, and the fact that the CSRC has far more regional offices. However, political influence, owing to interventions or pressure from various interest groups, often renders investigations ineffective.[188] And having more offices is not necessarily an advantage, as enforcement teams have been scattered around the country with insufficient manpower.[189]

With respect to outputs (securities enforcement actions and monetary sanctions), the observation is complicated. From an analysis of the total number of securities enforcement actions during the eight years between 2001 and 2008, it was found that China's figures were was slightly lower than its counterpart. This gap became more obvious when scaled by market capitalization. But, interestingly, fines imposed by the CSRC in 2008 were higher than those imposed by the SFC.

However, this data may convey a rather misleading picture of the market. Public enforcement strength is measured not only by the simple number of activities; it is highly correlated with the types of sanction and regulator themselves. From this perspective, several points are noteworthy.

Sanctions by China's regulators are more modest than those imposed in Hong Kong. Only 22 percent of all enforcement actions administered resulted in fines, as opposed to warning or informal reprimands.[190] Approximately 83 percent of eligible target companies subject to CSRC administrative sanctions have not been sued.[191] This is because the prospect of recovery is simply too small to justify the expense, time, and effort required in bringing a suit. Only a handful of cases have been brought to court and resulted in judgments ordering compensation to plaintiffs, and many of these have yet to be enforced. These problems suggest that the legal approach to investor protection in China is still relatively underdeveloped and insignificant to the whole economy.[192]

By contrast, Hong Kong prefers to use severe criminal penalties, even though pursuit of these may be costly.[193] In 2007, 74 persons in 72 disciplinary actions were charged in criminal proceedings, in which five persons were prosecuted for more than one offence.[194] Most were punished with jail sentences of six months or more, plus civil compensation. Similarly, more than 90 percent of enforcement actions resulted in prosecution during 2004–06.[195]

Most importantly, skepticism about public enforcement, particularly in developing countries, may be due to corruption among government officials – market regulators themselves. This is particularly true in China. The state plays the role of both referee and player; it controls a majority of shares in many listed companies, but is also responsible for drafting and enforcing regulations. The power of the CSRC and other regulators is daunting, and they may be susceptible to political influence, local protectionism, other forms of corruption, and similar problems.[196] Similarly, Hong Kong is also a jurisdiction with a concentrated ownership structure. Seventy percent of the large, publicly traded, companies in Hong Kong were family-controlled by the end of 1995, the highest percentage among other wealthy economies.[197] However, as discussed before, Hong Kong has employed huge public enforcement resources in financial markets so as to minimize the risks of insider control behavior. According to the Corruption Perception Index 2012, Hong Kong ranked 14 while China was ranked 80th.[198]

All in all, as far as the law in the books is concerned, Hong Kong has a strong market with stronger shareholder protection; China's stock markets are relatively weak, but it is moving towards high standards. There is still a gap in investor protection between the two jurisdictions at this moment, although China's capital markets are predicted to grow and prosper by building on the current structure and "piggybacking" international practices. As far as the law in action is concerned, variable data seems to show that China is not worse than Hong Kong. It implies that China may be committed to enforcement and has devoted significant resources to securities markets. However, unless some fundamental problems are resolved, throwing in more resources alone may not sufficiently enhance enforcement efficiency and effectiveness.

Notes

1 Palmer, Vernon Valentime (2005), "From Lerotholi to Lando: Some Examples of Comparative Law Methodology" in *American Journal of Comparative Law*, 53, p. 262.
2 Ibid, p. 290.
3 Örücü, Esin (2007), "Developing Comparative Law" in Örücü, Esin and Nelken, David (eds.), *Comparative Law A Handbook*, Oxford: Hart, p. 51.
4 La Porta, Rafael *et al.* (1997), "Legal Determinants of External Finance" in *Journal of Finance*, 52; La Porta, Rafael *et al.* (1998), "Law and Finance" in *Journal of Political Economy*, 106; La Porta, Rafael *et al.* (2000), "Investor Protection and Corporate Governance" in *Journal of Financial Economics*, 58; and La Porta, Rafael *et al.* (2008), "The Economic Consequences of Legal Origins" in *Journal of Economic Literature*, 46.
5 Jackson, Howell and Roe, Mark (2009), "Public and Private Enforcement of Securities Laws: Resource-Based Evidence" in *Journal of Financial Economics*, 93.
6 FSA (2009), "The Turner Review: A Regulatory Response to the Global Banking Crisis." pp. 47, 91–2. Online. Available at: www.fsa.gov.uk/pages/Library/Corporate/turner/index.shtml (laccessed 20 December 2012).
7 Kraakman, Reinier *et al.* (2009), *The Anatomy of Corporate Law: A Comparative and Functional Approach*, 2nd edn, Oxford: Oxford University Press, pp. 38–44.
8 Laurenceson, James and Chai, Joseph (2003), *Financial Reform and Economic Development in China*, Cheltenham: Edward Elgar, p. 83. It is composed of 15 documents about shareholding reforms, especially two *Opinions*, the *Standard Opinion on Companies Limited by Shares* and the *Standard Opinion on Limited Liability Companies*, which provided a solid foundation for the Company Law.
9 Clarke, Donald (2003), "Corporate Governance in China: An Overview" in *China Economic Review*, 14, p. 495.
10 Howson, Nicholas (1997), "China's Company Law: One Step Forward, Two Steps Back? A Modest Complaint" in *Columbia Journal of Asian Law*, 11, p. 128.
11 Xi, Duojun (2002), "Zhongguo Gongsifa Lifa yu Shishi de Jingyan, Wenti ji Wanshan Tujing" [The Experience, Problems and Improvements of China's Company Law's Legislation and Enforcement] in *Zhongnan Gongye Daxue Xuebao* [Journal of Mid-South Industrial University], 8, p. 87.
12 Cheng, Yangtie *et al.* (2005), "Steady as She Goes China's New Securities Law." December 2005/January 2006 *China Law & Practice*, 16.
13 Xiao, Xinrong *et al.* (2005), "Window Dressing of Chinese Securities Investment Funds." EMFA Conference Paper 2005, p. 9.
14 It was adopted by the Fifth Session of the Standing Committee of the Tenth National People's Congress on 28 October 2003 and came into force on 1 June 2004.
15 Speech made by Fulin Shang, president of CSRC, in a meeting with Xinhua reporters, see Xinhua website. Online. Available at: http://news.xinhuanet.com/newscenter/200310/28/content_1147747.htm (accessed 19 November 2008).
16 It was adopted by the 168th Executive Meeting of the State Council on 7 February 2007 and came into force on 15 April 2007. It is an overall amendment to the *Tentative Ordinance on Administration of Futures Trading*, which was issued by the State Council on 6 June 1999.
17 CO s. 2.
18 CO s. 332.
19 Stott, Vanessa (2005), *Hong Kong Company Law*, Hong Kong: Longman, p. 1.
20 CO s. 168BA.
21 See Tyler, Edward and Ho, John (2004), *HKLRD Review Series 2004*, Hong Kong: Sweet & Maxwell Asia, p. 3.
22 One representative example is the introduction of the statutory derivative action in

the CA 2006, s. 260. And other changes have also seen in the UK, for example, reduction of capital in private companies supported by solvency statement instead of the court, ss. 642–4; and one person company, s. 155.

23 Government of Hong Kong (2012), "Companies Ordinance Rewrite." Online. Available at: www.fstb.gov.hk/fsb/co_rewrite/eng/pub-press/consult.htm (accessed 20 December 2012).

24 Financial Services Bureau (1999), "Legislative Reform for the Securities and Future Market (Securities and Futures Bill 1999)," p. 1.

25 Ibid.

26 It is an ordinance to consolidate and amend the laws relating to financial products; the securities and futures market and the securities and futures industry; the regulation of activities and other matters connected with financial products; the securities and futures market and the securities and futures industry; the protection of investors; and other matters incidental thereto, or connected therewith, and for connected purposes. See SFO s. 1.

27 See Codes, Guidelines and Circulars on the SFC's website. Online. Available at: www.sfc.hk/web/EN/rule-book (accessed 20 December 2012).

28 See Listing Rules Volume Two Appendix 14. Available at: www.hkex.com.hk/eng/rulesreg/listrules/mbrules/vol.2.htm (last accessed 20 December 2012).

29 Hong Kong Stock Exchange (2011), "The Exchange Publishes Consultation Conclusions on Review of the Corporate Governance Code and Associated Listing Rules." Online. Available at: www.hkex.com.hk/eng/newsconsul/hkexnews/2011/111028news.htm.

30 Listing Rule 3.10A.

31 Kraakman *et al.*, op. cit., p. 42.

32 Art. 1 (3) of the Guiding Opinions.

33 Clarke, Donald (2006), "The Independent Director in Chinese Corporate Governance" in *Delaware Journal of Corporate Law*, 31.

34 Liao, Jing *et al.* (2009), "Board Structure Determinants and Efficiency, Evidence from the Implementation of Independent Director System in China." Massey University College of Business Research Paper No. 1, p. 19. Online. Available at: http://ssrn.com/abstract=1326169.

35 Clarke, Donald (2008), "The Role of Non-Legal Institutions in Chinese Corporate Governance" in Kanda, Hideki *et al.* (eds.), *Transforming Corporate Governance*, New York: Routledge, p. 177.

36 Xi, Chao (2009), *Corporate Governance and Legal Reform in China*, London: Wildy, Simmonds & Hill Publishing, p. 170.

37 Art. 4 (1) of the Independent Director Guidelines.

38 See a comparative view by Hopt, Klaus (2003), "Corporate Governance in Germany" in Hopt, Klaus *et al.* (eds), *Capital Markets and Company Law*, Oxford: Oxford University Press, p. 303.

39 The underlying influence on Chinese corporate and financial law is Roman-Germanic, via Germany. See Wood, Philip (2005), *Maps of World Financial law*, 5th edn, London: Allen & Overy, p. 45. Originally, the supervisory boards were places where large shareholders met to resolve their interests. An accident of drafting at the Nuremberg Conference in 1857 transformed what were previously described as administrative into supervisory boards. In 1884 the functions of the supervisory and the management board were separated by law, restricting the supervisory board to a controlling body and strengthening its fiduciary responsibilities. See Franks, Julian *et al.* (2006), "The Origins of the German Corporation – Finance, Ownership and Control" in *Review of Finance*, 10, pp. 540–2.

40 Wang, Jiangyu (2007), "The Strange Role of Independent Directors in a Two-tier Board Structure of China's Listed Companies" in *Compliance & Regulatory Journal*, 3, p. 49.

41 Xi, Chao (2007), "In Search of An Effective Monitoring Board Model: Board Reforms and the Political Economy of Corporate Law in China" in *Connecticut Journal of International Law*, 22, p. 44.
42 The 2004 Constitution as amended, Arts. 16 and 17, and the 2005 Company Law, as amended, Art. 18.
43 Art. 52 Company Law 2005.
44 Ibid., Art. 54.
45 Ho, Simon (2003a), "Corporate Governance in China." Hong Kong Baptist University Working Paper, p. 27. Online. Available at: www.hkbu.edu.hk/%7Ebus/simonho/index.htm (accessed 12 December 2009).
46 Davies, Paul (2002), *Introduction to Company Law*, Oxford: Oxford University Press, p. 113.
47 Art. 104 PRC Company Law 2005.
48 CO Cap 32, s. 116 (1). A resolution may be proposed and passed as a special resolution:

> (a) in the case of a resolution for voluntary winding up pursuant to section 228 (1) (b) in circumstances other than a member's voluntary winding up, at a meeting of which less than 21 days' notice but not less than 7 days' notice has been given; (b) in any other case, at a meeting of which less than 21 days' notice has been given.

49 Chen, Gongmeng *et al.* (2008), "Does the Type of Ownership Control Matter: Evidence from China's Listed Companies" in *Journal of Banking & Finance*, 32.
50 Dilution of monetary value occurs when the new shares issued are undervalued. Rights provide shareholders with protection against this dilution by giving them the first right to subscribe and, in the event that they decide not to subscribe, to sell their rights to other investors in the market. Additionally, rights prevent transfer of ownership to new shareholders from occurring without the prior agreement of existing shareholders. See Department of Trade and Industry (2005), "The UK 'Pre-emption Rights': Final Report 2005," pp. 9–12. Online. Available at: www.berr.gov.uk/files/file28436.pdf (accessed 20 December 2012).
51 The definition can be seen in the UK CA 2006, s. 561. At the EU level, pre-emption rights are governed by Art. 29 of the Second Company Law Directive 77/91/EEC of 13 December 1976.
52 Franks, Julian and Mayer, Colin (2002), "Governance as a Source of Managerial Discipline." National Bank of Belgium Working Paper 031. Online. Available at: www.nbb.be/doc/oc/repec/reswpp/WP31.pdf (accessed 20 December 2012).
53 Hong Kong Listing Rule 2.03(6).
54 For instance, see Davies, op. cit., pp. 145–8 and Franks and Mayer, op. cit., pp. 3–9.
55 The *Measures* was issued on 31 July 2006 by the CSRC, and came into force on 1 September 2006; the amendment came into force on 27 August 2008.
56 The code was formed in 1975, amended in 1992, 2002, and 2005. The code was intended to follow the approach of the City Code on Takeover and Mergers. See Ho, Betty (1997), "Rethinking the System of Sanctions in the Corporate and Securities Law of Hong Kong" in *McGill Law Journal*, 42, p. 616. According to the Listing Rule 14.78, all listed companies must comply with the Takeover Code.
57 The Hong Kong's Takeover Code 2005, 4.22; the China *Measures* 2006, Arts. 7–8; and the UK's Takeover Code 2006, Rule 21.
58 The Hong Kong Takeover Code, Rule 26; the China Securities Law, Art. 88 and the *Measures*, Art. 24; and the UK's Takeover Code 2006, Rule 9.
59 The Hong Kong Takeover Code, Rule 13.1; China's *Measures*, Art. 26; and the UK's Takeover Code, Rule 11.
60 MacNeil, Iain (2002), "Adaptation and Convergence in Corporate Governance: the Case of Chinese Listed Companies" in *Journal of Corporate law Studies*, 2,

p. 322. And Ho, Simon (2003b), "Corporate Governance in Hong Kong: Key Problems and Prospects." CUHK Centre for Accounting Disclosure and Corporate Governance Research Paper No. 1, p. 50. Online. Available at: http://ssrn.com/abstract=440924.

61 For example, according to the Combined Code, institutional investors have a responsibility to make considered use of their votes, and should enter into a dialogue with companies based on the mutual understanding of objectives. See the Combined Code 2008, s. 2, E.1 and E.3. Also see Gerke, Wolfgang *et al.* (2003), "Changing Role of Institutional Investors – A German Perspective" in Hopt, Klaus *et al.* (eds.), *Capital Markets and Company Law*, Oxford: Oxford University Press, p. 358.

62 Coffee, John (2007), "Law and the Market: the Impact of Enforcement" in *University of Pennsylvania Law Review*, 156, p. 296. The share ownership of institutional investors in the UK equity market has been over 50 percent since the early 1980s.

63 CSRC (2008), *China Capital Markets Development Report*, Beijing: China Financial Publishing House, p. 269.

64 Ibid., pp. 271–2.

65 China launched QFII in 2002 in a move to open up markets to the outside world. The original regulation on QFII was *Temporary Regulation on Domestic Securities Investment by Qualified Foreign Institutional Investors*, issued in November 2002, and replaced by *Regulation on Domestic Securities Investment by Qualified Foreign Institutional Investors*, issued in August 2006.

66 Zeng, Yamin and Zhang, Junsheng (2009), "The Dark Side of Institutional Shareholders Activism in Emerging Markets: Evidence from China's Non-Tradable Share Reform." Online. Available at: http://ssrn.com/abstract=1372428.

67 SFC (2004), "Understanding Investors in the Hong Kong Listed Securities and Derivatives Markets," p. 33. Online. Available at: www.sfc.hk/web/EN/published-resources/research-papers/market-reviews (accessed 20 December 2012).

68 Ibid.

69 Kraakman *et al.*, op. cit., p. 39.

70 Re *Smith v. Fawcett Ltd* [1942] Ch. 304 CA.

71 *Howard Smith v. Ampol Petroleum Ltd* [1974] AC 821 PC.

72 *Regal (Hastings) Ltd v. Gulliver* [1942] 1 ALL ER 738 HL.

73 Although there were recommendations to codify directors' duties in the form of a statutory statement, the Standing Committee on Company Law Reform considered the current state of law on fiduciary duties generally acceptable. It believes that there is merit in having a code of best practice which would serve as a guide to directors as to their duties, but the code of practice does not carry statutory force. In April 2006 the Companies Registry issued a set of "Non-statutory Guidelines on Directors' Duties." Directors are strongly advised to follow the guidelines. But it is worth noting that in the new Companies Bill 2011, the common law directors' duty of care has been codified.

74 The Listing Rules contain the Corporate Governance Code in Appendix 14.

75 Ho (2003b), op. cit., p. 25.

76 Dam, Kenneth (2006), "China as a Test Case: Is the Rule of Law Essential for Economic Growth?" University of Chicago Law & Economics, Olin Working Paper No. 275, p. 34. Online. Available at: http://ssrn.com/abstract=880125 (accessed 20 December 2012).

77 Lee, Rebecca (2007), "Fiduciary Duty without Equity: Fiduciary Duties of Directors under the Revised Company Law of the PRC" in *Virginia Journal of International Law*, 47, p. 925.

78 Clarke, Donald (2006), "Lost in Translation? Corporate Legal Transplants in China." GWU Law School Public Law Research Paper No. 213, pp. 14–16. Online. Available at: http://ssrn.com/abstract=913784 (accessed 20 December 2012).

79 *Foss* v. *Harbottle* (1843) 2 Hare 461. However, there are some exceptions to this

rule, which were set out by the Court of Appeal in *Edwards* v. *Halliwell* (1950) 2 ALL ER.

80 Romano referred to this type of litigation as a "stopgap" measure in corporate law. See Romano, Roberta (1991), "The Shareholder Suit: Litigation Without Foundation" in *Journal of Law, Economics & Organisation*, 7, p. 55.

81 Armour, John *et al.* (2009), "Private Enforcement of Corporate Law: An Empirical Comparison of the US and UK" in *Journal of Empirical Legal Studies*, 6.

82 The 2004 CO, Cap 32, ss. 168BA–168BK.

83 Derivative action is included in Art. 152 Chinese Company Law as amended. The *Mandatory Provisions for the Articles of Association of Companies Listed Overseas* provides the companies with certain remedies against directors, supervisors, and officers who breach their duties to the company. For more details regarding the evolution of the derivative action in China, refer to Chapter 7 of this book.

84 See Huang, Flora Xiao (2009), "Shareholder Revolt? The Statutory Derivative Action in China." Comparative Research in Law & Political Economy Research Paper No. 49/2009, pp. 13–19. Online. Available at: http://ssrn.com/abstract=1516448 (accessed 20 December 2012). Also see Tang, Xin (2008), "Protecting Minority Shareholders in China: A Task for Both Legislation and Enforcement" in Kanda, Hideki *et al.* (eds.) *Transforming Corporate Governance in East Asia*, London: Routledge, p. 146.

85 Tang, op. cit., p. 146.

86 CO, Cap 32, s. 168A.

87 CO, Cap 32, s. 142.

88 Art. 3.5 (d) *1993 Mandatory Provisions.*

89 Fair and efficient market behavior is a clearly stated requirement under the Market Abuse Directive, 2004/72/EC, of 29 April.

90 Chinese Securities Law 2005 Chapter 3 s. 4.

91 Zhu, Sanzhu (2007), *Securities Dispute Resolution in China*, Aldershot: Ashgate, pp. 159, 221.

92 Chinese Securities Law 2005, Arts. 79 and 171.

93 SFO, Cap 571, s. 245 (1).

94 SFO, Cap 571, s. 257 (1).

95 SFO, Cap 571, s. 303 (1).

96 SFO, Cap 571, Parts VIII and XIV.

97 The definition of insider dealing is widespread in much legislation such as the EC Market Abuse Directive, Arts. 2–4; the UK Financial Services and Markets Act (FSMA) s. 118; and the US SEC Rule 14e-3.

98 SFO, Cap 571, ss. 247 (1) and 287 (1).

99 Securities Law of China, Art. 74 (1) (directors, supervisors and officers of issuers), 74 (2) (substantial shareholders), 74 (3) (senior officers of the holding company of issues), 74 (4) (employees).

100 Ibid., Art. 74 (5) (regulatory officers).

101 Ibid., Art. 74 (6) (market professions and intermediaries).

102 Huang, Hui (2006), *International Securities Markets: Insider Trading Law in China*, Biggleswade: Kluwer Law, pp. 194–6. Regarding his second opinion, for example, directors or officers would not be viewed as insiders after they resigned from a company, which may potentially leave a hole in the law, since officers who have resigned may still hold some insider information and take advantage of it.

103 SFO, Cap 571, ss. 245 (2) and 285 (2).

104 Hsu, Berry Fong-Chung *et al.* (2006) *Financial Markets in Hong Kong*, Oxford: Oxford University Press, p. 392.

105 Huang (2006), op. cit., pp. 204–5.

106 SFO, Cap 571, ss. 271 and 292.

107 SFO, Cap 571, ss. 271 (1) and 292 (1).

108 Ibid.
109 Luo, Peixin *et al.* (2006), *Zuixin Zhengquan Fa Jiedu* [Studies on New Securities Law], Beijing: Peking University Press, pp. 124–5.
110 The *Provisions on the Real-Name Personal Saving Account System* were promulgated by the State Council of the PRC on 20 March 2000, and came into force on 1 April 2000.
111 Art. 6 *Provisions on the Real-Name Personal Saving Account System.*
112 SFO, Cap 571, s. 245.
113 Avgouleas, Emilios (2005), *The Mechanics and Regulation of Market Abuse*, New York: Oxford University Press, p. 173.
114 Chen, Grant and Zhang, Zhengyi (2007), "New Disclosure Standards for PRC Listed Companies" in *China Law and Practice*, April 2007, p. 1.
115 Outline of Part XV of the Securities and Future Ordinance (Cap 571) – Disclosure of Interest.
116 Ibid.
117 The *Measures*, Art. 3.
118 Ibid., Art. 46.
119 Ibid., Art. 16.
120 Ibid., Art. 50.
121 Ibid., Art. 55.
122 Ibid., Art. 56.
123 CO, Cap 32, ss. 121–3. It includes annual report and accounts, interim report, etc.
124 Ibid., s. 162A.
125 Ibid., s. 161 (1).
126 Ibid., ss. 38D and 48A.
127 These types of rules fall into two categories: notifiable transaction (Listing Rules Chapter 14) and connected transaction (Listing Rules Chapter 14A).
128 CG Report Rules, Rule 2.
129 CG Report Rules, Rule 3.
130 The *Measures*, Art. 5.
131 Ibid., Art. 20.
132 Ibid., Art. 30.
133 Ibid.
134 Ibid., Art. 37.
135 Ibid.
136 It was promulgated by the CSRC on 10 December 1997, then was replaced by the new version in 2001.
137 Art. 102 Securities Law 2005 and Art. 3 Administration Measures on Stock Exchange.
138 See the FSB website. Online. Available at: www.fstb.gov.hk/fsb/aboutus/welcome/index.htm (accessed 20 December 2012).
139 See the SFC website. Online. Available at: www.sfc.hk/sfc/html/EN/ (accessed 20 December 2012).
140 See Wan, Meng (2000), "The Securities System in China" in Joseph Norton *et al.* (eds.), *Financial Regulation in the Greater China Area: Mainland China, Taiwan and Hong Kong SAR*, Kluwer Law International: London, p. 117; and Wei, Yuwa (2005), "The Development of the Securities Market and Regulation in China" in *Loyola Los Angeles International and Comparative Law Review*, 27, pp. 497–8.
141 See Shi, Chenxia (2007), "Protecting Investors in China through Multiple Regulatory Mechanisms and Effective Enforcement" in *Arizona Journal of International & Comparative Law*, 24, p. 454. Also Sir Howard Davies identifies that the FSMA marks a formal shift in regulatory culture from the self-regulatory approach to a fully statutory basis, and the end of self-regulation. See Davies, Howard (2001), "Performing Financial Regulation: Progress and Priorities" in Ferran, Eilis and

Goodhart, Charles (eds.), *Regulating Financial Services and Markets in the 21st Century*, Oxford: Hart, pp. 17–24.

142 CSRC (1993), "Information Disclosure and Corporate Governance in China." Online. Available at: www.oecd.org/dataoecd/6/60/1931117.pdf (accessed 20 December 2012).

143 Arts. 115 and 118 Securities Law 2005.

144 Shi, op. cit., p. 478.

145 Art. 103 Securities Law 2005.

146 Ibid., Arts. 107 and 118.

147 Ibid., Arts. 55, 56, 60, 61.

148 Ibid, Art. 50 (1).

149 In 2002 Hong Kong's Financial Secretary Antony Leung replaced the territory's economic governing ethos of "positive non-intervention" with the new motto of "proactive market enabling." See Restall, Hugo (2002), "Riding the Subway to Statism" in *Wall Street Journal*, 13 March 2002.

150 See Wang, Chunge (2005), *Neidi Gongsi Xianggang Shangshi ji Liangdi Jianguan Hezuo Yanjiu* [The Companies from Mainland China Listed in Hong Kong and the Cooperation between Mainland China and Hong Kong's Supervisory Bodies], Beijing: Peking University Press, p. 131.

151 See the SFC website, "Our Role." Online. Available at: www.sfc.hk/web/EN/about-the-sfc/our-role (accessed 20 December 2012).

152 Ibid.

153 Art. 179 Securities Law.

154 Art. 53 Administrative Procedure Law. The Administrative Procedure Law was adopted by Second Session of the Seventh National People's Congress on 4 April 1989, and came into force on 1 October 1990.

155 Art. 9 Securities Law of China 2005.

156 Ibid., Art. 187.

157 Ibid., Art. 228.

158 Ibid., Art. 235.

159 Wang (2005), op. cit., p. 139.

160 See the Securities and Futures Appeals Tribunal website. Online. Available at: www.sfat.gov.hk/english/aboutus/intro/index.htm (accessed 20 December 2012).

161 See FSB (2010), "Process Review Panel for the Securities and Futures Commission." Online. Available at: www.fstb.gov.hk/fsb/topical/prp.htm (accessed 20 December 2012).

162 SFO, s. 245.

163 See the MMT website. Online. Available at: www.mmt.gov.hk/eng/home/home.htm (accessed 20 December 2012).

164 Jackson, Howell and Roe, Mark (2009), "Public and Private Enforcement of Securities Laws: Resource-Based Evidence" in *Journal of Financial Economics*, 93, p. 236.

165 Ibid.

166 La Porta, Rafael *et al.* (2006), "What Works in Securities Laws" in *Journal of Finance*, 61, p. 12. However, their argument attracted much criticism, for a summary, see Coffee, John (2007), "Law and the Market: The Impact of Enforcement" in *University of Pennsylvania Law Review*, 156, p. 258.

167 Jackson and Roe, op. cit.

168 Coffee, op. cit., p. 297.

169 For general discussions, see Roe, Mark (2006), *Political Determinations of Corporate Governance: Political Context, Corporate Impact*, Oxford: Oxford University Press; and Roe, Mark (2006), "Legal Origins, Politics, and Modern Stock Markets" in *Harvard Law Review*, 120.

170 In most cases companies or individuals are both fined and warned, while in a small number of cases the CSRC has imposed either only a warning or only a fine.

171 Art. 193 Securities Law 2005.
172 Ibid., Art. 233.
173 Ibid., Art. 102.
174 Ibid., Art. 55.
175 Ibid., Art 56.
176 SFO, s. 257.
177 Ibid., s. 252 (3).
178 Ibid., s. 303.
179 Jackson and Roe, op. cit., and Coffee, op. cit.
180 The number of personnel in the CSRC in 2007 and 2008 was 2,246 and 2,512 respectively. See CSRC Annual Report 2007 and 2008. The number of staff in the SFC in these two years was 442 and 478 respectively. See SFC Annual Report 2007–08 & 2008–09.
181 Data from World Federation of Exchanges. Online. Available at: www.world-exchanges.org/statistics/annual (accessed 20 December 2012).
182 Jackson and Roe, op. cit., pp. 210–11.
183 Jackson, Howell (2007), "Variation in the Intensity of Financial Regulation: Preliminary Evidence and Potential Implications" in *Yale Journal on Regulation*, 24, p. 280.
184 Liebman, Benjamin and Milhaupt, Curtis (2008), "Reputational Sanctions in China's Securities Market" in *Columbia Law Review*, 108, p. 942.
185 SFC (2009), "Annual Report 2008–2009," pp. 118–21. The fines were around HK$148 million. The currency exchange rate of HK$ to US$ is fixed at approximately 7.8.
186 CSRC (2009), "CSRC Annual Report 2008," pp. 34–5. The CSRC reported monetary sanctions in RMB320 million. The figure here is based on exchange rate of about RMB6.8 to US$ on 31 December 2008.
187 Shi, op. cit., p. 481.
188 Ibid.
189 CSRC (2008), op. cit., p. 279.
190 Pistor, Katharina and Xu, Chenggang (2005), "Governing Stock Markets in Transition Economies: Lesson from China" in *American Law and Economics Review*, 7, pp. 195–6.
191 Liebman and Milhaupt, op. cit., p. 943.
192 Ibid., p. 945.
193 Some commentators argue these sanctions can bring extra enforcement cost and opportunity cost (the cost of the beneficial activity foregone). See Fischel, Daniel and Ross, David (1991), "Should the Law Prohibit Manipulation in Financial Markets?" in *Harvard Law Review*, 105, pp. 522–3.
194 SFC (2009), "2007–2008 Enforcement Annual Report," p. 38.
195 SFC (2008), "2006–2007 Enforcement Annual Report," p. 32.
196 Anderson, Craig and Guo, Bingna, "Corporate Governance under the New Company Law (Part 2): Shareholder Lawsuits and Enforcement" in *China Law & Practice*, May 2006.
197 La Porta, Rafael *et al.* (1999), "Corporate Ownership around the World" in *Journal of Finance*, 54, pp. 491–2.
198 Transparency International (2012), "Corruption Perception Index 2012." Online. Available at: http://cpi.transparency.org/cpi2012/results (accessed 20 December 2012).

5 Chinese cross-listings in Hong Kong

Procedures and requirements

According to MacNeil and Lau the listing rules, the securities law, and the company law form a three tier structure of corporate regulation for cross-listing.[1] The listing rules is the top tier in a system of regulation for listed companies in which the lower tiers are represented by securities law and company law. The previous chapter has discussed the first two tiers (securities law and company law); this chapter turns to the third tier (listing rules).

The aims of this chapter are to: first, look at the listing requirements from both home and host jurisdictions in the Chinese/Hong Kong case; second, examine the strategies adopted to keep the market informed and protect investors; third, explore whether Hong Kong treats Chinese issuers differently due to their overwhelming significance, with China-related stocks accounting for more than 45 percent of the Hong Kong market capitalization since 2006; fourth, consider whether such cross-listing is indeed a case of bonding for Chinese companies to commit to a superior governance regime, or just a case of enabling them to escape from certain domestic listing requirements.

The chapter is structured as follows. The first part overviews the history of Chinese companies in Hong Kong and some related statistics. Section 5.2 examines the regulatory framework governing the listing of Chinese issuers in Hong Kong, with particular respect to the mechanisms used to protect shareholders. Section 5.3 provides an analysis of Chapters 19 and 19A of the Hong Kong Listing Rules. As a comparison, reflections on domestic public offerings and listings are given in Section 5.4. The final part concludes in Section 5.5.

5.1 Overview: history and statistics

The wave of H-share listings has been moving upwards since the first Chinese company listed on the Hong Kong Stock Exchange (HKSE) in 1993. The boom in Chinese overseas listings is due partly to the increasing prominence of the Chinese economy and partly to the increasing mobility of companies and capital in the era of globalization.

Historically, Hong Kong has been the preferred place of foreign listing for Chinese companies, in particular since its handover to China in 1997. In addition to the geo-cultural proximity and the Chinese language, other explanations are provided for why Chinese companies prefer to list in Hong Kong rather than in the US or the UK. For example, Yang and Lau argue that Hong Kong-listed companies may have a better information environment than those of other jurisdictions and are less financially constrained, which may be due to their ability to access the Hong Kong capital market for external financing.[2]

Tsingtao Brewery, the first Chinese company ever to issue equities outside China, began trading on the HKSE in July 1993. It was part of the first batch of nine companies approved for overseas listings in the same year, followed by a second batch of 22 companies which gained the requisite approval in late 1994.[3]

Before 1999, Chinese companies listed overseas were mainly the foreign listed arms of large SOEs. They were considered of vital importance to the national economy. More recently, more privately owned companies have ventured abroad and the H-share market has seen the entry of small and medium enterprises. Many of these are high-tech companies listed on Hong Kong's Growth Enterprise Market (GEM).

Equity-raising activities by Chinese companies are summarized in Table 5.1. At the end of 2012 a total of 172 Chinese companies were listed on the HKSE.[4] Those of the Industrial and Commercial Bank of China (ICBC) and the Bank of

Table 5.1 Market capitalization of H-shares (Main board and GEM) 1993–2011

Year	*Main Board*	*GEM*				
	Number of new issues	*Market capitalization (HKD million)*	*% of market*	*Number of new issues*	*Market capitalization (HKD million)*	*% of market*
1993	6	18,228.70	0.61			
1994	8	19,981.32	0.96			
1995	1	16,463.77	0.7			
1996	6	31,530.63	0.91			
1997	15	48,622.01	1.52			
1998	2	33,532.66	1.26			
1999	3	41,888.78	0.89	–	–	–
2000	3	85,139.58	1.78	3	991.69	1.47
2001	3	99,813.09	2.57	4	1,888.75	3.1
2002	4	129,248.37	3.63	10	2,393.01	4.58
2003	10	403,116.50	7.36	8	5,063.25	7.21
2004	8	455,151.75	6.87	8	6,376.35	9.56
2005	9	1,280,495.01	15.78	3	6,420.65	9.64
2006	17	3,363,788.46	25.39	3	14,952.03	16.82
2007	9	5,056,820.09	24.62	0	22,695.38	14.09
2008	6	2,720,188.76	26.53	1	11,550.65	25.57
2009	6	4,686,418.75	26.37	0	27,059.82	25.76
2010	12	5,210,324.73	24.88	0	20,154.24	14.97
2011	12	4,096,659.80	23.47	0	4,611.67	5.45
Total	140			40		

Source: Data & Statistics from the HKEx.

China (BOC) rank among the biggest ever IPOs in the world. Among these companies, 144 were listed on the Main Board, with total capitalization of HK$4,516 billion, which accounted for around one-fourth the market size. Twenty-eight of them were listed on the GEM with capitalization of HK$4.7 billion, covering around 5 percent of the market size.[5]

As shown in Table 5.1, market capitalization of H-shares on the Main Board has been rising, especially since 2002. The number has been accelerating rapidly and reached a peak in 2007 of over HK$5,057 billion of market capitalization, then decreased unexpectedly in the next year due to the credit crunch before reaching another peak in 2010. A similar pattern also appeared on the GEM. However, its significance has clearly been declining as seen from the figures for 2011.

There are internal and external aspects to the growth trend of H-shares. From a worldwide perspective, the global financial markets were damaged by the Asian financial crisis of 1997 and recovered a few years later. As the markets grew again, more money than ever flowed between countries and regions as investors sought opportunities outside their home market, resulting in a surge in cross-border IPO activities. Between 2003–07, the number of cross-border IPO listings increased more than sixfold from 44 to 297.[6] Nevertheless, the credit crunch reshaped the global financial sectors in 2008, so the IPO market experienced its lowest activity for 30 years.[7]

More importantly, internal pressure comes from China's increasing economic growth and the consequent appetite for capital. China's economy has grown strongly over the last decade with an average GDP growth of over 8 percent, far more dynamic than in other countries.[8] A decade ago, China's state-owned sector looked like an economic disaster. In the aftermath of the Asian financial crisis, average profit margins among Chinese SOEs fell close to zero. After ten years, in 2007, the combined profit of the 150 or so companies controlled by the state reached US$140 billion.[9] At the end of that year, out of the five largest companies in the world, three were SOEs: including PetroChina, China Mobile, and the ICBC. Incidentally, they are all listed in Hong Kong.

5.2 Listing requirements and procedures for Chinese/Hong Kong companies

In general, according to Hertig *et al.*, the objectives of listing rules are informed market pricing and the quality control of public issuers.[10] To achieve these two objectives, three strategies are employed: the rules and standards strategies, the entry strategy, and the trusteeship strategy.[11]

The rules and standards strategies attempt to directly regulate the substance of agency relationships.[12] But the functions of rules and standards are different. Rules require or prohibit specific behaviors, ex ante, while standards leave the precise determination of compliance to adjudicators after the fact. The entry strategy is in fact mandatory disclosure, to protect investors by requiring companies to disclose systemic information. The trusteeship strategy requires a neutral third party to exercise his or her own unconstrained best judgment in making a corporate decision.[13]

All major jurisdictions protect their capital markets and investors with a mix of the three strategies. No jurisdiction relies exclusively on one strategy. Rules and standards regulate what securities can trade on exchanges and what ongoing obligations companies have to comply with. The entry strategy begins the moment a security enters the market and continues as long as it is publicly traded. The trusteeship strategy screens out opportunistic agents in capital markets.

This is also the case in the Chinese/Hong Kong context. The three strategies set out a useful analytical framework for the next two sections. Both China and Hong Kong use these three legal strategies in regulating Chinese cross-listings in Hong Kong.

5.2.1 Home country regulation

China's financial law is said to be a hybrid model which was initially influenced by Germany and Japan and then imported key elements of Anglo-American law.[14] The experience of bringing China's SOEs to the HKSE is an important step in this harmonization process. Attempts have been made to adapt elements of foreign securities laws and regulations into the Chinese securities regulatory system. In the course of legal drafting, international institutions and foreign legal experts were invited to provide their advice and first-hand knowledge to help Chinese legislators. For example, in preparation for China's Securities Law 1998, the drafting team went to Hong Kong for consultations with securities law experts.[15]

A Legal experiences of the listing of Chinese companies in Hong Kong

When Chinese SOEs came to be listed, the primary concern of Hong Kong securities authorities was to ensure that the level of investor protection in Chinese SOEs was comparable to that applicable to companies incorporated in Hong Kong. At that time the principal protection afforded to investors was contained in the *Standard Opinion on Joint Stock Companies* ("the Standard Opinion"), a set of company regulations which operated before the Company Law 1993.[16] However, the *Standard Opinion* was very different from Hong Kong's corporate law and fell short of the shareholder protection which existed in Hong Kong. Hence, the regulatory bodies of China and Hong Kong enacted a series of regulations to reduce legal disparities in preparation for Chinese companies listing in Hong Kong.

Cross-border negotiations began early in the 1990s and were formalized by the Memorandum of Understanding (MoU). On 19 June 1993, a five-party *Memorandum of Understanding on Regulatory Cooperation* ("the 1993 MoU") was signed by the CSRC, the Shanghai Stock Exchange (SHSE), the Shenzhen Stock Exchange (SZSE), the Securities and Futures Commission (SFC) of Hong Kong, and the HKSE.[17] The signatories to the *1993 MoU* agreed to provide mutual assistance and exchange information in three areas: (1) to enhance investment protection and maintain market order; (2) to ensure compliance with each party's relevant laws and rules; (3) to facilitate consultation and cooperation by means of regular liaison and exchange of personnel.

An important outcome of the *1993 MoU* negotiations was the introduction of the 1993 *Mandatory Provisions for Articles of Association of Companies Listed in Hong Kong* ("the 1993 Mandatory Provisions") to be included in the articles of association of all Hong Kong-listed mainland companies.[18] The *1993 Mandatory Provisions* attempted to codify Hong Kong common law in those areas which Chinese company regulations did not adequately cover. It had ensured that all Chinese companies to be listed in Hong Kong had certain binding clauses in their articles of association which served to subject directors, supervisors, and senior management to a number of important of responsibilities to the company and its shareholders.

In addition, China launched the *Supplementary Provisions to the Standard Opinion* of *Joint Stock Companies* ("the Supplementary Provisions") which applied specifically to companies that wished to list in Hong Kong.[19] Article 2 of the *Supplementary Provisions* adopted the fundamental common law principle that the articles of association of a company constitute a legally binding contract for the company's actions and governs rights and obligations between the company and its shareholders. It provided that listed companies must not alter or delete the contents of the *1993 Mandatory Provisions*, except as otherwise provided by national company law and other relevant administrative regulations.[20] This was to ensure that the mandatory provisions would be included in the articles of association of Chinese companies listed in Hong Kong and would thus provide adequate protection to Hong Kong investors when they purchased the shares of Chinese companies.

At the same time the *Side Letters Concerning the Standard Opinion and the Supplementary Provisions*, dated 10 June 1993, were promulgated to the HKSE, which interpreted certain ambiguous provisions and attempted to relieve concerns from Hong Kong. For example, in response to the query that fiduciary duties did not exist in Chinese law, it explained that the phrase "directors' obligation of good faith and diligence to the company" in Article 62 of the *Standard Opinion* was similar to the fiduciary duties of Hong Kong law.

In relation to the Hong Kong side, a special separate chapter, Chapter 19A, was added to the Hong Kong Listing Rules in order to accommodate the primary listing of Chinese companies.[21] Chapter 19A imposes on Chinese issuers regulatory standards comparable to those imposed on existing issuers with a primary listing in Hong Kong, and aims to create standards of protection for shareholders in Chinese companies which are no less favorable than those enjoyed by investors in Hong Kong.

These laws and regulations resulting from the joint efforts made by China and Hong Kong removed legal barriers for Chinese companies to be listed on the HKSE. In July 1993 Tsingtao Brewery became the first SOE to be listed on the

HKSE, followed by eight other companies during 1994. In the light of this successful Hong Kong experience, the scale of international listings was expanded. In August 1994 the Shangdong Huaneng Electricity Company went public on the New York Stock Exchange; in March 1997 Datong Electric Power launched a share offering on the London Stock Exchange.

B The rules and standards strategies

1 THE 1994 SPECIAL PROVISIONS AND THE 1994 MANDATORY PROVISIONS

To facilitate and regulate the increasing number of Chinese international listings, the State Council, in accordance with Articles 85 and 155 of Company Law 1993, published the *1994 Special Provisions on Joint Stock Limited Companies Issuing Shares and Listing Overseas* ("the 1994 Special Provisions") and the *1994 Mandatory Provisions for the Articles of Association of Companies Listed Overseas* ("the 1994 Mandatory Provisions").[22] Both provided a national regulatory framework for overseas issuance and listing of shares by Chinese companies.

The *1994 Special Provisions* set out detailed requirements for all companies seeking a listing abroad, in particular in Hong Kong, and attempt to standardize the approval procedure and documentation requirements regarding overseas listing.

State Council Securities Committee's (SCSC) Approval: Under the *1994 Special Provisions*, any company seeking an overseas listing must obtain SCSC approval.[23] The approval process involves an assessment of various matters, including the ability of an issuer to generate sufficient foreign exchange to pay dividends to its overseas holders. Once the approval is granted, the application may be implemented within 15 months from the date of the approval, and the board of directors of an issuer may make detailed arrangements accordingly.[24]

Dual Disclosure Rules: The information disclosed within mainland China and abroad shall not be self-contradictory in content.[25] If there are disparities between the information revealed within and outside China, the company shall reveal the differences simultaneously at relevant stock exchanges.[26] Arguably, foreign investors became disillusioned when they found financial transparency in Chinese listed companies was not what they had expected. In the case of Tsingtao Brewery, it was discovered that funds raised through its flotation had been used to support other enterprises willing to pay high rates of interest instead of being used for expansion of the company as originally stated in the prospectus.[27]

Articles of Association: The *1994 Mandatory Provisions* were promulgated in the same month as the *1994 Special Provisions*. The *1994 Mandatory Provisions* evolved from an earlier version, the *1993 Mandatory Provisions for Articles of Association of Companies Listed in Hong Kong*. Indeed, there are a number of similarities between the *1994 Mandatory Provisions* and Table A articles of association in the Hong Kong CO, which helped to bring corporate governance standards within Hong Kong-listed Chinese companies more into line with those prevailing in other Hong Kong-listed companies.

The *1994 Mandatory Provisions* set out detailed rules for matters with which overseas investors are mostly concerned. These include legal status and effect of the articles of association; contracts between members and the company; shares and registered capital; rights and obligations of shareholders; qualifications and duties of directors, supervisors, and management personnel. Listed companies must not alter or delete the contents of the *Provisions*, although additions may be made. The contents which must be included in the articles of association of companies seeking a listing in Hong Kong are not required to be incorporated in the articles of association of companies listed in regions other than Hong Kong.[28]

One of the civil law characteristics of the *1994 Mandatory Provisions* is the absence of a memorandum. Under common law, the memorandum is the repository of a company's objectives and powers, and is particularly important in relation to a company's dealings with outsiders, such as creditors. The *1994 Mandatory Provisions* exclude the memorandum, and what may be called objectives and powers are covered in a few clauses in the articles. However, there is a current trend towards the abolition of the memorandum in common law countries. For example, from 1 October 2009, the memorandum no longer forms part of a company's constitution under the UK Companies Act 2006.[29] The memoranda of existing companies are automatically deemed to be part of a company's articles since then.

Directors' Duties: Directors, supervisors, managers, and other senior management personnel of a company have a duty of good faith and diligence to the company. The *1994 Mandatory Provisions* set out specific circumstances for determining the scope of fiduciary duties, such as the duty to act in the company's best interests, the duty not to make private gains by taking advantage of their position and power, and the duty to ensure the fair and equal treatment of shareholders.[30] The adoption of standard duties familiar to Western investors, in the form of mandatory provisions inserted in the articles of association, is one of the significant steps China made in its effort to bring securities regulation closer to international practice.

Shareholder Rights and Obligations: Article 7 of the *1994 Mandatory Provisions*, which deals with rights and obligations of shareholders, generally follows the relevant provisions of the Company Law 1993, but is more detailed. From the wording, it might imply that rights given to shareholders are wider than those given to directors. For instance, directors are only entitled to claim "rights concerning the affairs of the company" and not "rights and obligations."[31] Such an interpretation would be consistent with the general view of the intention of the Hong Kong provisions.

The *1994 Mandatory Provisions* also distinguish between obligations imposed on a shareholder and those imposed on a controlling shareholder. Article 46 only imposes a limited number of obligations on a shareholder; for example, to abide by the articles and pay subscription money. However, the term "obligations" under Article 47 appears to be much wider. A controlling shareholder cannot use his rights to vote "in a manner prejudicial to the interests of the shareholders generally or a portion of the shareholders."

In relation to controlling shareholders, the provisions are similar to those under English company law, except that under English common law some classes or sections of members may be outvoted by controlling shareholders.[32] The *1994 Mandatory Provisions* go further by stipulating that such a vote must be in the best interest of all shareholders.[33] Although it is possible to infer that controlling shareholders have the power to control a section of the remaining shareholders, on the face of the words of the provision, such an inference does not appear to be warranted.

Resolution of Disputes: Both the *1994 Mandatory Provisions* and the Hong Kong Listing Rules require an arbitration clause to be included in the articles of association. Whenever any disputes or claims arise between holders of foreign shares listed overseas and the company; or between holders of foreign shares listed overseas and the company's directors, supervisors, managers, or other senior officers; or between holders of foreign shares listed overseas and holders of domestic shares; the parties concerned may resolve the dispute through agreement between both parties, or refer it to arbitration.[34] An applicant requiring arbitration may select either the China International Economic and Foreign Trade Arbitration Commission or the Hong Kong International Arbitration Centre.[35]

2 RED-CHIPS

Before the promulgation of China's *Rules on Mergers and Acquisitions of Domestic Enterprises by Foreign Investors* ("the M&A Rules"), in 2006, the so-called red-chip model was a common method used by Chinese companies to seek listing on overseas stock exchanges.

In this model, the owner of a Chinese company would set up a special purpose vehicle (SPV) in a tax haven such as the Cayman Islands or Bermuda. The SPV would then acquire the shares of the Chinese company, with the result that it became the holding company of the Chinese company. Finally, the Cayman or Bermudian SPV would seek a listing on an overseas exchange.

However, the *M&A Rules* have made this model more cumbersome and may, in fact, have made it unworkable. The cost and uncertainty of red-chip model listings may well result in a reduction in their numbers and their importance.[36]

The main effects of the new *M&A Rules* are set out below.

Approval by the Ministry of Commerce (MoC): Pursuant to Article 11, if a domestic company or an individual intends to take over its domestic subsidiary company in the name of a foreign company which it established or controls, it is subject to examination and approval by the MoC. The *M&A Rules* also require that domestic companies or individuals have to apply to the MoC for permission before they can establish SPVs.[37] When SPVs acquire domestic companies, they again need to seek approval from the MoC.

Business license valid for one year: The MoC would issue to the domestic company an approval certificate with "equity held by an overseas special purpose vehicle, valid for one year from the date of issue of the business license."[38] If the listing cannot be completed within one year from the granting of this business license, the shareholding structure will be restored to its original situation. This time limit greatly increases the risks associated with overseas listings.

Approval by the CSRC:[39] In the past, a company intending to complete a red-chip listing had to obtain a "no comment letter" from the CSRC.[40] The new *M&A Rules* empower the CSRC to undertake an examination and approval instead. There are more than ten types of document which the applicant has to submit.[41] Compared with the submission of a legal opinion letter by a Chinese lawyer required in the "no comment letter," the *M&A Rules* are stricter.

To sum up, the new *M&A Rules* set out the procedure and approval process for red-chip listings. It hints that the regulators tend to be cautious and meticulous, and they will conduct overall control and examination in principle. In the long run these measures may hamper or even curtail red-chip listings.

C The trusteeship strategy: CSRC approval

Article 238 of the Securities Law 2005 provides that domestic companies seeking to offer directly or indirectly their shares in an overseas market must obtain approval from the securities regulator under the State Council, i.e., the CSRC. Once the approval for the issue of new H-shares is received from the CSRC, the applicant must amend its articles of association in accordance with Hong Kong requirements. Then the listing application is submitted to the HKSE.

The main requirements to be met for CSRC approval before submitting the necessary documents to the Hong Kong authorities are principally contained in: the *1994 Special Provisions*; the *1994 Mandatory Provisions*; the *1999 Circular on the Issues Concerning the Companies Applying for Overseas Listings*; the *1999 Guidelines on Examination, Approval and Supervision of Enterprises in China Applying to List on the Hong Kong Growth Enterprise Market*; the *1999 Several Opinions on Further Enhancing the Information Disclosure by Overseas Listed Companies*.

In essence, there are five stages involved in the review process by the CSRC before approving a company for cross-listing.

First, the CSRC solicits comments from the National Development and Reform Commission (NDRC) on national industrial policy and foreign investment policy. Meanwhile, the comments from the State-owned Assets Supervision and Administration Commission (SASAC) are also considered.

Second, if neither authority has any objections, issuers may submit application documents to the General Office of the CSRC. Pursuant to the *1999 Circular on the Issues Concerning the Companies Applying for Overseas Listings*, the documents which must be submitted to the CSRC, together with the application for overseas listings, include a report which outlines the applicant's business operation and shareholding structure, then details the intended use of the proceeds from the IPO; the business objectives for the future of the company to be listed; the risk factors involved and the costs or expenses incurred in the fundraising exercise. A sponsor's report is also required, which must contain an analysis of the feasibility of the listing and state the sponsor's intention to underwrite the securities of Chinese companies.

Third, the application documents are transferred to the Department of International Affairs of the CSRC via the General Office. The Department of International Affairs decides whether to accept the request. Once accepted, the General Office issues a notification to the applicant.

Fourth, the Department of International Affairs plays a vital role in the review process. It conducts interviews with the issuers and their intermediaries, presents feedback, and solicits opinions from other CSRC departments if necessary. Then it makes a final decision based on those documents and the feedback.

Fifth, if the applicant meets all requirements, the General Office issues a notification approval to the applicant. Otherwise, it issues a letter with explanation of reasons for refusal.

5.2.2 Host country regulation

Once CSRC approval for the Hong Kong listing is obtained, the H-shares listing applicant must still satisfy the Hong Kong authorities that the listing requirements have been met.

The Hong Kong legal and regulatory framework addressing offering and listing of shares is quite similar to the system prevalent in the UK prior to the enactment of the FSMA 2000 and the related transfer of responsibility for listing matters from the London Stock Exchange to the UK Listing Authority. However, there are certain differences, mainly in relation to the "dual-filing" system established by the SFO, under which all documents filed with the HKSE are also filed with the SFC, thereby bring them within the liability and enforcement framework of the SFO. In addition, there are continuing discussions over the need and methodologies for transferring increasing responsibility from the HKSE to the SFC.

Hong Kong uses three types of strategy to address public offerings and listings of company shares which comprise laws, regulations, and market practices.

- The Rules and Standards Strategies: Offering and Listing of Shares; Continuing Listing Obligations; GEM
- The Entry Strategy: Prospectuses and Related Liabilities
- The Trusteeship Strategy: Regulation of Sponsors and Compliance Advisers

A The rules and standards strategies: offering and listing of shares; on-going obligations of being listed; GEM

1 OFFERING AND LISTING OF SHARES

A company may invite offers from persons interested in subscribing to its shares. An invitation may be made to the public directly by the company or by public placement through brokers/placing agents. For direct offers for subscription, any document by which such an offer to the public is made will be deemed to be a prospectus issued by the company.[42] For a public placement, the prospectus may provide for the placing of shares through brokers/placing agents of the HKSE who sell the shares to clients at the issue price plus brokerage commission. This procedure is rarely used.

Chapter 8 of the Listing Rules (LR) sets out the basic conditions which have to be met as a prerequisite to the listing of equity securities. In particular, both the issuer and its business must be suitable for listing. The issuer must also normally have a trading record of not less than three financial years under substantially the same management. The expected total market capitalization at the time of listing must be at least HK$200 million and the total capitalization of securities held by the public must be at least HK$50 million. The issuer must also satisfy either the profit test in LR 8.05 (1), or the market capitalization/revenue/cash flow test in LR 8.05 (2), or the market capitalization/revenue test in LR 8.05 (3).

The HKSE may accept a shorter trading record period and/or may vary or waive the above requirements. Under LR 8.05A the HKSE will accept a shorter trading record under substantially the same management where the directors have sufficient experience of at least three years in the same line of business subject to management continuity for the most recent audited financial year. It may also vary the above requirements with respect to mineral companies (subject to Chapter 18 of the Listing Rules) and newly formed "project" companies (for example a company formed to construct a major infrastructure project).

In addition, a number of other requirements need to be met, including: latest financial period reported to be within six months before the date of the listing document; directors to satisfy the requirement of Chapter 3 of the LR; the company must maintain in Hong Kong a register of members maintained by an approved share registrar; etc.

2 CONTINUING LISTING OBLIGATIONS

The LR provide detailed provisions on post-listing events such as stabilization,[43] new share issues,[44] share repurchases,[45] minimum public holding,[46] suspension of trading,[47] and cancellation of listing.[48] For example, the Securities and Futures (Price Stabilizing) Rules (Cap 571W) exclude price stabilization action conducted in accordance with the Rules from the application of the market misconduct provisions in the SFO. They prescribe the circumstances in which the prices of certain securities offered to the public may be stabilized for a limited period and regulate such stabilizing action. Regarding share repurchase, the LR require that the company promptly advise the HKSE of any share repurchases it makes,[49] and that it complies with the requirements of the Code on Share Repurchases.[50]

Once listed, an issuer will face various continuing obligations. At the operational front line of the market in Hong Kong is the HKSE, which is responsible for administering the LR. The LR set out ongoing obligations that are imposed upon the issuers to maintain their listings. Additionally, the SFC plays an important role in regulatory oversight. Specifically, the HKSE and the SFC supervise the listed companies in four main areas including corporate governance, takeovers and mergers, market misconduct, and information disclosure.

It is worth recalling that Chapter 4 contains details about the regulatory framework in Hong Kong. But that chapter focuses on companies incorporated in Hong Kong rather than listed companies, especially for Chinese issuers. Therefore, the CO and the SFO are the main focus of that chapter. By contrast, this section is intended to stand alone, and focuses on the LR in order to avoid potential overlapping.

Corporate Governance: The HKSE requires listed issuers to ensure that they have adequate and effective systems of internal control covering financial and compliance matters. Independent non-executive directors and the audit committee are two main points of focus. Issuers are required to appoint at least three independent non-executive directors.[51] At least one of them must have appropriate professional qualifications or accounting or related financial management expertise. Additionally, issuers must establish an audit committee comprising non-executive directors only.[52]

Takeovers and Mergers: The *Code on Takeovers and Mergers* ("the Takeovers Code") is a non-statutory set of rules regulating all aspects of M&A transactions. It is administered by the Executive Director (the Executive) of the Corporate Finance Division of the SFC and enforced by the Takeovers and Mergers Panel ("the Panel").

The Executive is the primary entity responsible for the monitoring and investigation of takeovers.[53] The Executive is able to interpret the Takeover Code as to what constitutes appropriate behavior in a specific situation. In addition, it is also able to make rulings, either on its own initiative or upon request from concerned persons. As for the enforcement body, the primary functions of the Panel are to give rulings on the Takeover Code to review rulings given by the Executive, and to hear disciplinary matters.[54]

All persons accessing the markets in Hong Kong are required by the SFC to comply with the Takeover Code. Failure by a listed company to comply with it may entail a number of potential consequences including suspension or cancellation of its listing.[55]

The review of the disciplinary rulings of the Panel is undertaken by the Takeover Appeal Committee (TAC).[56] The TAC, as an appellate body, does not review the Panel's finding of facts but only determines whether a sanction imposed by the Panel is unfair or excessive.

Market Misconduct: Under the SFO, there are six types of market misconduct, namely: insider dealing, false trading, price rigging, market manipulation, disclosure of information about prohibited transactions, and disclosure of false or misleading information.[57]

Information Disclosure: In order to protect investors and to promote higher standards of financial reporting so that investors are able to make informed investment decisions, issuers are required to publish their financial results on a timely basis.

Main Board issuers must publish annual reports not later than four months after the end of the fiscal year, and half-yearly reports not later than three months after the end of the fiscal year. GEM issuers must publish annual reports not later than three months, half-yearly reports not later than 45 days, and quarterly reports not later than 45 days after the date upon which the financial period ended.

The LR set out the minimum financial information that a listed issuer must include in its preliminary announcement of results, interim reports, annual reports, listing documents, and circulars in relation to equity securities.[58]

3 THE GROWTH ENTERPRISE MARKET (GEM)

The GEM was formally launched in November 1999. The primary set of regulations concerning listing securities on it is the *Rules Governing the Listing of Securities on the Growth Enterprise Market of the Stock Exchange of Hong Kong Limited* ("GEM Rules").

The *GEM Rules* broadly follow the same approach and structure for admission to listing and continuing obligations as the Main Board. But the requirements for listing on the GEM are less demanding. For instance, the GEM has relatively low profit record or revenue or other financial standard requirements,[59] and companies must have had active business pursuits for the 24 months before listing application.

B The entry strategy: prospectuses and related liabilities

1 REQUIREMENTS FOR PROSPECTUSES

The specific content requirements under the LR and the CO are not mutually exclusive, and the requirements overlap as to content required. Special requirements apply as regards other types of listing and in respect of special companies such as mineral companies, non-Hong Kong issuers including Chinese issuers, and investment companies.[60]

Requirements for information differ on issuers, securities,[61] shareholders, and finance.[62] For example, information on issuers must include: general information about the issuers, such as its incorporation and constitution, and its advisers; information about the issuer's capital including shareholder voting rights and any other rights affecting capital (such as options); particulars of any other stock exchange on which any securities of the issuer are listed; details of any controlling shareholders of the issuer, including a statement explaining the way in which the issuer is satisfied that it is capable of carrying on its business independently of the controlling shareholder after listing.

2 PROSPECTUS LIABILITY

The LR provide that each of the directors of the company (including any person proposed or named as a director in the listing document) is required to accept responsibility for the information contained in the listing document and include in the listing document a statement to that effect.[63]

Civil liability Under the CO, civil liability is imposed on certain categories of persons to pay compensation to any person who applied for securities on the basis of statements made in the prospectus and who suffers loss by reason of an untrue or misleading statement in that prospectus.[64] There are exemptions restricting liability in some circumstances; such as where the prospectus was issued without their consent, or in relation to an untrue statement where a person had reasonable grounds *to* believe and *did* believe that the statement made was true.

Under the SFO, a person who makes a fraudulent, reckless, or negligent misrepresentation in a prospectus may be liable to pay compensation where a person has invested on the basis of that misrepresentation and who suffers a pecuniary loss as a result.[65] Further, market misconduct liability may arise in respect of the disclosure of false or misleading information that induces transactions.[66] The agreement between the company and the underwriters may also be a source of contractual liability as regards the prospectus.

Criminal liability Under the CO, criminal liability is imposed on any person who authorizes the issue of a prospectus containing an untrue statement or a material omission.[67] Such a person is liable to imprisonment for up to three years, and a fine of up to HK$700,000, unless he proves either that the statement was immaterial or that he had reasonable grounds to believe, and did at the time of the issue of the prospectus believe, that the statement was true.

In addition to the CO, a number of related provisions under the SFO may be relevant to a prospectus. First, where a person makes a fraudulent or reckless misrepresentation in a prospectus such person is liable to imprisonment of up to seven years and a fine of up to HK$1 million.[68] Second, a company is prohibited from issuing an advertisement in connection with an offer to the public unless authorized by the SFC.[69] Breach of the prohibition is an offence carrying penalties of up to three years' imprisonment and a fine of up to HK$500,000. Third, market misconduct may comprise the disclosure of false or misleading information that induces transactions.[70] The commission of an offence renders the person liable to imprisonment of up to ten years, and a fine to up to HK$10 million. In addition, the courts may make certain orders against such person including disqualifying that person as a director of a listed company for up to five years.

C The trusteeship strategy: regulation of sponsors and compliance advisers

1 SPONSORS

Every company seeking an IPO must appoint a sponsor; that is, a company or authorized financial institution, licensed or registered under applicable law to advise on corporate finance matters. The sponsor must be acceptable to the HKSE.[71]

The sponsor plays a dual role in relation to an initial listing. First, it acts as an adviser. Its services cover the commercial aspects of being listed including the marketing and pricing of shares, and the guidance of the company through the listing process. Second, it plays a watchdog role. Upon being appointed, the sponsor is required to give a signed undertaking to the HKSE. The undertaking requires the sponsor to "ensure that that information provided to the Exchange during the listing application process is true in all material respects and does not omit any material information."[72]

2 COMPLIANCE ADVISERS

Every company seeking an initial listing must also appoint a compliance adviser who must be acceptable to the HKSE.[73] The function of the compliance adviser is to assist the newly listed issuer through the early stages of its life as a listed company. In advising the company, the compliance adviser is required by the LR to guide the company as regards the requirements of the LR and other applicable laws and regulations.

5.3 A critical analysis of Hong Kong listing rules: Chapters 19 and 19A

In addition to all the above requirements, the LR contain rules applying to non-Hong Kong companies. Chapter 19 sets out the rules applying to non-Hong Kong issuers seeking either a primary or a secondary listing on the HKSE, while Chapter 19A is exclusively for Chinese issuers.

There are several reasons for the special treatment for the latter. First, a strong political and economic tie exists between China and Hong Kong. Second, Chinese stock companies were governed by the *Standard Opinion on Joint Stock Companies* which was different from the Hong Kong corporate law, in particular with reference directors' duties and shareholders' rights. Third, Chinese laws create different classes of domestic and foreign shares such as A-shares, B-shares, and H-shares, which potentially create separate markets in the shares of an issuer.

Below we will discuss additional requirements under Chapter 19 for overseas issuers, and the modifications under Chapter 19A for Chinese issuers. The discrepancies between the two will also be examined.

5.3.1 Chapter 19

The core requirement of Chapter 19 is that shareholders be given adequate protection, with a standard at least equivalent to that provided in Hong Kong. This requires a consideration of the laws of the jurisdiction in which the issuer is established, or in some cases, the constitutive documents[74] of the issuer. The listing document prepared by the issuer will need to summarize the relevant local laws and regulations as well as the issuer's constitutive documents insofar as the concerned shareholder rights, in each case highlighting any differences from that prevailing under the Hong Kong laws.

Additional requirements are concerned with localization: the presence of a person authorized to accept service in Hong Kong and the establishment of a Hong Kong shareholder register.

The HKSE will also be concerned to see that the reporting accountants are properly qualified and independent of the issuer, to the standards of independence issued by the International Federation of Accountants. Additionally, an audit must have been conducted at least to the standards required in Hong Kong or the International Auditing and Assurance Standards Board of the International Federation of Accountants.

In relation to secondary listings, the HKSE requires that (1) the primary listing is on a regulated market recognized by the HKSE; (2) the issuer has an adequate connection with the primary market; and (3) the primary market and the HKSE have entered into an agreement concerning their respective roles as regards the regulation of the issuer.

5.3.2 Chapter 19A

The HKSE will require the presence of a sufficient level of shareholder protection under Chinese laws and the constitutive documents of the issuer. A summary of those laws and protection is required in the listing document. In particular, the articles of association of the issuers must contain provisions which reflect the different nature of domestic shares and overseas listed foreign shares including H-shares (shares issued by Chinese companies listed on the HKSE)[75] and the different rights of their respective holders. When an issuer is to be dual-listed, an adequate "communication arrangement" must be in place between the HKSE and the other exchange. Given the particular regulatory arrangements in China, the HKSE also requires adequate cooperation with the relevant domestic securities regulatory authorities.

Since the HKSE realizes that investor protection standards are different in both jurisdictions, it sets out additional obligations for Chinese issuers. These measures impose stringent requirements on the issuers. Meanwhile, they enable investors to make an informed assessment of the activities of companies and the rights attaching to the shares.

One major concern for Chinese companies complying with the LR is accounting. This is largely because the accounting standards traditionally adopted in China are generally thought to be less rigorous than global accounting standards.[76] The HKSE is concerned with proper accounting and audit standards, auditor independence, and requires Chinese issuers to present their annual accounts in accordance with Hong Kong or International Financial Reporting Standards.

Second, a strict sponsor system is required. A new issuer must retain the services of a sponsor. An increased burden is placed on the sponsor to satisfy itself as to the suitability for listing of the issuer. In particular, the sponsor will need to be sure that the directors of the issuer understand their obligations under the LR, and applicable laws as directors of a listed company, and that they will act accordingly.[77] If the securities of the Chinese issuer are to be listed on any other stock exchange, the sponsor must make a written submission to the exchange, stating whether in the sponsor's opinion the issue's directors appreciate the differences as well as the similarities between H-shares and the shares listed on such exchanges and between the rights and obligations of holders of such shares.[78] The sponsor must also explain the way in which the Chinese issuer's directors propose to coordinate and comply in a timely manner with their obligations under the requirements of the HKSE and such other exchanges.

However, although under LR 3A.02 the legal requirement for a sponsor normally ends once the application has been listed, LR 19A.05 modifies this rule so as to require Chinese issuers to retain the services of a sponsor for at least one year. In its role after listing, the sponsor must inform the issuer on a timely basis of any amendment or supplement to the LR and any new or amended law, regulation, or code in Hong Kong applicable to such issuer.

Finally, it must be provided that disputes involving holders of H-shares are to be settled by arbitration. The LR and the *Mandatory Provisions* in China require an arbitration clause to be included in the articles of association.[79] A claimant may elect for arbitration to be carried out at either the Hong Kong International Arbitration Centre in accordance with its Securities Arbitration Rules, or the China International Economic and Trade Arbitration Commission in accordance with its rules.[80]

Under Chinese law, an arbitration award is final and binding on the parties.[81] A party seeking to enforce an award of the arbitration panel against a party who is not within China may apply to a foreign court with jurisdiction over the case for enforcement.[82] On 18 June 1999, an arrangement was made between Hong Kong and the Supreme People's Court for the mutual enforcement of arbitration awards. The arrangement came into force on 1 February 2000. Under this arrangement, awards made by Chinese arbitration authorities recognized under the Arbitration Ordinance of Hong Kong, can be enforced in Hong Kong. Conversely, Hong Kong arbitration awards are also enforceable in China.

Apart from some additional requirements, there is one important concession to Chinese issuers in Chapter 19A. For example, the exchange requires a new applicant to make disclosure where it has a controlling shareholder or a director with an interest in a counterpart's business.[83] A "controlling shareholder" means any shareholder or other person or group of persons together entitled to exercise, or control the exercise, of more than 30 percent of the voting rights in the company.[84] But Chinese governmental bodies, which are the controlling shareholders in many Chinese companies, are exempt.[85] Likewise, they are not treated as persons connected to the issuer.[86]

Under Hong Kong law, a Chinese governmental body is broadly defined to include the central government,[87] provincial-level governments,[88] and local governments immediately under the provincial-level governments.[89] Charity entities under the government which are engaging in commercial business or operating another commercial entity are excluded from this category.

This concession implies that the HKSE has tried to lower the barrier for Chinese issuers with a view to attracting more Chinese companies. The HKSE positioned itself as China's international exchange and the international home market for Chinese enterprises in its Strategic Plan 2007–09. At the end of May 2009, China-based companies, including H-shares and red-chips, constituted in aggregate over 50 percent of the Hong Kong market's capitalization of HK$6,983 billion.[90]

There is a danger here. An influx of Chinese companies which do not commit to higher standards may undermine Hong Kong's strong securities market image. Most Chinese listed companies are directly or indirectly controlled by the state. Meanwhile, government bodies are heavily involved in connected transactions. According to the *China Corporate Governance Report* by the SHSE, in 2001 the number of connected transactions was 12,225. In 2005, this number had doubled to 27,773. Of these transactions 78.94 percent were related to Chinese government bodies.[91]

So concessions to Chinese issuers and governmental bodies in this sense under the Hong Kong Listing Rules may lead to poor disclosure and a lack of transparency in ownership structure and connected transactions of Chinese companies. The risk of illegal activities, such as insider dealing and price manipulation, may rise. The concession clearly has the potential to undermine the primary goal of securities regulation, which is to maintain an orderly and efficient market.

5.4 Bonding or avoiding? Reflections on domestic public offerings and listings

Standards and procedures for approving Chinese overseas listings and screening of their applications by the HKSE, as well as continuous monitoring, have been discussed.

A particular question arises: in cross-listings, do Chinese issuers try to bond themselves to high standards, or do they try to avoid the domestic standards? Regarding this question, two hypotheses can be put forward: bonding and avoiding. The bonding hypothesis suggests that companies may list on a foreign stock market with a view to renting that market's better corporate governance system.[92] In contrast, the avoiding hypothesis proposes that issuers may prefer lower accounting standards in order to avoid stringent domestic regimes.[93] At the center of this debate is whether the entry standards and ongoing disclosure requirements of the host country are superior to those of the home country.

Specifically, in Chinese cross-listings, where the standards of Hong Kong LR exceed those of Chinese listing rules, then such listing may be motivated by a desire on a company's part to bond itself to the higher standards. Otherwise, this effect will not occur. Companies may nevertheless be motivated to cross-list under such circumstances simply to seek out greater liquidity available in a larger market.

To tackle this question, it is necessary to compare the different ways in which the two jurisdictions address public offerings and listings. As regards the appropriate comparative methodologies, the functional approach is adopted since the Chinese Securities Law and related CSRC regulations deal with matters similar to those dealt with by the Hong Kong LR. Hence, this section follows the previous structure in section 5.2.2 to explore the "bonding or avoiding" puzzle.

- The rules and standards strategies: offering and listing of shares; continuing listing obligations; the Growth Enterprise Board (GEB)
- The entry strategy: prospectuses and related liabilities
- The trusteeship strategy: regulation of sponsors and compliance advisers

A The rules and standards strategies: offering and listing of shares; continuing listing obligations; GEB

1 OFFERING AND LISTING OF SHARES

The Chinese Securities Law 2005 provides general requirements for an IPO of a company, such as having a well-operated organization, sound financial status, and no other major irregularity.[94]

Interestingly, one requirement for an IPO in China, which is absent in Hong Kong, is that 10 percent of shares of a state-owned company must be transferred to the National Council for the Social Security Fund (NCSSF) when the company launches an IPO.[95] The NCSSF is an institutional investor, set up by the central government in August 2000, for managing and operating social security assets. This requirement has two policy objectives. The first is to decrease state shares in public companies. The second is to inject more assets into the fund for better social security coverage.

Around the world there are two main types of systems for listing shares. One is the registration system, the other is the verification and approval system.[96] The former is simpler, and is found in the US, the UK, Hong Kong, Australia, Canada, Singapore, Germany, and France. As long as the applicant complies with all the prescribed listing requirements, no further procedures are required. In this system the market is the ultimate decisive factor. By contrast, under the verification and approval system, the relevant authority will examine and verify the documents for listing, and if necessary disallow the company's listing. Therefore, in practice, the authority has the power to decide whether a company can be listed or not. This system is adopted by China, New Zealand, Sweden, and Switzerland.

Since Hong Kong and China use different examination systems they differ significantly in listing requirements and approval procedures.

In Hong Kong, the HKSE is empowered to make listing rules prescribing the requirements for the listing of shares and securities.[97] Chapter 8 of the LR sets out the basic conditions which have to be met as a prerequisite to the listing of equity securities. When applicants are suitable for listing and pass the review process, they can list on the HKSE. At the next level is the SFC, which is responsible for detecting market malpractices. Its powers include the power to carry out, on its own initiative, or in cooperation with the HKSE, investigations into market misconduct.[98]

By contrast, under Article 7 of the Chinese Securities Law, the authorities in charge of approving securities are the CSRC and the "department authorized by the State Council." As the major rule-maker for listed companies, the CSRC enforces the rules concerning listing standards. The stock exchanges thus have very little control over an individual company's listing. This is a major difference from the Hong Kong system.

The criteria for the CSRC's approval include clean ownership,[99] sound operation compliance,[100] and independence.[101] Additionally, there are other specific conditions to be met such as a three-year track record,[102] a financial test,[103] and continuous profit-making capability.[104]

While all listing and trading matters are largely regulated by the CSRC, the two national stock exchanges have primary control over the daily trading of domestic shares, and receive and scrutinize listing applications.[105] Under Article 50 Securities Law, a stock exchange may specify listing conditions which are more stringent than those specified in the legislation, as long as those conditions are first approved by the CSRC.

2 CONTINUING LISTING OBLIGATIONS

Chinese law has specific provisions on post-listing events such as new share issues, share repurchases, minimum public holding, suspension of trading, and cancellation of listing. In addition, it provides ongoing requirements for listed companies on corporate governance, takeover, and other corporate matters.

Under Article 143 Company Law, a company may purchase its own shares in four situations: where it is reducing its registered capital; where it is merging with another company which holds shares of the company; where it will grant the shares as an incentive to its staff and workers; or where a shareholder who opposes a resolution on the merger or division of the company adopted at a shareholders' general meeting requests that the company purchase his or her shares.

To implement the Company Law, the CSRC promulgated two circulars regarding share repurchases: the *Administration of Repurchase of Public Shares by Listed Companies Procedures (Trial Implementation)* in 2005, and the *Supplementary Provisions on the Share Repurchase by Listed Companies by Means of Centralized Bidding* in 2008. The latter replaced the former in relation to share repurchase by means of centralized bidding. In addition, the Listing Rules of Shanghai and Shenzhen also specify identical procedures for share repurchases.[106]

To list its shares after the IPO, the issuer must have offered at least 25 percent of its total share capital to the public, except that an issuer with a total share capital of more than RMB400 million may only make a 10 percent public offering.[107]

In the past, the CSRC decided upon matters relating to the suspension and trading of a listed company's shares. However, this function has been shifted to stock exchanges under the Securities Law 2005.[108] Apart from general provisions prescribed in the Securities Law, each stock exchange can specify the circumstances of suspension.[109] Meanwhile, stock exchanges can decide to terminate the listing of a company's stocks under certain circumstances.[110]

Compared with Hong Kong LR, there are two distinguishing features of the Chinese listing framework. First, there is no relevant regulation regarding stabilization in China. Second, special requirements are imposed on new share issuances. When a company issues new shares, the relevant procedures are stipulated in Articles 134–7 Company Law 2005. Meanwhile, the company must satisfy the financial and corporate governance provisions under the Securities Law.[111] In addition, the CSRC sets out additional requirements for issuing new shares. For example, the weighted average net asset yield rate for the most recent three years must not be lower than 6 percent; there must be no transactions of large sums at the end of the recent period; the issue price must not be lower than the average company share price during the 20 transaction days prior to the announcement of the prospectus or the average price of the transaction day prior to the issuance.[112]

3 THE GROWTH ENTERPRISE BOARD (GEB)

The GEB is new in China. In the past, small Chinese enterprises mostly chose to list on the Hong Kong GEM, or the UK Alternative Investment Market (AIM). In 1999 the CSRC responded to a proposal by the SZSE, stating that "establishing a market for high-tech companies within the Shanghai and Shenzhen Stock Exchanges can be considered."[113] The interest in setting up a new market was fuelled by ex-Premier Zhu Rongji's visit to the US. It is believed that high-level officials were impressed by the success of Nasdaq. The State Council issued the *Decision of Strengthening Technological Innovation, Developing Advanced Science and Technology and Realizing Industrialization* in August 1999, emphasizing the need to foster a capital market conducive to the development of high and new technology industries.

A significant legal barrier then needed to be removed. The Company Law originally set strict requirements on, for example, size, profitability, and industry focus, for companies that were allowed to list and offer their shares to the public. In light of this, amendments were made to the Company Law at the end of 1999 to exempt high-tech companies from the requirements, leaving their applications to the discretion to the State Council.[114]

Ten years later, with the enactment of the *Tentative Measures for the Administration of the Initial Public Offering of Shares and the Listing thereof on the Growth Enterprise Board* on 31 March 2009, the GEB was finally created. It was also announced on the CSRC website that the CSRC and the Shanghai and Shenzhen stock exchanges would soon issue further rules to supplement the measures.

According to the new rules, which consist of 58 articles, issuers wishing to list on the board must be companies limited by shares. Also, they must have an operational history of at least three years, as well as a record of profits for the last two consecutive years. [115] Their net profit in the last two years should amount to at least RMB10 million, with profits continuing to grow.

B The entry strategy: prospectuses and related liabilities

1 PROSPECTUSES REQUIREMENTS

In order to allow investors to obtain as much knowledge about an issuer as possible, the CSRC has enacted a series of regulations guiding information disclosure. In particular, *Criteria No. 1 on the Content and Format of Information Disclosure by Companies Conducting Public Offer of Securities – Prospectus* ("the Prospectus Rule") was enacted on 18 May 2006. It contains a required content and format of the prospectus for IPOs and secondary offerings. All the information disclosed by the issuer in the prospectus and its abstract shall be true, accurate, and complete. In the case of any omission of matters that ought to have been disclosed, or any relevant subsequent events that occur after the submission of the draft prospectus, the issuer shall provide a written explanation to the CSRC and amend the prospectus to include such information in time.[116]

The Prospectus Rule specifies the information requirements to be included in a prospectus. They are: (1) general description of the offer; (2) basic information of the issuer; (3) risk factors; (4) the scope of business; (5) related parties transactions; (6) management personnel; (7) corporate governance; (8) financial position; and (9) business forecast.

Additionally, information disclosure required from listed companies can be found in periodical and ad hoc reports. The former include the annual report, interim report, and quarterly report. The latter should be disclosed in a timely manner when a company's securities and/or derivative prices may be substantially affected by any significant matters.

In this sense, contents and format requirements for prospectuses in China are broadly similar to those in Hong Kong. However, some differences exist in A-share and H-share listing documents and prospectuses which are prepared on the basis of different disclosure requirements.

First, accounts and financial information in the A-share prospectus are prepared in accordance with China's Generally Accepted Accounting Principles (GAAP), while those in the H-share prospectus are prepared in accordance with International Financial Reporting Standards (IFRS).[117] It is commonly said that Chinese accounting standards are lower than internationally recognized standards.

Next, the definitions of connected transactions are different under Chinese and Hong Kong laws, therefore different rules apply to the disclosure of connected transactions in the respective prospectuses. In China, related party transactions (or connected transactions in the Hong Kong terminology) involving the granting of corporate guarantees are all subject to stringent disclosure requirements and shareholder approval; none of these transactions are exempt from these requirements, regardless of the amounts involved.[118] In Hong Kong, by comparison, the granting of guarantees is only subject to the relatively less demanding benchmarks that trigger disclosure and approval procedures.[119]

Furthermore, according to investigations carried out by Chinese stock exchanges, information practice standards among domestically listed companies still suffer from serious problems including false disclosure, inaccurate information, and late disclosure.[120] During the period between 1996 and 2007, 461 cases were published by the CSRC, 52.9 percent of which related to late disclosure.[121]

2 PROSPECTUS LIABILITIES

The amended Securities Law states that the information disclosed by an issuer and listed company must be true, accurate, and complete, and must contain any false record, misleading statement, or major omission.[122] The *Several Provisions of the Supreme People's Court on Hearing Civil Compensation Cases Arising from False Statement on the Securities Market* has given a precise definition on what constitutes a false statement.[123] These are defined as statements made by the wrongdoers during regular information disclosure processes, such as in corporate reports, or announcements made through the media that influence investors to make calculations that result in significant detriment to their investment. On the other hand, a material omission is the failure of a fiduciary to disclose, either wholly or partially, any information required by law. The Securities Law clearly states the possible administrative penalties for the offence.[124] Meanwhile, the potential joint civil liabilities of the issuer, management personnel of the issuer, the sponsors, and underwriters are mentioned in Article 69 Securities Law. For offences involving criminal elements, the offenders can face imprisonment of up to five years.[125]

All the promoters, directors, and principal underwriters are required to sign the prospectus and verify that it contains no false or seriously misleading statements or major omissions, and promise to bear joint responsibility if it does.[126]

Where the prospectus contains any false record, misleading statement, or major omission that causes losses to investors, the issuer bears the liability of compensation. Any director or manager of the issuer held to be directly responsible is jointly liable to pay compensation, unless he is able to prove that he has no fault therein.[127] However, the Securities Law fails to address the details of penalties and compensation.

Under the *Provisions*, different rules apply to determine the liability of different defendants; some (promoters, issuers, listed companies, and controlling shareholders) are subject to strict liability, while others (underwriters, sponsors, intermediaries) are subject to a fault-based liability.[129] Where a false statement causes losses to investors, the investors have the right to claim a refund or compensation of the amount paid for the stock, plus interest.[130] For offences involving criminal elements, the offenders can face imprisonment of up to five years.[131]

C The trusteeship strategy: regulation of sponsors and compliance advisers

The sponsor systems in China and Hong Kong are similar. But Hong Kong separates compliance advisers from sponsors, while they are considered the same in China.

The Chinese sponsor system can be traced back to October 2003, when the CSRC promulgated the *Provisional Measures on the Sponsor System for Issuing and Listing of Securities*. Later, such Measures were embodied in the amendments to the Securities Law in 2005. Under Chinese law, sponsors and their representatives are required to recommend and guide securities issuers, to check through due diligence the truthfulness, accuracy, and completeness of the issuer's offering-related documents, and assist the issuer in establishing a stringent disclosure system.[132]

D A summary of the differences between Chinese and Hong Kong listing rules

A comparison of China and Hong Kong listing frameworks shows that cross-listing serves as a mechanism for Chinese companies to tie themselves to a stronger market. The listing requirements in Hong Kong are, to a large extent, more stringent and comprehensive than those in China, mainly in post-listing obligations and prospectuses. Although China is moving toward a better disclosure system, its practice still has serious problems.

However, the comparison also finds that cross-listing is a means for Chinese companies to avoid an overly regulated market. But they are attempting to escape from a malfunctioning market rather than domestically higher standards, as the avoiding hypothesis suggests. This could be interpreted by the different roles of their market authorities. The two jurisdictions use different offering systems. In Hong Kong, as long as the applicant satisfies all of the prescribed listing requirements by the HKSE, no further procedures are required. By contrast, the CSRC can decide upon major offering and listing matters, leaving the stock exchanges little control over them. This may create policy-driven markets. When domestic fundraising channels are restricted, companies find a way to list abroad. This idea can be supported by the CSRC decision to suspend all IPOs between September 2008 and June 2009 in order to stabilize the market and prevent investors from losing money in the economic downturn.[133] Faced with this restriction, Chinese companies were forced to raise funds through alternative channels, including cross-listing. During this period ten Chinese companies went public in Hong Kong.

Neither a purely bonding nor a purely avoiding theory can explain the complexity of the Chinese case. The driving forces behind Chinese cross-listings may come from both a desire to bond themselves to a stronger market with higher standards, but also from a desire to avoid over-regulated Chinese markets.

5.5 Concluding remarks

Jurisdictions adopt a mix of legal strategies in their listing rules to protect their capital markets and public investors. These include rules and standards strategies, the entry strategy (mandatory disclosure), and the trusteeship strategy. The general design of each legal strategy is similar across countries.[134]

The Chinese/Hong Kong case is no exception. H-share companies are subject to regulatory control from both jurisdictions. On the Chinese side, the rules and standards strategies in the form of the *1994 Special Provisions* and the *1994 Mandatory Provisions* regulate Chinese companies seeking to list overseas. Moreover, China develops the trusteeship strategy (CSRC approval) to control the quality of listing applicants. On the Hong Kong side, companies have satisfied rules and standards prescribed by the HKSE and the SFC, i.e., the requirements for the offering and listing of shares, and ongoing obligations. The applicant must also comply with mandatory disclosure. In addition, sponsors and advisers as third parties are empowered to screen companies which wish to enter the public markets.

While LR Chapter 19 requires overseas corporate issuers to be incorporated in a jurisdiction where the standards of shareholder protection are at least equivalent to those provided in Hong Kong, Chapter 19A is exclusively for Chinese issuers and includes certain additional requirements, modifications, and exceptions to Chapter 19. The existence of Chapter 19A may imply different standards of investor protection. In order to provide investors with adequate safeguards, certain stringent requirements have been imposed on Chinese issuers, such as the stricter sponsor system and higher accounting standards as well as the arbitration mechanism. However, these issuers are exempt from certain disclosure duties because Chinese governmental bodies are not considered a "controlling shareholder" under LR 19A.04. On the one hand, this is consistent with the findings in the preceding chapter that China has a relatively lower investor protection standard compared to Hong Kong. On the other hand, the concessions in Chapter 19A reveal that the HKSE, as a commercial organization, may compromise its standards to attract more business when it faces severe competition from other exchanges.

Comparing listing standards and requirements between China and Hong Kong, the findings are interesting and meaningful. In terms of substantive and procedural listing rules, Hong Kong is superior to China, in particular on information disclosure and ongoing requirements. In this sense, Chinese companies prefer higher standards with a view to linking themselves to a stronger market. However, the findings also reveal that Chinese companies want to escape from the domestic market because it is tightly controlled by the CSRC and influenced by the state. Overall, the Chinese case illustrates that the driving forces behind cross-listings are complicated and arise partly from a preference for higher standards and partly from a desire to avoid domestically malfunctioning markets.

This chapter has discussed the legal requirements and procedures of H-share listings, and the disparity between the two markets. The next chapter will examine the benefits received and problems encountered by H-share companies by means of general empirical evidence and case studies.

Notes

1 MacNeil, Iain and Lau, Alex (2001), "International Corporate Regulation: Listing Rules and Overseas Companies" in *International and Comparative Law Quarterly*, 50, p. 787.
2 Yang, Ting and Lau, Sie Ting (2006), "Choice of Foreign Listing Location: Experience of Chinese Firms" in *Pacific-Basin Finance Journal*, 14, pp. 325–6.
3 De Jonge, Alice (2005), "Solving Agency Problems in a Cross-border Environment: Ten Years of Chinese Companies Listings in Hong Kong" in Smyth, Russell *et al.* (eds.), *China's Business Reforms: Institutional Challenges in a Globalized Economy*, London: Routledge, p. 46.
4 From Data & Statistics of the HKSE. Online. Available at: www.hkex.com.hk/eng/stat/smstat/chidimen/chidimen.htm (accessed 20 December 2012).
5 Ibid.
6 Bauhinia Foundation Research Centre (2008), "Hong Kong as a Preferred IPO Hub: Are We on the Right Track?" p. 19. Online. Available at: www.bauhinia.org/publications.htm (accessed 20 December 2012).
7 The details of the IPO market in individual countries can be seen in a series of PricewaterhouseCoopers reports, e.g., *Greater China IPO Watch 2008*, *IPO Watch Europe: Review of the Year 2008*, and *2008 US IPO Watch*.
8 The average GDP growth in China from 1991 to 2007 is 10.4 percent. In 2007 it reached 11.4 percent while the average rate of worldwide GDP growth was 3.7 percent. See Chinese statistical yearbooks of different years compiled by the National Bureau of Statistics of China. After the credit crunch in 2007, China still managed to maintain a GDP growth of around 10 percent.
9 Dyer, Geoff and McGregor, Richard (2008), "China's Champions" in *Financial Times* (17 March 2008).
10 Hertig, Gerard *et al.* (2009), "Issuers and Investor Protection" in Kraakman, Reinier *et al.* (eds.), *The Anatomy of Corporate Law: A Comparative and Functional Approach*, Oxford: Oxford University Press, p. 276.
11 Ibid., p. 277.
12 Armour, John *et al.* (2009), "Agency Problems and Legal Strategies" in Kraakman, Reinier *et al.* (eds.), the *Anatomy of Corporate Law: A Comparative and Functional Approach*, Oxford: Oxford University Press, p. 39.
13 Ibid., p. 43.
14 Wood, Philip (2005), *Maps of World Financial Law*, 5th edn, London: Allen & Overy, p. 45. He chooses five key indicators to help position worldwide legal systems. These are insolvency set-off, marketability of contracts, securities interests, commercial trust, and tracing.
15 For details, see Zhu, Sanzhu (2000), *Securities Regulation in China*, New York: Transnational Publishers, p. 161.
16 The *Standard Opinion* was issued by the State Commission for Restructuring the Economic System (SCRES) on 15 May 1992, and came into force at the same time.
17 CSRC website, "Checklist of the Memoranda between the CSRC and the Overseas Regulatory Commissions." Online. Available at: http://old.csrc.gov.cn/n575458/n4001948/n4002030/4079126.html (accessed 9 October 2009).
18 The *1993 Mandatory Provisions* were issued on 10 June 1993 by the SCRES.
19 The *Supplementary Provisions* were issued on 23 May 1993 by the SCRES.
20 Ibid., Art. 2.
21 Chapter 19 Hong Kong Listing Rules deals with companies incorporated in common

law jurisdictions, such as Bermuda and the Cayman Islands, while Chapter 19A is solely concerned with companies incorporated in China.

22 The *Special Provisions* were enacted by the State Council and came into effect on 4 August 1994. The *Mandatory Provisions* were enacted by the SCRES and the Securities Commission (the predecessor of the CSRC) and came into effect on 27 August 1994.

23 Art. 5 *Special Provisions*.

24 Ibid., Art. 8.

25 Ibid., Art. 28 (1).

26 Ibid., Art. 28 (2).

27 Zhu, op. cit., p. 137.

28 The *1994 Mandatory Provisions*, Art. 164.

29 Companies Act 2006, s. 28.

30 The *1994 Mandatory Provisions*, Art. 116.

31 Ibid., Art. 7.

32 For more details, see Tokley, Ian and Ravn, Tina (1998), *Company Law and Securities Law in China*, Hong Kong: Sweet & Maxwell Asia, p. 108.

33 The *1994 Mandatory Provisions*, Art. 47.

34 Ibid., Art 163.

35 Ibid.

36 Fei, Guoping (2007), "Red-chip Listing and the Impact of the New Acquisition Regulations on it." Online. Available at: www.longandfield.com/en/publication/articles_detail.asp?a_id=34 (accessed 12 August 2010).

37 Art. 42 *M&A Rules*.

38 Ibid., Art. 45.

39 Ibid., Art. 40.

40 This stipulation was cancelled in June 2003 so that the CSRC did not intervene in this area until the M&A Rules was promulgated.

41 Art. 21 *M&A Rules*.

42 CO, s. 41.

43 The Securities and Futures (Price Stabilizing) Rules (Cap 571W).

44 LR 10.08.

45 LR 13.31 and LR 13.23.

46 LR 13.32.

47 Suspension may be imposed by the HKSE under the LR 6.01 or by the SFC under the Securities and Futures (Stock Market Listing) Rules, or may be requested by the company itself. Also LR Practice Note 11 provides further guidance on when dealing may be suspended.

48 Cancellation may occur voluntarily or involuntarily. A company may seek voluntarily to withdraw its listing, for example, where its shares are listed on another exchange. Cancellation may be imposed on the company by the SFC under the Securities and Futures (Stock Market Listing) Rules, or by the HKSE pursuant to the LR where the company is no longer suitable to remain listed.

49 LR 13.31.

50 LR 13.23 (2).

51 Chapter 3 Main Board of LR on Authorised Representative and Directors, and Chapter 5 of the GEM LR on Directors, Secretary and Corporate Governance matters.

52 Ibid.

53 Takeover Code, Introduction, paras 5–9.

54 Ibid., paras 10–13.

55 LR 13.23 (2) and 14.78.

56 SFO, s. 8 (1).

57 SFO, s. 245 (1). For details see Chapter 4.

58 For further details, see Chapter 4 and Appendix 16 of the Main Board LR and Chapter 7 for Main Board companies; and Chapter 18 of the GEM LR for GEM companies.
59 Two requirements are: (1) a positive cashflow generated from operating activities in the ordinary and usual course of business of at least HK$20 million in aggregate for the two financial years immediately preceding the issue of the listing document; and (2) market capitalization of at least HK$100 million at the time of listing.
60 LR, Chapter 18 for mineral companies; Chapter 19 for overseas issuers; Chapter 19A for Chinese issuers; and Chapter 21 for investment companies.
61 Information on securities must include: information about the securities for which listing is sought and the terms and conditions of their issue and distribution, including the total amount of the public or private issue and the number of securities offered; the underwriting arrangements; whether price stabilizing activities may be entered into in connection with an offering and the terms and duration on which the same shall be conducted; and the date on which dealings are expected to commence.
62 Financial information on the issuer must include: financial information about the group and the prospects of that group including commentary on the group's liquidity and financial resources and capital structure; an auditor's report for each of the three preceding years, the latest ending on a date not more than six months before the issue date of the prospectus; and a statement by the directors on the sufficiency of working capital and any materially adverse change in the financial or trading position of the group.
63 LR 11.12.
64 CO s. 40 (in relation to Hong Kong companies) and CO s. 342E (in relation to non-Hong Kong companies). An untrue statement includes a material omission: CO s. 41A (2) and s. 343 (2A).
65 SFO s. 108.
66 SFO s. 277.
67 CO s. 40A (in relation to Hong Kong companies) and CO s. 342F (in relation to non-Hong Kong companies).
68 SFO s. 107.
69 SFO s. 103.
70 SFO s. 298.
71 LR 3A.02.
72 LR 3A.04 (2).
73 LR 3A.19.
74 i.e., the memorandum and articles of association of the issuer.
75 For the definition of H-shares, refer to China's Share Categories in Table 3.1 of Chapter 3.
76 Fung, Eugene (1996), "Legal Implications of Foreign Listings for PRC Enterprises with Particular Reference to Hong Kong: Part 1" in *Company Lawyer*, 17, p. 37.
77 LR 19A.06 (1).
78 LR 19A.06 (2).
79 LR 19A.01, 19A.54 and the *Mandatory Provisions* Art. 163 (1).
80 The *Mandatory Provisions* Art. 163 (2).
81 The *Mandatory Provisions* Art. 163 (4) and China's Arbitration Law Art. 9.
82 China's Arbitration Law, Art. 72.
83 LR 19A.14.
84 Ibid.
85 Ibid.
86 LR 19A.19.
87 They include the State Council of China, state ministries and commissions, bureaus and administrations directly under the State Council, State Council offices and institutions, and bureaus supervised by state ministries and commissions.

88 They consist of provincial governments, municipalities directly under the central government, and autonomous regions, together with their respective administrative arms, agencies, and institutions.
89 They include prefectures, municipalities and countries, together with their respective administrative arms, agencies, and institutions.
90 Data is from "China Dimension" on the HKEx's website. Online. Available at: www.hkex.com.hk/data/chidimen/CD_MC.htm (accessed 20 December 2012).
91 SHSE (2006), *Guoyou Konggu Shangshi Gongsi Zhili* [China Corporate Governance Report: the Corporate Governance of State Holding Listed Companies], Fudan University Press, pp. 49 and 53.
92 See Chapter 2 of this book.
93 Licht, Amir (2003), "Cross-listing and Corporate Governance: Bonding or Avoiding" in *Chicago Journal of International Law*, 4, p. 142.
94 Art. 13 of Securities Law.
95 *Measures on the Transfer of State Shares to the NCSSF in Domestic Securities Markets* was issued jointly by the Ministry of Finance, the State Asset Supervision and Administration Commission, the CSRC, and the National Council for Social Securities Funds, and came into force on 19 June 2009.
96 Lau, Alex (2007), "A Study on Listing Applications in the People's Republic of China" in *Company Lawyer*, 28, p. 92.
97 LR 2.03.
98 SFO, s. 183.
99 Arts. 10 and 13 *Measures for the Administration of Initial Public Offering and Listing of Stocks*.
100 Ibid., Arts. 34, 35 and 37.
101 Ibid., Arts 14–19.
102 Ibid., Art 9. The issuer is required to have a consecutive business record of at least three years since its establishment, with the exception that the State Council may exempt this requirement.
103 Ibid., Art. 33. The test includes: (1) net profit: over RMB300 million in aggregate in the three-year trading record; (2) net cash flow: over RMB50 million in aggregate in the three-year trading record, or business revenue over RMB300 million in aggregate in the three-year trading record; (3) intangible assets: no more than 20 percent of the net asset value as at the end of the latest reporting period; (4) all loss made up, as at the end of the latest reporting period.
104 Ibid., Arts. 34, 35 and 37.
105 Arts. 48, 52–54 Securities Law.
106 Listing Rules of Shanghai Chapter XI, s. 6, and Listing Rules of Shenzhen Chapter XI, s. 6.
107 Art. 50 (3) Securities Law.
108 According to Article 55 of the Securities Law, there are five circumstances where trading can be suspended.
109 Shanghai Listing Rules, Chapter XIV, and Shenzhen Listing Rules, Chapter XIV.
110 Art. 56 Securities Law.
111 These include: (1) a complete and well-operated organization; (2) the capability to make profits continuously, and to have a sound financial status; (3) no false record in its financial statement over the latest three years, and no other major irregularity; (4) other requirements as prescribed by the CSRC. See Art. 13 Securities Law.
112 Art. 13 *Measures on Administration of the Offering of Securities by Listed Companies*.
113 "Chuanyeban Tuichu de Shinian Licheng Huigu" [The Ten Years of the GEB] in *People's Daily* (2008). Online. Available at: http://finance.people.com.cn/GB/8215/115194/115197/6858214.html (accessed 20 December 2012).
114 The Company Law 1999, Art. 229.

115 Art. 10 GEB Rules.
116 Art. 7 Prospectus Rule.
117 IFRS are standards, interpretations, and frameworks adopted by the IASB. Many of the standards forming part of IFRS are known by the older name of International Accounting Standards (IAS). For more discussion on the differences between Chinese and Hong Kong accounting standards, see section 6.3.1; for the development of the Chinese accounting system, see section 8.2.3.
118 Hong Kong Institute of Chartered Secretaries (2008), "A Comparative Study of Continuing Disclosure in Hong Kong and the PRC," p. 5. Online. Available at: www.hkics.org.hk/media/publication/attachment/2216_A&H.pdf (accessed 20 December 2012).
119 Ibid.
120 SHSE (2008), *Toumingdu yu Xinxi Pilu* [China Corporate Governance Report: Transparency and Information Disclosure], Shanghai: Fudan University Press, pp. 115–19.
121 Ibid., p. 120.
122 Art. 63 Securities Law.
123 This was issued by the Supreme People's Court on 9 January 2003. See Art. 17 of this rule for the definition.
124 Art. 193 Securities Law.
125 Art. 160 Criminal Law. The Criminal Law especially applies to information disclosure cases where "the amount involved is huge, and the consequences are serious, or if there are other serious circumstances," as stipulated in the law.
126 Art. 17 *Interim Provisions on the Management of the Issuing and Trading of Stocks*. Also Art. 55 *Measures for Administration of the Initial Public Offering and Listing of Shares*.
127 Art. 69 Securities Law.
128 This was issued by the SPC on 9 January 2003. See Art. 17 of this rule for the definition.
129 Arts 7, 21–28 *Several Provisions of the Supreme People's Court on Hearing Civil Compensation Cases Arising from False Statement in the Securities Market*.
130 The actual losses of the investors include: loss in investment margin; commission and stamp duty for the loss in investment margin. See ibid., Arts. 29 and 30.
131 Art. 160 Criminal Law.
132 For specific details, see Arts. 11, 26, 69 and 192 PRC Securities Law, and Arts. 4, 7, 10, 11 and 19 *Provisional Measures on the Sponsor System for Issuing and Listing of Securities*.
133 Waldmeir, Patti (2009), "Investors Prepare for Fresh Flood of Chinese Offerings" in *Financial Times* (17 June 2009).
134 Hertig, op. cit., p. 276.

6 Company-level evidence

Liquidity and bonding

Companies bonding themselves to more stringent markets might realize a "cross-listing premium" in the form of a higher value relative to their domestic peers, a phenomenon that has been empirically demonstrated in a study by Doidge *et al.*[1] This is a general phenomenon, and should not be exclusive to the US market, as long as the regulatory gap between home market and host market is sufficiently wide.[2] However, little research pays attention to the potential disadvantages of cross-listing. Every coin has two sides. Overseas listed companies may encounter certain problems and challenges, despite the potential gains from bonding premiums.

This chapter looks at the bonding phenomenon of Chinese cross-listed companies in Hong Kong from both sides: benefits *and* problems. In particular, what benefits do Chinese companies receive after cross-listing? How far do these benefits influence Chinese companies? And what kinds of weaknesses and challenges are Chinese companies facing when they comply with higher standards? Are there any regulatory implications resulting from the differences between compulsory compliance and voluntary compliance? All these issues are investigated by means of empirical evidence and case study.

This chapter is organized as follows. The next section outlines the methods employed and the data sources. Sections 6.2 and 6.3 look at the general empirical evidence, evaluating the benefits received and the difficulties encountered by H-share companies at the firm level (impacts at the market level are evaluated in the next two chapters). Individual cases are analyzed in Section 6.4. The final section concludes.

6.1 Methods and data

In conducting the case studies of H-share companies, the principle from general to specific is applied. As in the overall picture, it uses empirical evidence to explore the macro-level governance and financial performance of H-share companies. Issues under the categories of liquidity, financial performance, ownership diversification, management, and disclosure standards are examined. The potential drawbacks of cross-listing will also be assessed.

Next, the analysis turns to individual cases. Representative examples of Chinese companies are taken to disintegrate the macro-level evidence and to examine the specific consequences of the initial and post-listing compliance of a given company. Five cases are selected from 144 H-share companies that were on the Main Board of the HKSE as at the end of 2012.[3] They are: Tsingtao Brewery (Tsingtao), Kelon Electrical (Kelon), China Petroleum & Chemical Corporation (Sinopec), Industrial and Commercial Bank of China (ICBC), and BYD Auto (BYD). There are three main reasons behind the selection.

First, the listing of these five companies covers a broad period of time, spanning the years 1993, when the first ever Chinese enterprise listed abroad, to after 2000. The exact dates of listing are as follows: Tsingtao, 15 July 1993; Kelon, 23 July 1996; Sinopec, 19 October 2000; ICBC, 27 October 2006; and BYD, 31 July 2002. The first batch of H-share companies in 1993 was driven by policy and enjoyed a considerable amount of government financial and administrative support. Their objectives were probably related to political purposes such as the need to demonstrate the liberalization of China's stock markets.[4] In contrast, during the era of globalization, cross-listing has become a voluntary choice for companies wanting to obtain capital at a lower cost, while also increasing their international recognition. Thus, examples that cover different periods are worth investigating.

Second, both SOEs and private companies are considered. Among the five, three are SOEs (Tsingtao, Sinopec, and ICBC), one is a township and village enterprise (TVE) (Kelon), and one is a private enterprise (BYD). Such different ownership structures may have different growth curves and may demonstate specific issues. Chinese listed companies have been widely conceived as having a blockholder model, in which the state as the controlling shareholder should in theory possess the incentives to constrain the opportunistic behavior of managers. A study comprising SOEs and non-SOEs can reveal the way in which state involvement influences companies' operation and management.

Third, the selected sample covers different market sectors: brewing, electronics, car manufacture, banking, and petroleum refining.

Admittedly, the case study approach has its shortcomings; five examples cannot reveal the situation of all H-share companies. This chapter will therefore combine general empirical evidence with the specific case studies, an approach that will help to cover more spheres of Chinese listed companies.

The data for the case studies were gathered from publicly available sources including newspapers, annual reports, and scholarly articles.

This chapter uses the data to compare Chinese cross-listings to domestic listings, and especially makes reference to company performance before and after listing. Also, it provides a brief chronicle of the relevant companies from their emergence through to their latest developments or abrupt failings.

6.2 Liquidity: demand and supply side factors

As discussed in Chapter 2, it is necessary to stress that debt financing is still the dominant source of capital in China. Despite a surge in stock market listings, both domestically and overseas, the role of equity financing remains secondary.

Before 2000 a quota system existed in the domestic market. Only a limited number of companies and predetermined quantities of shares were listed. The state remains highly skeptical about introducing private ownership into companies, especially SOEs. But the Chinese banking system has been plagued by problems associated with bad loans, forcing the state to diversify fundraising channels for companies. One advantage of allowing companies to list overseas is that it relieves the pressure on the infant Chinese market. Funds raised overseas have constituted a major part of total funds raised by equity. Nonetheless, the peak of cross-listing actually took place between 2005–07 when the Shanghai Stock Exchange was already considerably well developed. This may imply that the motivations of cross-listed Chinese companies are not limited to liquidity. As discussed in Chapter 3, it seems that China has cautiously developed its stock market. Before it is fully comfortable about its experiment, listing on an overseas exchange has clearly been an interim solution to ease the financial pressure on a number of companies.

Following the success of the first batch of nine companies in 1993–94, a second batch of 22 companies was selected. In 1995, seven more companies were included. At the same time, the HKSE was increasingly dependent on Chinese companies. Between 1997–2002, HK$232.8 billion was raised from 73 Chinese IPOs.[5] Of this, HK$113.9 billion was raised for 50 H-share companies and HK$118.9 billion for red-chips. By contrast, just HK$80.5 billion (25.7 percent of the total) was raised by 358 non-Chinese companies. On average, each Chinese company raised HK$3.2 billion, significantly more than the overall average of HK$0.73 billion.

The connection between Hong Kong and China has been gaining in strength. The central government announced in 2004 that China would utilize overseas capital markets and strengthen financial cooperation with Hong Kong.[6] The Hong Kong government responded by publishing an Action Agenda, which echoed the Chinese plan and committed Hong Kong to playing a strategic role in China's financial reform and development.[7] The parties hoped that the two markets would become increasingly integrated. In 2006 Hong Kong became one of the largest IPO fundraising centers, handling the listings of mega-sized IPOs such as the Bank of China and ICBC. A comparison of the total funds raised by H-share and red-chip companies, since 1993, is given in Table 6.1. This reveals Hong Kong to be an important fundraising ground for China.[8]

6.3 Bonding and the potential drawbacks of cross-listing

This section concerns benefits received from, and difficulties encountered by, H-share companies at the general firm level.

6.3.1 Bonding premiums in the H-share market

Bonding practices may involve adopting stringent accounting standards, hiring reputable outside auditors, and diversifying ownership by introducing foreign

Table 6.1 Yearly total funds raised through IPOs, domestically and in Hong Kong, 1993–2009 (US$ billion)

	H-Share	*Red-chip*	*A-Share*	*Total*	*% of funds raised in HK*
1993	1.90	0.22	4.80	6.92	30.65
1994	1.03	0.16	1.16	2.35	50.64
1995	0.22	0.17	1.02	1.42	27.95
1996	0.76	0.38	3.54	4.69	24.49
1997	3.61	4.44	9.96	18.01	44.68
1998	0.23	0.02	9.40	9.65	2.59
1999	0.48	0.27	10.79	11.55	6.52
2000	6.03	5.02	18.45	29.50	37.47
2001	0.8	1.36	14.28	16.45	13.18
2002	2.18	2.37	9.42	13.97	32.56
2003	5.58	0.34	9.90	15.82	37.42
2004	4.81	1.65	10.10	16.56	39.05
2005	16.01	0.12	4.23	20.26	79.62
2006	36.03	0.34	30.91	67.27	54.06
2007	10.40	6.69	101.56	118.65	14.40
2008	5.39	0.00	14.89	20.28	26.57
2009	5.87	1.13	32.74	39.74	17.62

Source: based on Huang and Yeung (2012).

strategic investors. And, more importantly, companies can enhance their financial and governance performance in general.

A Macro-level improvements on governance and financial performance

A company's credit rating is widely used to signal a company's reputation and creditworthiness, given the lack of readily quantifiable variables in corporate governance structure and practices. Xinhua Finance (XFN), a leading Chinese financial agent, presents a credit rating report on Chinese domestically and internationally listed companies, mainly based on their management quality, organizational structure, disclosure practice, and relationship with the parent company and major shareholders. As the ratings use strictly international criteria, they therefore provide a useful proxy for assessing the extent to which cross-listed Chinese companies have improved their corporate governance. This report has been proven to have instructive content, and to influence investment decisions.[9]

According to XFN's Far East China Credit Ratings of August 2007,[10] 36 (23.8 percent) of the total 152 overseas listings were qualified for the Public Information (PI) rating, based on the publicly available information. In contrast, 164 (11.4 percent) of the 1434 domestic listings were qualified for the PI rating. Some 61.1 percent of overseas listings achieved a rating of A– or above, while the corresponding figure for domestic listings was just 28.6 percent. Few domestic listings achieved higher ratings (none at AAA, and only one AA+). But six overseas listings obtained above AA+. The disparity indicates that Chinese overseas listings distinguish themselves from their local peers with better governance and higher credit ratings.

Turning to the H-share market, the findings are in line with the general findings. Huang and Song compare the pre- and post-listing financial and operational performance of a sample of H-share companies by using accounting data.[11] They find that real sales and dividend payouts gradually increase after going public in Hong Kong. This shows that the market recognition effect of bonding may exist and that the corporate governance of H-share companies may have improved. Based on the result of the test on 53 SOEs in Hong Kong over the period from July 1993 to December 2002, Jia *et al.* found that listing led to an increase of 70 percent in real net profits, 80 percent in real sales, and 50 percent in capital spending, and a mild improvement in coverage ratios.[12] The findings further confirm China's incremental approach to development by emulating the developed markets. Companies have taken advantage of listing on more stringent markets.

B Ownership diversification

A common perception of Chinese companies is that, unless they fundamentally alter the ownership structure, they will not be able to provide sufficient assurance to investors that controlling shareholders and insiders would not expropriate them. As a result, some companies' stakes are sold to strategic investors before having an IPO or before issuing a secondary offering. From a political perspective, selling companies to foreign investors could signal that a government is committed to supporting market-oriented policies.[13] The Chinese government wished to use foreign listings to improve the quality of SOEs and to make them role models for domestic companies.[14]

This strategy has been common in the financial sector (see Table 6.2). The Chinese government faces intense pressure to open up the country's financial industry to foreigners as part of China's WTO entry commitments.[15] Foreign financial institutions, too, are also keen to enter the Chinese markets through capital tie-ups with local banks, thus explaining the spate of investments in Chinese banks.

C Stricter accounting rules and reputational intermediaries

From a bonding perspective, strict accounting rules and reliable intermediaries are two main areas of concern in attempts to improve company transparency and disclosure standards. A sound accounting system should aim at protecting the interests of investors and shareholders by monitoring the behavior of corporate insiders.[16] For the latter, entry into overseas markets exposes the issuers to the scrutiny of reputational intermediaries, including underwriters, auditors, debt rating agencies, and securities analysts. These can reasonably be viewed as financial watchdogs in uncovering financial deception, and hence a company that subjects itself to their scrutiny is arguably signaling its commitment to full and fair disclosure.

In the Chinese context, some companies voluntarily use International Financial Reporting Standards (IFRS) instead of China's own Generally Accepted Accounting Principles (GAAP), which focus more on how the government can collect tax from companies, with less emphasis on how to evaluate the company's performance and how to give equity holders the benefits to which they are entitled.[17] Table 6.3 lays out different accounting standards applied in different market segments. The accounting report for H-shares is prepared under either IFRS or the Hong Kong Financial Reporting Standards (HKFRS). By 2005, HKFRS became fully harmonized with IFRS, except for a few minor differences.[18] Company earnings determined according to Chinese GAAP are on average 20–30 percent higher than those based on IFRS.[19]

In the past few years the CSRC has eliminated, as much as possible, the differences between Chinese GAAP and IFRS. Most notably, with the release of the 1999 *Accounting System for Insurance Companies* and the 2000 *Accounting System for Securities Companies*, Chinese GAAP has become much closer to IFRS. However, there are still several major differences in content, format, and formulating institutions between the two. These differences, along with the differences in auditing practices, differentiate financial reporting in the A-share market from that in the H-share market.

Next, having finance reports audited by reputable intermediaries may constitute a bonding practice. Intermediaries in the Chinese financial market are generally state-owned entities.[20] They are controlled by the CSRC in respect of licensing, capital adequacy, and conduct of business. The policy of separation of the three pillars of the financial sector (banking, securities, and insurance) means that there is no functional integration of different types of business. Ownership links are, however, permitted.[21] The position is therefore quite different to that in Western markets, where the independent position of financial intermediaries such as investment banks allows them in principle to attach their reputation to transactions.

Chinese regulators realized the possible merits of having reputational intermediaries to ensure the accuracy and reliability of listed companies' financial reports. On 31 December 2001, the CSRC promulgated the *Temporary Measure Regarding Additional Auditing Requirement for Listed A-Share Companies*, requiring that all companies engaging in an IPO, and all current listed A-share companies conducting a secondary offering in China, have their annual reports audited by a "world renowned accounting firm." The "world renowned accounting firms" were actually the Big Five (Arthur Andersen, Deloitte, Ernst & Young, KPMG, and PricewaterhouseCoopers). However, this measure never came into force, partly due to Arthur Andersen's immediate implosion after the Enron scandal. The CSRC has certified several firms as authorized to provide the auditing service. However, the Big Four still dominate the auditing service for listed companies.[22]

Nevertheless, the effectiveness of independent intermediaries and their role as gatekeepers has been doubtful since the world was scandalized by the false accounting practices of Enron and WorldCom in 2002. This may be due to the

Table 6.2 Strategic investors in key Chinese banks (as of August 2009)

Key Chinese banks	*Investors*	*Investment amount (in USD billion)*	*% of shares*	*Timing of agreement*	*Notes*
Industrial and Commercial Bank of China (ICBC)	Goldman Sachs (US), Allianz (Germany), American Express (US)	3.78	10	April 2006	ICBC went public in Hong Kong and Shanghai on 27 October 2006.
Bank of China (BOC)	RBS (UK), Merrill Lynch (US), Li Ka-Shing Foundation (HK)	3.1	10	August 2005	BOC is currently listed on the HKSE.
	Temasek (Singapore)	3.1	10	August 2005	
	UBS (Switzerland)	0.5	1.6	September 2005	
	Asian Development Bank	0.075	0.24	October 2005	
	Bank of Tokyo-Mitsubishi UFJ (Japan)	0.3	1	January 2006	
China Construction Bank (CCB)	Bank of America (US)	2.5	9	June 2005	CCB is currently dual listed on the HKSE and the SHSE.
	Temasek Holdings (Singapore)	1.47	5.1	August 2005	
Bank of Communications (BoCom)	HSBC (UK)	1.75	19.9	August 2004	BoCom was listed on the HKSE in June 2005 and the SHSE in May 2007

Shanghai Pudong Development Bank	Citigroup (US)	0.07	5	2003	Citigroup was trying to raise that stake to 19.9% in 2005 (the plan was not successful and its stake never rose above 3.779%).
Shenzhen Development Bank	Newbridge Capital (US)	0.15	17.89	September 2004	China's Ping An Insurance Group was set to buy out Newbridge Capital's stake in Shenzhen Development Bank for US$1.68 billion in June 2009 (the bank finally merged with Ping An Bank, part of the Ping An group).
Minsheng Bank	The International Financial Corporation (IFC)	0.023	1.08	July 2004	
Huaxia Bank	Deutsche Bank and Sal Oppenheim Jr. and Cie KGaA (Germany)	0.33	14 (Deutsche took a 9.9% stake and Sal Oppenheim bought 4.1%)	October 2005	Deutsche Bank increased its stake to 13.7% in 2008.
	Pangaea Capital (Singapore)	0.12	6.9	September 2005	

Source: compiled from media news and relevant company annual reports.

Table 6.3 Accounting and auditing standard differences in different market segments

Share categories	*Accounting standards*	*Auditing firms*
A-shares	Chinese GAAP	Local auditing firms
B-shares	IFRS	Big 4 (PwC, EY, Deloitte and KMPG)
H-shares	IFRS/HKFRS	Big 4
AB-shares	Chinese GAAP and IFRS dual reporting	Local CPA and Big 4 dual auditing
AH-shares	Chinese GAAP and IFRS dual reporting	Local CPA and Big 4 dual auditing

fact that outside auditors are hired by insiders of the company, and report to them.[23] According to recent empirical research by Liu and Zhou, the auditing quality of the Big Four is no better than that of other Chinese auditing firms.[24] Consequently, the usefulness or otherwise of bonding through employing international intermediaries remains an open question.

D Independent directors

Another issue in the attempt to ensure better corporate governance for publicly listed companies is the role independent directors. Before 2001, no law or regulation required that any directors be independent of management. In August 2001 the CSRC promulgated the *Guiding Opinion about Establishing Independent Director System in Listed Companies* ("the Opinion"). The *Opinion* required that at least a third of a listed company board be made up of independent directors by 30 June 2003.[25] By the end of 2004 it was estimated that there were about 5,000 independent directors in China's 1,300 listed companies.[26] The amended Company Law 2005 strengthens the obligations of directors by including both "duty of loyalty" and "duty of care" in Article 148, though neither is defined very clearly.[27]

Empirical research shows that market response to the progress on independent directors in China is moderately positive, but in other countries is very ambiguous.[28] A joint survey by the Association of Board Secretaries of Listed Companies of Shanghai and the Shanghai Jinxin Institute of Securities Research, conducted in 2003, demonstrated that independent directors had helped to improve corporate governance, especially in terms of bringing professional expertise to the board and protecting the interests of minority shareholders.[29] Empirical research by the Corporate Governance Centre of Nankai University shows that the level of competence of independent directors has a positive relationship with the profitability, market value, and financial security of listed companies, and a negative relationship with the scale of illegal activities of companies.[30] Although the data may be limited and rudimentary, it is recognized that the introduction of the independent director system can make a difference in corporate governance in China.

Unfortunately, using independent directors as a bonding mechanism in Chinese listed companies has not been completely effective. The biggest problem is that of ensuring director independence. According to a survey by *China Securities Daily*, 27.5 percent of independent directors had been directly nominated by controlling shareholders. Furthermore, 52.5 percent of them revealed that their remuneration was determined by the company's senior managers, while the remuneration of 37.5 percent was decided by controlling shareholders. Clarke pointed out that "independent directors" in a Chinese context were better described as "non-executive directors" who represented controlling shareholders' interests against managerial wrongdoing.[31] Hence, the extent to which directors can represent minority shareholders is questionable. It is also questionable whether they will ever have the independence required to perform their jobs properly.

6.3.2 Mechanism for SOE reform

SOE reform revolved around a "2-R strategy." In a "retreat" strategy, control is normally sold directly to employees. Listing state-owned companies is generally a retaining strategy. Control will not be lost owing to the existence of non-tradable shares.

Before looking at an overseas listing, it is necessary to see how it compares with a domestic listing. Indeed, the majority of listed companies in China are transformed SOEs. According to a survey, of the 835 companies listed on the Shanghai Stock Exchange at the end of 2005, 662 had state shares, which accounted for 50.8 percent of the total shares.[32] This shows that the state still maintained control over these companies. A critical question is whether the core performance of SOEs and other state-controlled companies improved after their domestic listing. Empirical evidence suggests that operational performance, measured in terms of return on equity and earnings per share, declined on average after listing.[33] Furthermore, profitability deteriorated.[34] The cause of this failure can be attributed to various reasons. First, the logic of introducing private ownership is fundamentally flawed if the state retains the majority of shares. Political influence on internal decision-making persists. The majority of state-controlled listed companies had government officials as executive management. Their behavior is predominantly policy-driven rather than market-oriented. Conflicts of interest between the state's dual role, as owner and regulator, can hinder enforcement actions by public authorities. Second, the Chinese stock market is still dominated by small retail investors with short-term trading behavior who have no interest in the operation of companies. Outsourcing the regulatory role of the CSRC and the governance role of domestic shareholders, to overseas regulators and institutional investors respectively, seems to be a viable solution.

In cross-listings, the control of Chinese companies has never been lost to foreigners. For example, the majority of shares in the big four banks are owned by Central Huijin, a state-owned investment company owned by the government and the Ministry of Finance.[35] Oil company shares are mostly owned by their state parent companies.[36] Normally, only around 10–20 percent of shares in these companies are traded in Hong Kong. Even if they are dual-listed in China as well, the proportion of tradable domestic A-shares will be no more than that. According to a survey of the largest 30 listed companies in China, the overall percentage of tradable A-shares was only 28 percent in August 2008.[37] For those also listed in Hong Kong, the percentage could be under 10 percent. These companies include PetroChina (2.47 percent), Bank of China (3.65 percent), ICBC (5.96 percent), China Life Insurance (7.2 percent), and China CITIC Bank (8.64 percent).[38] The number of state-owned non-tradable shares is almost guaranteed to be far more than that of tradable shares. In this way, the state maintains absolute control over these companies.

Considering the lesson of the domestic market, such a partial privatization might not be so effective in improving the operational efficiency of SOEs. For Eastern Europe and Russia, it was presumed that the transfer of ownership rights from state to private hands would create a regime of transparent property arrangements; such a transfer was deemed a prerequisite for the establishment of a market economy.[39] For this to happen there must be more than a simple transfer of ownership from state to private individuals. Clear property rights must be present in the market. However, there are at least two problems in the context of China. First, there has not been a real separation of ownership and control because the state has never wanted to give up either its shareholding in, or influence over, many strategically important SOEs. Second, the first property law of China came into effect in 2007. It remains unclear how this law will work in the socio-political context of China, where socialism is still essentially the basic system.[40]

6.3.3 Potential drawbacks of cross-listing

While Chinese companies can benefit from going public in Hong Kong, it is also important to understand the drawbacks associated with overseas listing. Indeed, given the significant barriers discussed below, it is not easy to strike a balance between costs and benefits.

A Political limits of bonding

Underlying assumptions of the bonding hypothesis are that: on the whole, companies are free to choose whether they wish to be listed; and the cross-listing decision is made autonomously by companies. But this is not the case in China, at least not entirely.

The listing of Chinese companies in Hong Kong has from the very beginning been controlled by the Chinese government, through both legal and political means. It was the central government which picked the nine SOEs that became the first batch of H-shares companies. In 1994, a State Council regulation entitled *Special Provisions on Joint Stock Limited Companies Issuing Shares and Listing Overseas*, which is still in force, confirmed that overseas offering and listing of shares must be approved by the SCSC (later merged into the CSRC).

Throughout the 1990s, selection of the Chinese overseas listings was completely controlled by the central and local government through a quota system. The quota system was instituted in 1993 in China with the intention of curbing the potentially excessive investment demand in a premature market. Provincial governments and industry supervising bodies were assigned issue quotas. They would then recommend enterprises for listing within their given quotas, and the CSRC would review each listing applicant. The quota system allowed funds to be channeled towards important sectors such as natural resources, utilities, heavy industry, and manufacturing SOEs. However, this system was damaging in at least two ways.[41] First, the government regularly used it to manipulate market sentiment. Second, the whole process was inevitably vulnerable to lobbying and corruption.

Since July 1999 the CSRC has replaced the quota system with a verification and approval system under which an enterprise may directly approach the CSRC for application to seek overseas listing.[42] However, the CSRC still looks at consistency with state policies concerning industrial development, foreign investment, good corporate governance, and business management.[43]

Such heavy state involvement in the process of Chinese overseas listings would restrict the bonding effects. First, better corporate governance (particularly better disclosure) of H-share companies might have resulted from the Chinese state's "macro-level cross-benefit analysis."[44] Better disclosure by H-share companies may "reflect the effect of state initiated disclosure policies rather than management's response to firm-specific costs and benefits of disclosure."[45] The Chinese government might treat the overseas listed companies as Chinese international ambassadors and, as such, expose only its best companies to foreign markets. There are benefits associated with this practice. A policy that carefully selects and showcases companies signals to international investing communities that Chinese companies are willing to increase transparency and act as good corporate citizens. This may not only influence investor confidence but also pave a wider avenue for other issuers.[46]

Second, Chinese regulators purposely allocate the resources of listing companies by controlling the pace of Chinese companies listing in Hong Kong. For more than a decade after 1993, the Chinese government exposed only large, growth-oriented enterprises (most of which were SOEs) to foreign markets for listing. In 2006–07, when China's stock markets were experiencing their most sustained bull market, the CSRC encouraged Hong Kong listed Chinese companies (including both H-share and red-chip companies) to return to the domestic A-share market. This was partly under pressure from domestic investors, who wished to share those firms' profits; they had long been angry at the authorities for their decision to list overseas and pay dividends only to foreign investors.[47] During that period, 14 H-share companies issued A-shares in China's domestic market. At the same time, Chinese companies wishing to be listed overseas were asked by the CSRC to offer and list shares on the mainland stock markets simultaneously. Since December 2007 companies have been asked to issue and list A-shares first in China before being offered in Hong Kong. Clearly, the regulator's purpose was to keep the resources of listed companies in the mainland in order to foster the development of China's own securities market.[48]

B Agency problems and corporate frauds

Another problem that Chinese listed companies face is that of a conflict of interest between controlling shareholders and managers. Most executives do not own their company's stock. According to a survey by Bai *et al.*, the top five executives in listed Chinese companies in 2000 only owned 0.02 percent of their companies' shares.[49] Managers cannot take advantage of the gain in bonding, but do have to bear the increased legal risk; so they may lack incentives to facilitate bonding, even though the state, as the controlling shareholder, is willing to do so.

These conflicts of interest could lead to corporate fraud.[50] The insiders' incentives before and after listing are probably the same: to maximize their own interests a governance structure that would give them more leeway and less external control would serve their self-interest better than good corporate governance. In China's relatively brief corporate system history, fraud has been a recurring feature. David Webb, a shareholder advocate on the board of the HKSE, lays out a list of cases of bad governance at the senior level in which 20 Chinese listed companies, including H-shares and red-chip companies, incurred criminal penalties (see Table 6.4). Twenty-nine directors involved received prison sentences. These include several high-profile cases such as the arrest of Gu Chujin, the former chairman of Kelon, on charges of embezzlement; and Euro-Asia Agricultural Company Limited, the first Chinese private overseas company to be delisted from a foreign exchange.

C Difficulties in cross-border enforcement

The third problem is the extent to which Hong Kong's enforcement mechanisms are as effective as they are supposed to be. Theoretically, the Hong Kong financial system has developed for more than 100 years and should be able to offer much greater protection to shareholders than that of China, with its short history. In practice, unfortunately, this theoretically higher level of protection is handicapped by a lack of enforcement in cross-listings.

On the political point, the Chinese government is resistant to any external intervention in the running of Chinese SOEs, especially the banks. Professor Tomasic remarked: "The Constitution and the law proclaim the equality of all under the law, but in fact party and government cadres are more equal than ordinary citizens."[51]

On the legal point, a state's legal jurisdiction which deals with cross-border activities falls into three general categories: the power to enact laws; the power to adjudicate disputes; and the power to enforce legal orders and judgments.[52] When disputes arise, it may not be clear whether Hong Kong or China is the most appropriate forum. The assets of the Chinese companies are primarily located in China. Normally, cross-border enforcement of judgments is not easy.

Table 6.4 A jailbird list in Chinese listed companies in Hong Kong

Company name	*Director(s) jailed*
Bank of China Ltd.	Wang Xuebing
Beijing Capital International Airport Company Ltd.	Li Peiying
BOC Hong Kong (Holdings) Ltd.	Liu Jinbao
Changchun Da Xing Pharmaceutical Company Ltd.	Feng Zhen Wen and Li Xiu Jie
China Everbright Ltd.	Ch'ng Poh and Zhu Xiaohua
China Motion Telecom International Ltd.	Hau Tung Ying and Li Bin
China Petroleum & Chemical Corporation	Chen Tonghai
Chintex Oil and Gas Company Ltd.	James Coe
CITIC Ka Wah Bank Ltd.	Jin Deqin
Euro-Asia Agricultural (Holdings) Company Ltd.	Yang Bin
Guangnan (Holdings) Ltd.	Cen Ting Biao and Huang Xiao Jiang
Hisense Kelon Electrical Holdings Company Ltd.	Gu Chu Jun
Mandarin Resources Corporation Ltd.	Chim Pui Chung
Shanghai Electric Group Company Ltd.	Han Guozhang and Li Songjian
Shanghai Industrial Holdings Ltd.	Lu Da Yong
Shanghai Land Holdings Ltd.	Chau Ching Ngai (aka Zhou Zhengyi) Gong Beiying
Shanghai Merchants Holdings Ltd.	Mo Yuk Ping Gong Beiying Tsoi Hon Chung
Shenyin Wanguo (H.K.) Ltd.	Guan Jin Sheng
Skyworth Digital Holdings Ltd.	Stephen Wong Wang Sang Wong Pui Sing
Yeebo International Holdings Ltd.	Makie Hui Po Yuen

Source: Webb-site.com as of 30 September 2009.

Notes

1 A person in this list is a director of a past or present listed company, and has been convicted for crimes related to the company or its shares, or crimes which cast doubt on his or her suitability to be a director of a listed company.

2 As companies frequently change names, the names used here are those at the time of the offences or prosecution.

Even though an investor can get an award from a Hong Kong court, the enforcement of such award against a Chinese company outside Hong Kong is problematic. In particular, if disputes are related to SOEs, enforcement may be more complicated. China may be resistant to claim against some SOEs because of the political considerations mentioned above.

The solution to such problems is an agreement on reciprocal enforcement of judgments. The *Arrangement on Reciprocal Recognition and Enforcement of Judgements in Civil and Commercial Matters by the Courts of the Mainland and of the Hong Kong Special Administrative Region Pursuant to Choice of Court Agreements between Parties Concerned* ("the Arrangement"), was signed on 14 July 2006. It applies to final arbitration awards and certain commercial judgments (but is not applicable to orders for specific performance or injunctions). However, enforcement of a Hong Kong judgment may be refused by a Chinese court if it considers that enforcement is "contrary to the social and public interests of China." Additionally, the "exclusive jurisdiction" exception effectively restricts the types of disputes that fall under the *Arrangement*. For example, unless there is a valid agreement to arbitrate, Sino-foreign joint venture disputes are subject to the exclusive jurisdiction of PRC courts, which means that litigation in Hong Kong remains unavailable as an option in respect of Sino-foreign joint venture disputes (and indeed any other disputes where PRC courts are deemed to have exclusive jurisdiction).

At the regulatory level, on 2 April 2007 Hong Kong's SFC and the CSRC reached an agreement to enhance cross-border enforcement in the investigation of cross-border crimes and regulatory breaches.[53] Under this arrangement, if the Hong Kong SFC decides to seek information from a person located in mainland China, and such person refuses to comply with the SFC's request, the SFC may ask the CSRC for assistance and the CSRC will seek court sanctions against that person. In turn, the SFC will also exercise its powers to help the CSRC in investigations that have a Hong Kong element. However, observers criticize this agreement, claiming that it only deals with information exchange and that it is still very difficult to prosecute wrongdoers involved with Chinese listed companies in Hong Kong.[54]

D The failure of the HKSE as the investors' guardian

Nowadays, stock exchanges have moved from the older, state-owned continental European approach, and from member cooperatives in the Anglo-American approach, to the corporate model of ownership and governance. This would necessitate a reduction to their portfolio of regulatory duties.[55]

This is the case in Hong Kong. The HKSE owns and operates the only stock exchange and futures exchange in Hong Kong, and their related clearing houses. The HKSE performs a dual role. It is a listed company and it is also the regulator of Hong Kong's capital markets. In other words, on the one hand, it is a self-interested economic organization that supplies services to listing companies in exchange for fees. On the other hand, it is also the regulator that creates the listing rules and guidelines on directors' duties, disclosure, and enhances corporate governance and market quality. There is a potential conflict of interest here because of the commercial interests of the HKSE as a listed company, and its regulatory role. Will this potential conflict of interest result in the HKSE reducing regulatory standards when it comes to dealing with important Chinese companies, thereby putting itself at risk of undermining a strong securities market?

Recalling the previous chapter, LR Chapter 19A is exclusively for Chinese issuers, with Chinese government bodies exempted from the definition of "a controlling shareholder," and "connected persons of the issuer." The obvious aim is the lowering of barriers to attract more Chinese companies, and in particular SOEs. But the downside of the rule is the high possibility of poor disclosure and a lack of transparency in Chinese listed companies. Risks of market misconduct, such as insider dealing and price manipulation, may soar.

6.4 Five case studies: prizes and scandals

This section demonstrates the bonding of an individual company in practice. The five case studies may provide some evidence for the benefits derived from, and the challenges faced by, cross-listed Chinese companies.

6.4.1 Tsingtao Brewery (Tsingtao)

Tsingtao (HK 00168) was founded in 1903. Tsingtao products are sold in 62 countries, accounting for more than 50 percent of all China's beer exports. It deserves attention not only because it was the first enterprise chosen for overseas listing, but also because of an apparently successful mixture associated with its listing; active government support and the involvement of foreign investment.

A The listing

Tsingtao was listed on the HKSE on 15 July 1993. The listing generated a wave of investor enthusiasm for Chinese enterprise stocks.[56] The issue of 317,600,000 H-shares included a placing of 45,000,000 H-shares under a special arrangement with Anheuser-Busch International Holdings Inc., the world's largest brewery.[57] The arrangement gave Anheuser-Busch 5 percent of the total registered capital of Tsingtao. The H-share issue was followed by the A-share issue on the SHSE on 27 August 1993.[58]

By the end of 1993, the share structure of Tsingtao was: H-shares foreign investors including Anheuser-Busch, holding 38.64 percent; Qingdao State-owned Assets bureau ("SAB," later the Qingdao State-owned Assets Supervision and Administration Commission, "SASAC") controlling 44.42 percent; domestic individual holders of tradable A-shares, holding 11.11 percent; non-tradable legal person shares, comprising 5.93 percent (3.25 percent held by Shangdong Province Branch of Bank of China and 2.12 percent held by Qingdao Branch of China Construction Bank).[59] By October 1994 Tsingtao's share price had risen from its listing price of HK$2.80 to HK$10.40.

B Upgrading accounting and disclosure standards

As it issued both A-shares and H-shares, Tsingtao prepares and issues each fiscal year a primary set of financial statements based on the Chinese GAAP, but also provides restatement of a few key financial measures in accordance with Hong Kong GAAP. Hence, analyses of its financial reports based on the rules in China and Hong Kong may suggest the bonding effect of cross-listing in accounting.

Lin and Wang have tried to reveal the substantial discrepancies between the main accounting numbers reported by Tsingtao under Chinese GAAP and Hong Kong's standards.[60] In particular, under Chinese GAAP, the key measures of income before tax, net income, and earnings per share (EPS) were significantly higher than the numbers stated according to the Hong Kong rules; in fact, by a margin of between 30–60 percent in the four-year period 1995–98. The H-share numbers relating to income in all four years were lower than the A-share numbers. In addition, the total revenues reported for H-shares were considerately lower than those for A-shares. On the other hand, numbers relating to the company's H-shares total assets and net assets were higher than the comparable A-share numbers.

These data may hint that the company's revenues and earnings, based on Chinese GAAP, were substantially overstated, while assets were slightly understated in terms of the accounting and reporting rules prevailing in Hong Kong. Since this deficiency exists in Tsingtao, the quality of information disclosures by other companies in China may be even lower because most domestically listed companies have generally been subject to less stringent accounting and disclosure requirements compared to those listed in both China and abroad.

C Changing management structure

When the company began listing in 1993, Tsingtao's board had nine directors, of whom six were executive directors and three were non-executive directors. Two of the latter came from the state-controlled banking sector and had significant connections with local state-owned banks. The board has subsequently undergone several major changes. However, before 2003 members of the board were nominated in the main by the controlling shareholder: Qingdao SAB. The non-executive directors all held senior positions in local political and business entities.[61]

Following the 2003 conversion of the first tranche of convertible bonds issued to Anheuser-Busch (into 60,000,000 cross-listed shares), Anheuser-Busch held 9.91 percent of the total equity of Tsingtao. It became entitled to nominate one non-executive director and one supervisor to the board.[62] When Anheuser-Busch further increased its shareholding in April 2005, it nominated one additional director, taking two seats on Tsingtao's board. By the end of 2005, Tsingtao's board consisted of 11 members. They were the Chairman, the Vice-Chairman, three executive directors nominated by the Qingdao SASAC, two non-executive directors nominated by Anheuser-Busch and four independent directors nominated by the board.

Apart from its participation in board and supervisory committee meetings, Anheuser-Busch also played an active role on the special committees of the company, including the Strategy and Investment Committee, and the Audit and Finance Committee. Tsingtao has also established five Best Practice Exchange Groups with Anheuser-Busch to exchange experiences in enterprise systems and quality control. So far, Tsingtao has placed itself in a good position to benefit from the management experience and techniques of its international partner.

D Ownership diversification

Encountering pressure and competition from overseas markets, China lifted in September 1999 its then-existing Company Law restrictions on state-owned companies repurchasing their own shares abroad. Tsingtao had been named as one of a number of pilot H-share companies to carry out the first experimental share buyback plans.

After a series of meetings the Tsingtao board approved a new share issue of up to 20 percent of the issued H-shares of the company or carrying out share repurchase plans for up to 10 percent of issued H-shares.[63] In De Jonge's view, share buyback plans provide companies with more flexibility in global markets and allow them to operate in line with international standards.[64] Unfortunately, the share repurchase scheme never took place.

By a special resolution passed on 28 February 2001, the authorized ordinary share capital of the company increased from RMB900 million to RMB1 billion through the creation of 100 million A-shares of RMB1 each. These new A-shares were sold to the public at a price of RMB7.87 per share. Most of the new shares were listed in Shanghai on 7 March 2001, and the remaining 3,416,368 shares held by institutional investors were listed on 7 June 2001.[65]

Foreign investment in the company also increased. On 21 October 2001, Tsingtao entered into a Strategic Investment Agreement with Anheuser-Busch and agreed to issue an aggregate of approximately US$182 million worth of convertible bonds to Anheuser-Busch, in three tranches. Following the conversion of all these bonds into a total of 308,219,178 new H-shares, the registered capital of the company rose to 1,308,219,178 shares.[66] As a result, by the beginning of 2006 state-owned shares (non-tradable A-shares) in the company had fallen from 44.42 percent to 30.56 percent, and foreign-controlled shares (H-shares) had risen from 38.54 percent to 50.07 percent.[67] Control of Tsingtao has been transformed from the state to foreign investors.

E Summary

Tsingtao sets a good example for Chinese cross-listings and SOE reform. It was the first Chinese company selected by government to cross-list. After listing, it improved its accounting and disclosure standards by complying with Hong Kong law. Also, it introduced foreign institutional investors as a way of diversifying its shareholding structure and changing its management structure. The experience of Tsingtao reveals that cross-listing is a feasible way for Chinese companies to ride experience from outside in an effort to transform themselves into international companies.

6.4.2 Guangdong Kelon Electrical Holdings (Kelon)

Kelon (HK 00921) was founded in 1984 in Rongqi, a small town in Guangdong Province. Over a six-year period, Kelon became China's largest refrigerator and air conditioning manufacturer. It was called "China's Corporate Dragon," a successful example of a Chinese TVE arising from China's embracing of the market economy during the 1980s and 1990s.[68] Unlike traditional SOEs, TVEs are founded, financed, and directly controlled by very low level governmental organizations (townships and villages), but ones which exhibited a tremendous degree of pro-business attitude in supporting local entrepreneurs. However, Kelon suddenly collapsed in 2000.

The Kelon affair reveals a series of accumulated difficulties with regard to the corporate governance reform of Chinese listed companies. The company rose largely as a result of support from the local government, and it fell because of asset stripping by the local government.

This section provides a brief history of Kelon, from growth to failure, and gives an insight into the potential problems arising from Chinese listed companies.

A The rise of a TVE star

The predecessor of Kelon was the Guangdong Shunde Pearl River Refrigerator Factory, which was founded in 1984 through collaboration between a local entrepreneur, Wang Guoduan, and the township government of Rongqi. To seize the opportunity offered by the advent of economic liberalization in China, Rongqi township government provided capital of RMB90,000 and the security of a bank loan of RMB4 million for construction of a factory.[69] Pan Ning, a vice-head of the township, was assigned as general manager to work with Wang. In addition, the factory received much political support from the township, such as a production license.[70]

By 1991 Kelon was the top-selling refrigerator manufacturer in China. In terms of corporatization, Kelon was also a pioneer. As early as 1992 the company was become a shareholding company in which Rongqi township held 80 percent of the shares via a holding company called Rongqi Township Economic Development Company, with managers and employees offered the remaining 20 percent stake. Thus, a new company, Kelon Electrical Holdings, was formed.

Kelon's business peaked in 1996 when it issued shares in Hong Kong and subsequently listed domestically in Shenzhen in 1999. It charmed investors with its reputation for an advanced management style and its distance from the government, because it was a TVE.[71] In the post-listing years, profitability at Kelon steadily increased, with corresponsing boosts in sales and operating profits recorded between 1996 and 1999.

In conclusion, the success of Kelon has been correlated with the nature of TVEs, a mix of local governmental and private entrepreneurial ownership. On the one hand, the local government offered political and capital support to nurture the company, while on the other, private participation provided management with a good incentive to compete in the market. However, every coin has two sides; government intervention accelerated the company's growth, but also forced its collapse.

B The sudden collapse in 2000 and the subsequent corporate scandal

In 1998 the government arranged for Kelon to merge with two Shunde city home appliance manufacturers that were in debt. This merger imposed a considerable burden on Kelon. Meanwhile, its founder was about to retire and his successor was impatient to manage the new company.

Kelon's performance in 2000 was harmed by a record deficit. At the beginning of that year the company predicted an annual 11.7 percent growth in sales and RMB0.7 billion net income. But the year-end result could not match the target and Kelon reported a huge net loss of RMB0.83 billion, with a 30.9 percent sales decline. It was the first time in its history that Kelon had fallen into deficit. A further loss of more than RMB1.4 billion followed in 2001, leaving Kelon on the verge of collapse.

Accordingly, in June 2001, Rongqi town government made a decision to intervene in the management of Kelon, a decision that resulted in the resignation of the second CEO, and the appointment the town government's vice-mayor as Kelon's third CEO. On 31 October 2001, Kelon announced that its holding company, Guangdong Kelon (Rongsheng) Group, had signed a share transfer agreement with Shunde Greencool Enterprise Development, a shelf company owned by Gu Cuojun.[72] According to the agreement, the wholly-owned town government group released 20.6 percent of the 34.06 percent of shares it held, to Gu, at a price of RMB 2.7 per share, which made Gu the ultimate controller of Kelon. As a result, Gu was an executive director and Chairman of both Kelon and Greencool. He held approximately 26.43 percent and 62.59 percent of the total shares of Kelon and Greencool respectively.[73] In this way Kelon left the control of the town government and the privatization of Kelon was accomplished. In mid-2000, Gu succeeded in merging the commercial distribution and service segment into a company called Greencool Technology Holdings Ltd., and had this listed on Hong Kong's GEM.

Under Gu's ownership Kelon recovered quickly. Although profitability was less impressive, sales maintained a steady growth and reached an unprecedented level of more than RMB6 billion in 2003. But the good days did not last long. Gu started siphoning off capital to fuel his M&A spree, resulting in a cash drain and production setbacks.

The CSRC launched a fraud investigation into Kelon and its directors in May 2005, after a RMB60 million deficit revealed in the 2004 annual report caused widespread suspicion. The CSRC also conducted an investigation into Greencool in connection with the possible misappropriation of funds of Kelon. The investigation found that Kelon overstated its profit by RMB387 million, and revenues by RMB1.2 billion.[74] The CSRC also found that Gu was suspected of embezzling and misappropriating huge amounts of the company's assets, and accused him of manipulating the share price. The CSRC imposed a fine of RMB600,000 on Kelon for fraudulent accounting between 2002 and 2004, and imposed warnings and fines on Gu and other related directors.[75]

In Hong Kong, the HKSE conducted a hearing into connected transactions of Kelon and imposed a public censure on directors of the company for their respective breaches of the Director's Undertakings.[76] Subsequently, on 16 June 2005, Kelon announced the suspension of trading in H-shares due to the pending release of information concerning Gu being investigated for involvement in seizing company assets.[77] Gu and six other executives were later dismissed by the board of directors of Kelon. Gu also faced criminal prosecution, and on 30 January 2008 was sentenced to ten years of imprisonment and fined RMB6.8 million by the Foshan Intermediate People's Court.

In June 2006 disgruntled investors filed a lawsuit in the Guangzhou Intermediate People's Court against Kelon on the grounds of it having produced false information. Pursuant to the result of mediation made by the court in 2008, Kelon paid a total amount of RMB14,527,123 to the plaintiffs and bore all litigation costs.[78]

C Reasons for the failure

Liu and Sun attribute the failure of Kelon to the grabbing hand of the township government during the post-listing period.[79] Rongqi township government, via its Guangdong Kelon (Yongsheng) Group, diverted a total of RMB1.26 billion from the listed Kelon Electronics through a string of secretive related party transactions between 1997 and 2001. Table 6.5 displays the major fund diversions between Kelon and its parent company: Rongsheng Group. The controlling shareholder could either tunnel funds from its listed subsidiary or inject cash into the company for the benefit of all shareholders. As Table 6.5 shows, in 1997 Rongsheng Group contributed more than RMB100 million to Kelon. The dynamics, however, were reversed, and increasing levels of Kelon funds were expropriated by the Rongsheng Group, especially in 2000 and 2001. The cash asset stripping by the government gave a vital and final impact to the collapse of Kelon.

The arrival of Gu after the abrupt failure of Kelon could not save it. The entry of a new owner seems to have been a doubled-edged sword. On the one hand, Gu experienced initial success in turning the troubled Kelon into a fairly profitable business. On the other hand, Gu, like the previous owner, Rongqi township,

Table 6.5 Transactions between Kelon Electronics and Guangdong Kelon (Rongsheng) Group (1997–2001)

Year	*Kelon → Rongsheng*	*Rongsheng → Kelon*	*Balance (Kelon → Rongsheng, RMB)*
1997	308,373,000	410,299,000	–101,926,000
1998	7,163,622,000	7,106,870,000	56,752,000
1999	4,389,922,000	4,362,194,000	27,728,000
2000	4,599,826,000	4,496,662,000	103,164,000
2001	5,083,814,000	4,378,515,000	705,299,000

Source: Kelon Electronics (13 March 2002), "Announcement" cited in Liu and Sun (2006).

used his position as controlling shareholder to attempt to substitute rent-seeking for profit-making. Indeed, private ownership does not necessarily imply immunity from the generic agency problem in this system. Another example is the collapse of D'Long Ltd., China's largest private business group.[80]

The Kelon case also shows the changing role of local government, from being supportive in the initial stage, to predatory when the company went public. Government-dominated ownership is helpful when the company is a small start-up. However, once the company becomes bigger and less dependent on the support of the government, the situation changes dramatically. In particular, after the stock flotation the company is put in a difficult situation that demonstrates clearly the moral hazard problems of having the government as controlling shareholder, and the agency problem of management becoming more acute. In this case, the problems offset the benefits gained from government ownership.[81]

The case also implies that the agency problem of an expropriating block-holder is rooted in the institutional environment characterized by a relatively weak legal system and poor investor protection.[82] Chinese controlling shareholders seem to maximize the funds that they can tunnel from the listed companies when they exit. This needs appropriate regulation and enforcement to ensure that insiders cannot expropriate investor funds and damage the company's interests.

D The future: Hisense-Kelon

In 2006 Shangdong-based Hisense secured a 26.43 percent stake in Kelon for RMB680 million, becoming its largest shareholder. In 2007 the name of Kelon was changed after acquisition to Hisense-Kelon Electrical Holdings Limited.[83] Hisense started out as a manufacturer of household electrical appliances, but then turned its attention to the white goods business. The acquisition gives Hisense a foothold in refrigerator and air-conditioner manufacturing, both of which are Kelon's strong points. In addition, Hisense could strengthen its presence in southern China.

E Summary

The Kelon affair results from its corporate governance system, a system which was developed when China's economy was undergoing a complex transition which induced block shareholders to play a dual role (helping and appropriating) in controlling their publicly-owned companies. Kelon succeeded in its initial stages largely because of the support of its largest shareholder, the local government; and it collapsed on account of asset stripping by the town government. Although Kelon's huge losses were finally covered by the injection of private investment, courtesy of rapid development of private business in China, its future sustainability still remains uncertain; there is no guarantee that the new private owner will not tunnel assets away from the business when weak corporate governance is present.

The Kelon affair also exposes the ineptitude of the HKSE. During the period from 1997–2001 there were major fund diversions between Kelon and its government-controlled parent company (Rongsheng). But the HKSE did not investigate these connected transactions, or act accordingly, until 2005.

6.4.3 China Petroleum & Chemical Corporation (Sinopec)

Sinopec (HK 00386) is the first Chinese SOE to be listed in Shanghai, Hong Kong, New York, and London. It is also one of the largest integrated energy and chemical companies in China, whether measured by revenue, profit, market value, or market weight. However, in China, even in a well-structured company, corruption still exists.

A The listing, and ownership structure

Sinopec was founded on 25 February 2000 by China Petrochemical Corporation (Sinopec Group), which was itself incorporated by the state. Sinopec issued 16.78 billion shares on the stock exchanges of Hong Kong, New York, and London, on 18 and 19 October 2000. On 16 July 2001 it floated 2.8 billion A-shares on the SHSE.[84]

After the overseas and A-share listings, the state directly held 55.06 percent of shares in Sinopec Group. Together with legal person shares, state-related institutions held 77.42 percent of all shares.[85] Later, Sinopec Group acquired some of the shares held by legal persons. In the fall of 2006, Sinopec completed its conversion of non-tradable shares into tradable shares. It was one of the last major listed SOEs to do so. In conjunction with the share conversion, Sinopec Group further redeemed almost all remaining legal person shares. To compensate minority shareholders for the conversion, all A-share holders were given 2.8 newly tradable shares for every 10 shares they held. H-share holders, however, did not receive any compensation. Since 2001, the percentage of state-controlled shares owned by the parent company has actually increased substantially, in spite of the share compensation scheme: rising from 55.06 percent to 75.84 percent.[86] In the process, legal person shares have almost been eliminated, while minority shareholder ownership in Sinopec has increased only marginally.

The legal person share redemptions outweighed the state share dilution that occurred as an immediate consequence of non-tradable share reform. To date, the state's ownership control through Sinopec Group has been considerably enhanced rather than reduced. This gives the state stronger control of tremendous cash flows that can be used to finance government programs.

B Subsequent performance

Table 6.6 shows the earning and financial indicators of Sinopec between 2001 and 2006. As shown, Sinopec's net profit rate maintained a high level of around 4.6 percent in all six years. Business revenue, profits, and net return on assets

Table 6.6 Key financial indicators of Sinopec

	2001	*2002*	*2003*	*2004*	*2005*	*2006*
Primary Business Income (million RMB)	304,347	324,184	417,191	590,632	799,115	1,044,652
Net Profit (million RMB)	14,018	14,121	19,011	32,275	39,558	50,664
Net Profit Rate (%)	4.6	4.4	4.6	5.5	5.0	4.8
Net Return on Assets (%)	10.1	9.6	11.7	17.3	18.3	19.9
Earnings per Share (RMB)	0.162	0.163	0.219	0.372	0.46	0.58
Net Assets per Share (RMB)	1.604	1.690	1.879	2.149	2.58	3.05
P/E (times)	21.3	18.5	22.6	11.7	10.2	15.6
P/B (times)	2.15	1.78	2.63	2.03	1.87	3.10

Source: various Sinopec annual reports.

increased on a year-by-year basis, which indicates a trend of stable and sustainable development. Subsequently, investors in Sinopec in both domestic and overseas markets enjoyed substantial gains.

Compared with domestically listed companies, Sinopec is a market leader and is ranked first, not only in Fortune's Top 100 listed companies in China in 2009, but also in the "China Enterprise Competitiveness Report" issued by the Global Competitiveness Organization in 2008. From a worldwide perspective, the rank of Sinopec among Top Global 500 companies scaled by revenue, continues upwards: from 73rd position in 1999, to 9th in 2009 (Table 6.7). Its position in the petroleum refining industry is stable, and today Sinopec is Asia's biggest refiner of oil, supplying 80 percent of China's fuel.[87]

C Enhancement of governance efficiency

As a company dual-listed domestically and overseas, Sinopec is under much more stringent market supervision in comparison with domestically listed companies. It is regulated by a number of laws and regulators associated with the stock markets in which it is listed, such as the Sarbanes–Oxley Act (SOX) in the US, and the CO and the LR in Hong Kong. Its strict compliance with the laws, and mandatory supervision, leads to optimization in its decision-making processes and enhancement of its corporate governance.

This part focuses on two major governance areas: internal control and information disclosure.

INTERNAL CONTROL

After the enactment of the SOX in 2002, Sinopec established a team for internal control led by the Chairman, President, and CFO to promote the company's construction of an internal control system. Special organizations were set up within

Table 6.7 Sinopec's ranking in the Fortune Global 500

Year	*Global 500*	*Petroleum refining industry*	*Revenues (in US$ billion)*
1999	73	6	34.02
2000	58	5	41.88
2001	68	8	45.35
2002	86	8	40.39
2003	70	9	44.50
2004	54	9	55.06
2005	31	7	75.08
2006	23	7	98.79
2007	17	7	131.64
2008	16	7	159.26
2009	9	7	207.81

Source: Fortune Global 500 (2009).

headquarters and all subsidiaries, respectively responsible for implementation and management of internal control.

Meanwhile, Sinopec systemized all business and major events and finished the compilation of its "Internal Control Instruction."[88] The Instruction includes several parts; internal environment, risk evaluation, control activity, information and communication, internal supervision, and so forth.[89] Subsidiaries are requested to work out detailed implementation rules in accordance with different scenarios. Furthermore, the company updates itself in accordance with new supervision requests and operational and management demands to improve the internal control system. For instance, the 2009 Instruction consists of 18 categories; namely, procurement, budget, cost, marketing, investment, etc. It also contains 59 business procedures, covering all aspects of company management.[90]

INFORMATION DISCLOSURE

To improve the quality of information disclosure, Sinopec has established a communication mechanism to ensure qualified and standardized information collection and disclosure.[91] Specifically, information is collected in the following ways: the collection of the company's important legal texts; the preparation of periodic reports; the understanding of the company's operating mechanisms and conditions; and the establishment of financial operating information databases and an internal linear information dissemination network. Sinopec also set up a team for information disclosure, composed of directors from different departments, that decides on matters of major information disclosure.

In addition to abiding by rigorous information disclosure requirements set by different regulatory bodies in different countries, Sinopec also takes the initiative in disclosing required information in an honest and timely fashion, the aim being to help shareholders and other stakeholders make better decisions. For example, explanation meetings for analysts and the financial media are regularly held. In addition, Sinopec issues periodic reports to disclose public petrochemical industry information, environmental information, as well as the latest operational statistics. For its efforts in initiating information disclosure, Sinopec's financial reporting was awarded the "Best Annual Report in Asia" in 2002 and 2003, as well as "Best Annual Report and Other Corporate Literature" in 2005, and "Best Corporate Governance" in 2011.[92]

D Corruption

Unfortunately, the shadow of corruption at Sinopec has destroyed investors' confidence and cast doubt on the governance of this leading Chinese company. Its former Chairman, Chen Tonghai, was sentenced to death, albeit with a two-year reprieve. Chen had been a highest-level state enterprise leader, controlling the largest-scale companies; however, he also committed serious crimes involving the largest sums ever seen in recent years. He was involved in what is believed to be China's biggest ever bribery case.

Chen Tonghai had a close relationship with the government. He once worked as the mayor of Ningbo in Zhejiang province, and then as Deputy Commissioner of the State Planning Commission, before joining Sinopec in 1998. His father was Chen Weida, who held posts as Party Secretary of the Zhejiang Provincial Party Committee, and First Secretary of the Tianjin Municipal Party Committee. Chen Tonghai is well known within Sinopec as the "boss" and is inglorious for his opinion on expenditure. At a party meeting he once said: "We spend a million or two on entertainment every month, that's nothing, our company pays over RMB20 billion in taxes every year. If you don't know how to spend money, you won't know how to make money either."[93]

The investigation into Chen started in 2007, and he was expelled from the Party and the government and officially charged with corruption in January 2008. According to the verdict of Beijing No. 2 Intermediate People's Court, he took about RMB195.73 million in bribes from 1999 to June 2007, by taking advantage of his positions as Deputy General Manager and General Manager of the Sinopec Group, and Vice-Chairman and Chairman of Sinopec.[94] In return for bribes, he helped others seek illegal interests in the enterprise's operations, land transfers, and contracts.

"The handling of Chen's case sounded an alarm for the country's SOE leaders," the court said. It also said that state enterprise reforms should be accelerated to improve supervision of power and "unearth corruption from the roots."[95]

E Summary

As a huge SOE, the benefits of Sinopec's overseas listing are twofold. Not only can Sinopec gain extra capital, it can also learn from the monitoring systems of other prestigious markets such as Hong Kong and the US. Under their stringent market supervision and information disclosure systems, the market competitiveness of Sinopec has been enhanced by adaptation to different legal, regulatory, and market environments. In general, Sinopec has succeeded in improving its own corporate governance and financial performance after cross-listing.

However, even the leading Chinese company cannot escape from managerial corruption. The corruption of Chen mirrors a very serious and widespread phenomenon in Chinese SOEs. Corruption is mostly a consequence of SOE agency problems, reflected in the appointments system and the lack of supervision of power. For the former, the government normally selects its own representatives to operate SOEs and has the power to decide on the election and appointment of SOE managers. The switch from government official to SOE manager produces some basic problems with accountability, and has significantly shaped incentive structures. For the latter, in the view of Zhou and Wang, China lacks efficient monitoring so that there is a high risk of managers taking advantage of informational asymmetries.[96]

6.4.4 Industrial and Commercial Bank of China (ICBC)

ICBC (HK 01398) is the world's largest bank as measured by both market value and size of customer deposits.[97] It is one of China's "Big Four" state-owned commercial banks, alongside the Bank of China, the Agricultural Bank of China, and the China Construction Bank. At the end of 2011, ICBC had 408,859 employees, providing a wide range of financial products and services to 4.11 million corporate clients and 282 million individual customers through 16,648 outlets across China, 239 overseas subsidiaries, and a global network of more than 1,669 correspondent banks.

A Restructuring prior to listing

ICBC is an important example of how cross-listing in Hong Kong helped improve its internal structure. ICBC was the first company to offer and list shares concurrently on the HKSE (H-share) and the SHSE (A-share). In 2006 the CSRC and the China Banking Regulatory Commission gave written approval for the global offering and the application to list the company's shares on the HKSE. The proceeds were expected to be used to strengthen the capital base of the bank. The IPO of ICBC remained the largest in the world until 2010 when it was surpassed by that of the Agricultural Bank of China.[98]

The bank was converted from a state-owned commercial bank to a joint stock limited company on 28 October 2005. The legal name was changed from Industrial and Commercial Bank of China to Industrial and Commercial Bank of China Limited. All of the businesses, assets, and liabilities were assumed by the latter upon conversion.

As part of the financial restructuring in 2005 the Ministry of Finance (MoF) retained RMB124 billion of the bank's then existing capital; Huijin (an investment company owned by the government of China) made a capital contribution of US$15 billion to the bank; the bank disposed of certain non-performing assets to an aggregate amount of RMB705 billion at book value; the government contributed certain land use rights to the bank; and the MoF amended the terms of a special government bond issued by it to the bank.

B Ownership diversification

As an important step of the IPO, foreign strategic ownership was introduced into the bank. In exchange for a share in Chinese growth, foreign investors brought their experience, knowledge, and expertise. In 2006, Goldman Sachs, Allianz, and American Express subscribed for 16.48 billion, 6.43 billion, and 1.28 billion shares in ICBC respectively.[99] Together they were expected to hold around 7 percent of the equity interest in the bank after its listing.

The presence of strategic investors is hoped to result in a win-win outcome. From the Chinese perspective, banks can improve their capital base. They can diversify the risk associated with over-reliance on a single financial strategy that might turn out to be ill-suited to the task, or simply flawed. Meanwhile, it could lead to better performance, as the foreign investors will bring in their more advanced management, risk control techniques, and innovative products. For the purpose of protecting their own interests, strategic investors often enter into arrangements with the controlling shareholders to obtain certain rights such as board representation, information rights, rights against adversary charter amendments, and others. Simultaneously, the controlling shareholder can request that they provide strategic assistance in certain areas, including corporate governance. As a result, other minority shareholders get a free ride on the road towards improved and more transparent corporate governance.

While the need to introduce foreign capital and expertise into the state-owned banks is widely recognized, critics are querying whether the shares of these banks are being sold too cheaply in the process. As grounds for such "underselling" arguments, they refer to the fact that the price of state-owned bank shares sold to foreign investors are far below what they should be based on earnings. For instance, the ICBC's operating profit in 2004 amounted to RMB74.7 billion, which translated into some US$9 billion based on the foreign exchange rate at that time. At this profit level, a foreign financial institution acquiring a 10 percent stake in ICBC for US$3 billion would be able to recover the cost of its investment within four years. The rate of return would be even greater for foreign investors, considering an expected rise in the share price subsequent to the listing of ICBC.

C Inputs from foreign partners

An investment in ICBC by Goldman Sachs provides a good illustration. In conjunction with Goldman Sachs share purchase agreement, it obtained the right to nominate one director, as well as certain information rights, anti-dilution rights, and registration rights.[100] In addition, ICBC entered into a "strategic cooperation agreement" with Goldman Sachs and established "working procedures and processes," as well as "a joint steering committee" which is responsible for "the overall implementation of the strategic cooperation."[101] The President of ICBC and the Chairman of Goldman Sachs Asia co-chair the joint steering committee.

The strategic cooperation with Goldman Sachs aimed to leverage the respective strengths of Goldman Sachs and ICBC to enhance their businesses pursuant to the following guiding principles:[102]

- providing technical assistance, consultation and employee training to ICBC to help its continued development into a world class financial institution with long-term sustainable competitiveness and profitability;
- assisting ICBC in developing its corporate and management culture and improving its risk management system and corporate governance structure, and;
- assisting ICBC in developing non-lending products to further enhance its product and service offerings to customers, which also lays the foundation for the continuous development of attractive business opportunities.

The input from Goldman Sachs was meant to be comprehensive, with particular respect to corporate governance. It assisted ICBC in establishing measures that are consistent with international best practices. Such assistance consisted of consultation, training, and site visits regarding a variety of corporate governance issues, including ongoing disclosure and corporate governance obligations as a listed company.[103] In particular, the risk management of ICBC was strengthened through the listing. Goldman Sachs shared appropriate risk management tools and models with the bank and assisted it in developing its risk management systems and analytical models. In particular, ICBC separated the assessment, approval, and management functions in its credit risk management process.[104] The position of Chief Risk Officer was established to oversee risk management and make related decisions. Although the stake in the bank held by Goldman Sachs is not significant, its contribution towards enhancing the bank's governance and management is extensive. In theory, Goldman Sachs's involvement can be achieved without a listing in Hong Kong. In practice, Goldman Sachs might not have completed the deal in the absence of an exit strategy, which is essentially provided by the listing.

D Additional oversight

To prepare for the listing, and as a direct result of the listing, the bank has voluntarily subjected itself to comprehensive oversight. The original internal audit department was divided into separate departments, which consist of an internal control and compliance department that reports to the President, and an internal audit department that reports to the audit committee. As for external audits, ICBC was the first of the big four commercial banks to have an internationally recognized accounting firm audit of its domestic branches.[105] After its listing, China International Capital Corporation and Merrill Lynch Far East became the bank's joint Compliance Advisers in accordance with Rule 3A.19 of the Listing Rules. These two Compliance Advisers provide ICBC with services, including guidance and advice as to compliance with the requirements under the Listing Rules and other applicable laws, rules, codes, regulations, and guidelines.

E Summary

In fact, the acquisition of significant minority stakes by Western banks in three of China's big four banks in 2005 and 2006 was an important milestone. ICBC, Bank of China, and China Construction Bank each negotiated a private placement of shares with strategic foreign investors prior to offering their shares to the public and listing the companies on the HKSE. Several features can be found in these deals.[106] First, foreign investors were offered a minority stake that ruled out control. They were given an option to increase their stake to a maximum of 19.9 percent. Second, the foreign minority investors agreed to lock-up periods, typically three years unless otherwise agreed by the management and/or controlling shareholder: essentially the state. Finally, investors holding shares beyond a critical threshold were given the option of nominating directors to the bank's board.

In summary, the introduction of institutional investors has had two important functions. First, they have diversified the ownership structure of Chinese companies, although control is still largely retained by the state. Second, they have facilitated the process of organizational learning and management monitoring. Furthermore, similar to the requirements of independent non-executive directors, the introduction of foreign investors has laid the foundations for future legal/policy change.

6.4.5 BYD

A A snapshot of BYD

BYD (HK 01211) was established in Shenzhen, Guangdong province, in 1995 by Wang Chuanfu, a chemist and government researcher. Wang started BYD with a modest goal: to edge in on the Japanese-dominated battery business. "Importing batteries from Japan was very expensive," Wang said, "There were import duties, and delivery times were long."[107] In 2002 the company quickly became one of the world's largest manufacturers of cell phone batteries. On 31 July 2002, BYD was listed on the HKSE and set a record for the highest issue price among 54 H-shares.[108] In 2003 BYD officially entered the auto business by purchasing a bankrupt state-owned auto manufacturer, the Tsinchuan Automobile Company (now BYD Auto). The volume of sales was more than 193,000 units in 2008 despite the fact that most of its cars appear to have been imitations of Japanese vehicles.[109]

B Post-listing performance

The growth of BYD in revenue and net profit was dramatic during the period 2003–08. Revenue increased by US$3.5 billion;, in other words they jumped from US$0.5 billion in 2003 to approximately US$4 billion five years later.[110] Accordingly, net profit climbed at record pace, reaching US$230 million in 2007.[111]

2008 was a year of extreme global turbulence. According to the company's half yearly financial reports in 2008, BYD's profit was down 7 percent on the same period in the previous year due to rising material costs and declining cell phone sales.[112] But BYD continued to maintain its global leading position in rechargeable batteries with a year-on-year increase of 26 percent on turnover.[113]

C Strategic investment by Warren Buffett

BYD's breakthrough growth attracted Buffett's attention. Warren Buffet demonstrated a vote of confidence in BYD's commercialization of next-generation, environment-friendly electric vehicles and battery technology in general. The

American tycoon proposed to invest US$230 million to acquire a 10 percent stake of BYD in September 2008.[114] This would be Buffett's second China-based investment, after PetroChina.[115] This transaction took place via MidAmerican Energy Holdings, a subsidiary of Buffett's Berkshire Hathaway. It was hoped that the move would provide MidAmerican with a foothold in China's rechargeable battery market.

According to the agreement, MidAmerican Energy agreed to subscribe for 225 million H-shares of BYD at a price of HK$8 per share. MidAmerican had the right to nominate a non-executive director to the board, and proposed David Sokol, MidAmerican Chairman, for the role.

The benefits of the foreign investment were multiple. The subscription strengthened the financial position of BYD. Additionally, the introduction of a world renowned and substantial business conglomerate with extensive and diversified business experience as a strategic investor was believed to be advantageous to the BYD's future development. Furthermore, the entry of MidAmerican would facilitate BYD's strategy to extend its reach to the global market in respect of its rechargeable batteries, electric vehicles, and other environmentally friendly products.

D Improvements to corporate governance

BYD developed from a small private company into a leading international battery company, with worldwide branches and 130,000 employees. After listing on the HKSE in 2002, it set up a board of directors, including two executive directors, one non-executive director, and two independent non-executive directors under Hong Kong law.[116] They are responsible for formulating the strategic business direction of the company and overseeing its performance. BYD has adopted the Model Code for Securities Transactions by Directors of Listed Issuers, contained in Appendix 10 of the Hong Kong LR, as the company's code of conduct regarding securities transactions by its directors.[117] All directors complied with their obligations under the Model Code. Specified employees who are likely to be in possession of unpublished price-sensitive information about the company are also subject to this Model Code.

In furtherance of good governance, BYD has set up several committees: the audit committee, the remuneration committee, the nomination committee, and the strategy committee. Each committee reports regularly to the board of directors, addressing major issues and drawing up recommendations for the decision of the board.[118]

In particular, the audit committee plays a key role in the management of risk and is responsible for the company's internal control and for reviewing its effectiveness. With the development of the company, the audit committee has established various internal audit standard documents, including "Regulations on Internal Audit of the Company" and "Internal Control Standard of the Company," creating and implementing a standardized auditing practice flow for risk evaluation.[119]

Furthermore, BYD hires independent international auditors, such as Ernst & Young, for review and audit of its financial statements. This also ensures company information is reported in a fair and relatively reliable manner.

E Summary

The ability of BYD to catch up with many of its competitors, both in the battery industry and in the emerging electric car industry, has important implications for Chinese cross-listings. BYD's breakthrough perhaps comes from its effective corporate governance system and strategic investment by foreign investors. For the former, good corporate governance is an essential element in enhancing the confidence of shareholders, investors, and the community as a whole. In the case of BYD this is reflected by the introduction of independent directors, the clarification of directors' duties, the establishment of different committees, and the recruitment of international and independent auditors. For the latter, an increase in foreign ownership could help to lessen political control and mitigate agency problems in the company. In addition, strategic investment could increase BYD's reputation and facilitate its strategy of extending its reach into the global market.

6.5 Concluding remarks

Most if not all empirical results from previous studies have been based on the existence of bonding premiums in the form of company valuation and corporate governance. The examination of Chinese H-share companies in this chapter provides a non-trivial, alternative, qualitative-based test for the bonding argument, and observes that Chinese cross-listings in Hong Kong encounter potential problems and challenges, as well as benefits. This book, using general empirical evidence and specific case studies, therefore contributes to the bonding and cross-listing literature in important ways.

The benefit derived from raising funds in Hong Kong may be obvious. The general empirical evidence discussed above shows that companies can benefit from cross-listing, but that there are also risks. Among the various bonding mechanisms, the most effective to date have been diversification of the ownership structure and higher disclosure standards. The introduction of strategic investors enables cooperation and inter-organizational learning, but without transfer of control. Furthermore, companies can piggy-back better practices to improve their corporate governance, including adopting the stricter IFRS, hiring prestigious international auditors, and appointing independent directors.

On the other hand, many factors can serve to counteract the bonding effect of cross-listing: political restraints, agency problems and corporate fraud, difficulties in cross-border enforcement, and the inactive role of the HKSE. At the heart of these problems is the conflict of interest between controlling shareholders and managers. State ownership allows for a more direct form of monitoring of management, and minority investors are correspondingly less well protected.

Specific case studies are consistent with general empirical evidence. In the cases of Tsingtao and BYD, they succeeded in improving financial performance and corporate governance after listing on the HKSE. Nonetheless, state ownership and political influence are barriers that hinder improvement of corporate governance in Chinese companies. The negative effects of these factors are seen in two major ways. Government tends to change its role from "helping hand" to "grabbing hand" once companies go public, as illustrated by the Kelon case. With concentrated ownership comes a high probability of corporate fraud, expropriation of funds by the state, corruption, and false financial statements, as demonstrated by the cases of Kelon and Sinopec. ICBC looks like a very successful case; unlike Sinopec, no major scandals have emerged. One explanation may be that its listing on the HKSE is still relatively recent. Another possible reason could be that the corporate governance systems of financial institutions are generally more demanding.

Case studies also reveal that the commercial interests of the HKSE has led to an emphasis on profit, which has been detrimental to its duty to ensure the quality of issuers and safeguarding the interests of investors. In the collapse of Kelon and the scandal of Sinopec, the companies involved did not fulfill their disclosure obligation under Hong Kong law. But neither the HKSE nor the SFC commenced investigations until those companies were on the verge of collapse.

Overall, cross-listing is not a guaranteed way to succeed. Some companies achieved massive improvements in terms of corporate governance and prestige, characterizing themselves as successful examples of Chinese listed companies. By contrast, some failed, leaving behind many disgruntled investors who had little chance of recovering losses. To alleviate the potential problems caused by cross-listing, one of the possible remedies is for China to develop its own strong capital market based on a complex network of legal institutions. This is also the ultimate goal of Chinese cross-listing. How does cross-listing help China to achieve this goal by learning from Hong Kong? This issue is to be addressed in the next two chapters.

Notes

1 Doidge, Craig *et al.* (2004), "Why are Foreign Firms Listed in the US Worth More?" in *Journal of Financial Economics*, 71.

2 For supporting evidence in relation to Korea, see Dewenter, Kathryn *et al.* (2005), "Committing to Protect Investors in Emerging Markets: Can Local Exchange Provide Value-relevant Bonding Mechanisms?" University of Washington, Seattle, Working Paper. Online. Available at: http://ssrn.com/abstract=756866. For the Brazilian experience, see Pennacchi, George (2005), "Can Voluntary Market Reforms Promote Efficient Corporate Governance? Evidence from Firms' Migration to Premium Markets in Brazil." Working Paper. Online. Available at: http://ssrn.com/abstract=678282. For the Chinese experience see Sun, Qian *et al.* (2006), "Bonding Premium as a General Phenomenon." CUHK Working Paper. Online. Available at: http://ssrn.com/abstract=890962 (all accessed 20 December 2012).

3 For a list of H-share companies on the Main Board, see China Dimension of HKSE. Online. Available at: www.hkex.com.hk/eng/stat/smstat/chidimen/chidimen.htm (accessed 20 December 2012).
4 Su, Zhong (2007), "How Bourses Bring Democracy to China" in *Asia Times* (17 October 2007). Online. Available at: www.atimes.com/atimes/China/IJ17Ad01.html (accessed 20 December 2012).
5 SFC (2003), "IPO Activities in Hong Kong." Online. Available at: www.sfc.hk/web/EN/published-resources/research-papers/market-reviews (accessed 20 December 2012).
6 SFC (2007), "An Overview of the Major Events and Regulation of the Securities and Futures Markets between 1997 and 2007." Online. Available at: www.sfc.hk/web/EN/published-resources/research-papers/market-reviews (accessed 20 December 2012).
7 Ibid.
8 Huang, Flora and Yeung, Horace (2012), "Law and Finance: What Matters? Hong Kong as a Test Case" in *Asian Journal of Law and Economics*, 3.
9 Poon, Winnie and Chan, Kam (2008), "An Empirical Examination of the Informational Content of Credit Ratings in China" in *Journal of Business Research*, 61. Also see Tobin, Damian and Sun, Laixiang (2009), "International Listing as a Means to Mobilize the Benefits of Financial Globalization: Micro-level Evidence from China" in *World Development*, 37, p. 833.
10 As seen in Tobin and Sun, op. cit.
11 Huang, Guihai and Song, Frank (2005), "The Financial and Operating Performance of China's Newly Listed H-firms" in *Pacific-Basin Finance Journal*, 13.
12 Jia, Jin *et al.* (2005), "Privatization through an Overseas Listing: Evidence from China's H-share Firms" in *Financial Management*, 34.
13 Ibid.
14 On one occasion, when the former chairman of the CSRC, Zhou Daojong, talked with the CEOs of foreign listed SOEs, he said that:

> Overseas-listed companies are all outstanding enterprises that are representatives of their respective industries to an extent. I hope you can also be the models of listed companies. The behavior of an overseas-listed company is not only the company's own business, it relates to our country's image of reform and openness.... I hope you can solidly turn all your companies into world-class enterprises, bringing honor to the country.
>
> (26 May 1995, CSRC web news)

15 China joined the WTO at the end of 2001. The agreement entered into between China and the US preceding China's accession remains a good general guide to the obligations China assumed with its WTO partners. Regarding financial service, the Sino-US agreement provides that China will expand the scope and geographic opportunities for foreign banks to conduct local currency business.
16 Coffee, John (2001), "The Acquiescent Gatekeeper: Reputational Intermediaries, Auditor Independence and the Governance of Accounting." Columbia Law and Economics Working Paper No. 191, p. 2. Online. Available at: http://ssrn.com/abstract=270944 (accessed 20 December 2012).
17 For a comparison of Chinese and international accounting standards, see, e.g., Chen, Charles *et al.* (1999), "A Comparison of Reported Earnings under Chinese GAAP vs IAS: Evidence from the Shanghai Stock Exchange" in *Accounting Horizons*, 13; and Liu, Jianwei and Liu, Chunjiao (2007), "Value Relevance of Accounting Information in Different Stock Market Segments: The Case of Chinese A, B and H-shares" in *Journal of International Accounting Research*, 6.
18 Deloitte (2005), "Implementing Hong Kong Financial Reporting Standards: The Challenge for 2005." Online. Available at: ww.deloitte.com/view/en_CN/cn (accessed 10 December 2009).

19 Zhang, Yimin and Zhao, Ronald (2004), "The Valuation Differential between Class A and B Shares: Country Risk in the Chinese Stock Market" in *Journal of International Financial Management & Accounting*, 15, p. 45.

20 For a general discussion about Chinese intermediaries, see MacNeil, Iain (2002), "Adaptation and Convergence in Corporate Governance: The Case of Chinese Listed Companies" in *Journal of Corporate Law Studies*, 2, p. 321.

21 According to Article 6 of the Chinese Securities Law 2005, regulation of China's financial industry is subject to a model of separated regulation, placing securities, banking, and insurance industries under separate supervision and administration of, respectively, CSRC, the China Banking Regulatory Commission (CBRC) and the China Insurance Regulatory Commission (CIRC).

22 The Big Four now include Deloitte, Ernst & Young, KPMG, and Pricewaterhouse-Coopers.

23 Cai, Hua (2007), "Bonding, Law Enforcement and Corporate Governance in China" in *Stanford Journal of Law, Business & Finance*, 13, p. 94.

24 Liu, Feng and Zhou, Fuyuan (2006), "Guoji Wuda Yiweizhe Gao Shenji Zhiliang ma? – Lai zi Woguo A Gu Shichang de Chubu Zhengju" [Does the Big Five Mean Higher Auditing Quality: Preliminary Evidence from China's A Share Market], Asia and China Corporate Governance International Conference Group Working Paper.

25 The *Opinion*, s. 1 (3).

26 Yang, Hua (2005), "Overview of Governance of State-owned Listed Companies in China." OECD Proceedings of the Second Policy Dialogue on Corporate Governance in China, Beijing, 19 May 2005.

27 For comments on this provision, see *China Securities Daily* (28 July 2005), "Zhongguo Dudong Diaocha ji Zhidu Fansi" [Survey on China's Independent Directors and Reflections on the Institutions].

28 The evidence on the effectiveness of independent directors is mixed. Some find no positive linkage between this system and firm performance. For example, Brudney, Victor (1982), "The Independent Director – Heavenly City or Potemkin Village?" in *Harvard Law Review*, 95; Bhagat, Sanjai and Black, Bernard (2001), "The Non-Correlation between Board Independence and Long-term Firm Performance" in *Journal of Corporate Law*, 27.

29 Shanghai Director Committee of Listed Companies (2003), "Xianzhuang Diaocha: Duli Dongshi Zenmeyang le?" [A Survey of the Current Situation: What Happens to Independent Directors?] *China Securities Times* (7 August 2003).

30 Li, Weian *et al.* (2004), "Nankai Pandian Sannian Dudong Zhidu de Gongsi Zhili Jiazhi" [A Review of 3-year Independent Director System on Corporate Governance by Nankai] in *Zhongwai Guanli* [Sino-Foreign Management], 9.

31 Clarke, Donald (2006), "The Independent Director in Chinese Corporate Governance" in *Delaware Journal of Corporate Law*, 31, pp. 176–80. Clarke argues that independent directors in China cannot serve the purpose of improving corporate governance in China.

32 Shanghai Stock Exchange (2006), *Corporate Governance Report 2006*, Shanghai: Fudan University Press, p. 28.

33 Green, Stephen and Liu, Guy (2005), "China's Industrial Reform Strategy: Retreat and Retain" in Green, Stephen and Liu, Guy (eds.), *Exit the Dragon? Privatization and State Control in China*, Oxford: Blackwell, p. 30.

34 Ibid.

35 In October 2009, Central Huijin owned 35.42 percent, 67.53 percent, 57.09 percent and half of the stakes in ICBC, Bank of China, China Construction Bank, and Agricultural Bank of China respectively. The Ministry of Finance is another majority shareholder in ICBC, holding 35 percent of shares. For recent ownership statistics, visit the SINA Finance website. Online. Available at: http://finance.sina.com.cn (accessed 20 December 2012).

36 In October 2009, 75.84 percent of Sinopec was owned by the China Petrochemical Corporation, and 86.42 percent of PetroChina was owned by the China National Petroleum Corporation. Both companies are currently dual-listed in Shanghai and Hong Kong.
37 *China Securities Daily* (28 August 2008), "30 Percent of Shares in the Largest 30 Companies are Tradable."
38 Ibid.
39 See a comparison between former Soviet countries and China in Cao, Lan (2000), "Chinese Privatization: Between Plan and Market" in *Law and Contemporary Problems*, 63.
40 For general discussions, see for example, Zhang, Mo (2008), "From Public to Private: The Newly Enacted Chinese Property Law and the Protection of Property Rights in China" in *Berkeley Business Law Journal*, 5.
41 Green, Stephen (2003), *China's Stockmarket: A Guide to its Progress, Players and Prospects*, London: Economist, p. 161.
42 *The Circular on the Issues Concerning the Companies Applying for Overseas Listings* was promulgated by the CSRC on 17 July 1999.
43 Ibid., Art. 1.
44 Wang, Jiangyu (2009), "Regulatory Competition and Cooperation between Securities Markets in Hong Kong and Mainland China" in *Capital Markets Law Journal*, 4, p. 398.
45 Ferguson, Michael *et al.* (2002), "Voluntary Disclosure by State-owned Enterprises Listed on the Stock Exchange of Hong Kong" in *Journal of International Financial Management and Accounting*, 12, p. 142.
46 Ibid., p. 147.
47 Qiao, Xiaohui and Song, Yanhua (2009), "IPO Zairu Xiangjiang" [IPO again Entering Hong Kong], *Caijing Magazine* (30 March 2009), issue 7. Online. Available at: http://magazine.caijing.com.cn/2009–03–29/110129650.html (accessed 20 December 2012).
48 Wang, op. cit., p. 399.
49 Bai, Chongen *et al.* (2005), "Zhongguo Shangshi Gongshi Zhili Jieguo de Shizheng Yanjiu" [An Empirical Study on Corporate Governance of Chinese Listed Companies] in *Jingji Yanjiu* [Economic Research], 2.
50 For example, Chen, Guanting (2006), "Positive Research on the Financial Statement Fraud Factors of Listed Companies in China" in *Journal of Modern Accounting and Auditing*, 2; and Zhang, Yi (2006), "Law, Corporate Governance, Corporate Scandal in an Emerging Economy: Insights from China." Online. Available at: http://ssrn.com/abstract=957549 (accessed 20 December 2012).
51 Tomasic, Roman (1994), "Company Law and the Limits of the Rule of Law in China." Discussion Paper, Asia-Pacific Economic Law Forum.
52 Muchlinski, Peter (2007), *Multinational Enterprises and the Law*, 2nd edn, Oxford: Oxford University Press, p. 129.
53 SFC (2 April 2007), "Press Release: Cross Border Enforcement Enhanced." Online. Available at: www.sfc.hk/sfcPressRelease/EN/sfcOpenDocServlet?docno=07PR52 (accessed 20 December 2012).
54 See, e.g., "Regulators Broaden Ties" in *Wall Street Journal* editorial comment (4 April 2007), which quotes a comment from David Webb.
55 Avgouleas, Emilios (2005), *The Mechanics and Regulation of Market Abuse: A Legal and Economic Analysis*, Oxford: Oxford University Press, p. 28.
56 The issue caused a positive market response and was oversubscribed 110.5 times. See Tsingtao Brewery, "Annual Report 1993," p. 4.
57 Tsingtao Brewery (29 June 1993), "H-share Listing Prospectus," p. 15.
58 The tradable A-shares were issued at an issue price of RMB6.38 per share, and the issue raised approximately RMB638,000,000. See Tsingtao Brewery, "Annual Report 1994," p. 4.

59 Tsingtao Brewery, "H-share Listing Prospectus 1993" and "Annual Report 1995," p. 22.
60 Lin, Jun and Wang, Liyan (2001), "Financial Disclosure and Accounting Harmonization: Cases of Three Listed Companies in China" in *Managerial Auditing Journal*, 16, p. 268.
61 See Tsingtao Brewery, "Annual Report 1996," p. 33; and "Annual Report 2001," pp. 39–42.
62 Tsingtao (2 April 2003), "Announcement."
63 Tsingtao, "Annual Report 1999," p. 27. These meetings were the Extraordinary Shareholders' Meeting, a PRC Shareholders' Extraordinary Meeting, and a Foreign Shareholders' Meeting.
64 De Jonge, Alice (2008), *Corporate Governance and China's H-share Market*, Cheltenham: Edward Elgar, p. 146.
65 Tsingtao Brewery (2002), "Annual Report 2001," p. 21.
66 Total shares of Tsingtao included 399,820,000 state-owned shares held by Qingdao State-owned Assets Administration Office; 200,000,000 tradable shares domestically listed; 53,330,000 A-shares held by legal persons; and 655,069,178 listed overseas. See Tsingtao Brewery, "Annual Report 2005," p. 17.
67 Ibid.
68 Huang, Yasheng and Lane, David (2001), "Kelon: China's Corporate Dragon." Harvard Business School Case Study, No. 702–039.
69 Liu, Guy and Sun, Pei (2006), "The Rise and Fall of China's Corporate Dragon: Kelon and its Old and New Owners" in Mallin, Christine (ed.), *International Corporate Governance: A Case Study Approach*, Cheltenham: Edward Elgar, p. 220.
70 In the 1980s China operated a strict license system. Normally, only SOEs could be granted a manufacturing license.
71 Watanabe, Mariko (2002), "Holding Company Risk in China: A Final Step of State-owned Enterprises Reform and an Emerging Problem of Corporate Governance" in *China Economic Review*, 13, p. 377.
72 Greencool was founded in October 2001, so it was obvious that it was formed for ease of the planned acquisition. "Gu Cuojun" is a Cantonese spelling (in Hong Kong) while "Gu Chujun" is a Mandarin spelling (in China). Kelon was an H-share company, so "Gu Cuojun" was used in its annual reports in Hong Kong. This book is consistent with the annual report and therefore adopts Gu's Cantonese name.
73 Kelon (9 May 2005), "Clarification and Unusual Price and Volume Movement."
74 Kelon (4 July 2006), "Announcement in relation to Administrative Sanctions Imposed by the CSRC."
75 Ibid.
76 HKSE (29 March 2005), "Censures of Directors of Kelon."
77 For further details, see Kelon (9 January 2009), "Announcement on Development of Significant Litigation."
78 Ibid.
79 Liu and Sun, op. cit., pp. 222–8.
80 Ibid., p. 241.
81 Ibid., p. 233.
82 La Porta, Rafael *et al.* (2000), "Investor Protection and Corporate Governance" in *Journal of Financial Economics*, 58.
83 Hisense had earlier offered to acquire the stake with RMB900 million in cash, but later decided to reduce the price because auditing firms had found Kelon's assets to be much lower than that amount.
84 Sinopec website. Online. Available at: http://english.sinopec.com/about_sinopec/our_company/6as7tuvr.shtml (accessed 20 December 2012).
85 Mattlin, Mikael (2007), "The Chinese Government's New Approach to Ownership

and Financial Control of Strategic State-owned Enterprises." Bank of Finland, Institute for Economies in Transition, Discussion Paper.

86 Ibid.

87 For more details, see Fortune Global 500 (2009). Online. Available at: http://money.cnn.com/magazines/fortune/global500/2009/snapshots/10694.html (accessed 20 December 2012).

88 After compilation and testing in 2003, and trial implementation in 2004, the board of directors approved the Instruction at the end of 2004. 1 January 2005 marked comprehensive implementation of an internal control system in Sinopec.

89 For details, see Sinopec website. Online. Available at: http://english.sinopec.com/investor_center/corporate_governance/internal_control/ (accessed 20 December 2012).

90 Ibid.

91 Ma, Lianfu *et al.* (2008), "Overseas Listing, Voluntary Corporate Governance and Performance – A Case Study of Sinopec" in *Frontiers of Business Research in China*, 2, pp. 450–1.

92 For more awards, see Sinopec website. Online. Available at: http://english.sinopec.com/investor_center/corporate_governance/awards (accessed 20 December 2012).

93 Zhang, Peiyuan (2009), "Guanchang he Guoqi Haiyou Duoshao Chen Tonghai bei Yangzhe?" [How Many Chen Tonghai Fed by Government and SOEs?] in *Xinhua News* (13 August 2009).

94 *Xinhua News* (15 July 2009), "China Focus: Sinopec Ex-chairman Gets Death Sentence with reprieve after Reporting Others' Crimes."

95 Ibid.

96 Zhou, Mi and Wang, Xiaoming (2000), "Agency Cost and the Crisis of China's SOE" in *China Economic Review*, 11, p. 300.

97 See the website of ICBC. Online. Available at: www.icbc.com.cn/ICBC/About%20Us/Brief%20Introduction (accessed 20 December 2012).

98 PricewaterhouseCoopers (2009), "Greater China IPO Watch 2008," p. 11.

99 ICBC (2006), "Prospectus for Global Offering," p. 10.

100 Ibid., pp. 90–1.

101 Ibid.

102 Ibid., p. 91.

103 Ibid., p. 92.

104 Ibid., p. 87.

105 In 2002 Ernst & Young performed independent audits on the Shanghai and Zhejiang branches.

106 Pistor, Katharina (2009), "Banking Reform in the Chinese Mirror." Columbia Law and Economics Working Paper No. 354. Online. Available at: http://ssrn.com/abstract=1446930 (accessed 20 December 2012).

107 For a full interview with Wang Chuanfu, see Gunther, Marc, "Warren Buffett Takes Charge" in *Fortune* (13 April 2009).

108 For company profile and history, see BYD website. Online. Available at: www.byd.com/ (accessed 20 December 2012).

109 Wang, Hua (2009), "Betting on Chinese Electronic Cars? – Analyzing BYD's Innovation Capability." Conference Paper at 17th Gerpisa International Colloquium, Paris.

110 Gunther, op. cit.

111 Ibid.

112 BYD, "Annual Report 2008," p. 5.

113 Ibid.

114 BYD (19 September 2008), "Strategic Investment by MidAmerican Energy Holdings Company by way of Subscription of New H Shares and Resumption of Trading."

115 PetroChina (HK 0857) is the largest domestic oil company listed on the Hong Kong market. Buffet invested HK$1 billion in 2003 (US$128 million) for a shareholding of 6.7 percent.
116 BYD (22 July 2002), "Prospectus," pp. 102–4.
117 BYD, "Annual Report 2008," p. 24.
118 For their function and duties, see ibid., pp. 21–2.
119 Ibid., p. 23.

7 Market and legal development explanation

China's legal and regulatory reform

The general empirical evidence and the case studies presented in Chapter 6 suggest that cross-listing affects Chinese companies' governance and financial performance in a generally favorable manner, although some companies fail after listing. This chapter moves forward from the firm level to the market level. Cross-listing may affect not only cross-listed companies but, less directly, the laws and market institutions of their home country. As a result, it may lead to the convergence of the host market and the home market.

Numerous studies in the literature have been devoted to the investigation of common trends among stock markets. So far most of the studies have focused on developed markets. They find considerable evidence that supports the presence of long-term co-movements among equity markets.[1] With the trend towards internationalization of equity markets, the role of emerging equity markets becomes more important in the global capital market. Studies like those of Garrett and Spyrou extend the investigation to emerging markets, including those in the Latin American and Asia-Pacific regions.[2] However, few have included China in their studies, despite its growing importance in the world. One contribution of the remaining body of this book is to bridge the gap in the literature by giving cross-listing a market and legal system-level explanation, and seeing whether there exists any integration between the Chinese and Hong Kong stock markets.

Various factors may oblige Chinese legislatures to battle with international exchanges by enacting reform legislation. However, this race is doomed to be difficult as regards Hong Kong due to the existing regulatory gap between the Chinese and Hong Kong markets. However, when the Chinese markets deepen, the regulatory gap will be inevitably reduced along with minimizing bonding premiums. Consequently, cross-listing will become less attractive to companies. In spite of this, Hong Kong, because of its long historic roots in finance, may still have some core competencies to offer.

In light of the above, the next two chapters examine the role of cross-listing in Chinese legal and regulatory reform and in the integration of the Chinese and Hong Kong stock markets. Chapter 7 explores the extent to which China has improved its legal infrastructure and market institutions when facing fierce competition from other markets. Chapter 8 discusses the contributions of dual-listing and regulatory cooperation to such integration.

This chapter proceeds as follows. Section 7.1 explores the forces driving Chinese legal and regulatory reform. Sections 7.2 to 7.4 analyze Chinese company and securities law reform, issuance system reform, and non-tradable share reform, respectively. In addition, an assessment is provided for each reform. Section 7.5 contains a conclusion to this chapter.

7.1 Cross-listing driving China's legal and regulatory reform

7.1.1 Regulatory experimentation in Hong Kong: mandatory provisions

Regulatory dualism has been adopted in a few jurisdictions as a strategy to diffuse the tension between future growth and the pre-existing distribution of wealth and power.[3] By having two sets of company law at the same time, one for domestic companies and one for cross-listed companies, it is fair to say that this strategy has also been adopted by China. Yet the political motivation may be different. Unlike Brazil, where the current business elite may be the major force to oppose new reform, the Chinese state has been able to dictate the operation and regulation of the market throughout. Rather, regulatory experimentation may be a more sensible explanation. Chinese leaders have been skeptical of introducing the idea of market economy into their socialist state. With the goal of establishing a socialist market economy in mind, they have been unsure about how to proceed. Deng Xiaoping's famous phrase "crossing the river by feeling each stone" illustrates his prudence and sense of insecurity about economic reform.

The similarities between the *1994 Mandatory Provisions* and the new Company Law mean that lawmakers have drawn on the experience of cross-listed Chinese companies to formulate the new law. Table 7.1 summarizes the selected features of the old Company Law, the *Mandatory Provisions* and the new Company Law.[4]

From the table it can be seen that cross-listing Chinese companies might have helped the convergence of company law towards international practices, via regulatory dualism and subsequent harmonization. The Chinese state has used the *Mandatory Provisions* and cross-listed companies to advance company law. It is worth pointing out once again that both the first Company Law in China and the *Mandatory Provisions* came about at around the same time. The lawmakers had clearly contemplated the existence of international practices when drafting the first Company Law, but hesitated to incorporate them into it somehow.

Although cross-listing of Chinese companies in Hong Kong has played an important role by providing an experiment opportunity, other converging forces shaping the legal structures of China actually exist. First, regulatory competition from other jurisdictions, catalyzed by the possibility of multiple listings, might have helped. Second, the Chinese state might have been reluctant to accept wholesale foreign legal transplants. These could have complicated the considerations of lawmakers and the form and result of various reforms, and thereby the transition of China into a socialist market economy.

Table 7.1 Selected features of the three laws

Description	*Old company law*	*Mandatory provisions*	*New company law*
Fiduciary duty of directors, supervisors, and senior personnel	Duty of loyalty only	Duties of loyalty and care	Duties of loyalty and care
Fiduciary duty of controlling shareholders	N/A	Controlling shareholders (30% or more) must show good faith in exercising their rights	Controlling shareholders (50% or more) must show good faith in exercising their rights
Exit strategy	N/A	During a merger or split of company	1. fail to distribute profits; 2. merger or split of company; 3. renewal of operation term or dissolution
Information rights	Basic passive information right	Enhanced passive information right	Enhanced information right plus right of making inquiries
Private placement of shares	Not allowed	Allowed	Allowed
Pre-emptive rights	N/A	N/A (but provided by Hong Kong Listing Rules and recognized by the *Mandatory Provisions*)	Yes
Shareholder action	No mention of civil remedies	Disputes resolved through Chinese courts or arbitration	Derivative actions permitted and in some cases direct actions

7.1.2 Regulatory competition: a desire to nurture domestic markets

China has launched a wave of economic legislation in order to further its economic reform and to build up its legal system. It is a major part of China's current legal reform towards the rule of law.[5] Forces produced by economic development and the surge of cross-border activities help to impel Chinese law and regulatory reform.[6]

The internal impetus to this reform is the need for laws and regulations for the development of the market economy. It is understandable that, during the early period of economic reform before the 1990s, China enacted legislation mainly in the economic field so as to facilitate economic development and foreign trade. Areas covered included laws on foreign investment, foreign trade, banking, contract, and taxation. Since the 1990s, with the further development of China's economic reform and its increased international involvement, particularly after it endorsed the concept of market economy, legislation has been expanded to cover new areas in the economic field, including company law, securities, insurance, and intellectual property.

The external dynamic driving force consists of cross-border events, in particular cross-listing. However, existing empirical literature mostly concerns firm level evidence of the bonding phenomenon. The task of uncovering the way in which cross-listing might influence the home market's legal and institutional structure has rarely been explored. This is worth considering for three reasons.

First, listed companies may demand changes in local legal and market institutions, which will make these rules mesh better with those of the host jurisdictions.

Second, local securities, and legal and accounting professionals, may have an interest in promoting changes in local law to help maintain local trading. These groups' efforts may cause home country governance to converge with that of the host country. Whether they will succeed, however, is unclear. A move to laws in favor of dispersed ownership might be contrary to the interests of local banks and controlling shareholders, so they may have enough influence to block significant changes.[7]

Third, and more importantly, exchange motivation and issuer choice force regulatory regimes into competition. Stock exchanges are affiliated with marketplaces, have an interest in making higher profits, and often compete with one another to attract and retain listings. In addition, issuers can choose a regulatory regime from a menu of available options, which also increases regulatory competition. Arguably, in the Chinese context, this latter factor does not play a significant role since the choice of where to list is largely made by the Chinese government rather than by companies.

As a result, regulatory competition might lead to convergence in regulatory systems since companies wish to exploit global markets, and international shareholders require standard safeguards to protect them. From the viewpoint of countries and markets, they have an incentive to develop local securities laws in order to keep trading and its related revenue at home. They may therefore be forced to change their laws so that they can foster a market/corporate-friendly regime, or a strong investor protection regime, or even a mixture of both.

An example of a form of regulatory competition is legislative reform. One of the developments in China's legal framework was the promulgation by the CSRC of the Corporate Governance Code for Listed Companies ("the Code") in 2002.[8] The Code is mandatory for all listed companies and has been melded into the listing rules of the two stock exchanges. It stipulates the rights and responsibilities of shareholders, directors, management, and stakeholders. Disclosure of corporate governance practices is required in the annual report, along with disclosure of information on the controlling shareholder or the actual controller of the company.[9] This, to a certain extent, can reflect the Chinese adoption of a Western model of corporate governance.[10] For example, Article 31 of the Code introduces cumulative voting to elect directors. The Code also requires a listed company to establish a system of independent directors.[11]

More recently, amendments to the Company Law and the Securities Law strengthen the characteristic of adapting Western law into local conditions. Both amended laws seek to improve corporate governance in terms of board structure and shareholder rights.

In addition to legal reforms, regulatory changes are under way, including issuance system reform and non-tradable share reform. For the former, an ex ante review and approval system replaced the administrative quota system for public offering of shares. For the latter, the government promises to release many state-owned shares for general trading and make the market more accessible to foreign and domestic investors. This may be an example of an intention on the part of the Chinese to move towards Anglo-American dispersed ownership. Reduction of state-owned shares in the A-share market not only helps to eliminate legacy problems,[12] but also aims at improving resource allocation efficiency in China's capital markets, while narrowing the gap with international markets in terms of pricing and valuation of shares.

7.2 Chinese company and securities law reform

This section deals with the distinctive features of Chinese legal reform, then looks at legal transplants in Chinese corporate and securities law, and finally evaluates such reform.

7.2.1 Main characteristics of China's legal reform

A Legal transplants and selective adaptation

The idea of legal transplants broadly refers to the borrowing and transferring of laws and legal institutions between legal systems. No legal system is isolated. The Chinese legal system is no exception. Chinese legal reform reveals tensions between the Chinese government's effort to borrow legal norms and institutions from abroad and the need to protect local policy imperatives.[13] The process of borrowing involves a dynamic of selective adaptation by which foreign legal systems and practices are mediated by local norms. Selective adaptation is made possible by ways in which governments, elites, and other interpretive communities express their own preferences in the course of interpretation and application of practice rules.

Selective adaptation offers an insight into the processes by which China has attempted to join the international political economy on its own terms. A number of laws drafted by the National People's Congress (NPC) and its Standing Committee are the result of wide consultation with regard to the conventional practices and the laws of a particular foreign country. It has become an official attitude that China may, in developing its socialist market economy, boldly learn and adapt the legislative experience of economically advanced Western countries, and certain appropriate provisions may even be directly transplanted into Chinese legislation.[14]

The drafting of the 1993 Company Law was an example of combining China's own concepts and practices with those of Western countries. Various parts of the 1993 Company Law were specially designed for China, such as provisions with respect to SOEs and the functions of the Communist Party set up within companies. On the other hand, some concepts were drawn from different corporate law traditions. From the English/Hong Kong stream came the notion that a company must have at least two shareholders and, unless a stock company, fewer than 50 (English law on this point has changed to allow a sole promoter company).[15] From the German corporate tradition came the idea of a supervisory board. From the American notions of corporate management and justice came the concept that directors and managers could be personally liable for breaches of duty to the company and its shareholders.[16]

Likewise, the 1999 Securities Law imitated the US disclosure principle and numerous substantive provisions.[17] In the course of its drafting and amendment, international symposia were held with foreign experts from the US and Hong Kong as well as other jurisdictions.[18] For foreign securities regulation to be successfully applied in China, academics and law-makers emphasized that their adaptation should combine China's own conditions with foreign legal concepts and practices.

However, the success of legal transplant is subject to adaptations to local conditions. Potter argues that China is engaging in selective adaptation of international norms and the success of that exercise depends also on institutional capacity building.[19] In other words, the success of Chinese legal transplants depends not only on learning from the West, and designing laws, rules, and regulations which are suitable to the Chinese social and economic development and legal culture, but also on the supporting legal infrastructures such as the quality of judges and the independence and efficiency of the judiciary,[20] the doctrine of judicial precedent, and the appropriate mix of government regulation and self-regulation, as well as effective enforcement and remedies.[21]

B A mix of two corporate models

Corporate governance models can broadly be placed into two groups: the German/Japanese model (or the stakeholder model) and the Anglo-American model (or the shareholder model). The essential characteristics of the German/Japanese are: controlling shareholders; banks as shareholders; the two tier supervisory board; external markets; and the large involvement of employees in corporate management. The Anglo-American model is characterized by: dispersed shareholders; independent directors; developed securities markets; a sound legal system; and freedom of employment.[22]

What should be noted is that, although both models are recognized worldwide, neither is perfect.[23] A combination of the two models has therefore become a worldwide trend.[24]

This is the case in China. In the 1980s Chinese corporate governance reform was referred to SOE reform and greatly influenced by the German/Japanese model. For instance, Chinese enterprises are mainly controlled by the state as the majority shareholder, and employees participate in enterprise management.[25]

In terms of employment, Japan has a tradition of lifelong employment within one company, and in Germany there is a long-term employment system protected by labor laws and collective contracts. In China's planned economy, providing lifelong employment was one responsibility of Chinese enterprises.[26]

From the 1990s, corporate governance reform in China aims to establish a market economy and has been greatly influenced by the Anglo-American model. The government is much more focused on establishing an external control system for companies, such as securities markets, independent directors, and so on. In the meantime, non-tradable share reform intends to diversify concentrated ownership by selling state shares to the public. It implies that China is transforming towards a dispersed public shareholding.

The hybrid nature of the Chinese corporate model is the result of both historical and political factors. The historical factors involve the time at which China adopted a legal system and a corporate system. China established its legal infrastructure in the 1930s at a time when the dominant models were Germany/Japan. In the event a German based legal system was adopted. Chinese corporate restructuring was completed in the early 1990s when the US had just succeeded in winning the Cold War and at a time when the Japanese model of corporate ownership had come into question as a result of the bursting of the real estate bubble.

In addition to historical factors, political reasons may help to explain the choices made by China. The Anglo-American corporate law requires a skilled and powerful judiciary to interpret that law. However, the lack of pre-existing case law and a judiciary system in China may explain the attractiveness of the German/Japanese corporate model to the Chinese government. At the same time, the desire to allocate capital and mitigate agency problems in Chinese companies led to a preference for elements of the Anglo-American model.[27]

C Experimental legislation as precedents of national law

Another characteristic of Chinese legal reform is the use of experimental legislation in regional areas as precedents for drafting new laws at the national level.[28] The region (Hong Kong in this case) is forced to deal with new legal problems raised by the creation of the H-share market. These regional regulations help to move China's securities market and its corresponding regulatory framework from one stage to another and from a primitive to a more sophisticated framework.

For example, recognizing some of the previously unofficial practices adopted during the first listings of a few Chinese enterprises in Hong Kong, the Chinese authorities promulgated the *1994 Special Provisions*. The *1994 Special Provisions* expressed the government's willingness to adjust to different market environments and to fit in with common practices of overseas stock exchanges.[29] It permitted a company to grant an over-allotment option to the underwriter of a public issue of shares, to take up to 15 percent of the total shares to be issued by the company.[30] This is known as a "Green Shoe" option, allowing underwriters to participate in an issue from which they might otherwise be excluded.[31] This method had already been used by Shanghai Petrochemical Company, one of the first batch of H-share companies dealing with over-subscription for new share offerings. In mainland China, the *Tentative Opinion for Over-placement Option*, promulgated by the CSRC on 3 September 2001, served to formalize the legality of Green Shoe options and outline rules applicable to such options.

7.2.2 Legal transplants in China's company and securities laws

The previous section discussed Chinese legal reform in terms of a dynamic of legal transplant and selective adaptation of Western models, together with the use of experimental legislation as a model for subsequent national legislation. This section uses the Chinese Company Law (CCL) and the Securities Law (CSL) as examples to explain further.

The CCL and the CSL were originally promulgated in 1993 and 1998 respectively. Since their promulgation these two laws have played a critical role in facilitating SOE reform, establishing China's modern corporate system and securities market, and promoting the development of the socialist market economy in China. However, as China's economic reform progressed, serious deficiencies in these two laws were gradually exposed. Indeed, since the early 1990s, China has significantly deepened its market economy-oriented reforms and changed the socio-economic structure on which these two laws were originally based.[32] Hence, two amendments were made to the CCL in 1999 and 2005, and one amendment was made to the CSL in 2005.

Here it is neither possible nor necessary to discuss all of the changes to the CCL and the CSL. Only the more significant changes are examined below.

A Borrowing board structure

When the CCL was being formulated in the early 1990s, the drafters looked to both American and German models. In its basic structure, the CCL was modeled on the German dual board system for large public companies.[33] For example, the supervisory board, consisting of representatives of both shareholders and employees, monitors the board of directors and the senior management. However, the Chinese board structure is different from the German system in both the appointment method of the members of the board of directors, and in the accountability structure.[34] Directors are appointed by the general shareholders' meetings instead of the supervisory board; and they are made accountable to shareholders instead of the supervisory board.

INDEPENDENT DIRECTORS

Independent directors are regarded as an important element of legal and policy reform in the field of corporate governance. The Cadbury Report was a response to major corporate scandals associated with government failures in the UK (such as Robert Maxwell's executive abuses). The Cadbury Report recommended, along with subsequent similar reports and studies, a greater role for outside and independent directors. The last decade has seen a number of corporate law reforms in Japan designed to enhance the role of directors and auditors not tied to management.[35]

In the 1997 Articles of Association Guidelines, the CSRC brought in the notion of independent directors. The Guidelines provided listed companies with the option of having independent members sit on the board. The duties that independent directors discharge, however, was a matter for the articles of association to determine.[36] However, few listed companies seemed to be interested in having independent board members.[37]

In 1999 the *Opinions* jointly issued by the CSRC and the State Economic and Trade Commission required Chinese companies listed overseas to have a board of directors with more than half of its members from outside, among whom at least two had to be independent.[38]

The CSRC took an important step further in 2001 by introducing the *Guiding Opinions about Establishing Independent Director System in Listed Companies* in August. Covering all companies listed on Chinese stock exchanges (but not Chinese companies listed overseas), it constituted the most comprehensive measure taken to that date, or since, by the CSRC – or indeed by any Chinese governmental authority – to regulate internal corporate governance through the institution of the independent director. It was also portrayed unapologetically as something borrowed from US corporate law and practice, and as such involves many issues relevant to legal transplants.[39]

FIDUCIARY DUTY

In 1993 China's State Commission on the Reform of the Economic System (SCRES), a ministry-level government body, issued a letter to the HKSE.[40] In it, the SCRES solemnly assured the Exchange that the "directors' obligation of good faith and diligence to the company" in Article 62 of the *Standard Opinion* had a meaning similar to that of fiduciary duty under Hong Kong law.[41] However, it is questionable whether this interpretation is wholly accurate. If something very like the fiduciary duty of Hong Kong law were to exist in China, it would have to have been borrowed; this common law concept is founded on the law of trusts, which has no real counterpart in China.[42] Since there was no set of legal norms that could claim any existence outside of textbooks, it was believed that no such borrowing had occurred as of 1993 when the SCRES issued its letter.

Under the 1993 CCL, there was no separate and independent chapter on directors' duties and remedies for breach thereof. Provisions on directors' duties were scattered throughout the statute. Directors were only required to "perform their duties faithfully" (*zhongshi lvxing zhiwu*) under Articles 59 (1) and 123. The 1993 CCL mentioned a duty of loyalty, but no duty of care. This appeared to suggest that directors had to observe the articles of association of the company and were prohibited from committing a number of types of misconduct.[43]

Although these provisions were too general to be used to invoke impeachment action against a director, and therefore devoid of any practical significance, they did at least raise the discussion of whether they could be regarded as a step towards recognition of a concept of fiduciary duty such as that at common law.[44]

The *1994 Mandatory Provisions* use the term "good faith and diligence" in the *Standard Opinion*, and make up for the shortcomings of the CCL by the reinforcement of directors' duties in public companies. Three breakthroughs have been made. First, the common law concept of "duty of care" was introduced into China as "diligence" in the *1994 Mandatory Provisions*. Article 115 defines the term "diligence" to mean that in exercising their rights or executing their duties, directors and managers must follow the same standard of care and skill as a "reasonable person" would follow. The term "reasonable person" is a concept newly introduced into Chinese law. Second, Article 116 sets out specific circumstances for determining "good faith and diligence" for avoiding conflicts of interest. These include, but are not limited to: the duty to act honestly in the best interests of the company; the duty to use their powers within the authorized scope of office; and the duty to avoid a conflict of interest in the 12 items of obligation. Third, remedies for directors committing breaches while serving in public companies are provided in Article 127.

Amendments to the CCL of 2005 adopt essential elements of the *1994 Mandatory Provisions* and transform them into a national law. This is very similar to the UK law. The Companies Act 2006 provides a statutory statement of codified directors' duties in Sections 171 to 177, which replace the common law and equitable fiduciary duties of directors. The statutory expression of the duties is essentially the same as the duties established by case law, the only major exception being the new procedure for dealing with conflicts of interest.

The amended CCL expressly obliges directors, supervisors, and senior officers of Chinese companies to uphold "duties of loyalty and diligence" to their companies under new Article 148. Article 148 (2) is a general duty imposed on directors. Under this duty, company officers are prohibited from taking bribes or other illegal payments, and they must not misappropriate company property. This duty is an extension to the duty of care. Article 149 further provides a list of prohibited actions by a director or senior officer.

On 30 January 2007 the CSRC published the *Measures on Administration of the Information on Disclosure of Listed Companies*, implementing the amended CCL and CSL's stricter new requirements on information disclosure.[45] The *Measures* require disclosure of information by personnel at all levels of listed companies. Listed companies, their issuers, directors, supervisors, and senior managers are responsible for ensuring the authenticity, accuracy, completeness, and timing of the information disclosed.

This clearly corresponds to Article 68 of CSL, as amended, which requires the directors, supervisors, and senior officers of a listed company to ensure that the information disclosed by the company is true, accurate, and complete. They even need to sign written confirmation with respect to the regular reports of the company. All these clearly lay down the basis of civil claims from investors.

B Borrowing mechanisms of shareholder protection

RIGHT TO KNOW

The right to know is important because it will enable a shareholder to make informed decisions. The 1993 CCL also provided this right to shareholders. A shareholder had the right to read and examine the articles of association of the company, the minutes of shareholders' meetings, and the financial accounting reports of the company.[46] Financial accounting reports included the balance sheet, the profit and loss statement, a statement on changes in the financial position of the company, a statement explaining the financial situation of the company, and a statement regarding the distribution of profits.[47] However, accounting books of the company were not covered. This would leave a gray area in the matter of information disclosure.

In order to strengthen the protection of shareholders' right to know, and increase the supply of information to minority shareholders, the amended CCL has granted shareholders the right to inspect corporate books and records.[48]

The methods that shareholders can utilize to exercise their right to know vary according to the type of company involved. The amended CCL distinguishes companies limited by shares from limited liability companies. As a side note, it can be said that the former are public companies while the latter are private companies.

In a limited liability company, the amended CCL reaffirms the rights of shareholders to review and copy a wide range of documents: the company's articles of association, register of shareholders, corporate bond counterfoils, minutes of shareholders' general meetings, resolutions of the board of directors and the supervisory board, financial accounting reports, and the account books.

But in a company limited by shares, there is no mention of "accounting books." Articles 65–7 of CSL, as amended, provide that shareholders of listed companies have access to information about the company, including: operating conditions, major litigations, background of directors, supervisors, senior management and their shareholdings profile, issued stocks, debenture bonds, and major events which can greatly influence the price of the stock.

The reason for this disparity is that a company limited by shares has a higher capitalization than that of a limited liability company, especially now in a growing capital market.[49] In China's bullish stock market of 2006, the number of investor accounts reached a new record of 82 million and kept rising to 143 million by the end of 2007.[50] Most of them were short-term individual investors who held small numbers of shares and were concerned about profits rather than the long-term development of the company. On the other hand, the major shareholders who really cared about the operation of the company usually participated in company management. They had authority to inspect accounting books through their management activities. Therefore, in practice, even if the law allows shareholders of companies limited by shares access to accounting books, this provision also does not have too much significance.

DERIVATIVE ACTIONS

Derivative action is an important shareholder protection mechanism in the sense that when wrongdoers are in control of the company, the individual shareholders can still commence legal action on behalf of the company.

One common view is that the law did not authorize any derivative action before the amended CCL. The 1993 CCL barely played any role in preventing misconduct by the controlling shareholders and directors, or in protecting minority shareholders.[51]

Article 111 was the only provision in the 1993 CCL which enabled shareholders to initiate action against corporate misconduct.[52] But it failed to indicate whether the law directly permitted derivative lawsuits. Furthermore, this article was ineffective in protecting shareholders. It was vague, obscure, and difficult to apply because there was no regulation regarding applicable procedures, and it did not elaborate the circumstances under which an action could be initiated. The only remedy available to plaintiff shareholders was through an injunction. Damages could not be awarded.[53] Furthermore, the types of actionable infringements provided for were excessively narrow.[54] Since this was a typical direct action, only companies could be considered as defendants. Senior management, controlling shareholders, and other potential wrongdoers were excluded from the scope of liability even if it had been their personal illegal activities that had harmed the interests of the company and its minority shareholders.

Although the law remained silent on derivative action in the 1993 CCL, disputes between controlling shareholders and minority shareholders have been common in China since 1998. Shareholders have found it difficult to bring actions when a controlling shareholder has infringed the company's interests due to a lack of legislation applicable to shareholder actions. In the case of Chengdu Hongguang Industrial Shareholding Company, investors sued the directors after the CSRC published the *Enforcement Notice of the CSRC against Chengdu Hongguang Industrial Co. in relation to Severe Breach of Regulation*[55] in 1998. But the court refused the claim due to there being an "inappropriate plaintiff."[56] Similarly, Shenzhen Intermediate People's Court dismissed the appeal from an investor, Xinxian Zhao, against the director of Sanjiu Medical & Pharmaceutical Company in 2003.

Unlike the CCL conservative approach to the protection of minority shareholders, the CSRC has taken a more aggressive step. It enacted the 2002 Corporate Governance Code for Listed Companies in an effort to improve corporate governance in public companies. Directors, supervisors, or managers who, in violation of law, administrative regulation, or the bylaws of the company, cause damages to the company, are liable for such damages. Shareholders have the right to require the company to institute legal proceedings for damages according to the law.[57]

The introduction of the statutory derivative action in the amended CCL in 2005 is a significant experiment in attempting to establish an investor-friendly legal regime. New Article 150 provides that a director, supervisor, or any senior officer is liable for any losses of the company if he/she violates any provisions of laws, or administrative regulations, or the articles of association of the company in performance of his/her official duties. Additionally, Article 152 provides certain procedural rules, which allow shareholders individually or collectively holding at least 1 percent of the company's shares to bring a lawsuit against the management for maladministration. And Article 153, as amended, allows shareholders to bring a direct action against management if they violate laws, administrative regulations, or the company's articles of association.

Regarding the CSL, prior to its amendment it provided civil liability only for misrepresentations made during securities' issuance and trading.[58] The amended CSL specifies civil remedies for a number of additional violations, including matters involving corporate governance. For example, amended Article 76 provides civil remedies for insider trading by stating that "if an act of insider trading causes investors to incur a loss, the person so acting shall be liable for damages in accordance with the law."

After the amended CCL came into force, the SPC announced that its interpretations of the CCL would be enacted in several instalments. On 28 April 2006, the *Provisions on Several Issues concerning the Application of the PRC Company Law (1)* (the "Company Law Interpretations") was enacted. The *Company Law Interpretations* address several procedural issues regarding the application of the amended CCL to civil lawsuits, and clarify certain issues related to the standing requirement for shareholders who seek to initiate derivative lawsuits. Two years later the SPC promulgated the second *Provisions on Several Issues concerning the Application of the PRC Company Law (2)*, with an emphasis on company dissolution and liquidation.[59] A derivative action may also be brought when any member of the liquidation committee violates a law or regulation and thus causes losses to the company in the course of liquidation.[60] Even after a company has been liquidated and struck off the register, a shareholder can still sue a member of the liquidation group.[61] In the foreseeable future, the SPC's interpretations will further address the vague or missing components of the derivative lawsuit procedure.

STRENGTHENED VOTING (DECISION AND APPOINTMENT) RIGHTS

The 1993 CCL adopted a simple "one share one vote" mechanism for shareholders' voting rights. In this system minority shareholders would not have a say in most cases. As the protection of minority shareholders' interests is a crucial element for a sound corporate governance system, it is important for the CCL to introduce a more balanced voting mechanism in which minority shareholders' interests can be effectively protected. The cumulative voting mechanism adopted in some Western countries, for example, may offer a solution for the reform of the CCL in this area.

For the first time, the 2002 Corporate Governance Code for Listed Companies (the "Corporate Governance Code") borrowed the cumulative voting system.[62] Article 31 stipulates:

> The shareholders' meeting, in the course of the election of directors, shall positively carry out the cumulative voting system. The listed company whose 30% or more shares are held by its proprietary shareholder shall adopt the cumulative voting system. A listed company that adopts the cumulative voting system shall stipulate the implementing rules of this system in its bylaws.

This provision was codified in amendments to the CCL in 2005.[63] The cumulative voting system allows shareholders to cast all of their votes for a single nominee for the board of directors when the company has multiple openings on its board.[64] The provisions also give minority shareholders a greater opportunity to oust the management of a company limited by shares. Furthermore, the amended CCL makes it easier for minority shareholders to participate in companies' decision-making processes.[65] Article 40, as amended, allows shareholders representing 10 percent of all votes cast (previously 25 percent was required under the 1993 CCL) to propose an extraordinary meeting. Also, shareholders individually or collectively holding 3 percent (previously 5 percent) or more of the shares of the company can propose a motion and submit it to the general meeting via the board of directors under Article 103.

EXIT RIGHT

Controlling shareholders may try to prevent minority shareholders from realizing the value of their investments by withholding dividends or by forcing them out of the business on unfavorable terms.[66] An exit right enables minority shareholders to sell their shares back to the company, or other shareholders.

The system of exit right in China was first introduced in the regulation of overseas listed companies, before extending to all companies incorporated in China by national legislation. The earliest version appeared in the *1994 Mandatory Provisions* for overseas companies. Shareholders who oppose a merger or division plan have the right to require the company or shareholders who are in favor of such a proposal to purchase their shares at a fair price.[67] Similar provisions existed in the *1997 Guidelines for the Articles of Association of Listed Companies* for A-share and B-share companies.[68] When a company merges or divides, directors of the company have an obligation to protect the lawful interests of those who object to the merger or division plan.[69]

Finally, Chinese legislators adopted this system in the amended CCL. Article 75 CCL, as amended, grants investors the right to request that the company purchase their shares at a reasonable price when they vote against a relevant resolution, if: the company has not paid dividends for five consecutive years, or; the company merges, is divided, or transfers its main property, or; the company's operation term is renewed after its expiration, or; events triggering dissolution occur. However, this remedy is less relevant in the context of a public company; the same result can usually be achieved by shareholders selling their shares on the stock market.

7.2.3 Evaluation of company and securities law reform

As observed above, Chinese legal reform has adopted a cautious, gradual, and incremental approach, in contrast with the reform undertaken in countries in Eastern Europe and the former Soviet Union. It often uses overseas listings as trials and then codifies successful experiences into national legislation in order to develop its capital markets. The goal of Chinese leadership is not to transform the entire political and legal system, but to deepen Chinese capital markets as rapidly as possible within the basic framework of socialism and the existing political system.[70]

Amendments to the CCL and the CSL 2005 are an aggregate of Chinese legal reform on capital markets. They introduce provisions protecting minority shareholders and improving corporate governance.

According to the report released by the Institute of World Economics and Politics of the Chinese Academy of Social Science, compared with 2005, Chinese corporate governance standards gained an overall improvement in 2006.[71] This improvement was mainly in the areas of information disclosure and certain shareholder rights, including voting rights and the right to know. But companies performed better on the mandatory requirements for compliance and monitoring, such as information disclosure and transparency, than on less prescriptive items such as responsibilities of directors.[72]

Furthermore, the report revealed that governance standards improved in form rather than in substance.[73] The institution of independent directors and the introduction of derivative actions are two instances. Independent directors do not function as hoped because the nomination procedure prevents minority shareholders from appointing their representatives to the board. Similarly, the rules of derivative action have been adopted by Article 152 of CCL, but implementation has yet to be issued by the SPC so that Chinese courts find it difficult to deal with such lawsuits in practice.

The reason for the failure of some legal transplants may be that legal reform was initiated from regulatory requirements rather than from market pressure. The Chinese authorities hoped to achieve immediate results by learning the superficial procedures from developed markets. But they ignore many important systematic factors and have not taken into account specific features of the Chinese institutional and legal environment that affect the viability of any legal borrowings.

7.3 Issuance system reform

The Chinese IPO market has transformed from a tightly controlled system to a more market-oriented system. Reforms include: the abolition of the listing quota system and its replacement by the approval system; the improvement of the transparency and efficiency of the share issuance approval procedure; and the allowance of more market participation in IPO pricing by using market-driven pricing mechanisms.

7.3.1 Replacing the quota system with the approval system

Figure 7.1 shows the way in which the Chinese issuance system developed from 1990 to the present. Between 1990 and 2000, when China's capital markets began to develop, public offerings of shares were subject to administrative approval from the authorities. As discussed in Chapter 3, the Chinese authorities' main purpose in developing a stock market was to raise capital for the development of China's SOEs and to facilitate the reconstruction of SOEs.[74] Each year's volume of equity issuance was determined by the government and this was then divided up among the provinces and ministries by means of the listing quota system.

Certainly the listing quota system had a number of useful functions.[75] Without it, the stock market would have been swamped with share offerings from myriad companies desperate to tap into investment capital markets. The quota system also allowed funds to be channeled towards important sectors such as natural resources, utilities, heavy industry and manufacturing SOEs, and away from light industry, real estate, and finance. In the early days of China's stock markets, it was nearly impossible for any private enterprises to be approved and listed on the stock exchange. Until March 1998, only one non-SOE, Sichuan New Hope Agriculture Stock Company, received the Chinese government's approval to list. It subsequently became the first listed private enterprise.[76]

However, the listing quota system was damaging in at least two ways.[77] First, the government regularly used it to manipulate market sentiment. Second, the whole process was inevitably vulnerable to lobbying and corruption. For instance, the Chinese media reported that at least 12 companies from Jiangsu province had bribed regulators to gain market listings during the 1990s.[78]

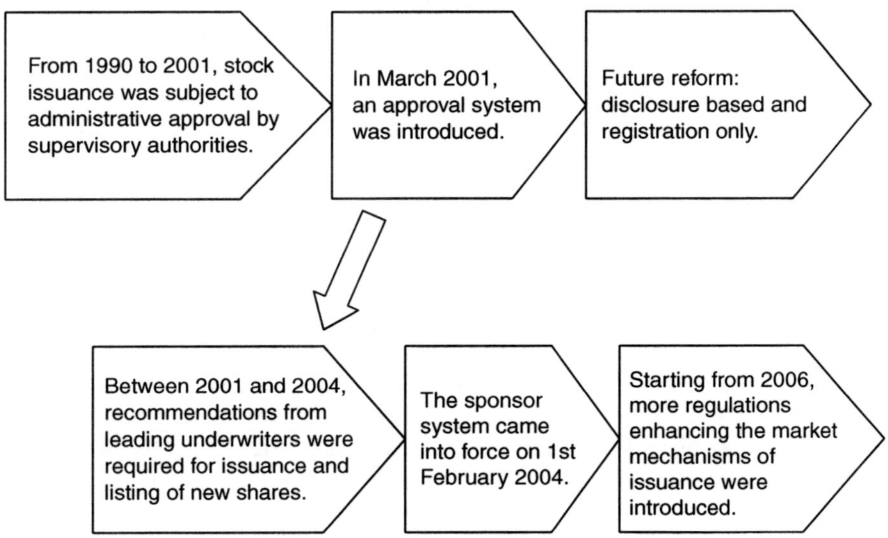

Figure 7.1 The evolution of China's issuance system (source: based on CSRC (2008), p. 219).

In 2001 an approval system replaced the listing quota system. This is a significant change, but is still appreciably different from the registration system common in most developed markets. The new system required pre-issuance mandatory information disclosures and post-issuance investigations.

7.3.2 Improving the transparency and efficiency of the share issuance procedure

A regulatory system for supervising public offerings was developed with simplified and standardized procedures. The Public Offering Review Committee ("the Committee"), established in September 1999, was responsible for providing professional opinions on the performance of companies applying for public offering. The Committee was composed of 80 members drawn from the CSRC, other government agencies, stock exchanges, and academia. The establishment of the Committee marked the beginning of issuance system reform. But its operations were secret and the identities of the Committee members confidential, a practice questioned by market participants as it generated corruption.[79]

To improve the transparency of the share issuance approval system, three measures have been introduced. The first is the enactment of the *Provisional Measures on the Sponsor System for Issuing and Listing of Securities*, which replaces the leading underwriter recommendation system with a quota ceiling for each underwriter.[80] The second is the creation of an accountability mechanism for controlling sponsor institutions and sponsor representatives. The third is the enactment of the *Provisional Measures on Public Offering Review Committee*, promulgated by the CSRC in December 2003, to restructure the Committee. The size of the Committee was reduced from 80 to 25. Prior to each Committee meeting, the CSRC would inform the public of the identities of the participating members and the supplementary information of applicants. The final decision of the meeting was made public.

These measures abolished the members' secrecy rule, replaced anonymous voting with real-name voting by committee members, and defined the accountability and supervision mechanisms for Committee members. The provisions also ensured that all stakeholders under the verification and approval system for issuance shared responsibilities and risks, marking the first step towards a market-oriented system.[81]

To increase efficiency, the CSRC promulgated the *Measures on the Public Offering Review Committee* ("POR Measures") in 2006, replacing the *Provisional Measures*. The *POR Measures* set out a three-stage approval process for new issuance. The first step follows the filing of application documents by the sponsor, and involves preliminary examination and verification by the CSRC Issuance Department. The second step involves an ad hoc meeting held by an issuance verification commission consisting of five members (selected from a group of five CSRC officers and 20 external experts). The ad hoc issuance verification commission is in charge of examining the application documents prepared by the issuer, its accountants, financial advisers, legal counsel, and valuation institution. Finally, following the examination, the commission makes a recommendation to the CSRC, which will then approve or disapprove the application, mainly based on the commission's report. The reforms of the Committee have upgraded the professionalism and transparency of the issuance examination process and have also augmented public supervision and issuance efficiency.

The *POR Measures* were amended in 2009 because the GEB was created in the same year.[82] The Committee is divided into the Main Board Committee, the GEB Committee and the Committee for M&A and Restructurings. A member of one committee may not hold a concurrent post on another committee.

While all listing and trading matters are largely regulated by the CSRC and the Committee, the two national stock exchanges have primary control over the daily trading of domestic shares and receive and scrutinize listing applications.[83] Under the amended Article 50 of CSL, a stock exchange may specify listing conditions which are more stringent than those specified in the legislation, as long as those conditions are first approved by the CSRC. Also, the sponsor system can provide additional safeguards for investors. The Chinese sponsor system was established in October 2003 when the CSRC promulgated the *Provisional Measures on the Sponsor System for Issuing and Listing of Securities*. Later, it was embodied in the amended Securities Law. Under this law, sponsors and their representatives are required to recommend and guide securities issuers, check the truthfulness, accuracy and completeness of the issuer's offering-related documents, and assist issuers in establishing a stringent information disclosure system.[84]

7.3.3 Introducing market-driven pricing mechanisms

Pricing mechanisms in China have changed many times, from face value issuance to the fixed price method, then to book-building.

In the middle of the 1980s the issuance of stocks was under strict government control and stocks were issued at a price equal to their face value. Starting in the 1990s, stocks were sold for prices above face value. People began to be interested in purchasing stocks as they gained more knowledge about the capital market. Then a fixed price earnings (P/E) ratio method, predetermined by the CSRC, was used to decide the issue price of an IPO.

In July 1999 the CSRC introduced a cumulative auction method to determine IPO pricing. Article 28 of the 1998 CSL provided that the offering price should be first negotiated between issuers and underwriters and then approved by the relevant authorities. In theory, this method should have brought the IPO pricing more into line with market demand and better reflect the valuation of the new issuer. This may work well for developed markets, but did not work on the Chinese IPO market. Investors, in particular retail investors, were not capable of judging the valuation. This resulted in some overvalued IPOs with very high P/E ratios in 2000.[85] The cumulative price inquiry method, with an upper limit set for the offering's P/E ratios, was introduced in July 2001. The objective was to cool down overheated IPOs with excessively high P/E ratios by putting a cap on pricing. However, this restriction was applied across all industries, ignoring the characteristics of different market sectors. This distorted the market mechanism and created an imbalance in market supply and demand.[86]

From January 2005, China borrowed the book-building method, the most popular practice for IPO pricing. This method allows underwriters to seek bids from institutional investors and the final negotiated price is used for the retail offering. The CSRC promulgated the *Circular on Several Issues concerning the Book-building Procedure for IPOs*,[87] removing government approval for the share issuance price and replacing it with a book-building process, which augmented market supervision over stock issuance. The *2006 Administration Measures for Securities Issuance and Underwriting* accomplished several goals.[88] These included introducing key regulations on the book-building process, pricing and share allotment during the IPO, improving the book-building process, and stepping up supervision of the issuers, securities firms' other intermediaries, and investors at the share issuance.

But the book-building process in China is a little different from that used in developed markets like the US.[89] In China, underwriters do not have allocation rights. After the book-building price inquiry is completed, if the total amount of valid purchase above the issue price is greater than the total number of shares to be offered in the rights issue to the inquiry targets, the issuer and its sponsor institution must offer shares in the rights issue on a pro rata basis for all valid purchases above the issue price. The percentage of the rights issue must be the number of shares to be offered in the rights issue to the inquiry targets divided by the total amount of valid purchases above the issue price. In the US, underwriters usually have allocation rights. Second, in China, after the book-building price inquiry is completed, the issuer and its sponsor institution must offer the remaining shares to the public at the same price. The latter in fact belongs to the fixed pricing method, which is different from the US method.

Although the book-building process constitutes a major step towards marketization, there is still a big problem – underpricing in the Chinese IPO market. There are three main reasons for Chinese underpricing. First, companies with a long delay between the issue of the IPO shares and the subsequent listing of those shares are likely to price the IPO cheaply.[90] This underpricing is required in order to compensate investors for the uncertainty attached to a long listing process. Second, there are a limited number of enterprises that can be verified and approved to issue stocks each year.[91] As a result, the demand in the primary market becomes relatively intense. Limited supply and huge demand constitute a major feature of Chinese stock markets. Third, when state or quasi-state ownership is high, agency costs increase and liquidity decreases. Therefore, greater underpricing may be needed to compensate investors for their increased risk exposure.

7.3.4 Evaluation of issuance system reform

The reform of the stock issuance system aims to transform capital markets from being government-driven to market-driven, and attempts to enhance market discipline and transparency.

Table 7.2 shows that the number of IPOs in China fluctuated in the ten-year period from 2002 to 2011. A-share IPOs increased to 71 after the abolition of the quota system in 2001, and remained steady for several years. But the year 2005 was a turning point; the number of A-share IPOs followed a downward trend. The financial crisis further reduced IPO activities in 2008. The capital markets in China regained slight momentum in 2009 as the economy gradually recovered.

The boom of A-share IPOs in 2002–04 implies that the quota system had previously restricted the fundraising activities of certain companies. That is why there was an immediate boost after abolition. Afterwards, the number of IPOs should have been determined entirely by supply and demand factors dictated by the market.

But the state has not refrained from maintaining tight market control. For example, there was a nine-month ban on IPOs in the second half of 2008 because the government wanted to stabilize capital markets and prevent meltdown.[92] The formal quota system might have been abolished, but the state can still interfere with the market using alternative administrative measures.

7.4 Non-tradable share reform towards a market-oriented economy

Dispersed shareholding structures are common around the world and typically grant different rights to shareholders.[93] Yet an unparalleled feature of the shareholding structure in China is that of non-tradable shares entitling the holders to exactly the same voting and cashflow rights assigned to the holders of tradable shares, but which cannot be traded publicly even if the company is listed.

7.4.1 Background

Non-tradable shares can be dated back to the early experiment of corporate shareholding restructuring, when listed companies promised in the IPO prospectus or the public announcement for listing that shares owned by shareholders prior to the public offering would remain unlisted and non-tradable. Typically these shares belong to the state, or to domestic financial institutions ultimately owned by central or local government.

The predominance of non-tradable shares caused several problems for the market.[94] First, the limited free float available made the domestic market extremely illiquid, volatile, and thus prone to market manipulation and insider trading. Second, the holders of tradable shares were typically minority shareholders with

Table 7.2 The number of A-share IPOs (2002–11)

2002	*2003*	*2004*	*2005*	*2006*	*2007*	*2008*	*2009*	*2010*	*2011*
71	67	61	3	13	26	6	9	28	39

Sources: based on PricewaterhouseCoopers, "Greater China IPO Watch" (various years).

limited power to affect management decisions. Third, the inefficiency of the domestic market induced many high value Chinese companies to list overseas. This adversely affected domestic investors. Prevented from investing in the best companies, they were stuck with holdings in the less well performing local companies.

With the expansion of Chinese markets, non-tradable shares are on the reform agenda; their predominance raises concerns over China's commitment to market-oriented principles, market stability, and protection of minority shareholder rights. Chinese authorities have tried to deal with the problem of non-tradable shares on several occasions, in particular in 1999 and 2001. In the first attempt, two companies were selected to sell their state shares to public shareholders. The experiment was not well received by investors, and within 15 days of the announcement of the transfer program the share price of the two companies fell about 40 percent.[95] The second attempt in 2001 also failed badly, reportedly because the proposal envisaged equal pricing for tradable and non-tradable shares.

7.4.2 Mechanisms of the reform and its implementation

In 2004 the issue was again addressed by the State Council, which promulgated the *Several Opinions on Promoting the Reform and Opening-up and the Stable Development of the Capital Market* as the basis of non-tradable share reform.[96] This document states that stable steps should be taken to solve the circulation problem of non-tradable shares.[97] On 29 April 2005, the CSRC announced a new pilot program, inviting a first batch of four companies to transform their shares by compensating existing shareholders through various methods such as bonus shares, cash, and options.[98] This attempt was different from previous ones because both tradable and non-tradable shareholders were invited to negotiate on the terms of the scheme. Such flexibility seemed to work well. Subsequently, a second pilot program was initiated, involving 42 companies who accounted for 10 percent of overall stock market value. Two months later, the program was successfully accomplished.

Learning from successes and failures of previous experiments, the CSRC promulgated the *Measures on Administration of Split Share Structure Reform of Listed Companies* on 5 September 2005, requiring listed companies to convert non-tradable state-owned shares into tradable ones.

According to the *Measures*, the reform can be roughly divided into four stages: initiation, negotiation, approval, and implementation.[99]

1. Initiation

The process typically starts with a proposal for floating non-tradable shares put forward by their holders. If a consensus fails to be achieved, the motion can also be raised independently or jointly by the shareholders who hold two-thirds or more of the non-tradable shares.[100]

2. Negotiation

The reform proposal must be adequately disclosed and consulted upon with the holders of tradable shares. If adjustments to the reform plan are necessary, the board of directors may make them. If no adjustments are necessary, a shareholder's meeting will be held. The board of directors is required to publicize the details of the meeting twice or more.[101] Trading in the shares of the stock is subsequently suspended.

3. Approval

Negotiation will be followed by a vote on the proposal by all shareholders and by holders of tradable shares respectively. The proposal may only be passed if at least two-thirds of the shareholders vote, and at least two-thirds of holders of tradable shares endorse the proposal.[102] If the proposal is accepted the board must publicize the timetable for actual implementation of the reform.

4. Implementation

The sale of non-tradable shares of any company is subject to two provisions: (1) within 12 months of the date of implementing the reform scheme, these shares cannot be traded; (2) after expiration of the 12-month period, the shareholders of these shares who own 5 percent or more of the total amount of shares of a listed company, can sell no more than 5 percent of the total amount of shares of the company within 12 months and no more than 10 percent within 24 months.[103] Compensation plays an important role in the process of implementation. It may be in the form of cash, warrants, or bonus shares. The terms of compensation vary from company to company but are generally based on the assumption of a substantial price drop in the aftermath of the reform.

7.4.3 Evaluation of non-traedable share reform

The reform was remarkable not only for solving legacy structure problems in the market but also for paving the way for further innovation and dispersed ownership. The shareholdings of the largest shareholders in Chinese listed companies could be eliminated through non-tradable share reform.

As Table 7.3 shows, among the sample of 916 listed companies there were a total of 356 companies controlled by those largest shareholders who held over 50 percent of the shares.[104] After the reform, the number of such companies decreased to 74. By the end of 2007, 1,298 companies listed on the SHSE and SZSE had either initiated or completed the process of non-tradable share reform, accounting for 98 percent of the total listed companies that were subject to the reform.[105] This was a good attempt to establish the normal function of stock markets which had previously been hampered by a large amount of non-tradable shares.

Table 7.3 Shareholding of the largest shareholders of 916 sample listed companies before and after the reform

Shareholding of the largest shareholders	*Before the reform (April 2005)*		*After the reform (December 2006)*	
	Number of companies	*Percentage*	*Number of companies*	*Percentage*
Below 10%	8	0.87	24	2.62
10–20%	49	5.35	125	13.65
20–30%	217	23.69	243	26.53
30–40%	139	15.17	178	19.43
40–50%	147	16.05	172	8.77
50–60%	184	20.09	20	13.10
Over 60%	172	18.78	54	5.9
Total	916	100	916	100

Source: based on Zhang and Chu (2007).

However, it remains to be seen whether the reform will be successful. For the largest 30 companies in China, the overall percentage of tradable A-shares was only 28 percent as of August 2008.[106] For some of them, the percentage could be under 10 percent.[107] This illustrates that the state is particularly cautious in unwinding the non-tradable shares of the largest, and usually more important, SOEs. The crucial stage was in 2009 and 2010 when US$1,300 billion of shares, accounting for more than 60 percent of total non-tradable shares, could potentially be unlocked and sold.[108]

The number of companies in the Top 100 Chinese listed companies, with government or government agencies rather than other types of organization as the largest shareholder, increased from 10 in 2009 to 28 in 2010.[109] This illustrates that the share restructuring of major Chinese listed companies might have augmented, rather than changed, the state ownership model, despite the introduction of full circulation.

7.5 Concluding remarks

Chinese cross-listings in Hong Kong constitute a form of regulatory competition in which issuers opt into higher standards without seeking to escape the law of their local jurisdiction. Such competition seems to have beneficial effects, one of which is legal and regulatory reform.

China's capital markets have undergone dramatic changes since the first listing in Hong Kong in 1993. Specifically, a series of reforms and improvements have been conducted in an effort to optimize the market function and improve infrastructures.

The development of China's company and securities laws is a prime example of the transplant phenomenon. Formal convergence can be seen in the importation of Western legal norms and institutions into China via cross-listing. The concepts of independent directors and fiduciary duties, as well as mechanisms of shareholder protection such as cumulative voting and derivative actions, are all examples of legal transplantation. The borrowings have strengthened shareholder rights and improved corporate governance to a significant extent. However, these improvements might not be in substance but rather in form. The main reason for the failure of some legal transplants is that Chinese legal reform is initiated by regulators rather than the by the market. Regulators may indeed hope to achieve immediate results, but they have done so without actual regard for the underlying market demands and legal environment in China.

Meanwhile, reform of the stock issuance system took place in three areas: the replacement of the administrative approval system by the approval system for the public offering of stocks; the development of simplified and standardized procedures for supervising public offerings; and the strengthening of transparency and disclosure by the adoption of international accounting standards. The reform means that the capital markets have been gradually transformed from being government-driven to being market-driven. However, whether the state is fully committed to market-driven mechanisms remains doubtful.

On the market front, the government continues to carry out non-tradable share reform. It is also reducing state ownership in public companies and is paving the way for a dispersed market and internationalization. Nonetheless, the problem of state control remains acute. The willingness of the government to relinquish control of SOEs is doubtful. Three years after the implementation of the reform, just 10 percent of the unlocked non-tradable shares had actually been sold in the market.[110] Conflicts of interest between the state as owner of many listed companies, and the state as regulator, persist.

Notes

1 For example, MacDonald, Ronald and Taylor, Mark (1991), "Exchange Rates, Policy Convergence, and the European Monetary System" in *Review of Economics and Statistics*, 73; and Corhay, Albert and Rad, Alireza (1994), "Daily Returns from European Stock Markets" in *Journal of Business and Finance and Accounting*, 21.

2 Garrett, Ian and Spyrou, Spyros (1999), "Common Stochastic Trends in Emerging Equity Markets" in *Manchester School*, 67.

3 Gilson, Ronald *et al.* (2010), "Regulatory Dualism as a Development Strategy: Corporate Reform in Brazil, the U.S., and the EU." Stanford Law and Economics Olin Working Paper No. 390. Online. Available at: http://ssrn.com/abstract=1541226 (accessed 20 December 2012).

4 See section 7.2.2 for in-depth discussions.

5 The Amendment to the Constitution Law of 1999 expressly endorsed the concept of the rule of law by stipulating that "the People's Republic of China implements law to govern the state and construct the socialist country with rule of law." This endorsement can be regarded as a milestone in China's overall legal reform. Since that date, the term "rule of law" has frequently been used in China's political, economic, and social life.

6 Lubman, Stanley (1996), "The Future of Chinese Law" in Lubman, Stanley (ed.), *China's Legal Reforms*, Oxford: Oxford University Press, p. 1.

7 Other reasons provided by Ribstein include: (1) reforms may hurt stakeholder groups such as labor or consumers who have power in companies under the more

communitarian governance; (2) home country securities industry professionals who lost business from cross-listing may have different interests from local capitalists and others who gain from cross-listing by reducing their cost of capital. See Ribstein, Larry (2005), "Cross-listing and Regulatory Competition" in *Review of Law and Economics*, 1, p. 117.

8 The Code was issued 10 January 2002, and came into force on the same day.

9 Yet Liebman has pointed out that the Chinese media, including the business press, often fails to provide an independent source of information despite some de facto autonomy. Commercialization of the media may create conflicting pressures to highlight sensational cases of abuse and at the same time to suppress unfavorable information about potential advertisers and locally important enterprises. See Liebman, Benjamin (2005), "Watchdog or Demagogue? The Media in the Chinese Legal System" in *Columbia Law Review*, 105.

10 MacNeil, Iain (2002), "Adaptation and Convergence in Corporate Governance: the Case of Chinese Listed Companies" in *Journal of Corporate Law Studies*, 2, p. 307.

11 The Code, s. 5.

12 According to the CSRC's report, the problematic legacy of the non-tradable shares stemmed mainly from a lack of consensus on shareholding systems in the early years; a lack of clarity over the role and functions of the securities markets, and a lack of awareness of how to manage state assets through capital markets. See CSRC (2008), *China Capital Markets Development Report*, Beijing: China Financial Publishing House, p. 204.

13 Potter, Pitman (2004), "Legal Reform in China: Institutions, Culture, and Selective Adaptation" in *Law & Society Inquiry*, 29, p. 478.

14 Zhu, Sanzhu (2000), *Securities Regulation in China*, New York: Transnational Publishers, p. 157.

15 Nee, Owen (1994), "China's Company Law Sets out the Next Stage of Reform" in *International Financial Law Review*, 13, p. 13.

16 Ibid.

17 Tang, Xin (2008), "Protecting Minority Shareholders in China: A Task for Both Legislation and Enforcement" in Kanda, Hideki *et al.* (eds.), *Transforming Corporate Governance in East Asia*, London: Routledge.

18 Art, Robert and Gu, Minkang (1996), "Securitisation of State Ownership: Chinese Securities Law" in *Michigan Journal of International Law*, 18, p. 123; Fu, Jian and Yuan, Jie (2006), *PRC Company & Securities Laws*, Singapore: CCH Asia, p. 24.

19 Potter, op. cit.

20 Despite many improvements in the judicial system since 1978, concerns over judicial independence from state influence and the parties involved, and inefficiency, still remain. See Ma, Josephine (2005), "Corrupt Courts Seen as Biggest Threat" in *South China Morning Post* (10 March 2005).

21 Goo, Say Hak and Carver, Anne (2008), "Low Structure, High Ambiguity: Selective Adaptation of International Norms of Corporate Governance Mechanisms in China" in Nakamura, Masao (ed.), *Changing Corporate Governance Practices in China and Japan*, Hampshire: Palgrave Macmillan, p. 208.

22 For example, see Coffee, John (2001), "The Rise of Dispersed Ownership: The Roles of Law and the State in the Separation of Ownership and Control" in *Yale Law Journal*, 111, p. 3.

23 For the problems of the stakeholder model, see Roe, Mark (2000), "Political Preconditions to Separating Ownership from Corporate Control" in *Stanford Law Review*, 53, pp. 556–7. For the problems of the shareholder model, see Blair, Margaret (1995), *Ownership and Control: Rethinking Corporate Governance for the Twenty-First Century*, Washington DC: The Brookings Institution, p. 250.

24 Governance systems in Germany, Japan, and the US show signs of convergence toward each other. See Coffee, John (1999), "The Future as History: The Prospects

for Global Convergence in Corporate Governance and its Implications" in *Northwestern University Law Review*, 93; Hansmann, Henry and Kraahman, Reinier (2001), "The End of History for Corporate Law" in *Georgetown Law Journal*, 89. However, institutional persistence such as politics and path dependence exists in corporate governance.

25 According to the Law on Industrial Enterprises Owned by the Whole People, enterprises should be managed in a democratic way in the form of the staff and workers' congress, which has rights over issues ranging from discussing enterprise development plans, to electing the factory director. This law was adopted by the First Session of the Seventh National People's Congress on 13 April 1988 and came into force on 1 August 1988.

26 Before the introduction of the employment contract system in 1986, employment for workers was usually for life in Chinese enterprises.

27 Yang, Pengfei (2007), "The Two Models of Corporate Governance and the Institutional Reform of Chinese Enterprises" in Nakamura, Masao (ed.), *Changing Corporate Governance Practices in China and Japan*, Hampshire: Palgrave Macmillan, pp. 17–19.

28 De Jonge, Alice (2008), *Corporate Governance and China's H-Share Market*, Cheltenham: Edward Elgar, p. 29.

29 Ibid, p. 33.

30 The problems of this system were costly and time-consuming. Moreover, in many cases the distribution of the wining applications was largely over before it began, as most of the successful applications had already been allocated to friends and family of those involved in the listing process. See ibid., p. 36.

31 Tokley, Ian and Ravn, Tina (1998), *Company and Securities Law in China*, Hong Kong: Sweet & Maxwell Asia, p. 88.

32 Wang, Baoshu and Huang, Hui (2006), "China's New Company Law and Securities Law: An Overview and Assessment" in *Australian Journal of Corporate Law*, 19, p. 230.

33 Hopt, Klaus (1997), "The German Two-Tier Board: A German View on Corporate Governance" in Hopt, Klaus and Wymeersch, Eddy (eds.), *Comparative Corporate Governance: Essays and Materials*, Berlin: Walter de Gruyter & Co, p. 3; and Hopt, Klaus (1998), "The German Two-Tier Board: Experience, Theories, Reforms" in Hopt, Klaus *et al.* (eds.), *Comparative Corporate Governance – The State of the Art and Emerging Research*, New York: Oxford University Press, p. 227.

34 Xi, Chao (2009), *Corporate Governance and Legal Reform in China*, London: Wildy, Simmonds & Hill Publishing, p. 151.

35 Clarke, Donald (2006), "Lost in Translation? Corporate Legal Transplants in China." GWU Law School Public Law Research Paper No. 213, p. 9.

36 Art. 112 Guidelines 1997.

37 In 1998 only 16 out of 851 domestic listed companies had independent directors. See Yu, Zhongzhi (2001), "Dongshihui, Gongsi Zhili yu Jixiao- dui Zhongguo Shangshi Gongsi de Jingyan Fenxi" [The Board of Directors, Corporate Governance and Performance – An Empirical Analysis on Chinese Listed Companies] in *Zhongguo Shehui Kexue* [China Social Science], 3, p. 36.

38 *The Opinions on Further Promoting Standardized Operation and Deepening Reforms of Companies Listed Overseas* were issued on 26 March 1999, art. 6.

39 Clarke, op. cit., p. 10.

40 The *Side Letters Concerning the Standard Opinion and the Supplementary Provisions* dated 10 June 1993.

41 The *Standard Opinion on Joint Stock Companies* is a set of company regulations which operated before the Company Law 1993. It was issued by the SCRES on 15 May 1992 and came into force at the same time.

42 Clarke, op. cit., p. 15.

43 A few examples of a director's duties could be found in arts. 59 to 62 of CCL 1993.
44 Lee, Rebecca (2007), "Fiduciary Duty Without Equity: Fiduciary Duties of Directors under the Revised Company Law of The PRC" in *Virginia Journal of International Law*, 47, p. 901. Also, Tokley and Ravn, op. cit., pp. 91–102.
45 Chen, Grant and Zhang, Zhengyi (2007), "New Disclosure Standards for PRC Listed Companies" in *China Law & Practice* (April 2007).
46 Arts. 32 and 110 CCL 1993.
47 Art. 175 CCL 1993.
48 Art. 34 CCL 2005.
49 Wang, Jingyi and Wang, Peng (2009), "Discussion about Shareholders' Right to Information" in *Journal of Politics and Law*, 2, p. 45.
50 CSRC (2008), "Summary of Investor Accounts (1993–2007)." Online: Available at: www.csrc.gov.cn/pub/newsite/xxfw/cbwxz/tjnj/zqqhtjnj/2008/main/nj2007/6–1.htm (accessed 20 December 2012).
51 In the Company Law 1993, there were almost no restrictions on the controlling shareholder. For example, there were no fiduciary duties, no cumulative voting, and no restriction on voting in the case of a related party transaction. See Li, Xiaoning (2007), *A Comparative Study of Shareholders' Derivative Actions: England, the United States, Germany and China*, Deventer: Kluwer, pp. 252 and 254.
52 It provided that: "If a resolution adopted by the shareholders' general committee or the board of directors violates the relevant national statutes or administrative regulations, or infringes rights and interests of shareholders, a shareholder is entitled to bring a suit to the People's Court to enjoin such illegal act or infringing act."
53 Li, op. cit., p. 266.
54 Deng, Jiong (2005), "Building an Investor-Friendly Shareholder Derivative Lawsuit System in China" in *Harvard International Law Journal*, 46, pp. 357–8.
55 The CSRC published the *Notice* on 20 November 1998, stating that Hongguang had made false profit claims, obtained listed company status by fraud, had failed to disclose important events, and misappropriated funds. The CSRC issued a disgorgement order and fined Hongguang and related professional intermediaries. See the CSRC website. Online. Available at: http://old.csrc.gov.cn/n575458/n575667/n642011/2006010.html (accessed 2 September 2009).
56 Sun, Hong (2005), "Gudong Daibiao Susong Fengchao Bijin" [A Wave of Shareholders Representative Actions is Coming] in *China Securities Journal* (26 December 2005).
57 Art. 4 Corporate Governance Code.
58 Anderson, Craig and Guo, Bingna (2006), "Corporate Governance under the New Company Law (Part 1): Fiduciary Duties and Minority Shareholder Protection" in *China Law & Practice* (April 2006).
59 The *Provisions of the Supreme People's Court on Some Issues about the Application of the Company Law of the People's Republic of China (II)* was promulgated by the SPC on 5 May 2008 and came into force on 19 May 2008.
60 Ibid., art. 23.
61 Ibid.
62 The *Code of Corporate Governance for Listed Companies* was issued on 7 January 2002 by the CSRC and the China Council for the Promotion of International Trade.
63 Art. 106 CCL as amended.
64 In normal voting, shareholders may not give more than one vote per share to any single nominee. For example, if the election is for four directors and one person holds 500 shares (with one vote per share), under the normal method he could vote a maximum of 500 shares for any one candidate (giving him 2,000 votes total – 500 votes per each of the four candidates). With cumulative voting, he could choose to cast all 2,000 votes for one candidate, making it easier to get his preferred candidate elected.

65 Anderson and Guo, op. cit.
66 Ibid.
67 Art. 149, *1994 Mandatory Provisions*.
68 The *1997 Guidelines* were promulgated by the CSRC on 16 December 1997. It was replaced by the *2006 Guidelines*, which were promulgated by the CSRC and came into force on 20 March 2006.
69 Art. 173, *1997 Guidelines*.
70 Bell, Michael *et al.* (2003), *China at the Threshold of a Market Economy*, Washington DC: International Monetary Fund, p. 4.
71 Lu, Tong *et al.* (2006), "Corporate Governance Assessment on the Top 100 Chinese Listed Companies," p. 7. Online. Available at: www.iwep.org.cn (accessed 6 September 2010).
72 Ibid, p. 8.
73 Ibid, p. 10.
74 Dong, Fuying (1998), "Fazhan Ziben Shichang yu Gaige Guoyouqiye" [Capital Market Development and SOE Reform] in Li, Yining (ed.), *Zhongguo Ziben Shichang Fazhan de Lilun yu Shijian* [the Theory and Practice of Capital Market Development in China], Beijing: Beijing University Press, pp. 109–10.
75 For the advantages and disadvantages of the quota system, see Green, Stephen (2003), *China's Stockmarket: A Guide to its Progress, Players and Prospects*, London: Economist, p. 162.
76 Cai, Hua (2007), "Bonding, Law Enforcement and Corporate Governance in China" in *Stanford Journal of Law, Business & Finance*, 13, p. 105.
77 Green, op. cit., p. 162.
78 Ibid.
79 CSRC, op. cit., p. 220.
80 Channel restrictions: the system under which the number of the stock issuance channels held by securities firms was assigned by the CSRC. The CSRC only accepted a new IPO application from a securities firm after that firm's previous application was approved. This system aimed at controlling the number of IPO companies being simultaneously recommended by securities firms. After the implementation of the sponsor system in February 2004, the CSRC used both systems during a transitional period till January 2005, when the channel restriction system was formally abolished.
81 CSRC, op. cit., p. 221.
82 The *Amendments to Measures on the Public Offering Review Committee* was issued by the CSRC on 14 June 2009 and came into force on the same day.
83 Art. 48 CSL.
84 Arts. 11, 26, 69 and 192 CSL and arts. 4, 7, 10, 11 and 19 *Provisional Measures on the Sponsor System for Issuing and Listing of Securities*.
85 Fujian Mindong Electric Power (stock code 000993) was listed in Shenzhen Stock Exchange with a record high P/E ratio of 88.69 on 31 July 2000.
86 Cheung, Yan-leung *et al.* (2009), "How Regulatory Changes Affect IPO Underpricing in China" in *China Economic Review*, 20, p. 695.
87 The *Circular* was promulgated by the CSRC on 7 December 2004 and came into force on 1 January 2005.
88 The *Measures* were issued by the CSRC on 17 September 2006 and came into force on 19 September 2006.
89 For the disparities in book-building between China and the US, see Huang, Fangliang (2007), "China's Initial Public Offering Pricing Mechanisms: A Complicated Way of Improvement with A Short History" in *International Journal of Business and Management*, 2, p. 128.
90 Chen, Gongmeng *et al.* (2004), "IPO Underpricing in China's New Stock Market" in *Journal of Multinational Financial Management*, 14, p. 284.

91 Huang (2007), op. cit., p. 129.
92 Waldmeir, Patti (2009), "Investors Prepare for Fresh Flood of Chinese Offerings" in *Financial Times* (17 June 2009).
93 Faccio, Mara, and Lang, Larry (2002), "The Ultimate Ownership of Western European Corporations" in *Journal of Financial Economics*, 65.
94 For drawbacks of non-tradable shares, see Cai, Jinghan *et al.* (2007), "What will Privatization Bring: The Nontradable Share Issue Reform in China." Working Paper Series, p. 2. Online. Available at: http://ssrn.com/abstract=981682. Also, see Beltratti, Andrea and Bortolotti, Bernardo (2007), "The Nontradable Share Reform in the Chinese Stock Market." FEEM Working Paper No. 131.06. Online. Available at: http://ssrn.com/abstract=944412 (both accessed 20 December 2012).
95 Beltratt and Bortolotti, op. cit., p. 3.
96 This document was issued by the State Council on 31 January 2004. Apart from the non-tradable share problem, it also addresses eight other issues such as perfecting the existing regulatory framework, improving the quality of listed companies, and cooperation of various departments, etc.
97 For more details regarding the process of the non-tradable share reform, see Yeung, Horace (2009), "Non-tradable Share Reform in China: A Review of Progress" in *Company Lawyer*, 30.
98 The first four pilot companies were Tsinghua Tongfang, Hebei Jinniu Energy Resources, Shanghai Zi Jiang Enterprise Group, and Sany Heavy Industry. Only Tsinghua Tongfang failed to pass its reform proposal due to floating shareholders' discontent about compensation. The other three accomplished the transfer program successfully, in two months.
99 For details about procedure rules, see Yeung, op. cit., p. 341.
100 Art. 5 *Measures*.
101 Art. 13 *Measures*.
102 Art. 16 *Measures*.
103 Art. 27 *Measures*.
104 Zhang, Gaosheng and Chu, Shanna (2007), "Guquan Fenzhi Gaige Hou Shangshi Gongsi Guquan Jiegou de Bianhua jiqi dui Gongsi Zhili Jizhi de Yingxiang" [The Influence of Split Share Structure Reform on Ownership Structure and Corporate Governance] in *Xiandai Jingji* [Modern Economics], 62.
105 CSRC, op. cit., p. 208.
106 *China Securities Daily* (28 August 2008), "30 Jia Dashizhi Gongsi jin Sancheng Xianshou Gu yi Liutong" [30 Percent of Shares in the Largest 30 Companies are Tradable].
107 Ibid.
108 Lynch, Jake (2008), "Insight: Chinese Bubble won't Burst yet" in *Financial Times* (7 April 2008).
109 Protiviti Consulting (2010), "Corporate Governance Assessment Summary Report on the Top 100 Chinese Listed Companies for 2010," p. 17. Online. Available at: www.protiviti.com/zh-CN/Headlines/Documents/2010 (accessed 30 August 2010).
110 Lynch, op. cit.

8 Implications of Chinese cross-listings

Market integration via dual-listing and regulatory cooperation/competition

Chapter 7 dealt with the Chinese legal reform aspect of integration of the Chinese and Hong Kong stock markets influenced by cross-listing. This chapter examines other factors which contribute to the integration of the two markets. Section 8.1 concerns a new trend of H-share companies partially returning to the domestic market by becoming dual-listed in China and Hong Kong. Advantages of the dual-listing model, its problems, and its influences on the two markets are discussed. Section 8.2 examines the way in which regulatory cooperation, CEPA, and international standards foster integration. Section 8.3 considers the more general issue of the competitive and complementary relationship between the two jurisdictions, an issue that is sparked by the desire to promote Shanghai as an international financial center. Section 8.4 discusses the future of China from the perspective of law and finance. The final part concludes.

8.1 Alleviating the market gap by dual-listing

Cross-listing between China and Hong Kong differs from cross-listing elsewhere. Usually, companies first list their shares on their domestic market, then go public again outside their home market. In contrast, most Chinese companies choose to list their H-shares first before partially returning to list their domestic A-shares on the Chinese stock markets. More recently, a new trend has appeared in which some Chinese companies simultaneously issue A- and H-shares, or even A-shares first.

In 2006 ICBC became the first company to dual-list in Hong Kong and Shanghai. It was followed by the China CITIC Bank Corporation in 2007. In the same year, China Railway Corporation diverged from the norm by listing in Shanghai first, and then in Hong Kong shortly afterwards.[1] By the end of 2012, 82 out of 172 H-share companies had issued A-shares.[2] This section explains the appeal of the A/H share models, the reason for the price disparity between them, and suggests corresponding measures and policies to reduce that price gap.

8.1.1 The attraction of dual-listing

The principal attractions of dual-listing from a Chinese policy perspective include: reinforcement of the domestic market with quality stock which had previously preferred overseas markets; the raising of governance standards for domestically listed companies; and the acceleration of the development of the domestic markets.[3]

A simultaneous flotation in Hong Kong and China would limit political pressure on the Chinese government, which is facing a nationalist backlash against foreigners buying significant stakes in domestic companies.[4] The two previous listings of Chinese state-owned banks in Hong Kong, ICBC and BOC, not only provoked criticism from economic nationalists but also from mainland institutions frustrated at seeing overseas investors buying stakes in well-known Chinese companies into which they could invest. Retail investors in China have also been angered by the ability of Hong Kong investors to profit from Chinese IPOs in which they cannot participate.

For issuers, apart from pricing considerations, concurrent dual-listings can bring about benefits, including quicker access to both exchanges and wider sources of capital, as well as lower costs associated with listings separated by a short time gap.

Dual-listings would also enable domestic investors, generally prohibited from investing overseas, to share in the growth of some of the best domestic companies. Moreover, assuming that a simultaneous offering is conducted at an identical offer price, domestic investors would be given the chance to invest in the same underlying assets at the same price as overseas investors, rather than at the typical premium seen when the A-share offering occurs later than the initial H-share offering. There has been domestic criticism that the state was selling off company shares to foreigners at a deep discount.[5] Certain highly successful IPOs, such as China Construction Bank in October 2005, provided pre-IPO strategic investors with shares far below their nominal value. But such criticisms might have been less vocal had domestic investors been able to participate in the offerings.

8.1.2 Factors contributing to the A/H-share price disparity

In theory, there should be little difference between shares listed on two or more stock exchanges. However, one disconcerting feature of Chinese dual-listed companies is a large and persistent price difference. The weighted average premium of A-shares over H-shares fell from some 830 percent in 2000 to 22 percent by the end of 2005.[6] The AH Premium Index is an index measuring the absolute price premium (or discount) of A-shares over H-shares for the largest and most liquid Chinese companies with A/H dual-listings.[7] In 2007, A-shares in dual-listed companies enjoyed a premium over their H-share counterparts ranging from 10 percent to 260 percent with a market capitalization-weighted average of over 50 percent.[8] The Index reached 133.24 points on its debut, 9 July

2007. This indicated that dual-listed companies' share prices in Shanghai were 33.24 percent higher than their counterparts in Hong Kong. But the AH Premium Index has been declining ever since and it reached 100.38 points as of the end of 2012, indicating that the A/H share price disparity may have ceased. Two major reasons may account for this phenomenon: first, the A-share market rapidly dropped, which was influenced by the Chinese government's tight credit and house control policies; second, the overseas stock markets, including Hong Kong, stayed relatively strong, which drove the H-share market to perform better than the A-share market.

Some researchers have attempted to understand factors accounting for the price diversity. Restrictions on foreign investor access to A-shares and mainland investor access to H-shares, coupled with the relatively small supply of A-shares, are often found to be the main reasons explaining the price differences.[9] Before the implementation of the Qualified Domestic Institutional Investors (QDII) scheme, domestic Chinese investors were only allowed to trade A-shares.[10] Moreover, the supply of A-shares was not enough to meet local investor demand, resulting in a premium for A-shares. However, when the QDII was introduced, it was believed that some of the demand would move to the HKSE, resulting in a decrease in A-share prices and an increase of H-share prices.

Additionally, several explanations are offered for the discount on foreign markets from both micro and macro perspectives.

Micro factors include information asymmetry. This can be caused by factors such as availability of reliable information, speed of information flows, language barriers, and different accounting standards.[11] Information asymmetry may result in a certain group of investors being disadvantaged and thus less willing to pay. Firm size can be an influential factor in information asymmetry because larger companies tend to have better information disclosure systems and attract more analysts to follow the news of their stocks. However, some scholars argue that this hypothesis does not entirely apply to the Chinese case because information asymmetry has become a relevant factor only recently, possibly attributable to the listing of some very large companies during 2006.[12]

There is also some evidence in support of the differential risk hypothesis, which postulates that the price premium can be explained by relative riskiness of assets because A-and H-share investors have different risk profiles. Market commentaries often suggest that mainland investors are more speculative, for example, having a higher risk appetite or being less risk averse, and hence may be more willing to pay a higher price for an asset at the same level of risk. In contrast, Hong Kong investors tend to be relatively more risk averse.[13] Certainly, there is still a question as to why investors are willing to pay a higher price for more volatile stocks. However, this appears to be consistent with Ma's results. He finds that the premium is positively related to A-share flotation, leading him to the conclusion that this is due to the risk-taking behavior of domestic investors.[14]

From a macro perspective, macroeconomic imbalance has arguably affected the prices of A- and H-share markets in at least three ways.[15] First, an undervalued currency has provided strong motivation for foreign investors to acquire H-shares as a proxy for RMB assets. Second, the external imbalance resulting from an undervalued RMB has been manifested in a rising internal imbalance as evidenced by rapidly growing bank deposits. With a limited choice of financial products available domestically, stock investment, in addition to real estate investment, has offered a convenient and feasible alternative to bank deposits for the majority of mainland investors. Finally, as China's trade surplus continues to rise, the opportunities for mainlanders to retain their foreign currency proceeds outside the mainland, so as to avoid capital controls, have increased. This in turn reflects increased ability of mainlanders to arbitrage by purchasing H-shares of the same stock whenever they find the discount offered by H-shares attractive enough.

8.1.3 Convergence of A/H-share prices

Such large price gaps for the two types of shares highlight the segmentation of the two capital markets and raises questions about the efficiency of price discovery and resource allocation in these markets. Hence, efforts have been made by both Hong Kong and the mainland to strengthen the linkages between the two markets with a view to reducing the price gaps and developing an integrated financial market to help sustain rapid economic growth in China.

McGuinness and Birtch offer a summary of measures and policies which contributed to the convergence story during the period from 2001 to 2005.[16] They cover a wide range of areas such as accounting and disclosure, regulation/role of government, corporate governance, and macroeconomic factors. Most of the measures attempt to reduce A-share prices and raise H-share prices. Non-tradable share reform and the implementation of the QDII are the principal factors. As noted by McGuinness and Ferguson, the flagging A-share market of 2001–05 stemmed from the announcement of the conversion of non-tradable state-held shares into tradable A-shares.[17] It awoke investors to the real possibility of subsequent swingeing cuts in state-related holdings. On the other side, the strong performance of the H-share market in the same period owed much to a firming up of expectations surrounding capital control liberalization via a QDII scheme designed to allow controlled and limited capital outflow from the mainland into Hong Kong.

In the past two years the regulatory authorities of the Chinese and Hong Kong markets have been more realistic and have done more to amplify the linkage of the two markets. One significant target would be the restrictions on currency convertibility, particularly in the mainland capital account, and other limitations relating to prudential or financial stability concerns, which restrict the mobility of users and providers of financial services, and of capital and financial instruments, between the two jurisdictions.

In order to lift those restrictions, Joseph Yam, former Chief Executive of the Hong Kong Monetary Authority, called for the creation of a channel between the two to foster better integration.[18] The channel would have the effect of pooling the various financial markets of the two jurisdictions, providing much greater liquidity and much more efficient price discovery.

As an illustration of how such a channel could be built, the approval process of the QFII could be synchronized with that of the QDII, either to bring about a zero net inflow and outflow of funds, or, if necessary, to allow a net inflow or a net outflow to achieve a better balance of international payments. Another example is the creation of derivative instruments in the form of certificates of ownership of shares listed on Shanghai, Shenzhen, and the HKSE. Such certification could be traded on both markets with an arbitrage mechanism to equalize prices.[19]

Indeed, the gap between the share prices of dual-listed Chinese companies has been minimized, as shown earlier. It is likely that the two markets will tend towards further integration that will allow them to function as one and enjoy the benefits of a single, much larger market.[20]

8.2 Regulatory cooperation and international standards integration

The regulatory cooperation and competition relationship between the securities markets in China and Hong Kong must be understood in the context of the "One Country Two Systems" formula, an arrangement that defines the political relationship between them. Under the Hong Kong Basic Law and the Chinese Constitution, with the exception of foreign relations and defense matters Hong Kong is guaranteed its independent legislature, judiciary, and legal system, as well as full economic autonomy.[21] Given this, Hong Kong is actually treated as a de facto state and an independent economy within the sovereign state of China, both by the Beijing government and the international community. Under these circumstances it is natural to assume a strong competitive relationship between the Hong Kong and Chinese economies.

Competition indeed exists, especially between Hong Kong and Shanghai. Shanghai has made enormous strides towards achieving its ambition of becoming a global financial center. On 29 April 2009, the Chinese government unveiled a plan for establishing Shanghai as an international financial and shipping hub by 2020. In order to implement the plan, the *Draft Regulations of Shanghai Municipality on Promoting the Building of International Financial Center* came into force on 1 August 2009.[22] This means that the city's ambition has become a national project and the central and local governments will combine resources to achieve it. As a result, it will present a direct threat to Hong Kong's financial status, although Chinese officials and commentators assert that a country as big as China can accommodate two global financial hubs.[23]

This rivalry between the two cities may create a dilemma for Chinese policymakers. On the one hand, China cannot let Hong Kong fall. Hong Kong is vital not only because it contributes significantly to China's economic growth by serving as a platform for Chinese companies to raise funds, and as a window towards international markets, but also because it is a showcase for the success of "One Country, Two Systems."[24] On the other hand, Chinese regulators demonstrate a certain degree of ambivalence towards Hong Kong. Beijing might be happier to see Shanghai, which sits squarely under its absolute sovereign and administrative control, take pole position. This would be compatible with the economic strength of the country and the international status of the RMB.

In a nutshell, the regulatory relationship between the mainland and Hong Kong is competitive, albeit complementary. Below we will examine aspects of regulatory cooperation, while Section 8.3 will discuss the competitive relationship.

8.2.1 Regulatory cooperation between China and Hong Kong

A At the national level

MEMORANDUM OF UNDERSTANDING (MoU)

Recalling Section 5.2, regulatory cooperation between China and Hong Kong was established in the early 1990s. The 1993 MoU was signed by the five parties, namely the CSRC, the SFC, the SHSE, the SZSE, and the HKSE. They agreed to provide mutual assistance and exchange information for the enhancement of investment protection; the compliance of relevant laws and rules; and the facilitation of consultation and cooperation by means of regular liaison and exchange of personnel.

Another *Memorandum of Understanding on Regulatory Cooperation Concerning Futures* (the "1995 MoU") was signed between the CSRC and the SFC on 4 July 1995. According to the *1995 MoU*, the two securities authorities began exchanges, cooperation, and law enforcement assistance between China and Hong Kong.

On 30 March 2007, the CSRC and the SFC signed and exchanged the *Side Letters to the 1995 MoU* (the "Side Letters") under which the SFC could require CSRC's assistance in investigations conducted in China.[25] Under the new arrangements, the SFC may request assistance from the CSRC in obtaining information in China for the purposes of SFC investigations. A person may face sanctions if he refuses to comply with a request to provide assistance. This power for the CSRC to compel the provision of information has been made possible by the amended Securities Law.[26] Previously, the SFC had to rely on the CSRC seeking voluntary cooperation from persons from whom information was sought. The SFC will also be able to exercise its investigatory powers to help the CSRC in probes that have a Hong Kong element.

Although the *Side Letters* mention exchange of information and mutual assistance in law enforcement, they constitute more an expression of a desire to cooperate than an actual binding agreement.[27] However, even assuming for the moment that some of the provisions of the *Side Letters* are legally binding, they could hardly be enforced through dispute settlement because, first of all, they do not have a dispute settlement mechanism; second, it is probably not politically feasible to refer a dispute between the central government and the Hong Kong government to a third party.[28]

China and Hong Kong are also subject to the *Multilateral Memorandum of Understanding Concerning Consultation and Cooperation and the Exchange of Information* (the "MMoU") adopted by the International Organization of Securities Commissions in May 2002. The *MMoU*, which aims to facilitate cross-border enforcement and exchange of information, enables signatories to receive assistance from other foreign signatories to pursue investigations. Compared to the MoU, the *MMoU* is much more detailed, containing more specific procedures pertaining to requests for assistance and response to such requests, as well as on consultation regarding mutual assistance and exchange of information; although the provisions of the *MMoU* "are not intended to create legally binding obligations or supersede domestic laws."[29]

MUTUAL ENFORCEMENT OF ARBITRATION AWARDS

The China *1994 Mandatory Provisions* and the Hong Kong LR require arbitration clauses to be included in the articles of association of H-share companies.[30] A claimant may elect for arbitration to be carried out at either the China International Economic and Trade Arbitration Commission or the Hong Kong International Arbitration Centre.[31]

Reciprocal enforcement of arbitration awards between the two regions is governed both by the *Convention on the Recognition and Enforcement of Foreign Arbitral Awards* of 1958 ("the New York Convention") and by the *Arrangement concerning Mutual Enforcement of Arbitral Award between the Mainland China and the HKSAR* of 1999 ("the Arrangement").[32] The *Arrangement* means that arbitration awards made on the mainland by recognized bodies under the Arbitration Law of China are enforced in Hong Kong. Likewise, awards made in Hong Kong under the Arbitration Ordinance are enforced by mainland courts.

Despite some clarification by the Supreme People's Court (SPC) in 2006,[33] there was continued uncertainty as to whether or not ad hoc arbitration awards rendered in Hong Kong or by foreign arbitration institutions such as the International Court of Arbitration of the International Chamber of Commerce (ICC), can be considered as Hong Kong arbitration awards under the *Arrangement.* With the publication of the latest *Circular of the SPC on Issues Relevant to the Enforcement of Hong Kong Arbitral Awards in the Mainland* ("the Circular"), this matter has been cleared up.[34]

The *Circular* confirms that two types of arbitration awards (ad hoc awards rendered in Hong Kong and those rendered in Hong Kong by foreign arbitration institutions) are both Hong Kong awards and can thus be enforced in the mainland according to Article 7 of the *Arrangement.*[35] This means that local people's courts have jurisdiction to review such awards and can also set aside or refuse to enforce them if the courts find relevant legal grounds to do so pursuant to the *Arrangement.*

The *Circular* is a positive development. It is likely to boost Hong Kong's development as a seat for international dispute resolution. Some industry experts have predicted that the clarification brought by the notification of the SPC will reinforce the position of the ICC and make it more attractive for administering cases relating to China.[36]

While the approach adopted by the SPC is to be welcomed, there are three issues to be further clarified.

The first issue is the nationality of an award. Earlier SPC statements have indicated that the Chinese courts recognize the place of arbitration as an important factor when determining whether it can enforce an arbitration agreement. Although the *Circular* does seem to hint, by references to the ICC in Hong Kong, that the seat of arbitration is more important than the institution's home country, its lack of detail and explanation means that any inferences drawn can be little more than speculation. It is difficult to conclude that the SPC has now adopted a new approach under which the "nationality" of arbitration awards will automatically follow the seat of arbitration rather than the place where the arbitration institution is established.[37] For example, would an ICC award rendered in the mainland be classified as a Chinese award or a foreign award?

The second issue concerns the enforceability of interim awards.[38] It is not clear whether the "award" mentioned in the SPC *Circular* is intended to refer to an interim award as well as a final award. Interim awards are temporary measures adopted by the arbitration tribunal prior to the issuance of the final award, usually to preserve certain assets or evidence, or to order a party to take or refrain from taking certain actions.[39] The key feature is that an interim award is provisional and temporary and may be revoked by any final award rendered thereafter. Chinese law is silent as to the enforceability of interim awards. Unfortunately, there is no such concept under the Civil Procedural Law[40] and the Arbitration Law[41] of China, and arbitration tribunals do not have the power to grant interim measures. In China, interim measures are exclusively within the remit of the Chinese courts.

The third issue concerns the enforceability of partial awards, meaning those which deal with one or more issues in a case, but not with the entirety of matters in dispute.[42] This is also a concept which does not exist under Chinese law and, to date, no publicly available case law has addressed the issue. A partial award, though, is different from an interim award in that it usually represents a final decision of the arbitration tribunal.

B At the regional level

The Guangdong provincial government and the Hong Kong government signed the *Framework Agreement on Hong Kong/Guangdong Cooperation* ("the Framework Agreement") on 7 April 2010.[43] The *Framework Agreement* gives a blueprint for forging a closer partnership between the two. It is a bridge built between the two systems and a significant embodiment of the principle of "One Country Two Systems."[44]

The *Framework Agreement* aims to create a new world class economic zone, with plans to create an advanced global manufacturing and modern services base, an international aviation, shipping and logistics hub, a high quality living area, and a world class metropolitan cluster.

According to the *Framework Agreement*, Hong Kong and Guangdong will speed up the construction of cross-boundary infrastructure facilities, optimize the business environment, and enhance personnel, cargo, information, and capital exchanges so to establish an international aviation hub, shipping center, and logistics center in the area; one that will feature lower costs and high efficiency. The *Framework Agreement* also stresses the development of green economy, ecological conservation, and the improvement of the living environment, among other goals.

Under the *Framework Agreement*, cooperation on finance is the focus for 2010. The main strategies are to enhance Hong Kong's position as an international financial center and to expedite the development of the financial services industries in Guangdong. This aims at building an international financial center with Hong Kong taking the lead with its financial systems, to be supported by resources and services in the Pearl River Delta cities.

The *Framework Agreement* has two important effects. First, it is endorsed by the State Council and translates the macro policies regarding Hong Kong/Guangdong into concrete measures,[45] laying a foundation for incorporating the related initiatives into the twelfth National Five-Year Plan. Second, it sets clear targets and development positioning for Hong Kong/Guangdong cooperation and outlines specific policies and measures so as to keep local industries and the general public better informed of the latest economic development and policies of the two places, so that they can build on the existing competitiveness and seize opportunities for expansion.

However, problems and obstacles exist in the establishment process of the integrated economic zone. Some are attributable to the differences between the two places: their political systems, economic policies, legal systems, and public administration systems. But some arise from other factors. They include: problems in cross flows in key areas; problems in coordinating the planning and construction of major public infrastructure facilities; problems of similar industry structures and excessive competition; problems of unaligned functions of cities. It is necessary to address the consequences of these problems.[46]

8.2.2 Integration contribution by the CEPA

One of the main factors which facilitates the integration of the Hong Kong and Chinese stock markets is the mutual recognition of professional qualifications. This was partly achieved by the *Closer Economic Partnership Arrangement* (CEPA). This is a forward-looking arrangement, as both China and Hong Kong/Macau have agreed to pursue further trade liberalization measures through consultation under its terms and conditions.[47] The objective of the *CEPA* is to strengthen trade and investment cooperation between the mainland and Hong Kong/Macau, and promote joint development of the two sides.

On 29 June 2003, the *CEPA* between the mainland and Hong Kong was signed and came into force. A similar agreement between the mainland and Macau was signed on 18 October 2003. Annual supplements have been signed between the mainland and Hong Kong. The most recent, Supplement VIII, was signed on 13 December 2011.

The *CEPA* covers market access to 18 service industries. Supplement I, agreed on 27 August 2004 between the mainland and Hong Kong, further relaxed market access conditions for Hong Kong services and service suppliers in the following areas: legal, accounting, medical, audiovisual, construction, distribution, banking, securities, transport, freight forwarding agencies, and individually owned stores.[48] Under Supplement I it agreed that eight more areas should be opened up for preferential access to Hong Kong service suppliers from 1 January 2005. In other words, the mainland was committed to opening a total of 26 sectors to Hong Kong with the *CEPA* and its Supplement I combined. It is expected that Supplement IX (currently under consultation) will cover 48 service sectors in total (together with previous supplements), strengthening cooperation in areas of finance, trade, and investment facilitation, and further promoting the mutual recognition of professional qualifications in the two places.[49]

Under the *CEPA* and its Supplements, securities intermediaries in Hong Kong and China have held discussions and reached a consensus in respect of collaboration on examinations, mapping of China/Hong Kong qualifications, arrangements for approval of qualifications, regulatory cooperation, and investigations.[50]

In line with the *CEPA* and its Supplements, the following opening-up measures have been implemented.[51] Since 1 January 2004 licensed professionals from Hong Kong applying for securities and futures practitioner qualifications in mainland China have only needed to participate in training and pass exams in legal knowledge. They do not need to pass exams on professional knowledge. Since 1 January 2005 qualified service providers from Hong Kong have been allowed to hold up to a 49 percent equity state in futures brokerage companies in the mainland. Since 1 January 2006 qualified mainland securities companies participating in innovative pilot programs have been allowed to set up subsidiaries in Hong Kong in accordance with relevant regulations. Qualified mainland futures companies have been permitted to operate futures businesses in Hong Kong, including setting up subsidiaries. Since 1 January 2008 qualified mainland fund management companies have been allowed to set up subsidiaries in Hong Kong to operate relevant businesses.

Gary Cheung, Chief Executive of the Hong Kong Securities Institute (HKSI), said

> Through taking the relevant training courses, Chinese practitioners can gain a better understanding of the regulatory framework and law governing the Hong Kong securities and futures markets, hence boosting their industry expertise … it is our hope that the examination will encourage talents in China and Hong Kong to learn from each other and exchange expertise, helping to lay a solid foundation for assimilation into the global financial markets.[52]

Indeed, the mutual recognition of professional qualifications between the securities and futures industries in China and Hong Kong encourages communication and the exchange of knowledge between practitioners. The collaboration also facilitates the cooperation between securities regulatory bodies, and the linkage and development of markets between both sides.

As commented on by Lucinda Wong, Director of Licensing, SFC, *CEPA* has brought the financial services industry of the mainland and Hong Kong much closer. Such cooperation effectively promotes the flow of expertise across the border, and cultivates a sound environment in which securities and futures practitioners can excel in their professionalism, enhancing the globalization and modernization of the securities markets.[53]

8.2.3 International standards integration

International standards, codes, and best practice can help to harmonize and sometimes standardize the systems and models adopted in the mainland and Hong Kong. One practical example of this is China's desire to converge domestic accounting standards with international ones. Another example is convergence on clearing and settlement.

A Adoption of international accounting standards

Information asymmetry increases agency costs as shareholders might not be fully informed about business risks. On the one hand, management obtains more detailed information than outsiders; on the other hand, information asymmetry reflects the advantage of the division of work between shareholders and management. To resolve the problem, many countries have regulated mandatory disclosure in securities laws in an effort to enhance information transparency.

As observed in Chapter 6, Chinese overseas companies adopt stricter accounting standards and employ reputational intermediaries when entering the Hong Kong market. This section explores the way in which this trend spreads to the Chinese domestic market.

There was no unified accounting system in China before the 1990s. Different standards, such as branch accounting standards, corporate accounting standards, and corporate accounting regulations applied simultaneously. In addition, different uses of accounting standards caused inaccuracies when a company went public or a company was involved with foreign investment.

When Chinese companies came to Hong Kong for listing, it was time-consuming and costly for them to convert their existing accounts to Hong Kong accounting standards. Moreover, foreign investors complained that Chinese accounting procedures were difficult to understand and under-regulated by Western standards. Bringing Chinese accounting standards into line with international accounting standards, therefore, became an urgent task in order to clarify the financial status of a listed Chinese company for foreign investors and to meet the tough listing requirements of overseas exchanges. When the first nine SOEs listed on the HKSE, they were required by the CSRC to comply strictly with Hong Kong accounting standards.[54] In particular, their financial reports had to include discrepancies arising from variations between Chinese and Hong Kong accounting standards.[55]

Furthermore, to bring Chinese regulatory standards up to international standards, Articles 24–26 of the *1994 Special Provisions* deal with the appointment and removal of accountants of overseas-listed Chinese companies. By adapting the law and practice of Hong Kong, Article 25 requires that if the shareholders' general meeting proposes the renewal or non-renewal of the services of the accountants, the accountants who may be removed or whose services may not be renewed should be given advance notice. The accountants have the right to present their views at the shareholders' general meeting. If the accountants resign on their own accord they are required to inform the shareholders' general meeting before they do so as to whether there is any evidence of impropriety within the company.

In the meantime, general accounting reform was under way in China. A significant step was taken in 1993 towards rationalizing China's enterprise accounting system. Impressive progress has been made toward the convergence of its Generally Accepted Accounting Principles (GAAP)[56] with the International Financial Reporting Standards (IFRS).

The development of the Chinese accounting system can be broadly divided into four stages.

The first stage (the 1992 GAAP) was from 1992 to 1997. Throughout this stage all A-share companies were required to follow the *Experimental Accounting System for Joint Stock Limited Enterprises* and the *Accounting Standards for Business Enterprises* (1992), which established a single set of accounting principles.[57] This was regarded as a landmark reform which substantially facilitated Chinese companies, including listed companies, to deal with foreign investors in Chinese companies, including listed companies.

The second stage (the 1998 GAAP) was from 1998 to 2000, represented by the adoption of the *Accounting System for Joint Stock Limited Enterprises* (1998). This regulation replaced the 1992 Chinese GAAP and was enacted specifically to eliminate discrepancies between Chinese GAAP and IFRS.[58] In addition, during this period, A-share companies were required to follow the Chinese Accounting Standards promulgated by the Ministry of Finance and the Accounting Law promulgated by the State Council in 1995.

The third stage (the 2001 GAAP) took place from 2001 to 2005, represented by the *Accounting System for Business Enterprises*. It moved Chinese accounting standards further toward convergence with the IFRS.[59] For example, inventory valuation at the lower of cost or market was optional in the 1998 GAAP but mandatory in the 2001 GAAP. The recognition of impairment losses was required only for investment in the 1998 GAAP, but it was also required for property, plant, equipment, intangible assets, construction in process, and investment property in the 2001 GAAP.

However, twenty-first century corporate scandals in Europe and the US, in particular at Enron, have shocked investors. The accounting system appeared incapable of delivering the information shareholders required, and markets and systems were threatened. This is relevant to the case of the Chinese stock markets. In an effort to deter potential corporate fraud, the CSRC invited international accounting firms like KPMG, PricewaterhouseCoopers, and Deloitte to engage in so-called "supplementary auditing" or "dual auditing" and deter the collusive practices of the domestic accounting firms and stock companies.[60] However, such measures have not realized a deterrent effect. PricewaterhouseCoopers and Deloitte were charged with breaches of accounting obligations in the cases of Jinzhou Port and Kelon Electronics.[61] Although it was the stock companies who were blamed at first, differences between the domestic accounting system and international accounting standards were questioned.

The fourth stage (the 2006 GAAP) began with the introduction of the *Chinese Accounting Standards for Business Enterprises* (2006).[62] The 2006 GAAP is substantially in line with the IFRS, except for certain modifications which reflect China's unique circumstances and environment.[63] All Chinese listed companies were required to start using it in their 2007 annual financial statements. The use of the *Standards* was expanded to all SOEs in 2008 and then to all large and medium sized companies in China in 2009.

The benefits of these accounting reforms for China are clear. The 2006 GAAP, incorporating accounting principles familiar to investors worldwide, would encourage investor confidence in China's capital markets and financial reporting. And it could serve as an additional spur for investment from both domestic and foreign sources of capital. For Chinese companies which are increasingly playing a global role, the acceptance of the new *Standards* should also reduce the cost of complying with the accounting regimes of the different jurisdictions in which they operate.[64] Meanwhile, it provides a good chance for Chinese stock companies to enhance their image by better information disclosure.

Nevertheless, concerns have been raised over the applicability of IFRS to Chinese accounting practices. Chen *et al.* found that convergence under 1998 Chinese GAAP did not immediately eliminate or significantly reduce the earnings gap between 1998 Chinese GAAP- and IFRS-based net incomes of Chinese listed companies.[65] Tang noted that compliance with a set of accounting standards depended not only on the acceptance of the constituency, but also on the competence of the audit profession which made judgments on the way in which they had been applied.[66]

Concerns have also been expressed over the effect of the Chinese preparers' level of competence. Again, as Tang points out, most accountants received an education incompatible with the new approaches.[67] This is even more so the case with management. These concerns call into question the relevance of China's convergence efforts.

B Clearing and settlement

In the financial markets, clearing and settlement systems refer to the arrangements for the clearing and subsequent settlement of transfer of funds or securities between financial institutions.[68] These funds or securities may be denominated in local or foreign currencies, and the transfer may take place within the same jurisdiction or cross-border.

The present inefficiencies of cross-border arrangements are the result of a lack of global technical standards, the existence of differing business practices, and inconsistent fiscal, legal, and regulatory underpinnings.[69] Specifically, a report commissioned by the EU identified 15 barriers, divided into technical or market barriers, barriers related to tax procedures, and legal barriers.[70] International bodies like the International Securities Services Association, the G30, and the Committee on Payment and Settlement Systems have issued international standards and best practices which help to overcome those barriers for cross-border clearing and settlement system. As China and Hong Kong are members of the above groups, this process will eventually help to facilitate the integration of clearing and settlement systems.

However, the main obstacle to cross-border clearing and settlement is the non-convertibility of the RMB on capital accounts and transactions. Hong Kong's RMB business used to be restricted to individual customers, with deposit business offered solely to Hong Kong residents, excluding business entities and non-residents. Hong Kong became the first place outside China to conduct personal RMB business under a Memorandum of Cooperation signed in November 2003. This implies that Hong Kong's business was of small-retail scale only. Subsequently, a limited scale of integration has been facilitated by the establishment of the Real Time Gross Settlement linkages with Shenzhen and Guangdong in relation to the clearing and settlement of Hong Kong and US dollars. Further, some clearing banks were appointed to conduct RMB business in Hong Kong.[71]

A breakthrough came in August 2010 when announcement of a pilot scheme was made for the RMB clearing bank and other eligible institutions outside China to invest in the interbank bond market in China. Furthermore, in 2011, enterprises in China were allowed to conduct and settle overseas direct investment in RMB, and banks in Hong Kong can provide RMB funds to facilitate such transactions. On the other hand, in the same year, the arrangement for foreign enterprises to conduct and settle foreign direct investment into China in RMB was formalized. This means that in addition to deposit-taking and currency exchange, Hong Kong is able to conduct a full range of RMB-related business such as remittance, lending, and securities, and is committed to becoming a premier offshore RMB business center.[72]

8.3 Regulatory competition: will Shanghai replace Hong Kong?

From previous discussions, a considerable level of integration between the two markets has been seen. Will this integration ultimately lead to a reversal, with Shanghai overtaking Hong Kong? Similarly, the question "Shanghai another Hong Kong?" posed by Wong, reflects the worry of many that the rise of Shanghai will lead to the demise of Hong Kong.[73] In particular, legalizing Shanghai as an international financial center in the State Council's regulation is increasingly pressurizing the spatial distribution of financial activity in the two jurisdictions.[74]

The following part shows that this prediction seems rather premature. It is developed with reference to historical evidence, the current range and intensity of financial activity in the two centers, and their limits and constraints. The extent to which Shanghai and Hong Kong can be considered complementary financial centers is also assessed.

8.3.1 Shanghai and Hong Kong: past and present

A Coexistence in the last century

From a historical perspective, Shanghai and Hong Kong were both well-known internationally as leading business and economic centers in Asia. However, Shanghai was no competition for Hong Kong during the last century.

Reed measured global financial centers based on the number of local bank headquarters and their international links and then ranked them during the period from 1900 to 1980, generally at five-year intervals.[75] These variables may be far from ideal, but they do have the advantage of having been assembled on a consistent basis for most of the century.[76] In his ranking, London and New York were in the top positions while Asian financial centers fell into the second or third tier. With respect to the three Asian centers of Hong Kong, Shanghai, and Tokyo, Figure 8.1 shows that Hong Kong started the century as the pre-eminent Asian center, only to fall behind Shanghai, and then Tokyo, before World War II. Then,

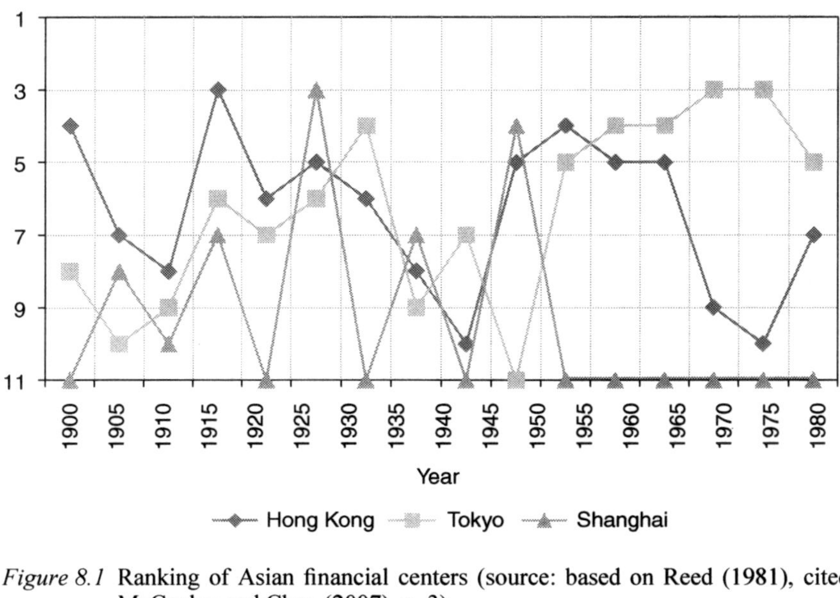

Figure 8.1 Ranking of Asian financial centers (source: based on Reed (1981), cited by McCauley and Chan (2007), p. 3).

after 1960, Tokyo emerged as the pre-eminent center in Asia. Reed placed Shanghai ahead of Hong Kong in just two years: 1925 and 1947. But even apart from World War II and the Mao years, Shanghai did not make the international top ten in 1900, 1920, and 1930, while Hong Kong was always placed.

History also shows us that the two have, in reality, been partners, supporting each other through their own unique circumstances and propeling each other forward. For example, in the 1950s the migration of Shanghai citizens to Hong Kong, along with their entrepreneurial and industrial skills, as well as their capital, helped to revive the local economy after the war, turning the city into an industrial, manufacturing, and shipping hub.[77] A few decades later, as Hong Kong became more affluent and labor costs increased, most of the local factories relocated to the mainland. That move contributed to the mainland's rise as "the factory for the world" for all types of goods, and transformed Hong Kong into the service economy that it is today.

B Shanghai and Hong Kong today

Hong Kong's status as China's international financial center of global significance remains as strong as ever. Shanghai is already a national financial center of China but it is still some way behind the world's leading financial centers in terms of market openness, market size, and the variety and sophistication of products available. Foreign exchange trading in China, for example, was less than 1 percent of that in London (Table 8.1). And while the Shanghai Stock Exchange was ahead of the London Stock Exchange in terms of market capitalization, it was less than one-fourth of the latter in terms of the amount of capital raised, and less than one-tenth of the New York Stock Exchange in terms of turnover.

Nevertheless, Shanghai is catching up with Hong Kong and other leading financial centers on qualitative counts. According to the latest Global Financial

Table 8.1 Shanghai's position among the world financial markets

(In US$ billion)	*Shanghai*	*Hong Kong*	*Tokyo*	*New York*	*London*
Stock market					
Capitalization (Mar 2009)	1,863	1,307	2,611	7,946	1,676
Turnover (2008)	2,587	1,629	5,586	33,639	6,474
Capital raised (2008, IPO plus secondary issues)	28	52	11	151	125
Bonds outstanding (domestic, end 2008)	2,210	50	11,077	24,622	1,223
FX market turnover (April 2007, daily average)	9	175	238	664	1,359
Banks' external assets (end 2008)	N/A	789	2,575	2,600	5,639

Centre Index (GFCI), Hong Kong ranked third in the table behind London and New York among the world's 77 financial centers in September 2012 (Table 8.2).[78] The GFCI evaluates the world's financial centers on the basis of a qualitative assessment by financial services professionals, incorporating such factors as the availability of skilled personnel, the tax, legal and regulatory environment, access to information, customers, and international financial markets.

By contrast, Shanghai is the biggest faller, down 31 points, falling out of the top 10. This illustrates that Shanghai has not established its image firmly. Shenzhen used to secure fifth place in the GFCI (2009), due to very strong support from Asian respondents, but by 2012 it had slipped considerably from that ranking. It is worth noting that over 80 percent of respondents who assessed Shenzhen in 2009 were mainly based in Hong Kong. Many view the city as a natural mainland partner to Hong Kong. It implies that Shenzhen is not very well connected outside Asia.

8.3.2 Competitive edge and constraints of the two centers

In the city's run-up to becoming an international financial center, Shanghai has clear advantages over many of its competitors. It has the back-up of one of the world's most dynamic economies. Between 1998 and 2008, China's economic growth averaged 9.6 percent a year; among the fastest in the world. In 2011 China overtook Japan as world's second largest economy.

But Shanghai also has its limits. A report by Hang Seng Bank, a principal member of the HSBC Group, outlines China's constraints and weaknesses with

Table 8.2 The world's top financial centers (previous ranking and score in brackets)

City	*Ranking*	*Score*	*Indicators*
London	1 (1)	785 (781)	• People: availability of skilled personnel, flexibility of the labor market, business education, and the development of human capital • Business environment: regulation, tax rates, levels of corruption, economic freedom, the ease of doing business • Market access: levels of securitization, volume and value of trading in equities and bonds, and the clustering effect of having many firms involved in the financial services sector together in one center • Infrastructure: cost and availability of buildings and office space, other infrastructure factors such as transport • General competitiveness: overall competitiveness in terms of more general economic factors such as price levels, economic sentiment, and how centers are perceived as places to live
New York	2 (2)	765 (772)	
Hong Kong	3 (3)	733 (754)	
Singapore	4 (4)	725 (729)	
Zurich	5 (6)	691 (689)	
Seoul	6 (9)	685 (686)	
Tokyo	7 (5)	684 (693)	
Chicago	8 (7)	683 (688)	
Shanghai	19 (8)	656 (687)	
Shenzhen	32 (32)	637 (638)	

Source: Z/Yen Group and Qatar Financial Centre Authority (2012), "Global Financial Center Index."

regard to its financial center status.[79] Most obvious is capital control, the presence of which inevitably limits the business volume of China's financial market. The inconvertibility of the RMB further restricts business volume in areas such as foreign exchange trading and IPO listing. Other constraints include controls on information and foreign participation. How far the mainland can, or is willing to, remove those constraints will be the key to the extent to which Shanghai can catch up with the world's leading financial centers by 2020.

Some weaknesses, such as the lack of skilled personnel, are easier to overcome, given the right incentives. Nor will an inadequate legal and regulatory environment be a hindrance to foreigners, as witnessed by the phenomenal inflow of FDI to the mainland in the 1990s. Other constraints, however, will need more time to overcome.

On the other hand, Hong Kong has significant strengths: a good foundation, mature mechanisms and thorough legal systems, better corporate governance, a large pool of financial talents such as fund managers and financial analysts, a mix of Eastern and Western cultures, rapid information dissemination, and a free flow of capital.[80]

But the big challenge for Hong Kong is a lack of talent.[81] Hong Kong's 6.8 million strong labor force has leveraged its creativity and skills to the limit. Companies in Hong Kong, whether local or foreign, have complained about the shortage of talent and skills and of the high wages they have to pay. They complained when the economy was booming before the onset of the Asian financial crisis and they still complain in the current economic recession. Part of the problem is that education and training must be even more focused on augmenting skill sets with a wider regional orientation. Another crucial issue is how much talent one can obtain from the labor force of a city economy. More investment in education and training cannot be the whole answer. Hong Kong desperately needs an influx of talent and skilled manpower, but is being hampered by a "Goretex border" – the current border allows resources from Hong Kong to flow into the mainland but restricts the flow of resources in the opposite direction. With increasing economic integration between the Chinese mainland and Hong Kong, the question of free movement of labor has been placed on the agenda. In this respect, Shanghai has a natural advantage, partly because of its well-educated labor force and partly because of its unfettered access to China's vast pool of talent.[82]

8.3.3 The rise of Shangkong

Hong Kong's role as China's international financial center does not appear to have been eclipsed since its return to Chinese sovereignty. Shanghai's role is growing, but the gap between the two cities remains considerable and Hong Kong continues to have an important role to play in managing China's financial resources and risk.

Shanghai and Hong Kong – with their distinct appeal – can achieve better results together than on their own. Garten, a Yale professor, recently said that for

China to make a major step towards becoming a global financial hub, ties between Hong Kong and Shanghai should be boosted.[83] He added that in the future the established centers of New York and London could be competing with "Shangkong," (a partnership between Shanghai and Hong Kong) especially in the aftermath of the global financial crisis. The global financial gravity would shift from the West to the East. Furthermore, an eclipse of the dollar would be mirrored by a rise in the use of the RMB, which also would guarantee Shangkong's prominence.

8.4 Law and finance: what will be the future of China?

The correlation between law and financial development are at the core of law and finance studies.[84] There are two questions; what is the role of financial markets in China's development, and how will China develop its financial markets to achieve its aims?

8.4.1 Financial markets and economic development

A stock market existed in China before the communist regime. The first stock market was established in Shanghai in the 1890s. At that time, Shanghai was considered one of the premier international finance centers of the Far East. At its peak, the shares of 76 companies were admitted for trading, 22 of them banks.[85] In 1949, when the communist government came to power, stock exchanges were viewed as one of the most prominent symbols of an oppressive capitalist regime and were forced to close down. State-owned banks have since become the sole representatives of the financial sector in the country. In fact, banks still intermediate nearly 75 percent of the capital in China, a significantly higher proportion than in other Asian countries (43 percent in India, 35 percent in Japan and 33 percent in South Korea) and the United States (only 19 percent).[86] This is understandable since an efficient banking system is usually a greater priority for a developing economy. A stock market relies on an elaborate array of institutions that are difficult to establish at an early stage of economic development.[87] However, the non-performing loans in China's banking system have driven Chinese leaders to consider a shift away from heavy reliance on the state-controlled banking system.

The problem of the Chinese bank-centered system can be explained by several factors. First, state-controlled banks have continued to account for 83 percent of bank assets in China since the new millennium.[88] The state ownership of banks has reduced competition and lessened the pressure on them to operate on a commercial, profit-oriented basis. Second, there is a lack of good internal credit assessment capabilities in many banks. The reason behind most of the non-performing loans in the past was the directed lending policies of the government to fund SOEs, regardless of their profitability. Third, these state-owned banks have a decentralized structure. Lending decisions are made at the local branch level, which is susceptible to influence from local government and favoritism towards local SOEs. This diffuse structure of banks, and many SOEs, makes it difficult for banks to collect and share useful information and make informed lending decisions.

Other than the predominantly state-owned banking system, the SOE system is another product of the communist regime in China. In 2003, the State Council approved the foundation of the State-owned Assets Supervision and Administration Commission (SASAC) with a view to separating the government's social and public management functions from its role as the investor of the state-owned assets.[89] This is intended to accelerate the reform and restructuring of the SOEs. Meanwhile, it also performs some substantive duties in relation to the operation of SOEs such as appointing, removing, and evaluating the executives of the enterprises. In 2010 the SASAC oversaw over 120 large SOEs. The formation of the SASAC was regarded by the state as a centralized effort to improve the socialist market economy.[90] Before that its duties were carried out by different organizations such as the State Economic and Trade Commission, Work Committee of Enterprises of the Communist Party of China Central Committee, the Ministry of Finance, as well as the Ministry of Labor and Social Security. For SOEs that are not managed by the SASAC, the local government established the Bureau of State Asset Management (BSAM) to manage state assets. Although the SASAC and BSAM are tasked with separating government functions from enterprise management, and relieving themselves of social and public duty burdens, government and political interferences continue to take place through them because they are still staffed with bureaucrats and Party Committee members.[91] Alternatively, it has been suggested that shifting the ownership of state shares from government agencies such as the SASAC and BSAM, to the corporate form of SOE, may result in better monitoring of top executives.[92]

Furthermore, new fundraising channels are required to finance emerging private economic activities. The process of economic liberalization in China started when the Communist Party began to focus its work on "social modernization" in 1979, and recognized that China's economy had underperformed for many years.[93] The most important aspect of modernization was the change in policy away from the state's control of the economy and towards the gradual recognition of the role of private companies. In the past the economy of China was centrally planned. Public ownership was the dominant form of ownership. These SOEs were financed either from the state budget directly, or indirectly through the state-controlled banking system. There was simply no demand for a capital market. This changed with the ideological shift in China away from a centrally planned economy towards a market economy. Public ownership began to be supplemented with private ownership. From 1994 onwards, following the enactment of China's first company law, the Anglo-American company system, with its feature of the separation of ownership and management, has become the key factor in economic reform in China. The step that China took to provide additional funding resources was to establish securities exchanges.

8.4.2 A roadmap for further legal reforms

Proper regulation is instrumental to market growth. The separation of the functions of ownership and control has been viewed as a cure for the ills of SOEs.[94] Such separation essentially means greater autonomy for the SOEs. The *Law on Industrial Enterprises Owned by the Whole People*, an early draft of the Company Law 1993, reaffirmed the Communist Party's explicit desire that the ownership and management of SOEs "be appropriately separated."[95] This law assigned managerial responsibility to enterprise managers, but preserved the roles of the Communist Party and government agencies in controlling business operations. State control could then be maintained by the following means. First, each company was required to have a Communist Party representative responsible for promoting party principles. Second, government agencies retained the authority to appoint managers.

It is worth noting that the Chinese Constitution originally recognized only socialist ownership.[96] In 1988 an amendment of the Constitution expressly authorized the development of a private economy.[97] The economic reform saw a shift from the strict adherence to socialist principles to a partial recognition of Western capitalist business. One of the experiments was a possible form of capital ownership by the workers in the SOEs, a joint state-private model. Gradually, small individual and household businesses emerged. Indeed, the state's efforts to stimulate private industry were successful. The number of workers employed in private companies rose to approximately 15 million in 1993 from just 3.7 million in 1988.[98] In a nutshell, the imminent task of the state was to design a regulatory framework to accommodate restructured SOEs and a much smaller, albeit emerging, private sector.

A Demand arising from the corporatization of SOEs

The ideological dilemma faced by the Chinese Communist Party was a choice between a strictly socialist model, a partially privatized model, and a laissez-faire capitalist model. China has not been shy in reiterating its commitment to socialism. The first pronouncement of the Company Law 1993 stated the purpose of "maintaining the social economic order and promoting the development of a socialist market economy." It appeared that a laissez-faire economy was not an option. By contrast, the initiation of economic reform was meant to move society away from socialism. It seemed that somewhere in between was the way to go. In Chinese terms, the path to reform by recasting Western corporate law was an attempt "to make a foreign construction readily adaptable to serving China, in the course of building socialism."[99] Control over industry and production has not been completely shifted from the state sector to private hands. China's economic reform has not been the privatization experienced by many former communist countries in the Soviet Union. Instead, it has been a process of corporatization, which entailed the adoption of corporate form, restructuring, and instituting stock ownership, but without necessarily relinquishing the state's controlling interest in the means of production.[100] The mechanism adopted by the state to prevent the loss of control is the creation of non-tradable shares. This has been discussed in depth in previous sections.

In a concentrated ownership setting, governance mechanisms are particularly important for controlling the behavior of managers. The largest shareholders should, in theory, have well-defined rights prescribed by law and the incentives and sufficiently large stakes to perform their monitoring role effectively. Protecting minority shareholders from the opportunistic expropriation of management or controlling shareholders was not the chief concern of the Chinese legal framework because it did not fit the reality of China's prevailing state ownership.[101] The majority stakes held by the state meant that shareholders had little hope of exercising their decision-making and appointment rights in a meaningful way.

However, the monitoring problem in many SOEs has been the absence of an ultimate principal.[102] The state as the majority shareholder plays an ineffective role in monitoring the behavior of managers because it is a collective body. The theoretical owner of a SOE is the government or the "people as a whole." In practice, one tactic the Chinese government used was the assignment of state-owned shares to local state property administration departments. Nonetheless, their behavior was governed purely by political considerations or the private benefits of government officials instead of commercial merits. There has been no "real" ownership. There has been no body within the state with sufficient and appropriate incentive to carry out a monitoring function. The ambiguous alignment of risk bearing and control has rendered the ownership structure of the state's interests extremely unclear. Managers have often been allowed to seize control and become the de facto controlling shareholder. Fundamentally, enforcement against the improper conduct of managers can be difficult. The state's dual role of regulator and blockholder of many listed firms has been problematic.[103] Meanwhile, the minority shareholders have limited power to affect managerial decisions. Potential majority-minority and principal-agent conflicts have been acute in the state sector.

B Demand arising from the emergence of private economic activities

One goal of company law should be to enable the organization of economic activities in the private sector. Unfortunately, the early Company Law was both restrictive and ambiguous. It was "pervaded with the attitude of making decisions on behalf of people."[104] Entrepreneurs were not given the opportunity to work out an efficient arrangement according to their own terms. Once again, this problem lay in the Company Law's overwhelming orientation towards the corporatization of SOEs. The company form contemplated by the Company Law was not one formed by a group of private entrepreneurs, who contract among themselves for an optimal set of rules. Rather, it was the SOE model.

A key feature was the state's control over the privilege of incorporation. Government departments, with the authority granted by the State Council or the provinces, had to approve the establishment of a company.[105] Similarly, public stock offerings required the State Council's permission.[106] The processes of the incorporation, operation, and capitalization of a business were matters of governmental control and permission, not of right. The transition from the planned economy to the socialist market economy, in theory, should be a shift from the priority of public law to the priority of private law.[107] In essence, the traditional legal culture of China emphasized public law and was state-centered. By contrast, a market economy should predominantly be governed by private law, the foundation of which includes the essential elements of a contract, such as the will, rights, and responsibilities of parties, as well as effective enforcement mechanisms. The corporate form, as an example of contract, will need all these elements to function properly. The socialist market economy in China presented a slightly different circumstance. The vast majority of companies continued to be state-owned, accustomed to dealing only with other government-owned entities.

More importantly, the early law provided for privately owned companies in only a preliminary and general manner. For example, vague legal terms such as "principles of voluntariness, equality, fairness, and good faith" seemed to permit further administrative or judicial determinations.[108] The ownership patterns and structures of collectively owned enterprises were heterogeneous. Although the state became "well aware that clearly defined ownership rights will be a major factor in further development," how to devise a regulatory framework to cater for different types of company and their different characteristics was left unresolved.[109] The lack of theoretical debate and empirical study of the domestic demands contributed to the unsophisticated nature of the law. Most of the provisions were tailored to dealing with issues surrounding SOEs. The capital requirement for incorporation, the requirement for internal structures and the management of companies, and qualifications and duties of directors and supervisors, all reflected the government's strong control over SOEs.[110] The needs of private companies or collectives were not properly addressed. The early Company Law lagged behind the rapid development of China's economic reform soon after its enactment. The incompatibility between its design and the actual situation in China worsened in the new millennium, as the number of privately owned businesses grew while the number of state-owned entities dropped rapidly. A drastic update of the law has been necessary.

8.4.3 Redefining the position of Hong Kong

China Railway's listing in Shanghai first, and then Hong Kong, in 2007, seemed to be a turning point. A strong political signal was sent out, that the future Hong Kong listing of a Chinese company might no longer be the primary one. The importance of this signal was twofold. First, it signified the end of the learning process of Chinese companies in Hong Kong and made clear that a foreign listing is optional. Second, the status of Shanghai rose above Hong Kong for the first time.

Undeniably, Hong Kong has been a successful experiment ground for China. The reforms in China have generally been carried out in phases. First, they were applied to a small selection of participants. If successful, they were extended.

In the past, foreign ownership in major Chinese companies was only a dream. However, through listing in Hong Kong, foreign strategic investors in these companies are now common. This experiment of introducing foreign ownership was further expanded on 26 May 2003. UBS and Nomura became the first two foreign entities to obtain a Qualified Foreign Institutional Investor (QFII) license. This symbolized a formal start to the long-awaited scheme that enabled foreigners to ride on the back of China's growth, without first going through Hong Kong.

Hong Kong has significantly helped the development of China's market. At the same time, it has capitalized on the China factor. Thanks to the influx of Chinese companies, Hong Kong was crowned as the IPO capital of the world for three years, dwarfing London and New York, before falling to fourth position in 2012.[111] However, there are some indications that the role of cross-listing will decline in the future. First, as formally recognized by the State Council, China is committed to developing Shanghai into an international finance center. Second, with the listing of the last of the big four Chinese banks (the Agricultural Bank of China) in Hong Kong in July 2010, almost all giant state-owned companies have already been listed in Hong Kong. There will definitely be a shortage of attractive new Chinese issuers in Hong Kong in the future.

This is further evidenced by the HKSE's move to look for alternative sources of new issuers. For example, Russian company UC Rusal, the world's largest aluminium producer, listed in Hong Kong in 2010. It claimed to be the first Russian IPO there. Yet there were regulatory hurdles to overcome; Hong Kong Listing Rules Chapter 19 made no mention of Russian companies (the fact that Rusal is actually incorporated in Jersey has undoubtedly helped a lot).[112] European companies such as L'Occitane en Provence, Samsonite, and Prada have also raised funds in Hong Kong.

Until late 2006, the HKSE would accept listing applications from only companies incorporated in a few jurisdictions such as Hong Kong, China, the Cayman Islands, and Bermuda.[113] Since October 2006 it has approved 14 other acceptable overseas jurisdictions under the Hong Kong Listing Rules, including Australia, Brazil, British Virgin Islands, Canada (British Columbia and Ontario), Cyprus, Germany, the Isle of Man, Japan, Jersey, Luxembourg, Singapore, the UK and the US (California). Most recently, in January and then in March 2011, it started to include Italy and France as acceptable overseas jurisdictions.

Alternatively, Hong Kong may consider attracting smaller Chinese issuers. It is reported that the CSRC plans to drop its requirement that Chinese companies listing in Hong Kong must meet certain size criteria: RMB400 million in net assets, an offering size of US$50 million, and RMB60 million in profits in the year before listing.[114] First, it is an apparent effort to ease fundraising pressure on the domestic market in China by encouraging more companies to float shares in Hong Kong. Second, this is in line with the CSRC's intention to move away from merit regulation and toward US-style disclosure regulation.

Furthermore, whilst the rivalry between Hong Kong and Shanghai may be too intense to form a convincing partnership, Shenzhen, a neighboring city, could be a better option. Following the State Council's agreement in principle on

The Overall Development Plan for the Qianhai Shenzhen–Hong Kong Modern Service Industry Cooperation Zone (2010), it officially approved preferential policies to facilitate the development of the zone on 27 June 2012. Plans for Qianhai's development envision four modern service industries, including finance, modern logistics, information service, and science and technology services, along with other professional service sectors.[115] Finally, the HKSE is also in the process of broadening its range of products and services. One example will be its acquisition of the London Metal Exchange.[116] Adapting to change is always the core competency of Hong Kong and the people there.

8.5 Concluding remarks

This chapter has examined the integration between the Chinese and Hong Kong stock markets, resulting, to a significant degree, from the cross-listing of Chinese companies in Hong Kong. Since Chinese legal reform has been previously discussed, this chapter focuses on the role of dual-listing and regulatory cooperation/competition in this process.

Dual-listings are driving forces to alleviate the gap between China and Hong Kong's stock markets, both in terms of market size and regulatory quality. Although various factors lead to high underpricing levels in Chinese IPOs, a set of measures have been taken, and policies formulated, in an attempt to converge A/H share prices. These include accounting and discourse, regulation/role of government, corporate governance, and macroeconomic factors.

Regulatory cooperation at the national and regional levels, and international standards, also accelerate harmonization of the two markets. First, the MoUs and mutual enforcement of arbitration awards, as well as the regional agreement on Hong Kong/Guangdong, greatly strengthen regulatory cooperation of the two markets. Second, the *CEPA* facilitates the mutual recognition of qualification of financial intermediaries between China and Hong Kong. Third, the adoption of international standards and practices, such as international accounting standards and the clearing and settlement system, can help to harmonize or even standardize the two financial systems.

With the narrowing regulatory gap between China and Hong Kong, connections have been made: Beijing declared that Shanghai would be a major global financial center in the next decade, and cooperation between Hong Kong and Shanghai is growing. The concern arises as to whether Shanghai is threatening Hong Kong. But history reveals a considerable amount of synergy between them. The inevitable economic integration of the two economies might eventually lead to the establishment of a common market that combines the economic resources of China and the supply-side strengths of Hong Kong. In the foreseeable future, New York and London might be vying with a new competitor: Shangkong. Nonetheless, even if the partnership does not work, Hong Kong will very likely remain a leading financial center for the foreseeable future. Meanwhile, whilst Shanghai is developing very quickly, China must continue to improve the regulatory system to keep up with the momentum of growth.

Notes

1 The company was listed in Shanghai on 3 December 2007 (stock code 601390), and in Hong Kong on 7 December (stock code HK 00390).
2 A list of H-share companies is available via the HKSE website. Online. Available at: www.hkex.com.hk/eng/stat/smstat/chidimen/chidimen.htm (accessed 20 December 2012). This list is used to check against the list of A-share companies.
3 Herbert Smith LLP (2006), "A New Model: How the Listing of Companies in both Hong Kong and China could Work in the Future" in *International Financial Law Review*, 25, p. 36.
4 Tucker, Sundeep and Dyer, Geoff (2006), "ICBC's Dual-listing Plan is Vote for Shanghai" in *Financial Times* (13 July 2006).
5 For example, see the case of ICBC in Chapter 6.
6 SFC (2005), "Trading of the 31 Mainland Companies which Issued Both A-shares and H-shares." Online. Available at: www.sfc.hk/web/EN/published-resources/research-papers/market-reviews. It is worth noting that in 2005 there were only four companies with H-share premiums.
7 The AH Premium Index was launched by the Hang Seng Bank on 9 July 2007. It is designed to provide the market with a simple and easy-to-follow barometer to measure the price difference between A-shares and H-shares. Online. Available at: www.hsi.com.hk/HSI-Net/HSI-Net (accessed 20 December 2012).
8 Hong Kong Monetary Authority (2007), "Price Convergence between Dual-listed A and H Shares" in *China Economic Issues*, July 2007, p. 2. Online. Available at: www.info.gov.hk/hkma/eng/research/cei/2007/CEI-200706.pdf (accessed 16 October 2009).
9 Chan, Kalok and Kwok, Johnny (2005), "Market Segmentation and Share Price Premium: Evidence from Chinese Stock Markets" in *Journal of Emerging Market Finance*, 4, p. 59. Also, Yeung, Winghim and Zhou, Jing (2007), "Changes in Regulation and Prices of Dual-listed Stocks in China," p. 7. Online. Available at: http://ir.lib.sfu.ca/handle/1892/9454 (accessed 20 December 2012).
10 On 14 April 2006, the CSRC announced that domestic Chinese investors were allowed to trade in foreign stock exchanges through the QDII. This scheme was also being extended to the HKSE on 11 May 2007. Since then, domestic Chinese investors are allowed to trade stock listed in Hong Kong through QDII, while the initial amount of money that can be flowed into the HKSE was estimated to be HK$56.7 billion. See Yeung and Zhou, op. cit., p. 7.
11 Bailey, Warren and Jagtiani, Julapa (1994), "Foreign Ownership Restrictions and Stock Prices in the Thai Capital Market" in *Journal of Financial Economics*, 36. For the Mexican market, see Domowitz, Ian, *et al.* (1997), "Market Segmentation and Stock Prices: Evidence from an Emerging Market" in *Journal of Finance*, 52.
12 Fong, Tom *et al.* (2007), "Share Price Disparity in Chinese Stock Markets." HKMA Working Paper 11/2007, p. 10. Also, for more empirical evidence, see Chan and Kwok, op. cit., p. 55.
13 Chan and Kwok, op. cit., p. 55.
14 Ma, Xianghai (1996), "Capital Controls, Market Segmentation and Stock Prices: Evidence from the Chinese Stock Market" in *Pacific Basin Finance Journal*, 4.
15 Fong *et al.*, op. cit., p. 4.
16 McGuinness, Paul and Birtch, Thomas (2008), "The 2001–2005 Price Convergence in the A- and H-shares of Chinese State-owned Enterprises: A Story of Unprecedented Economic, Regulatory and Political Change" in *Journal of Finance Regulation and Compliance*, 16, p. 248.
17 McGuinness, Paul and Ferguson, Michael (2005), "The Ownership Structure of Listed Chinese State-owned Enterprises and its Relation to Corporate Performance" in *Applied Financial Economics*, 15.
18 Yam, Joseph (2007), "Linking the Mainland's and Hong Kong's Financial Markets

(II)." Viewpoint, HKMA, February 2007. Online. Available at: www.info.gov.hk/hkma/eng/viewpt/20070201e.htm (accessed 17 October 2009).

19 Ibid.

20 For reasons and benefits to link the two financial markets, see ibid.

21 Hong Kong Basic Law, arts. 2, 13 and 14. Also, Constitution Law of China, art. 31.

22 Pursuant to the regulations, Shanghai will join forces with state financial administrative departments to optimize the composition of financial market players and establish different types of institutional investors, through the foundation of such instruments as securities investment funds, social insurance funds, insurance assets, enterprise annuity funds, and trusts.

23 Cheung, Gary (2009), "Finance Chief Plays down Shanghai Threat – Room Enough for HK and its Mainland Rival" in *South China Morning Post* (27 March 2009).

24 Wang, Jiangyu (2009), "Regulatory Competition and Cooperation between Securities Markets in Hong Kong and Mainland China" in *Capital Markets Law Journal*, 4, p. 388.

25 SFC (2 April 2007), "Press Release: Cross Border Enforcement Enhanced." Online. Available at: www.sfc.hk/sfcPressRelease/EN/sfcOpenDocServlet?docno=07PR52 (accessed 20 December 2012).

26 Art. 230, the Securities Law of China 2005.

27 Wang, op. cit., p. 390.

28 Ibid.

29 *MMoU*, art. 6 (a).

30 The *1994 Mandatory Provisions*, art. 163 (1) and the Hong Kong LR, Chapter 19A.54.

31 The *1994 Mandatory Provisions*, art. 163 (2).

32 The *Arrangement* was signed on 21 June 1999 and came into force on 24 January 2000.

33 The *Interpretation of the SPC Concerning Some Issues on Application of the Arbitration Law of the PRC* was promulgated by the SPC on 23 August 2006 and came into force on 8 September 2006.

34 The *Circular* was promulgated by the SPC and came into force on 30 December 2009.

35 Article 7 *Arrangement* mirrors Article V of the New York Convention, listing limited grounds on which enforcement and recognition of awards may be refused.

36 For example, ICC (2010), "Enforcement in Mainland China of ICC Arbitral Awards Rendered in Hong Kong." Online. Available at: www.iccwbo.org/court/arbitration/index.html?id=34693 (accessed 21 April 2010); and *China Law & Practice* (2010), "Court Clarifies Enforcement of Hong Kong Arbitral Awards." March 2010 issue.

37 *China Law & Practice*, op. cit.

38 Herbert Smith, LLP (2010), "Recent International Arbitration Developments." Online. Available at: www.herbertsmith.com/NR/rdonlyres/C7A10A47-AAEC-4BF1-A686-E6AE73FAD018/14586/0304Recentintlarbdev.html (accessed 21 April 2010).

39 The UNCITRAL Rules (Article 26), ICC Rules (Article 23.1) and HKIAC Rules (Article 24.2), among others, all make provision for interim measures in arbitrations which are governed by those rules.

40 The Civil Procedure Law of China was adopted on 9 April 1991 at the Fourth Session of the Seventh National People's Congress, came into force on 28 October 2007, was amended on 28 October 2007, and the amended law came into force on the same day.

41 The Arbitration Law of China was adopted on 31 August 1994 at the Ninth Session of the Standing Committee of the Eighth National People's Congress and came into force on 1 September 1995, was amended on 27 August 2009, and the amended law came into force on the same day.

42 Herbert Smith LLP, op. cit.

43 See Hong Kong Government (7 April 2010), "Signing Ceremony of Framework Agreement on Hong Kong/Guangdong Cooperation Held in Beijing." Press Release. Online. Available at: www.info.gov.hk/gia/general/201004/07/P201004070113.htm (accessed 20 April 2010).

44 See comments on the *Agreement* by Henry Tang, former Chief Secretary for Administration of Hong Kong, in *China Daily* (9 April 2010), "A Bridge Built for Two Systems."

45 The National Development and Reform Commission promulgated the *Outline of the Plan for the Reform and Development of the Pearl River Delta* in January 2009, specifying Hong Kong/Guangdong cooperation as a national policy.

46 Bauhinia Foundation Research Centre (2008), "Creating a World-Class Pearl River Delta Metropolis – Accelerating Economic Integration between Guangdong and Hong Kong: Executive Summary," pp. 10–11. Online. Available at: www.bauhinia.org/publications/GD-HK_ES.pdf (accessed 20 December 2012).

47 Under *CEPA*, consultation and negotiation are carried out by the steering committee and the liaison offices and working groups set up under it. See art. 19 of *CEPA*.

48 Art. 2 (1) Supplement I.

49 For further details, see the latest development of the *CEPA*. Online. Available at: www.tid.gov.hk/english/cepa/further_liberal.html (accessed 20 December 2012).

50 SFC (21 November 2003), "Closer Economic Partnership Arrangement – Arrangements relating to Qualifications of Securities and Future Industry Practitioners." Press Release. Online. Available at: www.sfc.hk/sfcPressRelease/EN/sfcOpenDocServlet?docno=03PR257 (accessed 20 December 2012).

51 For full details, see CSRC (2009), "Annual Report 2008," pp. 40–41.

52 HKSI (29 December 2004), "Mutual Recognition of Professional Qualification Marks New Page in Mainland-Hong Kong Coalition." Press Release. Online. Available at: www.hksi.org/eng/news/news_20041229.html (accessed 5 April 2010).

53 Ibid.

54 See the speech by Jiange Li, former Vice-Chairman of the CSRC, "The Chinese Stock Market in Transition to a Market Economy," at the China Economic Association (CEA) annual conference at the London School of Economics. The paper was published by the CEA as one of its Discussion Paper Series.

55 Starting in 2005, Hong Kong Financial Reporting Standards (HKFRS) are identical to IFRS. While Hong Kong had adopted many of the earlier IAS as Hong Kong standards, some had not been adopted, including IAS 32 and IAS 39. And all of the December 2003 improvements and new and amended IFRS issued in 2004 and 2005 came into force in Hong Kong beginning in 2005, although there are several minor wording differences between HKFRS and IFRS.

56 GAAP refers to the standard framework of guidelines for financial accounting used in any given jurisdiction: generally known as Accounting Standards. GAAP includes the standards, conventions, and rules accountants follow in recording and summarizing transactions, and in the preparation of financial statements.

57 For the motivations and processes leading to the promulgation of the Accounting Standards for Business Enterprises and its conceptual content, see Kazenski, Paul and Wong, Yin Ling (1994), "Unifying Accounting in the People's Republic of China" in *International Journal of Accounting*, 29.

58 Chen, Shimin, *et al.* (2002), "Evidence from China on Whether Harmonized Accounting Standards harmonized Accounting Practices" in *Accounting Horizons*, 16, p. 184.

59 For comparisons between the 1998 and 2001 Chinese GAAP with the IFRS, see Peng, Songlan, *et al.* (2008), "Does Convergence of Accounting Standards Lead to the Convergence of Accounting Practices?" in *International Journal of Accounting*, 43, p. 453. This comparison reflects the progress towards convergence.

60 Jiang, Qingyun (2007), "Monitoring Problems versus Fiduciary Duties in Chinese Stock Companies: An Economic and Comparative Analysis on Corporate Governance" in Eger, Thomas (eds.), *Economic Analysis of Law in China*, Cheltenham: Edward Elgar, pp. 210–12.
61 PricewaterhouseCoopers was charged in 2001 for issuing an audit report relating to a fraudulent financial scheme run by by Jinzhou Port; Deloitte was charged in 2006 for approving the fraudulent financial scheme of Kelon Electronics.
62 *The Accounting Standards for Business Enterprises* was issued by the Ministry of Finance on 15 February 2006 and came into force on 1 January 2007.
63 For similarities and differences of the new *Standards* and IFRS, see Deloitte (August 2006), "China's New Accounting Standards: A Comparison with Current PRC GAAP and IFRS." Online. Available at: www.iasplus.com/dttpubs/0607 prcifrsenglish.pdf (accessed 15 April 2010).
64 Ibid, p. 1.
65 Chen *et al.*, op. cit.
66 Tang, Yunwei (2000), "Bumpy Road Leading to Internationalization: A Review of Accounting Development in China" in *Accounting Horizons*, 14, p. 98.
67 Ibid.
68 See speech by Yam, Joseph (8 July 2004), "Commencement of the Clearing and Settlement Systems Ordinance." Online. Available at: www.info.gov.hk/hkma/eng/viewpt/20040708e.htm (accessed 13 April 2010).
69 CPSS-IOSCO Joint Task Force (November 2004), "Recommendations on Central Counterparties," p. 6. Online. Available at: www.bis.org.publ.cpss64.pdf (accessed 15 April 2010).
70 Ibid.
71 The RMB Real Time Gross Settlement (RTGS) system was upgraded from the RMB Settlement System in June 2007 with the Bank of China (Hong Kong) Limited as its clearing bank. The clearing bank maintains a settlement account with the People's Bank of China and is a member of China's National Automated Payment System (CNAPS). The RMB RTGS system in Hong Kong can be regarded as a technical extension of CNAPS in mainland China, but governed by Hong Kong laws.
72 Hong Kong Monetary Authority (2012), "Hong Kong: The Premier Offshore Renminbi Business Center." Online. Available at: www.hkma.gov.hk/media/eng/publication-and-research/hkrmb/hkma-rmb-booklet.pdf (accessed 20 December 2012).
73 Wong, Richard (2002), "Shanghai: Another Hong Kong?" HK Centre for Economic Research. Online. Available at: www.hktdc.com/info/mi/a/ef/en/1X005RK7/1/Economic-Forum (accessed 20 December 2012).
74 The *Opinions on Boosting Development of Modern Service and Advanced Manufacture Industry and Establishing International Financial and Shipping Center in Shanghai* was promulgated by the State Council on 14 April 2009.
75 Specifically, Reed adopted five variables: local bank headquarters, local bank direct links, private banks, foreign bank offices, foreign bank direct links. See Reed, Howard (1981), *The Pre-eminence of International Financial Centers*, New York: Praeger, pp. 9–12.
76 McCauley, Robert and Chan, Eric (2007), "Hong Kong and Shanghai: Yesterday, Today and Tomorrow." Bank of International Settlements Research Paper, p. 2. Online. Available at: www.bis.org/repofficepubl/arpresearch_fs_200803.01.pdf (accessed 20 December 2012).
77 For further details, see Arculli, Ronald (2009), "Shanghai-Hong Kong: Not a Zero-sum Game." Speech as HKEx Chairman at Macquarie's China/Hong Kong Conference. Online. Available at: www.hkex.com.hk/press/speech/sp090518.htm (accessed 11 October 2009).

78 Z/Yen Group and Qatar Financial Centre Authority (2012), "Global Financial Centre Index." Online. Available at: www.zyen.com/PDF/GFCI%2012.pdf (accessed 20 December 2012).
79 Leung, Bill and Yim, Joanne (2009), "Shanghai's Future as an International Financial Centre." Treasury Division of Hang Seng Bank. Online. Available at: www.hangseng.com/ermt/eng/fxmv/pdf/ecof_e_2009jun.pdf (accessed 20 December 2012).
80 Further to comments by Fang Zheng, Chairman of the SFC, see Xu, Ke (2007), "Hong Kong Eyes Link-up with Mainland Bourses" in *Caijing Magazine* (28 June 2007).
81 Wong, op. cit.
82 Ibid.
83 Garten, Jeffrey (2009), "From NyLon to Shangkong" in *Financial Times* (10 May 2009).
84 Siems, Mathias (2007), "Legal Origins: Reconciling Law & Finance and Comparative Law" in *McGill Law Review*, 52, p. 57.
85 Brayshaw, Robin and Teng, Z. (1995), "Re-emergence of the Chinese Stock Market" in Blake, John and Gao, Simon (eds.), *Perspectives on Accounting and Finance in China*, London: Routledge, p. 93.
86 McKinsey Global Institute (2008), "Mapping Global Capital Markets Fourth Annual Report," p. 19. Online. Available at: www.mckinsey.com/insights/mgi/research/asia (accessed 20 December 2012).
87 See, for example, Allen, Franklin, and Gale, Douglas (2000), *Comparing Financial Systems*, London: MIT Press.
88 McKinsey Global Institute (2006), "Putting China's Capital to Work: The Value of Financial System Reform," p. 35. Online. Available at: www.mckinsey.com/insights/mgi/research/asia (accessed 20 December 2012).
89 SASAC (22 May 2003), "China State-owned Assets Management System Reform Entering New Stage." Online. Available at: www.sasac.gov.cn/n2963340/n2964727/n2974401/2976097.html (accessed 20 December 2012).
90 Ibid.
91 Tan, Lay Hong and Wang, Jiangyu (2007), "Modelling an Effective Corporate Governance System for China's Listed State-Owned Enterprises: Issues and Challenges in a Transitional Economy" in *Journal of Corporate Law Studies*, 7, p. 175.
92 Ibid., p. 176.
93 MacNeil, Iain (2002), "Adaptation and Convergence in Corporate Governance: The Case of Chinese Listed Companies" in *Journal of Corporate Law Studies*, 2, p. 297.
94 Clarke, Donald (2003), "Corporate Governance in China: An Overview" in *China Economic Review*, 14, pp. 497–500.
95 The law was enacted by the National People's Congress in 1988.
96 Constitution of China 1982, art. 6.
97 See art. 11 of the Constitution 1988, which provides the following, "the state permits the private sector of the economy to exist and develop within the limits prescribed by law. The private sector of the economy is a complement to the socialist public economy."
98 Art, Robert and Gu, Minkang (1995), "China Incorporated: the First Corporation Law of the People's Republic of China" in *Yale Journal of International Law*, 20, p. 281.
99 Ibid., p. 280.
100 Ibid., pp. 279 and 283.
101 Tang, Xin (2008), "Protecting Minority Shareholders in China: A Task for Both Legislation and Enforcement" in Kanda, Hideki *et al.* (eds.), *Transforming Corporate Governance in East Asia*, London: Routledge, p. 141.
102 Clarke, op. cit., p. 499.

103 Fu, Jian and Tomasic, Roman (2006), "Legal Regulation and Corporate Governance in China's Top 100 Listed Companies" in *Company Lawyer*, 27.
104 Clarke, op. cit., p. 500.
105 Company Law 1993, art. 77.
106 Ibid., art. 85.
107 Chen, Albert (1996), "The Developing Theory of Law and Market Economy in Contemporary China" in Wang, Guiguo and Wei, Zhenying (eds.), *Legal Developments in China: Market Economy and Law*, Hong Kong: Sweet & Maxwell, p. 11.
108 Lubman, Stanley (1999), *Bird in a Cage: Legal Reform in China after Mao*, California: Stanford University Press, p. 186.
109 Ibid., pp. 186–7.
110 Fu, Jian and Yuan, Yie (2006), *PRC Company and Securities Laws: A Practical Guide*, Singapore: CCH, p. 9.
111 Noble, Josh (2012), "Hong Kong Loses IPO Crown" in *Financial Times* (17 December 2012).
112 Yeung, Horace (2011), "From Further North: The Case of Rusal's (Russian Aluminium) Listing in Hong Kong" in *International Company and Commercial Law Review*, 22.
113 Orrick (2011), "Listing of Italian and French Companies on the Hong Kong Stock Exchange." Online. Available at: www.orrick.com/fileupload/3521.htm (accessed 20 December 2012).
114 Ren, Daniel and Chan, Ray (2012), "Rules to be Relaxed to Help Mainland Firms List in Hong Kong" in *South China Morning Post* (18 December 2012).
115 KPMG (2012), "China Alert – Issue 18." Online. Available at: www.kpmg.com/cn/en/issuesandinsights/articlespublications/newsletters/chinaalerts/pages/default.aspx (accessed 20 December 2012).
116 HKSE (2012), "HKEx Begins New Chapter in its Development." Online. Available at: www.hkex.com.hk/eng/newsconsul/hkexnews/2012/1212065news.htm (accessed 20 December 2012).

9 Conclusion

In this final chapter, the key points discussed so far will be summarized, with a view to providing answers to the questions set out in Chapter 1. In particular, from a macro perspective, this chapter seeks to conclude the impact of cross-listing on the past, present, and future of the Chinese market.

9.1 Summary of key points

Cross-listing is the result of demand meeting supply. When a domestic market cannot cater for the needs of its companies, these companies will look for alternative options, of which cross-listing is one.

Using the framework of analysis in Chapters 3 and 4, it has been concluded that China's market development has been hindered by the poor quality of its domestic law and its enforcement, particularly during the period when the market was newly established. Over the past 15 years the law has been frequently updated; however, enforcement remains a concern. This is partly because of the conflicting role of the state as both the controlling shareholder of many companies and the regulator of the market. China's inexperience of running a market has also meant that the judiciary might not have known how to proceed with shareholder litigation. Moreover, the persistence of political influences, personal *guanxi*, and corruption in China has reduced the degree of certainty and predictability that law can provide. All these appear to be a sign of a weak market.

By contrast, thanks to its strong roots in finance and a colonial legacy of an English legal system, Hong Kong has been able to build its prominence as an Asian financial center. Nonetheless, the market is still largely dominated by family-owned businesses. This implies that majority-minority conflicts remain. The situation has not been helped by the influx of many state-owned Chinese companies since the 1990s. Another concern is that the private enforcement of corporate and securities law in Hong Kong has not been common. This lack of private enforcement has been partly remedied through the active policing by public regulators in Hong Kong. This should mean that wrongdoers face both high ex ante and ex post risks of sanctions. By investing abundant resources into public enforcement, the commitment of Hong Kong to maintain a strong market is unquestionable.

There is much that China can learn from Hong Kong through cross-listing. To examine the existing theories, namely liquidity and bonding, on the motivations to cross-list, and assess if they are capable of explaining Chinese cross-listings, Chapter 2 introduced a new concept: "spurring." This describes the extent to which cross-listing can help the development of a market through regulatory competition, as well as active learning by cross-listed companies and home state regulators from the host state. Chapters 6 to 8 then explored which of these motivational factors were the most relevant to Chinese companies listing in Hong Kong. A summary of important findings is given below.

A Liquidity

Liquidity is of relevance, but not of utmost importance. Following the twin strategies of reform and opening-up, the Chinese banking system was plagued by non-performing loans. The burden of supporting SOEs became increasingly heavy. This was not helped by the poor performance of various SOEs and a lack of financing channels available in China. For example, the HK$190 million raised by Tsingtao from the issue of shares in Hong Kong and China was not invested in expansion as promised in the prospectus.[1] Instead, Tsingtao loaned the proceeds to third parties. This incident reflected a triangular debt problem which involves the practice of SOEs borrowing and lending among themselves to weather difficult times. In fact, even after the launch of domestic exchanges, the Hong Kong Stock Exchange (HKSE) has remained an important equity financing channel for Chinese companies.[2]

Indeed, there might not have been a shortage of liquidity in the domestic market at all. Turnover at the Chinese exchanges is high compared with other seasoned exchanges.[3] This creates the unique situation of the shares of a dual-listed Chinese company being more expensive in China (A-shares) than in Hong Kong (H-shares). This is because even though the underlying fundamentals of the shares are essentially the same, they are different products traded in separate markets. Enormous demand in the A-share market has pushed share prices upwards. The A/H-share price discrepancies were discussed in depth in Chapter 8.

B Bonding

To prove bonding, there must be two elements. First, the entry standards and ongoing requirements in the host country should exceed those of the home country's stock exchange. Second, the action should be motivated by a desire to attract cheaper external finance and other benefits than would be the case for a home listing (which is weakly regulated) alone.

By comparing the entry and ongoing requirements of a listing in China and in Hong Kong (in Chapter 5) it is clear that there has been a regulatory gap between the two jurisdictions. At the same time, this gap has narrowed over time as the law in China has constantly improved. Nonetheless, good law is meaningless without it being enforced (using ex ante and ex post threats of sanctions).

The major problem of enforcement in China is that the state, on the one hand, is the major shareholder of many listed companies and, on the other hand, is the market regulator. There is an inherent conflict of interests between the two roles.

Cross-listing seems to be a trusteeship strategy in action. The HKSE and SFC of Hong Kong are more impartial law enforcers than the CSRC, which is under the control of the State Council of China. Still, one concern is that the Hong Kong regulators might sacrifice quality for revenues, considering that Chinese companies are now important for the Hong Kong market. The existence of Hong Kong Listing Rule Chapter 19A might be an indication that concessions are offered to Chinese issuers. The HKSE has stressed that the purpose of Rule 19A is to clarify that the Listing Rules apply to Chinese issuers as much as they do to Hong Kong ones and those of other overseas issuers. Indeed, certain stringent standards have been imposed exclusively upon Chinese companies. Examples include a special arbitration mechanism and the requirement for a longer period of notice prior to the shareholders' general meeting. Meanwhile, they are exempt from certain disclosure duties because Chinese governmental bodies are not considered a "controlling shareholder" under Listing Rule 19A.04. It is hard to say whether the overall effects of these variations will contribute to better or worse shareholder protection.

In relation to cheaper finance, Chinese issuers can obtain a higher valuation domestically than in Hong Kong because of the bonding effect of a Hong Kong listing. Unfortunately, there is no hard empirical evidence to support this statement. However, soft evidence revealed the benefits of bonding. Chapter 6 showed that cross-listed Chinese companies have shown observeable improvements in creditworthiness, disclosure and transparency, independent directors, foreign strategic partnerships, and international reputation.

In summary, bonding seems a more comprehensive convincing factor to motivate the cross-listing of Chinese companies than liquidity alone. However, this is still not an entirely satisfactory explanation.

C Spurring

Spurring fills the gaps left by the liquidity and bonding theories to offer a market and legal system level explanation. Cross-listing has been used by the Chinese state as part of an integrated strategy of development. The study finds that cross-listing not only affects Chinese companies themselves, regardless of their success or failure, but also pushes China and Hong Kong to converge their capital market regulatory frameworks. The influences are mutual, although the major one is from Hong Kong to China.

At the micro level, cross-listing is a mechanism by which Chinese companies can piggyback Hong Kong's legal and market institutions. In other words, it is a way for Chinese companies and China itself to benefit from another jurisdiction's law without necessarily importing it directly.

At the macro level, regulatory competition between China and Hong Kong instigated by cross-listing is leading to convergence of their legal systems and stock market integration. A series of reforms and improvements have been carried out in China in an attempt to optimize market function and improve legal infrastructures. Legal and regulatory reform, dual-listing, and regulatory cooperation are three methods of achieving convergence with international legal principles and practices. Legal and regulatory reform increases the prospects of success for legal transplants. It can be seen that the main features of Chinese law are based upon the civil law tradition and Western influence. Chinese law is moving towards commonly accepted international practices, albeit operating in a very different political, social, and economic context.

Examples of Chinese legal and regulatory reform include: amendments to the Chinese Company Law and the Securities Law; the reform of the issuance system; and the reform of the non-tradable share system. These reforms promote market liquidity and efficiency, and show that China's markets are in a process of gradual transformation from being government-driven to being market-driven. In these reforms, China adopts a cautious and gradual approach. Key elements of Western corporate law and market principles have been tested in H-share companies first, then spread to other Chinese companies, and finally embodied in national law. In the meantime, China emphasizes "Chinese characteristics" with the dynamism of selective adaptation by which the Hong Kong legal system and practices are mediated by Chinese local norms.

In addition to legal and regulatory reform, dual-listing and regulatory cooperation could also integrate the two markets. Dual-listing is a driving force to reduce the gap between China and Hong Kong's stock markets, both in terms of the size of the market and regulatory quality. This harmonization is also facilitated by regulatory cooperation in information exchange, cross-border enforcement, and mutual recognition of securities participants. Nonetheless, intrinsic rivalry exists between financial markets such as Shanghai and Hong Kong.

9.2 Why is China different?

The reason why spurring is particularly relevant in the context of Chinese cross-listings is because the decision to list has been made jointly at the company and the government levels. By contrast, the decision to list is typically made at the company level. As discussed in Chapter 2, the process of financial and institutional deepening can be market-led and/or government-led. In the Chinese case, in addition to market demands, the state's control of businesses and its commitment to reform have been the dominant forces behind spurring.

Corporate governance involves a set of relationships among a company's management and its board, shareholders, and other stakeholders.[4] The process of decision-making and control over company resources can be viewed as the resulting equilibrium between three major and separate forces: capital, labor, and management. Capital is the group that holds property rights, such as shareholders, or that otherwise makes financial contributions to the company, such as creditors. In the context of China, the major player in this group is the state because it can influence company's decisions through its shareholdings and its role as the major lender via state-owned banks. Capital can entail financial and strategic interests. Financial interests are predominant when investment is motivated by the prospect of a financial return on investment. By contrast, strategic interests are prevalent when investment is motivated by non-financial goals: for example, a strategic alliance between companies.

The extent of employees' ability to influence corporate decision-making and control company resources varies across countries. Labor participation is politically important in economies such as Germany and Japan. By contrast, Anglo-American companies tend to follow a manager-oriented model. Substantial discretion is generally granted to the managers of large business corporations. This can lead to the problem of managerial opportunism. The central insight here, as observed by Licht, is that corporate decisions on cross-listing are generally made by managers.[5] The agency problem lies in ensuring that mangers are responsive to owners' interests rather than pursuing their own personal interests.

The position of the capital group in China is larger than the other two groups. The state is the owner of, and major lender to, many companies. The dominant position of state ownership has been helped by the existence of non-tradable shares. According to the World Bank Enterprise Survey in 1992, SOEs were limited in their authority to recruit employees and even more limited in their authority to appoint senior managers.[6] Alteration to the enterprises' capital stock must be made jointly by the state and enterprise.[7] The process of corporatization has been distinctly different from that of privatization. Control has been retained by the state, especially in strategically important industries. There has been no clear separation between the state and SOEs. For example, Article 4 of the Company Law 1993 reads, "the ownership of state-owned assets in a company shall vest in the state."

Furthermore, in addition to state shareholders (both governmental organizations and other SOEs), political control can also be directly exerted by local committees and governments, ministries, and the central government. The Communist Party's ability to exist and operate in companies is confirmed by law.[8]

As a result, a decision made by companies in China might not necessarily be based on purely commercial calculations. That is reflected by the list of nine companies published by the State Council of China, which was the first batch of companies ever to issue equities overseas. These companies were "selected" by the state, instead of making a cognitive choice of their own. The move coincided with the decision of the fourteenth Communist Party Congress in 1992 to actively foster financial markets, including bond and equity markets. The role of cross-listing in the reform, and steady development of the capital markets in China, has recently been formally recognized and reaffirmed. Shanghai, designated the future "Manhattan of China", has been urged to explore opportunities to work with Hong Kong, based on the existing financial cooperation framework between the two jurisdictions.

9.3 Implications for future research

Finally, it may be important to reiterate the contributions of this book and explain how the theories and findings discussed via the case of Chinese cross-listing can be generalized to other countries. This book applied two existing theories to the Chinese case (liquidity and bonding) regarding the motivations for cross-listing. It was found that these two theories can explain the benefits of cross-listing at the company level. However, Chinese cross-listing has indeed helped in the development of the domestic market and the corporate and financial law systems. At a result, this book came up with the concept of "spurring" to explain cross-listing from market and institutional perspectives. It is uncertain to what extent spurring can be generalized unless a next wave of cross-listing occurs. For example, the bonding hypothesis was developed in the late 1990s to explain "the sudden growth in popularity of ADRs in the early 1990s ... a consequence of state privatizations of formerly state-owned enterprises, which swept across Europe and South America, beginning in the late 1980s."[9] When an academic faces a phenomenon, the first step is normally to look for previous explanations. That is why the bonding hypothesis was applied in this book. If that is a new problem, then it will be necessary to state an explanation. That is why "spurring" appeared. Afterwards, this explanation may be used to test against subsequent cases. The bonding hypothesis has clearly reached a more advanced stage than the "spurring" one, in terms of its development. Even though a new wave of cross-listing has not occurred yet, the following three conditions may be useful to serve as the preconditions for the application of "spurring" to other cases. First, the number of companies involved must be significantly large. Otherwise, the market demand to call for any changes may be weak. Second, the state should somehow participate in the process. This can illustrate the state's commitment to reform by learning from overseas markets. In the Chinese case, the state is the owner of many SOEs and is the primary decision-maker behind the listing. However, for other countries, state involvement may be understandably less direct, perhaps restricted to merely encouraging companies to cross-list. Third, there should be a considerable development/regulatory gap between two markets. Otherwise, the learning of the "weaker" market will be limited or less readily observeable. However, it should also be noted that the relationship between Hong Kong and China is unique owing to the existence of a "One Country Two Systems" principle. The distinctive geopolitical proximity of the two jurisdictions means that any subsequent cases of spurring may not be as strong as the ones investigated here.

Notes

1 Freund, Elizabeth (2005), "FIZZ, FROTH, FLAT: The Challenge of Converting China's SOEs into Shareholding Corporations" in *Review of Policy Research*, 18, p. 100.
2 See Table 6.1 in Chapter 6.
3 For example, the turnover ratios for both the SHSE and the SZSE were around 900

percent, higher than those of the US (129 percent), the UK (142 percent), Germany (146 percent), Japan (119 percent), and Korea (210 percent). See CSRC (2008), *China Capital Markets Development Report*, Beijing: China Financial Publishing, p. 272.

4 Definition from the OECD Principle of Corporate Governance.

5 Licht, Amir (2003) "Cross-listing and Corporate Governance: Bonding or Avoiding" in *Chicago Journal of International Law*, 4, p. 148.

6 Jefferson, Gary *et al.* (1999), "Structure, Authority and Incentives in Chinese Industry" in Jefferson, Gary and Singh, Inderjit (eds.), *Enterprise Reform in China: Ownership, Transition, and Performance*, New York: Oxford University Press, p. 46.

7 Ibid.

8 See art. 17 in Company Law 1993 and art. 19 in Company Law 2005. Companies are required to establish Party Committees.

9 Coffee, John (2002), "Racing Towards the Top?: The Impact of Cross-Listings and Stock Market Competition on International Corporate Governance" in *Columbia Law Review*, 102 , p. 1772.

Bibliography

Allen, Franklin and Gale, Douglas (2000), *Comparing Financial Systems*, London: MIT Press.

Allen, Franklin, Qian, Jun, and Qian, Meijun (2005), "Law, Finance, and Economic Growth in China," *Journal of Financial Economics*, 77.

Allen, Franklin, Qian, Jun, and Qian, Meijun (2007), "China's Financial System: Past, Present, and Future" in Rawski, Thomas and Brandt, Loren (eds.), *China's Great Economic Transformation*, Cambridge: Cambridge University Press.

Ammer, John, Holland, Sara, Smith, David, and Warnock, Francis (2005), "Look at Me Now: What Attracts U.S. Shareholders?" Board of Governors of the Federal Reserve System International Finance Discussion Paper No. 815. Online. Available at: http://ssrn.com/abstract=556208.

Anderson, Craig and Guo, Bingna (2006), "Corporate Governance under the New Company Law (Part 1): Fiduciary Duties and Minority Shareholder Protection" in *China Law & Practice* (April 2006).

Anderson, Craig and Guo, Bingna (2006), "Corporate Governance under the New Company Law (Part 2): Shareholder Lawsuits and Enforcement" in *China Law & Practice* (May 2006).

Arculli, Ronald (2009), "Shanghai-Hong Kong: Not a Zero-sum Game." Speech as HKEx chairman at Macquarie's China/Hong Kong Conference. Online. Available at: www.hkex.com.hk/press/speech/sp090518.htm.

Armour, John, Deakin, Simon, Sarkar, Prabirjit, Siems, Mathia, and Singh, Ajit (2009), "Shareholder Protection and Stock Market Development: An Empirical Test of the Legal Origins Hypothesis" in *Journal of Empirical Legal Studies*, 6.

Armour, John, Hansmann, Henry, and Kraakman, Reinier (2009), "Agency Problems and Legal Strategies" in Kraakman, Reinier *et al.* (eds.), the *Anatomy of Corporate Law: A Comparative and Functional Approach*, Oxford: Oxford University Press.

Armour, John, Hertig, Gerrard, and Kanda, Hideki (2009), "Transactions with Creditors" in Kraakman, Reinier *et al.* (eds.), *The Anatomy of Corporate Law: A Comparative and Functional Approach*, 2nd edn, Oxford: Oxford University Press.

Art, Robert and Gu, Minkang (1995), "China Incorporated: The First Corporation Law of the People's Republic of China" in *Yale Journal of International Law*, 20.

Art, Robert and Gu, Minkang (1996), "Securitization of State Ownership: Chinese Securities Law" in *Michigan Journal of International Law*, 18.

Asia Today (20 July 1994), "Zhongguo Gongsifa Jijiang Shishi" [The Chinese Corporate Law Will Come into Force].

Avgouleas, Emilios (2005), *The Mechanics and Regulation of Market Abuse*, New York: Oxford University Press.

Bai, Chongen *et al.* (2005), "Zhongguo Shangshi Gongshi Zhili Jieguo de Shizheng Yanjiu" [An Empirical Study on Corporate Governance of Chinese Listed Companies] in *Jingji Yanjiu* [Economic Research], 2.

Bailey, Warren and Jagtiani, Julapa (1994), "Foreign Ownership Restrictions and Stock Prices in the Thai Capital Market" in *Journal of Financial Economics*, 36.

Bauhinia Foundation Research Centre (2008), "Hong Kong as a Preferred IPO Hub: Are We on the Right Track?" Online. Available at: www.bauhinia.org/publications.htm.

Bauhinia Foundation Research Centre (2008), "Creating a World-Class Pearl River Delta Metropolis – Accelerating Economic Integration between Guangdong and Hong Kong: Executive Summary." Online. Available at: www.bauhinia.org/publications/GD-HK_ES.pdf.

Bell, Michael, Khor, Hoe Ee, and Kochhar, Kalpana (2003), *China at the Threshold of a Market Economy*, Washington DC: International Monetary Fund.

Beltratti, Andrea and Bortolotti, Bernardo (2006), "The Nontradable Share Reform in the Chinese Stock Market." FEEM Working Paper No. 131.06. Online. Available at: http://ssrn.com/abstract=944412.

Benos, Evangelos and Weisbach, Michael (2004), "Private Benefits and Cross-listings in the United States" in *Emerging Markets Review*, 5.

Berkman, Henk, Cole, Rebel, and Fu, Jiang (2009), "Expropriation through Loan Guarantees to Related Parties: Evidence from China" in *Journal of Banking and Finance*, 33.

Berkowitz, Daniel, Pistor, Katharina, and Richard Jean-Francois (2003), "Economic Development, Legality and the Transplant Effect" in *European Economic Review*, 47.

Berle, Adolf and Means, Gardiner (1991), *The Modern Corporation and Private Property*, London: Transaction Publishers.

Bhagat, Sanjai and Black, Bernard (2001), "The Non-Correlation between Board Independence and Long-term Firm Performance" in *Journal of Corporate Law*, 27.

Black, Bernard (2001), "The Legal and Institutional Preconditions for Strong Securities Markets" in *UCLA Law Review*, 48.

Black, Bernard and Kraakman, Reinier (1996), "A Self-enforcing Model of Corporate Law" in *Harvard Law Review*, 109.

Blair, Margaret (1995), *Ownership and Control: Rethinking Corporate Governance for the Twenty-First Century*, Washington DC: The Brookings Institution.

Brayshaw, Robin and Teng, Z. (1995), "Re-emergence of the Chinese Stock Market" in Blake, John and Gao, Simon (eds.), *Perspectives on Accounting and Finance in China*, London: Routledge.

Brudney, Victor (1982), "The Independent Director – Heavenly City or Potemkin Village?" in *Harvard Law Review*, 95.

BYD (2002), "Prospectus."

BYD (2008) "Strategic Investment by MidAmerican Energy Holdings Company by way of Subscription of New H Shares and Resumption of Trading."

BYD (2009), "Annual Report 2008."

Cai, Fang, Lin, Yifu, and Li, Zhou (2001), *State-owned Enterprise Reform in China*, Hong Kong: Chinese University Press.

Cai, Hua (2007), "Bonding, Law Enforcement and Corporate Governance in China" in *Stanford Journal of Law, Business & Finance*, 13.

Cai, Jinghan, Li, Yuming, and Xia, Le (2007), "What will Privatization Bring: The

Nontradable Share Issue Reform in China." Working Paper Series. Online. Available at: http://ssrn.com/abstract=981682.

Cao, Lan (2000), "Chinese Privatization: Between Plan and Market" in *Law and Contemporary Problems*, 63.

Cassis, Youssef (2006), *Capitals of Capital*, Cambridge: Cambridge University Press.

Chan, Kalok and Kwok, Johnny (2005), "Market Segmentation and Share Price Premium: Evidence from Chinese Stock Markets" in *Journal of Emerging Market Finance*, 4.

Cheffins, Brian (2001), "Does Law Matter? The Separation of Ownership and Control in the United Kingdom" in *Journal of Legal Studies*, 30.

Cheffins, Brian (2003), "Law as Bedrock: The Foundations of an Economy Dominated by Widely Held Public Companies," in *Oxford Journal of Legal Studies*, 23.

Chen, Albert (1992), *An Introduction to the Legal System of the People's Republic of China*, Singapore: Butterworths (Asia).

Chen, Albert (1996), "The Developing Theory of Law and Market Economy in Contemporary China" in Wang, Guiguo and Wei, Zhenying (eds.), *Legal Developments in China: Market Economy and Law*, Hong Kong: Sweet & Maxwell.

Chen, Charles, Gul, Ferdinand, and Su, Xijia (1999), "A Comparison of Reported Earnings under Chinese GAAP vs IAS: Evidence from the Shanghai Stock Exchange" in *Accounting Horizons*, 13.

Chen, Chien-Hsun and Shih, Hui-Tzu (2002), *The Evolution of the Stock Market in China's Transnational Economy*, Cheltenham: Edward Elgar.

Chen, Gongmeng, Firth, Michael, and Kim, Jeong-Bon (2004), "IPO Underpricing in China's New Stock Market" *Journal of Multinational Financial Management*, 14.

Chen, Gongmeng, Firth, Michael, Gao, Daniel, and Rui, Oliver (2005), "Is China's Securities Regulatory Agency a Toothless Tiger? Evidence from Enforcement Actions" in *Journal of Accounting and Public Policy*, 24.

Chen, Grant and Zhang, Zhengyi (2007), "New Disclosure Standards for PRC Listed Companies" in *China Law and Practice* (April 2007).

Chen, Guanting (2006), "Positive Research on the Financial Statement Fraud Factors of Listed Companies in China" in *Journal of Modern Accounting and Auditing*, 2.

Chen, Jinghan (2005), "Corporatization of China's State-owned Enterprises and Corporate Governance" in Brown, David and MacBean, Alasdair (eds.), *Challenges for China's Development – An Enterprise Perspective*, London: Routledge.

Chen, Shimin, Sun, Zheng, and Wang, Yuetang (2002), "Evidence from China on Whether Harmonized Accounting Standards Harmonized Accounting Practices" in *Accounting Horizons* , 16.

Chen, Zhiwu (2003), "Capital Markets and Legal Development: The China Case" in *China Economic Review*, 14.

Cheng, Yangtie, Xu, Alan, and Zhong, Allen (2005), "Steady as She Goes China's New Securities Law" in *China Law & Practice*, 16 (Dec 2005/Jan 2006).

Cheung, Gary (2009), "Finance Chief Plays down Shanghai Threat – Room Enough for HK and its Mainland Rival" in *South China Morning Post* (27 March 2009).

Cheung, Yan-Leung, Jing, Lihua, Rau, Raghavendra, and Stouraitis, Aris (2005), "Guanxi, Political Connections, and Expropriation: The Dark Side of State Ownership in Chinese Listed Companies." City University of Hong Kong Working Paper.

Cheung, Yan-leung, Ouyang, Zhiwei, and Tan, Weiqiang (2009), "How Regulatory Changes Affect IPO Underpricing in China" in *China Economic Review*, 20.

China Daily (9 April 2010), "A Bridge Built for Two Systems."

China Law & Practice (March 2010 issue), "Court Clarifies Enforcement of Hong Kong Arbitral Awards."
China Securities Daily (28 July 2005), "Zhongguo Dudong Diaocha ji Zhidu Fansi" [Survey on China's Independent Directors and Reflections on the Insitutions].
China Securities Daily (28 August 2008), "30 Jia Dashizhi Gongsi jin Sancheng Xianshou Gu yi Liutong" [30 Percent of Shares in the Largest 30 Companies are Tradable].
China Securities Regulatory Commission (1993), "Information Disclosure and Corporate Governance in China." Online. Available at: www.oecd.org/dataoecd/6/60/1931117.pdf.
China Securities Regulatory Commission (2008), *China Capital Markets Development Report*, Beijing: China Financial Publishing.
China Securities Regulatory Commission (2008), "Summary of Investor Accounts (1993–2007)." Online: Available at: www.csrc.gov.cn/pub/newsite/xxfw/cbwxz/tjnj/zqqhtjnj/2008/main/nj2007/6–1.htm.
China Securities Regulatory Commission (2009), "Annual Report 2008."
Chiu, Stephen and Lui, Tai-Lok (2009), *Hong Kong Becoming a Chinese Global City*, London: Routledge.
Clarke, Donald (2003), "Corporate Governance in China: An Overview" in *China Economic Review*, 14.
Clarke, Donald (2006), "The Independent Director in Chinese Corporate Governance" in *Delaware Journal of Corporate Law*, 31.
Clarke, Donald (2006), "Lost in Translation? Corporate Legal Transplants in China." GWU Law School Public Law Research Paper No. 213. Online. Available at: http://ssrn.com/abstract=913784.
Clarke, Donald (2008), "The Role of Non-Legal Institutions in Chinese Corporate Governance" in Kanda, Hideki *et al.* (eds.), *Transforming Corporate Governance*, New York: Routledge.
Coffee, John (1999), "The Future as History: The Prospects for Global Convergence in Corporate Governance and Its Implications" in *Northwestern University Law Review*, 93.
Coffee, John (2001), "The Acquiescent Gatekeeper: Reputational Intermediaries, Auditor Independence and the Governance of Accounting." Columbia Law and Economics Working Paper No. 191. Online. Available at: http://ssrn.com/abstract=270944.
Coffee, John (2001), "The Rise of Dispersed Ownership: The Role of Law and the State in the Separation of Ownership and Control" in *Yale Law Journal*, 111.
Coffee, John (2002), "Racing towards the Top? The Impact of Cross-listings and Stock Market Competition on International Corporate Governance" in *Columbia Law Review*, 102.
Coffee, John (2007), "Law and Market: the Impact of Enforcement" in *University of Pennsylvania Law Review*, 156.
Cookson, Robert (2011), "Hopes High that Prada's IPO will Set the Style for Hong Kong" in *Financial Times* (2 February 2011).
Corhay, Albert and Rad, Alireza (1994), "Daily Returns from European Stock Markets" in *Journal of Business and Finance and Accounting*, 21.
CPSS-IOSCO Joint Task Force (2004), "Recommendations on Central Counterparties." Online. Available at: www.bis.org.publ.cpss64.pdf.
Dam, Kenneth (2006), "China as a Test Case: Is the Rule of Law Essential for Economic Growth?" University Chicago Law & Economics, Olin Working Paper No. 275. Online. Available at: http://ssrn.com/abstract=880125.

Davies, Howard (2001), "Performing Financial Regulation: Progress and Priorities" in Ferran, Eilis and Goodhart, Charles (eds.), *Regulating Financial Services and Markets in the 21st Century*, Oxford: Hart.

Davies, Paul (2002), *Introduction to Company Law*, Oxford: Oxford University Press.

De Jonge, Alice (2005), "Solving Agency Problems in a Cross-border Environment: Ten Years of Chinese Companies Listings in Hong Kong" in Smyth, Russell, Tam, On Kit, Warner, Malcolm, and Zhu, Cherrie Jiuhua (eds.), *China's Business Reforms: Institutional Challenges in a Globalized Economy*, London: Routledge.

De Jonge, Alice (2008), *Corporate Governance and China's H-share Market*, Cheltenham: Edward Elgar.

Deloitte (2005), "Implementing Hong Kong Financial Reporting Standards: The Challenge for 2005." Online. Available at: ww.deloitte.com/view/en_CN/cn.

Deloitte (2006), "China's New Accounting Standards: A Comparison with Current PRC GAAP and IFRS." Online. Available at: www.iasplus.com/dttpubs/0607prcifrsenglish.pdf.

Deng, Jiong (2005), "Building an Investor-Friendly Shareholder Derivative Lawsuit System in China" in *Harvard International Law Journal*, 46.

Deng, Xiaoping (1994), "Shehui Zhuyi he Shichang Jingji bu Cunzai Genben Maodun" [There is No Fundamental Contradiction between Socialism and a Market Economy], in *Selected Works of Deng Xiaoping (Volume III)*, Beijing: Foreign Language Press.

Department of Trade and Industry (2005), "The UK Pre-emption Rights: Final Report 2005." Online. Available at: www.berr.gov.uk/files/file28436.pdf.

Dewenter, Kathryn, Kim, Chang-soo, and Lim, Ungki (2005), "Committing to Protect Investors in Emerging Markets: Can Local Exchange Provide Value-relevant Bonding Mechanisms?" University of Washington, Seattle, Working Paper. Online. Available at: http://ssrn.com/abstract=756866.

Djankov, Simeon and Murrell, Peter (2002), "Enterprise Restructuring in Transition: A Quantitative Survey" in *Journal of Economic Literature*, 40.

Doidge, Craig, Karolyi, George Andrew, and Stulz, Rene (2004), "Why are Foreign Firms Listed in the US Worth More?" in *Journal of Financial Economics*, 71.

Doidge, Craig, Karolyi, George Andrew, and Lins, Karl (2009), "Private Benefits of Control, Ownership, and the Cross-Listing Decision" in *Journal of Finance*, 64.

Domowitz, Ian, Glen, Jack, and Madhavan, Ananth (1997), "Market Segmentation and Stock Prices: Evidence from an Emerging Market" in *Journal of Finance*, 52.

Dong, Fuying (1998), "Fazhan Ziben Shichang yu Gaige Guoyouqiye" [Capital Market Development and SOE Reform] in Li, Yining (ed.), *Zhongguo Ziben Shichang Fazhan de Lilun yu Shijian* [The Theory and Practice of Capital Market Development in China], Beijing: Beijing University Press.

Dyer, Geoff (2007), "Chinese Regulators Impose Fine" in *Financial Times* (15 May 2007).

Dyer, Geoff (2007), "Beijing Cracks Down on Insider Trading" in *Financial Times* (24 May 2007).

Dyer, Geoff and McGregor, Richard (2008), "China's Champions" in *Financial Times* (17 March 2008).

Edison, Hali and Warnock, Francis (2008), "Cross-Border Listings, Capital Controls, and Equity Flows to Emerging Markets" in *Journal of International Money and Finance*, 27.

Editorial Comments (4 April 2007), "Regulators Broaden Ties" in *Wall Street Journal*.

Faccio, Mara and Lang, Larry (2002), "The Ultimate Ownership of Western European Corporations" in *Journal of Financial Economics*, 65.

Fei, Guoping (2007), "Red-chip Listing and the Impact of the New Acquisition Regulations on it." Online. Available at: www.longandfield.com/en/publication/articles_detail.asp?a_id=34.

Ferguson, Michael, Lam, Kevin, and Lee, Grace (2002), "Voluntary Disclosure by State-owned Enterprises Listed on the Stock Exchange of Hong Kong" in *Journal of International Financial Management and Accounting*, 12.

Financial Services Authority (2009), "The Turner Review: A Regulatory Response to the Global Banking Crisis." Online. Available at: www.fsa.gov.uk/pages/Library/Corporate/turner/index.shtml.

Financial Services Bureau (1999), "Legislative Reform for the Securities and Future Market (Securities and Futures Bill 1999)."

Financial Services Bureau (2010), "Process Review Panel for the Securities and Futures Commission." Online. Available at: www.fstb.gov.hk/fsb/topical/prp.htm.

Fischel, Daniel and Ross, David (1991), "Should the Law Prohibit Manipulation in Financial Markets?" in *Harvard Law Review*, 105.

Fong, Tom, Wong, Alfred, and Yung, Ivy (2007), "Share Price Disparity in Chinese Stock Markets." HKMA Working Paper 11/2007.

Franks, Julian and Mayer, Colin (2002), "Governance as a Source of Managerial Discipline." National Bank of Belgium Working Paper 031. Online. Available at: www.nbb.be/doc/oc/repec/reswpp/WP31.pdf.

Franks, Julian, Mayer, Colin, and Wagner, Hannes (2006), "The Origins of the German Corporation – Finance, Ownership and Control" in *Review of Finance*, 10.

Freund, Elizabeth (2005), "FIZZ, FROTH, FLAT: The Challenge of Converting China's SOEs into Shareholding Corporations" in *Review of Policy Research*, 18.

Friedman, William (2002), "One Country, Two Systems: The Inherent Conflict between China's Communist Politics and Capitalist Securities Market" in *Brooklyn Journal of International Law*, 27.

Fu, Jian and Tomasic, Roman (2006), "Legal Regulation and Corporate Governance in China's top 100 Listed Companies" in *Company Lawyer*, 27.

Fu, Jian and Yuan, Jie (2006), *PRC Company & Securities Laws*, Singapore: CCH Asia.

Fung, Eugene (1996), "Legal Implications of Foreign Listings for PRC Enterprises with Particular Reference to Hong Kong: Part 1" in *Company Lawyer*, 17.

Garrett, Ian and Spyrou, Spyros (1999), "Common Stochastic Trends in Emerging Equity Markets" in *Manchester School*, 67.

Garten, Jeffrey (2009), "From NyLon to Shangkong" in *Financial Times* (10 May 2009).

Gerke, Wolfgang, Bank, Matthias, and Steiger, Max (2003), "Changing Role of Institutional Investors – A German Perspective" in Hopt, Klaus and Wymeersch, Eddy (eds.), *Capital Markets and Company Law*, Oxford: Oxford University Press.

Gilson, Ronald, Hansmann, Henry, and Pargendler, Mariana (2010), "Regulatory Dualism as a Development Strategy: Corporate Reform in Brazil, the U.S., and the EU." Stanford Law and Economics Olin Working Paper No. 390. Online. Available at: http://ssrn.com/abstract=1541226.

Goo, Say Hak and Carver, Anne (2008), "Low Structure, High Ambiguity: Selective Adaptation of International Norms of Corporate Governance Mechanisms in China" in Nakamura, Masao (ed.), *Changing Corporate Governance Practices in China and Japan*, Hampshire: Palgrave Macmillan.

Goodstadt, Leo (2010), "The Global Crisis: Why *Laisser-faire* Hong Kong Prefers Regulation." Hong Kong Institute for Monetary Research Paper No. 01/2010. Online. Available at: www.hkimr.org/cms/upload/publication_app.

Green, Stephen (2003), "China's Stock Market: Eight Myths and Some Reasons to be Optimistic." The China Project Working Paper No. 6. Online. Available at: http://ssrn.com/abstract=431200.

Green, Stephen (2003a), *China's Stockmarket: A Guide to its Progress, Players and Prospects*, London: The Economist.

Green, Stephen (2003b), "Better Than a Casino: Some Good News from the Frontline of China's Capital Market Reforms." China Project Working Paper No. 6. Online. Available at: http://ssrn.com/abstract=431200.

Green, Stephen and Liu, Guy (2005), "China's Industrial Reform Strategy: Retreat and Retain" in Green, Stephen and Liu, Guy (eds.), *Exit the Dragon? Privatization and State Control in China*, Oxford: Blackwell.

Gunther, Marc (2009), "Warren Buffett Takes Charge" in *Fortune* (13 April 2009).

Hansmann, Henry and Kraakman, Reinier (2001), "The End of History for Corporate Law" in *Georgetown Law Journal*, 89.

Herbert Smith LLP (2006), "A New Model: How the Listing of Companies in both Hong Kong and China could Work in the Future" in *International Financial Law Review*, 25.

Herbert Smith LLP (2010), "Recent International Arbitration Developments." Online. Available at: www.herbertsmith.com/NR/rdonlyres/C7A10A47-AAEC-4BF1-A686-E6AE73FAD018/14586/0304Recentintlarbdev.html.

Heritage Foundation (2012), "2012 Index of Economic Freedom." Online. Available at: www.heritage.org/index/countries.cfm.

Hertig, Gerrard, Kraakman, Reinier, and Rock, Edward (2009), "Issuers and Investor Protection" in Kraakman, Reinier, Armour, John, Davies, Paul, Enriques, Luca, Hansmann, Henry, Hertig, Gérard, Hopt, Klaus, Kanda, Hideki, and Rock, Edward (eds.), the *Anatomy of Corporate Law: A Comparative and Functional Approach*, Oxford: Oxford University Press.

Ho, Betty (1997), "Rethinking the System of Sanctions in the Corporate and Securities Law of Hong Kong" in *McGill Law Journal*, 42.

Ho, Simon (2003a), "Corporate Governance in China." Hong Kong Baptist University Working Paper. Online. Available at: www.hkbu.edu.hk/%7Ebus/simonho/index.htm.

Ho, Simon (2003b), "Corporate Governance in Hong Kong: Key Problems and Prospects." CUHK Centre for Accounting Disclosure and Corporate Governance Research Paper No. 1. Online. Available at: http://ssrn.com/abstract=440924.

Hoepen, M. (1995), "Accounting in China: A Case of Vanishing Cultural Influence" in Blake, John and Gao, Simon (eds.), *Perspectives on Accounting and Finance in China*, London: Routledge.

Hong Kong Government (2009), *Yearbook 2008*, Hong Kong: Information Services Department.

Hong Kong Government (2010), "Signing Ceremony of Framework Agreement on Hong Kong/Guangdong Cooperation Held in Beijing." Press Release. Online. Available at: www.info.gov.hk/gia/general/201004/07/P201004070113.htm.

Hong Kong Government (2012), "Companies Ordinance Rewrite." Online. Available at: www.fstb.gov.hk/fsb/co_rewrite/eng/pub-press/consult.htm.

Hong Kong Institute of Chartered Secretaries (2008), "A Comparative Study of Continuing Disclosure in Hong Kong and the PRC." Online. Available at: www.hkics.org.hk/media/publication/attachment/2216_A&H.pdf.

Hong Kong Monetary Authority (2007), "Price Convergence between Dual-listed A and H Shares" in *China Economic Issues*, July 2007. Online. Available at: www.info.gov.hk/hkma/eng/research/cei/2007/CEI-200706.pdf.

Hong Kong Monetary Authority (2012), "Hong Kong: The Premier Offshore Renminbi Business Center." Online. Available at: www.hkma.gov.hk/media/eng/publication-and-research/hkrmb/hkma-rmb-booklet.pdf.

Hong Kong Securities and Investment Institute (2004), "Mutual Recognition of Professional Qualification Marks New Page in Mainland-Hong Kong Coalition." Press Release. Online. Available at: www.hksi.org/eng/news/news_20041229.html.

Hong Kong Stock Exchange (1999), "The Way Forward." A Strategic Plan.

Hong Kong Stock Exchange (2005), "Censures of Directors of Kelon."

Hong Kong Stock Exchange (2011), "The Exchange Publishes Consultation Conclusions on Review of the Corporate Governance Code and Associated Listing Rules." Online. Available at: www.hkex.com.hk/eng/newsconsul/hkexnews/2011/111028news.htm.

Hong Kong Stock Exchange (2012), "HKEx Begins New Chapter in its Development." Online. Available at: www.hkex.com.hk/eng/newsconsul/hkexnews/2012/1212065news.htm.

Hopt, Klaus (1997), "The German Two-Tier Board: A German View on Corporate Governance" in Hopt, Klaus and Wymeersch, Eddy (eds), *Comparative Corporate Governance: Essays and Materials*, Berlin: Walter de Gruyter & Co.

Hopt, Klaus (1998), "The German Two-Tier Board: Experience, Theories, Reforms" in Hopt, Klaus, Kanda, Hideki, Roe, Mark, Wymeersch, Eddy, and Prigge, Stefan (eds.), *Comparative Corporate Governance – The State of the Art and Emerging Research*, New York: Oxford University Press.

Hopt, Klaus (2003), "Corporate Governance in Germany" in Hopt, Klaus and Wymeersch, Eddy (eds.), *Capital Markets and Company Law*, Oxford: Oxford University Press.

Howie, Fraser and Walter, Carl (2003), *Privatizing China: The Stock Markets and Their Role in Corporate Reform*, Singapore: John Wiley & Sons.

Howson, Nicholas (1997), "China's Company Law: One Step Forward, Two Steps Back? A Modest Complaint" in *Columbia Journal of Asian Law*, 11.

Hsu, Berry, Arner, Douglas, Tse, Maurice, Johnstone, Syren, Li, Laurence, and Lejot, Paul (2006) *Financial Markets in Hong Kong*, Oxford: Oxford University Press.

Hu, Yebi (1993), *China's Capital Market*, Hong Kong: The Chinese University Press.

Hua, Jinyang, Miesing, Paul, and Li, Mingfang (2006), "An Empirical Taxonomy of SOE Governance in Transitional China" in *Journal of Management and Governance*, 10.

Huang, Fangliang (2007), "China's Initial Public Offering Pricing Mechanisms: A Complicated Way of Improvement with A Short History" in *International Journal of Business and Management*, 2.

Huang, Flora Xiao (2009), "Shareholder Revolt? The Statutory Derivative Action in China." Comparative Research in Law and Political Economy Research Paper No. 49/2009. Online. Available at: http://ssrn.com/abstract=1516448.

Huang, Flora Xiao (2010), "Modernizing the Chinese Capital Market: Old Problems and New Legal Response" in *International Company and Commercial Law Review*, 21.

Huang, Flora Xiao and Yeung, Horace (2012), "Law and Finance: What Matters? Hong Kong as a Test Case" in *Asian Journal of Law and Economics*, 3 (1).

Huang, Guihai and Song, Frank (2005), "The Financial and Operating Performance of China's Newly Listed H-firms" in *Pacific-Basin Finance Journal*, 13.

Huang, Hui (2006), *International Securities Markets: Insider Trading Law in China*, Biggleswade: Kluwer Law.

Huang, Yasheng and Lane, David (2001), "Kelon: China's Corporate Dragon." Harvard Business School Case Study, No. 702–039.

Huang, Yiping (2001), *China's Last Steps across the River: Enterprise and Banking Reforms*, Canberra: Asia-Pacific Press.

Hutchens, Walter (2003), "Private Securities Litigation in China: Material Disclosure about China's Legal System?" in *University of Pennsylvania Journal of International Economic Law*, 24.

IMD (2012), "World Competitiveness Yearbook 2012." Online. Available at: www.imd.org/research/publications/wcy/upload/scoreboard.pdf.

Industrial and Commercial Bank of China (2006), "Prospectus for Global Offering."

International Chamber of Commerce (2010), "Enforcement in Mainland China of ICC Arbitral Awards Rendered in Hong Kong." Online. Available at: www.iccwbo.org/court/arbitration/index.html?id=34693.

Jackson, Howell (2007), "Variation in the Intensity of Financial Regulation: Preliminary Evidence and Potential Implications" in *Yale Journal on Regulation*, 24.

Jackson, Howell and Roe, Mark (2009), "Public and Private Enforcement of Securities Laws: Resource-based Evidence" in *Journal of Financial Economics*, 93.

Jefferson, Gary, Zhang, Ping, and Zhao, John (1999), "Structure, Authority and Incentives in Chinese Industry" in Jefferson, Gary and Singh, Inderjit (eds.), *Enterprise Reform in China: Ownership, Transition, and Performance*, New York: Oxford University Press.

Jia, Jin, Sun, Qian, and Tong, Wilson (2005), "Privatization through an Overseas Listing: Evidence from China's H-share Firms" in *Financial Management*, 34.

Jiang, Qingyun (2007), "Monitoring Problems versus Fiduciary Duties in Chinese Stock Companies: An Economic and Comparative Analysis on Corporate Governance" in Eger, Thomas (ed.), *Economic Analysis of Law in China*, Cheltenham: Edward Elgar.

Johnson, Simon, La Porta, Rafael, Lopez-de-Silane, Florencio, and Shleifer, Andrei (2000), "Tunneling" in *American Economic Review*, 90.

Kanda, Hideki and Milhaupt, Curtis (2003), "Re-examining Legal Transplants: The Director's Fiduciary Duty in Japanese Corporate Law" in *American Journal of Comparative Law*, 51.

Kazenski, Paul and Wong, Yin Ling (1994), "Unifying Accounting in the People's Republic of China" in *International Journal of Accounting*, 29.

Keith, Ronald and Lin, Zhiqiu (2001), *Law and Justice in China's New Market Place*, Hampshire: Palgrave.

Kelon (2005), "Clarification and Unusual Price and Volume Movement."

Kelon (2006), "Announcement in relation to Administrative Sanctions Imposed by the CSRC."

Kelon (2009), "Announcement on Development of Significant Litigation."

Kose, M Ayhan, Prasad, Eswar, Rogoff, Kenneth, and Wei, Shang-Jin (2006), "Financial Globalization: A Reappraisal." IMF Working Paper (WP/06/189). Online. Available at: www.nber.org/papers/w12484.

Kose, M Ayhan, Prasad, Eswar, Rogoff, Kenneth, and Wei, Shang-Jin (2007), "Financial Globalization Beyond the Blame Game: A New Way of Looking at Financial Globalization Reexamines its Costs and Benefits" in *Finance and Development*, 44.

KPMG (2012), "China Alert – Issue 18." Online. Available at: www.kpmg.com/cn/en/issuesandinsights/articlespublications/newsletters/chinaalerts/pages/default.aspx.

Kraakman, Reinier, Armour, John, Davies, Paul, Enriques, Luca, Hansmann Henry, Hertig, Gérard, and Hopt, Klaus (2009), *The Anatomy of Corporate Law: A Comparative and Functional Approach*, 2nd edn, Oxford: Oxford University Press.

La Porta, Rafael; Lopez-de-Silane, Florencio; Shleifer, Andrei (1999), "Corporate Ownership around the World" in *Journal of Finance*, 54.

La Porta, Rafael, Lopez-de-Silane, Florencio, and Shleifer, Andrei (2006), "What Works in Securities Laws" in *Journal of Finance*, 61.

La Porta, Rafael, Lopez-de-Silane, Florencio, and Shleifer, Andrei (2008), "The Economic Consequences of Legal Origins" in *Journal of Economic Literature*, 46.

La Porta, Rafael, Lopez-de-Silane, Florencio, Shleifer, Andrei, and Vishny, Robert (1997), "Legal Determinants of External Finance" in *Journal of Finance*, 52.

La Porta, Rafael, Lopez-de-Silane, Florencio, Shleifer, Andrei, and Vishny, Robert (1998), "Law and Finance" in *Journal of Political Economy*, 106.

La Porta, Rafael, Lopez-de-Silane, Florencio, Shleifer, Andrei, and Vishny, Robert (2000), "Investor Protection and Corporate Governance" in *Journal of Financial Economics*, 58.

Lardy, Nicholas (1998), *China's Unfinished Economic Revolution*, Washington DC: Brookings Institution Press.

Lau, Alex (2007), "A Study on Listing Applications in the People's Republic of China" in *Company Lawyer*, 28.

Lau, Justine and Mitchell, Tom (2006), "Investors are Betting on Chinese IPOs" in *Financial Times* (31 May 2006).

Laurenceson, James and Chai, Joseph (2003), *Financial Reform and Economic Development in China*, Cheltenham: Edward Elgar.

Lee, Rebecca (2007), "Fiduciary Duty without Equity: Fiduciary Duties of Directors under the Revised Company Law of the PRC" in *Virginia Journal of International Law*, 47.

Legrand, Pierre (1997), "The Impossibility of 'Legal transplants'" in *Maastricht Journal of European and Comparative Law*, 4.

Legrand, Pierre (2001), "What Legal Transplant?" in Nelken, David and Feest, Johannes (eds.), *Adapting Legal Cultures*, Oregon: Hart Publishing.

Leung, Bill and Yim, Joanne (2009), "Shanghai's Future as an International Financial Centre." Treasury Division of Hang Seng Bank. Online. Available at: www.hangseng.com/ermt/eng/fxmv/pdf/ecof_e_2009jun.pdf.

Li, Qing and Ye, Weiqiang (2007), "Bamai Gaowen Gushi" [Diagnose the Market Fever] in *Caijing Magazine* (11 June 2007), issue 187. Online. Available at: www.caijing.com.cn/2007–06–11/100021866.html.

Li, Weian, Tang, Yuejun, Xie, Yongzhen, and Zhang, Guoping (2004), "Nankai Pandian Sannian Dudong Zhidu de Gongsi Zhili Jiazhi" [A Review of the 3-year Independent Director System on Corporate Governance by Nankai] in *Zhongwai Guanli* [Sino-Foreign Management], 9.

Li, Xiaoning (2007), *A Comparative Study of Shareholders' Derivative Actions: England, the United States, Germany and China*, Deventer: Kluwer.

Liang, Bin (2008), *The Changing Chinese Legal System, 1978-Present*, London: Routledge.

Liao, Jing, Young, M.R., and Qian, S. (2009), "Board Structure Determinants and Efficiency, Evidence from the Implementation of Independent Director System in China." Massey University College of Business Research Paper No. 1. Online. Available at: http://ssrn.com/abstract=1326169.

Licht, Amir (1998), "International Diversity in Securities Regulation: Roadblocks on the Way to Convergence" in *Cardozo Law Review*, 20.

Licht, Amir (2003), "Cross-listing and Corporate Governance: Bonding or Avoiding" in *Chicago Journal of International Law*, 4.

Liebman, Benjamin (2005), "Watchdog or Demagogue? The Media in the Chinese Legal System" in *Columbia Law Review*, 105.

Liebman, Benjamin and Milhaupt, Curtis (2008), "Reputational Sanctions in China's Securities Market" in *Columbia Law Review*, 108.

Lin, Jun and Wang, Liyan (2001), "Financial Disclosure and Accounting Harmonization: Cases of Three Listed Companies in China" in *Managerial Auditing Journal*, 16.

Lin, Thomas (2004), "Corporate Governance in China: Recent Developments, Key Problems, and Solutions" in *Journal of Accounting and Corporate Governance*, 1.

Liu, Feng and Zhou, Fuyuan (2006), "Guoji Wuda Yiweizhe Gao Shenji Zhiliang ma? – Lai zi Woguo A Gu Shichang de Chubu Zhengju" [Does the Big Five Mean Higher Auditing Quality: Preliminary Evidence from China's A-Share Market], Asia and China Corporate Governance International Conference Group Working Paper.

Liu, Guy and Sun, Pei (2003), "Identifying Ultimate Controlling Shareholders in Chinese Public Corporations: An Empirical Survey." Royal Institute of International Affairs, Asia Program Working Paper No. 2. Online. Available at: www.chathamhouse.org/publications/papers/view/107671.

Liu, Guy and Sun, Pei (2006), "The Rise and Fall of China's Corporate Dragon: Kelon and its Old and New Owners" in Mallin, Christine (ed.), *International Corporate Governance: A Case study Approach*, Cheltenham: Edward Elgar.

Liu, Jianwei and Liu, Chunjiao (2007), "Value Relevance of Accounting Information in Different Stock Market Segments: The Case of Chinese A, B and H-shares" in *Journal of International Accounting Research*, 6.

Liu, Qiao and Lu, Zhou (2007), "Corporate Governance and Earnings Management in the Chinese Listed Companies: A Tunneling Perspective" in *Journal of Corporate Finance*, 13.

Liu, Ruidong (2007), "Quanguo Zhengquan Diyi An Chenai Luoding, 6800 Ren Jieshou Tiaojie" [The First National Securities Case Settled Down, 6800 Persons Accepted Mediation]. Online. Available at: www.chinacourt.org/html/article/200709/12/264338.shtml.

Lu, Tong; Zhong, Jiiyin; Kong, Jie (2006), "Corporate Governance Assessment on the Top 100 Chinese Listed Companies" in *China Economist*, 3. Online. Available at: www.iwep.org.cn/cccg/en/publications.htm.

Lubman, Stanley (1996), "The Future of Chinese Law" in Lubman, Stanley (ed.), *China's Legal Reforms*, Oxford: Oxford University Press.

Lubman, Stanley (2000), *Bird in a Cage: Legal Reform in China after Mao*, California: Stanford University Press.

Luo, Peixin and Lu, Wendao (2006), *Zuixin Zhengquan Fa Jiedu* [Studies on New Securities Law], Beijing: Peking University Press.

Lynch, Jake (2008), "Insight: Chinese Bubble won't Burst yet" in *Financial Times* (7 April 2008).

Ma, Josephine (2005), "Corrupt Courts Seen as Biggest Threat" in *South China Morning Post* (10 March 2005).

Ma, Lianfu, Chen, Deqiu, and Gao, Li (2008), "Overseas Listing, Voluntary Corporate Governance and Performance – A Case Study of Sinopec" in *Frontiers of Business Research in China*, 2.

Ma, Xianghai (1996), "Capital Controls, Market Segmentation and Stock Prices: Evidence from the Chinese Stock Market" in *Pacific Basin Finance Journal*, 4.

MacDonald, Ronald and Taylor, Mark (1991), "Exchange Rates, Policy Convergence, and the European Monetary System" in *Review of Economics and Statistics*, 73.

MacNeil, Iain (2002), "Adaptation and Convergence in Corporate Governance: The Case of Chinese Listed Companies" in *Journal of Corporate Law Studies*, 2.

MacNeil, Iain and Lau, Alex (2001), "International Corporate Regulation: Listing Rules and Overseas Companies" in *International and Comparative Law Quarterly*, 50.

Malkiel, Burton and Taylor, Patricia (2008), *From Wall Street to the Great Wall: How Investors Can Profit from China's Booming Economy*, New York: W.W. Norton & Company.

Mattlin, Mikael (2007), "The Chinese Government's New Approach to Ownership and Financial Control of Strategic State-owned Enterprises." Bank of Finland, Institute for Economies in Transition, Discussion Paper.

McCauley, Robert and Chan, Eric (2007), "Hong Kong and Shanghai: Yesterday, Today and Tomorrow." Bank of International Settlements Research Paper. Online. Available at: www.bis.org/repofficepubl/arpresearch_fs_200803.01.pdf.

McGregor, Richard (2007), "Chinese Put Stock in Lady Luck" in *Financial Times* (12 May 2007).

McGuinness, Paul and Birtch, Thomas (2008), "The 2001–2005 Price Convergence in the A- and H-shares of Chinese State-owned Enterprises: A Story of Unprecedented Economic, Regulatory and Political Change" in *Journal of Finance Regulation and Compliance*, 16.

McGuinness, Paul and Ferguson, Michael (2005), "The Ownership Structure of Listed Chinese State-owned Enterprises and its Relation to Corporate Performance" in *Applied Financial Economics*, 15.

McKinsey Global Institute (2006), "Putting China's Capital to Work: The Value of Financial System Reform." Online. Available at: www.mckinsey.com/insights/mgi/research/asia.

McKinsey Global Institute (2008), "Mapping Global Capital Markets Fourth Annual Report." Online. Available at: www.mckinsey.com/insights/mgi/research/asia.

Meyer, Jennifer (1994), "Let the Buyer Beware: Economic Modernization, Insurance Reform, and Consumer Protection in China" in *Fordham Law Review*, 62.

Milhaupt, Curtis and Pistor, Katharina (2008), *Law and Capitalism*, London: The University of Chicago Press.

Minow, Nell and Monks, Robert (2004) *Corporate Governance*, Oxford: Blackwell.

Morck, Randall (1996), "On the Economics of Concentrated Ownership" in *Canadian Business Law Journal*, 26.

Morck, Randall and Yeung, Bernard (2003), "Agency Problems in Large Family Business Groups" in *Entrepreneurship Theory and Practice*, 27.

Muchlinski, Peter (2007), *Multinational Enterprises and the Law*, 2nd edn, Oxford: Oxford University Press.

Nee, Owen (1994), "China's Company Law Sets out the Next Stage of Reform" in *International Financial Law Review*, 13.

Noble, Josh (2012), "Hong Kong Loses IPO Crown" in *Financial Times* (17 December 2012).

Orrick (2011), "Listing of Italian and French Companies on the Hong Kong Stock Exchange." Online. Available at: www.orrick.com/fileupload/3521.htm.

Orts, Eric (2001), "The Rule of Law in China" in *Vanderbilt Journal of Transnational Law*, 34.

Örücü, Esin (2007), "Developing Comparative Law" in Örücü, Esin and Nelken, David (eds.), *Comparative Law A Handbook*, Oxford: Hart.

Palmer, Vernon Valentime (2005), "From Lerotholi to Lando: Some Examples of Comparative Law Methodology" in *American Journal of Comparative Law*, 53.

Peng, Songlan, Tondkarb, Rasoul, van der Laan Smith, Joyce, and Harless, David (2008), "Does Convergence of Accounting Standards Lead to the Convergence of Accounting Practices?" in *International Journal of Accounting*, 43.

Pennacchi, George (2005), "Can Voluntary Market Reforms Promote Efficient Corporate Governance? Evidence from Firm's Migration to Premium Market in Brazil." Working Paper. Online. Available at: http://ssrn.com/abstract=678282.

People's Daily (2008), "Chuanyeban Tuichu de Shinian Licheng Huigu" [The Ten Years of the GEB]. Online. Available at: http://finance.people.com.cn/GB/8215/115194/115197/6858214.html.

Perera, Shalini (2010), *Corporate Onwership and Control: Corporate Governance and Economic Development in Sri Lanka*. Series on Economic Development and Growth, Vol. 6, London: World Scientific Publishing.

Pistor, Katharina (2009), "Banking Reform in the Chinese Mirror." Columbia Law and Economics Working Paper No. 354. Online. Available at: http://ssrn.com/abstract=1446930.

Pistor, Katharina and Xu, Chenggang (2005), "Governing Stock Markets in Transition Economies: Lessons from China" in *American Law and Economics Review*, 7.

Poon, Winnie and Chan, Kam (2008), "An Empirical Examination of the Informational Content of Credit Ratings in China" in *Journal of Business Research*, 61.

Potter, Pitman (2004), "Legal Reform in China: Institutions, Culture, and Selective Adaptation" in *Law & Society Inquiry*, 29.

PricewaterhouseCoopers (2009), "Greater China IPO Watch 2008."

Protiviti Consulting (2010), "Corporate Governance Assessment Summary Report on the Top 100 Chinese Listed Companies for 2010." Online. Available at: www.protiviti.com/zh-CN/Headlines/Documents/2010.

Qiao, Xiaohui and Song, Yanhua (2009), "IPO Zairu Xiangjiang" [IPO again Entering Hong Kong] in *Caijing Magazine* (30 March 2009), issue 7. Online. Available at: http://magazine.caijing.com.cn/2009–03–29/110129650.html.

Qian, Xuefeng (1993), "Riding Two Horses: Corporatising Enterprises and the Emerging Securities Regulatory Regime in China" in *UCLA Pacific Basin Law Journal*, 12.

Qian, Yingyi (1995), "Reforming Corporate Governance and Finance in China" in Aoki, Masahiko and Kim, Hyung-Ki (eds.), *Corporate Governance in Transitional Economies*, Washington DC: World Bank.

Ramos, Sofia (2003), "Competition Between Stock Exchanges: A Survey." FAME Research Paper No. 77. Online. Available at: http://ssrn.com/abstract=410727.

Reed, Howard (1981), *The Pre-eminence of International Financial Centers*. New York: Praeger.

Ren, Daniel and Chan, Ray (2012), "Rules to be Relaxed to Help Mainland Firms List in Hong Kong" in *South China Morning Post* (18 December 2012).

Restall, Hugo (2002), "Riding the Subway to Statism" in *Wall Street Journal* (13 March 2002).

Ribstein, Larry (2005), "Cross-listing and Regulatory Competition" in *Review of Law and Economics*, 1.

Roe, Mark (2000), "Political Preconditions to Separating Ownership from Corporate Control" in *Stanford Law Review*, 53.

Roe, Mark (2003), *Political Determinant of Corporate Governance*, Oxford: Oxford University Press.

Roe, Mark (2006a), *Political Determinations of Corporate Governance: Political Context, Corporate Impact*, Oxford: Oxford University Press.

Roe, Mark (2006b), "Legal Origins, Politics, and Modern Stock Markets" in *Harvard Law Review*, 120.
Romano, Roberta (1991), "The Shareholder Suit: Litigation Without Foundation" in *Journal of Law, Economics & Organization*, 7.
Ruskola, Teema (2000), "Corporations and Kinship" in *Stanford Law Review*, 52.
Seidman, Ann and Seidman, Robert (1996), "Drafting Legislation for Development: Lessons from a Chinese Project" in *American Journal of Comparative Law*, 44.
Securities and Futures Commission (SFC) (2002), *Securities Regulation in Hong Kong*, Hong Kong: SFC.
Securities and Futures Commission (SFC) (2003a), "IPO Activities in Hong Kong." Online. Available at: www.sfc.hk/web/EN/published-resources/research-papers/market-reviews.
Securities and Futures Commission (SFC) (2003b), "Closer Economic Partnership Arrangement – Arrangements relating to Qualifications of Securities and Future Industry Practitioners." Press Release. Online. Available at: www.sfc.hk/sfcPressRelease/EN/sfcOpenDocServlet?docno=03PR257.
Securities and Futures Commission (SFC) (2004), "Understanding Investors in the Hong Kong Listed Securities and Derivatives Markets." Online. Available at: www.sfc.hk/web/EN/published-resources/research-papers/market-reviews.
Securities and Futures Commission (SFC) (2005), "Trading of the 31 Mainland Companies which Issued Both A-shares and H-shares." Online. Available at: www.sfc.hk/web/EN/published-resources/research-papers/market-reviews.
Securities and Futures Commission (SFC) (2006), "Positioning of Hong Kong amid Reforms in the Mainland Financial Markets." Online. Available at: www.sfc.hk/sfc/html/EN/research/research/research.html.
Securities and Futures Commission (SFC) (2007a), "An Overview of the Major Events and Regulation of the Securities and Futures Markets between 1997 and 2007." Research Paper No. 36. Online. Available at: www.sfc.hk/web/EN/published-resources/research-papers/market-reviews.
Securities and Futures Commission (SFC) (2007b), Press Release. "Cross Border Enforcement Enhanced." Online. Available at: www.sfc.hk/sfcPressRelease/EN/sfcOpenDocServlet?docno=07PR52.
Securities and Futures Commission (SFC) (2008), "2006–2007 Enforcement Annual Report."
Securities and Futures Commission (SFC) (2009), "2007–2008 Enforcement Annual Report."
Securities and Futures Commission (SFC) (2009), "Annual Report 2008–2009."
Shanghai Director Committee of Listed Companies (2003), "Xianzhuang Diaocha: Duli Dongshi Zenmeyang le?" [A Survey of the Current Situation: What Happens to Independent Directors?] in *China Securities Times* (7 August 2003).
Shanghai Stock Exchange (SHSE) (2003), *China Corporate Governance Report*, Shanghai: Fudan University Press.
Shanghai Stock Exchange (SHSE) (2006), *Guoyou Konggu Shangshi Gongsi Zhili* [China Corporate Governance Report: the Corporate Governance of State Holding Listed Companies], Shanghai: Fudan University Press.
Shanghai Stock Exchange (SHSE) (2008), *Toumingdu yu Xinxi Pilu* [China Corporate Governance Report: Transparency and Information Disclosure], Shanghai: Fudan University Press.

Shi, Chenxia (2007), "Protecting Investors in China through Multiple Regulatory Mechanisms and Effective Enforcement" in *Arizona Journal of International & Comparative Law*, 24.

Shleifer, Andrei and Vishny, Robert (1997), "A Survey of Corporate Governance" in *Journal of Finance*, 52.

Siems, Mathias (2005), "Numerical Comparative Law – Do We Need Statistical Evidence in Law in Order to Reduce Complexity?" in *Cardozo Journal of International & Comparative Law*, 13.

Siems, Mathias (2007), "Legal Origins: Reconciling Law & Finance and Comparative Law" in *McGill Law Review*, 52.

Siems, Mathias (2008), *Convergence in Shareholder Law*, Cambridge: Cambridge University Press.

Singh, Ajit (1990), "The Stock Market in a Socialist Economy" in Nolan, Peter and Fureng, Dong (eds.), *The Chinese Economy and its Future: Achievement and Problems of Post-Mao Reform*, Cambridge: Polity Press.

State-owned Assets Supervision and Administration Commission (SASAC) (2003), "China State-owned Assets Management System Reform Entering New Stage." Online. Available at: www.sasac.gov.cn/n2963340/n2964727/n2974401/2976097.html.

Stott, Vanessa (2005), *Hong Kong Company Law*, Hong Kong: Longman.

Stulz, Rene (1999), "Globalization of Equity Markets and the Cost of Capital" in *Journal of Applied Corporate Finance*, 12.

Su, Zhong (2007), "How Bourses Bring Democracy to China" in *Asia Times* (17 October 2007). Available at: www.atimes.com/atimes/China/IJ17Ad01.html.

Sun, Hong (2005), "Gudong Daibiao Susong Fengchao Bijin" [A Wave of Shareholders Representative Actions is Coming] in *China Securities Journal* (26 December 2005).

Sun, Qian, Tong, Wilson, and Wu, Yujun (2006), "Bonding Premium as a General Phenomenon." CUHK Working Paper. Online. Available at: http://ssrn.com/abstract=890962.

Tan, Lay Hong (1998), "Legal Issues in China's Bifurcated Securities Markets" in *Company Lawyer*, 19.

Tan, Lay Hong and Wang, Jiangyu (2007), "Modelling an Effective Corporate Governance System for China's Listed State-Owned Enterprises: Issues and Challenges in a Transitional Economy" in *Journal of Corporate Law Studies*, 7.

Tang, Xin (2008), "Protecting Minority Shareholders in China: A Task for Both Legislation and Enforcement" in Kanda, Hideki; Kim, Kon-Sik; Milhaupt, Curtis (eds.), *Transforming Corporate Governance in East Asia*, London: Routledge.

Tang, Yunwei (2000), "Bumpy Road Leading to Internationalization: A Review of Accounting Development in China" in *Accounting Horizons*, 14.

Taylor, Phil (2009), "Anything but an Easy Ride for Shanghai" in *China Law and Practice* (June 2009).

Tenev, Stoyan and Zhang, Chunlin (2002), *Corporate Governance and Enterprise Reform in China: Building the Institutions of Modern Markets*, Washington DC: World Bank.

Teubner, Gunther (1998), "Legal Irritants: Good Faith in British Law or How Unifying Law Ends Up in New Divergences" in *Modern Law Review*, 61.

Tobin, Damian and Sun, Laixiang (2009), "International Listing as a Means to Mobilise the Benefits of Financial Globalization: Micro-level Evidence from China" in *World Development*, 37.

Tokley, Ian and Ravn, Tina (1998), *Company Law and Securities Law in China*, Hong Kong: Sweet & Maxwell Asia.

Tomasic, Roman (1994), "Company Law and the Limits of the Rule of Law in China." Discussion Paper, Asia-Pacific Economic Law Forum.
Tomasic, Roman (1995), "Company Law and the Limits of the Rule of Law in China" in *Australian Journal of Corporate Law*, 4.
Transparency International (2012), "Corruption Perception Index 2012." Online. Available at: http://cpi.transparency.org/cpi2012/results.
Tsingtao Brewery (1993), "H-share Listing Prospectus."
Tsingtao Brewery (1994), "Annual Report 1993."
Tsingtao Brewery (1995), "Annual Report 1994."
Tsingtao Brewery (1996), "Annual Report 1995."
Tsingtao Brewery (1997), "Annual Report 1996."
Tsingtao Brewery (2000), "Annual Report 1999."
Tsingtao Brewery (2002), "Annual Report 2001."
Tsingtao Brewery (2003), "Announcement."
Tsingtao Brewery (2006), "Annual Report 2005."
Tucker, Sundeep and Dyer, Geoff (2006), "ICBC's Dual-listing Plan is Vote for Shanghai" in *Financial Times* (13 July 2006).
Tucker, Sunny (2007), "On Asia: Shareholder Activism Taking Root in Asia" in *Financial Times* (13 April 2007).
Tyler, Edward and Ho, John (2004), *HKLRD Review Series 2004*, Hong Kong: Sweet & Maxwell Asia.
Uddin, Hamid and Wong, Ann (1998), "The Stock Market II: The Trading Market" in Ho, Simon, Scott, Robert, and Wong, Kie Ann (eds.), *The Hong Kong Financial System: A New Age*, Oxford: Oxford University Press.
Waldmeir, Patti (2009), "Investors Prepare for Fresh Flood of Chinese Offerings" in *Financial Times* (17 June 2009).
Wan, Meng (2000), "The Securities System in China" in Norton, Joseph, Li, C.J., and Huang, Yangxin (eds.), *Financial Regulation in the Greater China Area: Mainland China, Taiwan and Hong Kong SAR*, Kluwer Law International: London.
Wang, Baoshu and Huang, Hui (2006), "China's New Company Law and Securities Law: An Overview and Assessment" in *Australian Journal of Corporate Law*, 19.
Wang, Chunge (2005), *Neidi Gongsi Xianggang Shangshi ji Liangdi Jianguan Hezuo Yanjiu* [The Companies from Mainland China Listed in Hong Kong and the Cooperation between Mainland China and Hong Kong Supervisory Bodies], Beijing: Peking University Press.
Wang, Hua (2009), "Betting on Chinese Electronic Cars? – Analysing BYD's Innovation Capability." Conference Paper at 17th Gerpisa International Colloquium, Paris.
Wang, Jiangyu (2007), "The Strange Role of Independent Directors in a Two-tier Board Structure of China's Listed Companies" in *Compliance & Regulatory Journal*, 3.
Wang, Jiangyu (2008), "An Overview of China's Corporate Law Regime." Online. Available at: http://ssrn.com/abstract=1222061.
Wang, Jiangyu (2009), "Regulatory Competition and Cooperation between Securities Markets in Hong Kong and Mainland China" in *Capital Markets Law Journal*, 4.
Wang, Jingyi and Wang, Peng (2009), "Discussion about Shareholders' Right to Information" in *Journal of Politics and Law*, 2.
Wang, Wallace (1992), "Reforming State Enterprises in China: The Case for Redefining Enterprise Operating Rights" in *Journal of Chinese Law*, 6.
Watanabe, Mariko (2002), "Holding Company Risk in China: A Final Step of State-owned Enterprises Reform and an Emerging Problem of Corporate Governance" in *China Economic Review*, 13.

Watson, Alan (1993), *Legal Transplants an Approach to Comparative Law*, 2nd edn, Athens: University of Georgia Press.

Watson, Alan (1996), "Aspects of Reception of Law" in *American Journal of Comparative Law*, 44.

Watson, Alan (2000), "Legal Transplants and European Private Law" in *Electronic Journal of Comparative Law*, 4.4 Online. Available at: www.ejcl.org/44/art44–2.html.

Wedeman, Andrew (2003), "Corporate Capitalism in Socialist China" in Gomez, Edmund and Hsiao, Hsin-Huang (eds.), *Chinese Enterprise, Transnationalism and Identity*, London: Routledge.

Wei, Yuwa (2005), "The Development of the Securities Market and Regulation in China" in *Loyola of Los Angeles International and Comparative Law Review*, 27.

Williams, Mark (2005), *Competition Policy and Law in China, Hong Kong and Taiwan*, Cambridge: Cambridge University Press.

Wong, Richard (2002), "Shanghai: Another Hong Kong?" HK Centre for Economic Research. Online. Available at: www.hktdc.com/info/mi/a/ef/en/1X005RK7/1/Economic-Forum.

Wood, Philip (2005), *Maps of World Financial Law*, 5th edn, London: Allen & Overy.

World Bank (1995), *China – The Emerging Capital Market: Volume II*, Washington DC: World Bank.

Xi, Chao (2006a), "Institutional Shareholder Activism in China (Part I)" in *International Company and Commercial Law Review*, 17.

Xi, Chao (2006b), "Case Note: Private Enforcement of Securities law in China: Daqing Lianyi Co v Zhong Weida and Others (2004) Heilongjiang High Court" in *Journal of Comparative Law*, 1.

Xi, Chao (2007), "In Search of An Effective Monitoring Board Model: Board Reforms and the Political Economy of Corporate Law in China" in *Connecticut Journal of International Law*, 22.

Xi, Chao (2009), *Corporate Governance and Legal Reform in China*, London: Wildy, Simmonds & Hill Publishing.

Xi, Duojun (2002), "Zhongguo Gongsifa Lifa yu Shishi de Jingyan, Wenti ji Wanshan Tujing" [The Experience, Problems and Improvements of China's Company Law's Legislation and Enforcement] in *Zhongnan Gongye Daxue Xuebao* [Journal of Mid-South Industrial University], 8.

Xia, Mei, Grub, Phillip, and Lin, Jianhai (1992), *The Re-Emerging Securities Market in China*, London: Quorum Books.

Xiao, Xinrong, Cheng, Peng, and Chen, Jean (2005), "Window Dressing of Chinese Securities Investment Funds." EMFA Conference Paper.

Xinhua News (2009), "China Focus: Sinopec Ex-chairman Gets Death Sentence with reprieve after Reporting Others' Crimes."

Xu, Ke (2007), "Hong Kong Eyes Link-up with Mainland Bourses" in *Caijing Magazine* (28 June 2007).

Yam, Joseph (2004), "Commencement of the Clearing and Settlement Systems Ordinance." Online. Available at: www.info.gov.hk/hkma/eng/viewpt/20040708e.htm.

Yam, Joseph (2007), "Linking the Mainland's and Hong Kong's Financial Markets (II)." Viewpoint, HKMA, February 2007. Online. Available at: www.info.gov.hk/hkma/eng/viewpt/20070201e.htm.

Yang, Hua (2005), "Overview of Governance of State-owned Listed Companies in China." OECD Proceedings of the Second Policy Dialogue on Corporate Governance in China, Beijing, 19 May 2005.

Yang, Pengfei (2007), "The Two Models of Corporate Governance and the Institutional Reform of Chinese Enterprises" in Nakamura, Masao (ed.), *Changing Corporate Governance Practices in China and Japan*, Hampshire: Palgrave Macmillan.
Yang, Ting and Lau, Sie Ting (2006), "Choice of Foreign Listing Location: Experience of Chinese Firms" in *Pacific-Basin Finance Journal*, 14.
Yeung, Horace (2009), "Non-tradable Share Reform in China: A Review of Progress" in *Company Lawyer*, 30.
Yeung, Horace (2010), "Just Another Casino? The Case of Launching the Growth Enterprise Board in China" in *International Company and Commercial Law Review*, 21.
Yeung, Horace (2011), "From Further North: The Case of Rusal's (Russian Aluminium) Listing in Hong Kong" in International Company and Commercial Law Review, 22.
Yeung, Winghim and Zhou, Jing (2007), "Changes in Regulation and Prices of Dual-listed Stocks in China." Online. Available at: http://ir.lib.sfu.ca/handle/1892/9454.
Yu, Dongzhi (2001), "Dongshihui, Gongsi Zhili yu Jixiao: dui Zhongguo Shangshi Gongsi de Jingyan Fenxi" [The Board of Directors, Corporate Governance and Performance – An Empirical Analysis on Chinese Listed Companies] in *Zhongguo Shehui Kexue* [China Social Science], 3.
Z/Yen Group and Qatar Financial Centre Authority (2012), "Global Financial Centre Index." Online. Available at: www.zyen.com/PDF/GFCI%2012.pdf.
Zeng, Yamin and Zhang, Junsheng (2009), "The Dark Side of Institutional Shareholders Activism in Emerging Markets: Evidence from China's Non-Tradable Share Reform." Online. Available at: http://ssrn.com/abstract=1372428.
Zhang, Gaosheng and Chu, Shanna (2007), "Guquan Fenzhi Gaige Hou Shangshi Gongsi Guquan Jiegou de Bianhua jiqi dui Gongsi Zhili Jizhi de Yingxiang" [The Influence of Split Share Structure Reform on Ownership Structure and Corporate Governance] in *Xiandai Jingji* [Modern Economics], 62.
Zhang, Mo (2008), "From Public to Private: The Newly Enacted Chinese Property Law and the Protection of Property Rights in China" in *Berkeley Business Law Journal*, 5.
Zhang, Peiyuan (2009), "Guanchang he Guoqi Haiyou Duoshao Chen Tonghai bei Yangzhe?" [How Many Chen Tonghai Fed by Government and SOEs?] in *Xinhua News* (13 August 2009).
Zhang, Yi (2006), "Law, Corporate Governance, Corporate Scandal in an Emerging Economy: Insights from China." Online. Available at: http://ssrn.com/abstract=957549.
Zhang, Yichen and Yu, Da (1994), "China's Emerging Securities Market" in *Columbia Journal of World Business*, 29.
Zhang, Yimin and Zhao, Ronald (2004), "The Valuation Differential between Class A and B Shares: Country Risk in the Chinese Stock Market" in *Journal of International Financial Management & Accounting*, 15.
Zhou, Mi and Wang, Xiaoming (2000), "Agency Cost and the Crisis of China's SOE" in *China Economic Review*, 11.
Zhu, Sanzhu (2000), *Securities Regulation in China*, New York: Transnational.
Zhu, Sanzhu (2005), "Civil Litigation Arising from False Statements on China's Securities Market" in *North Carolina Journal of International Law and Commercial Regulation*, 31.
Zhu, Sanzhu (2007), *Securities Dispute Resolution in China*, Aldershot: Ashgate.

Index

Page numbers in *italics* denote tables, those in **bold** denote figures.